The Journalist's Guide to American Law

MW01033596

How do you report on the latest sensational criminal trial or newest controversial legislation without a basic understanding of how the American legal system works?

This easy-to-use guidebook offers an overview of American law that should be found on the desk of any journalism student or professional journalist. It provides an overview of major legal principles and issues in simple terms for journalists who cover any aspect of the legal system. *The Journalist's Guide to American Law* can be used in two ways: first, as a sit-down read that gives an overview of American law; and second, as a reference that can be used every day under deadline pressure for a specific purpose. Every feature of the book is designed to serve both functions. The book's organization captures both the bird's-eye view of a subject; and, alternatively, permits a quick review of a given section when the professional needs to understand a distinct concept. The areas covered range from professional concerns such as the First Amendment, cameras in the courtroom, sunshine laws, and access to government documents, to general legal matters such as the institutions of law and the law-making function of the judiciary; core constitutional principles such as separation of powers and judicial review; and how courts function.

The book is ideal for use in general newswriting and reporting courses, particularly those with a focus on legal or court reporting, and may also be used as a supplementary text in Media Law courses.

John T. Nockleby, Laurie L. Levenson, Karl M. Manheim, F. Jay Dougherty, Victor J. Gold, Allan P. Ides, and **Daniel W. Martin** are all faculty members at Loyola Law School, Los Angeles, which annually hosts the Journalist Law School, a fellowship program for professional journalists.

The Journalist's Guide to American Law

John T. Nockleby
Laurie L. Levenson
Karl M. Manheim
F. Jay Dougherty
Victor J. Gold
Allan Ides
Daniel W. Martin

Routledge
Taylor & Francis Group

NEW YORK AND LONDON

First published in paperback in 2014

First published 2013
by Routledge
711 Third Avenue, New York, NY 10017

and by Routledge
2 Park Square, Milton Park, Abingdon, Oxon OX14 4RN

Routledge is an imprint of the Taylor & Francis Group, an informa business

© 2013, 2014 Taylor & Francis

Library of Congress Cataloging-in-Publication Data

The journalist's guide to American law / By John T. Nockleby . . . [et al.].
    p. cm.
  Includes bibliographical references and index.
  1. Law—United States.   2. Journalists—United States—Handbooks,
manuals, etc.   3. Journalists—Legal status, laws, etc.—United
States.   I. Nockleby, John T.

KF386.J68   2012
349.73—dc23   2012024156

ISBN: 978-0-415-88471-6 (hbk)
ISBN: 978-0-415-88472-3 (pbk)
ISBN: 978-0-203-84097-9 (ebk)

Typeset in Sabon
by Apex CoVantage, LLC

Contents

LAURIE L. LEVENSON

Preface

This book has many parents. Nearly a decade ago, working in partnership with a number of bar organizations, the Civil Justice Program at Loyola Law School created the *Journalist Law School*, a four-day boot camp in law for professional journalists who cover the courts and legal system. Each year the JLS attracts hundreds of applicants for 35 Fellowships, and has proven to be the most exciting teaching most of us do. Indeed, this book was inspired by our work with scores of Journalist-Fellows who represent all types of media.

The authors are all law professors, but most of us have worked with journalists for years. Indeed, collectively we have given thousands of press interviews on a wide variety of subjects. Many of us teach constitutional law, and have a special concern for the First Amendment protections accorded those who report on matters of public concern, including legal matters. We hope this book continues to support the work of journalists and others who wish to understand the legal system in a more comprehensive way.

We would be remiss if we didn't also tell a story about how a chance lunch led to the creation of the Journalist Law School, and eventually this book. A number of years ago, John Nockleby was invited to a lunch with the incoming President of an influential bar organization, the American Board of Trial Advocates, or ABOTA. We knew that the ABOTA was a highly-selective group of some of the finest trial lawyers in the country, whose membership hailed from every state. In their professional life, some ABOTA members represent large companies and insurers; others represent individuals and small businesses. More recently, the organization had become active in promoting civic education in high schools, helping teachers gain a deeper understanding of the legal system, and supporting public education about the law, particularly the jury system and judicial independence.

The incoming President of ABOTA was Donna Melby, a partner in a major Los Angeles law firm. When Donna heard about our idea for the Journalist Law School, she immediately took it to ABOTA. As a result, the organization got behind the idea and used their brains, connections and muscle to turn the idea into reality. Indeed, without the support of ABOTA and the ABOTA Foundation, the JLS would not have come into existence and this book would not have been written. We are deeply grateful to all the members, but especially to current and past presidents of ABOTA and the ABOTA Foundation: Mick Callahan; John V. Phelps; Mark Robinson; Lewis Sifford; Craig Lewis; Bill Callaham; Mike McGuire; Bill Sieben; Bill Ginsberg; Charles Baumberger; Wylie Aiken; Tom Harkness; Joel Collins; Harry Widmann; Pat Simek; Ron Rouda; Gordon Rather; Tom Girardi; John Holcomb; Robert Stone; Gil Jones; Bob Barbagelata; Bob Baker; Ed Nevin; and of course, Donna Melby.

We continue to receive support for the JLS from many other organizations that have made wonderful contributions to the success of the program. These include the Conference of Chief Justices (CCJ); the National Center for State Courts (NCSC); the Los Angeles County Bar Association (LACBA); the California Federal -State Judicial Council; the Consumer Attorneys Association of Los Angeles (CAALA); the Defense Research Institute (DRI); the American Association for Justice (AAJ); the Consumer Attorneys Association of California (CAOC), and many local ABOTA Chapters from around the country. We are deeply appreciative of all the support from these organizations.

We also want to thank our faculty colleagues who have generously given of their time to participate in producing the JLS. Each year over 50 lawyers, judges, and law faculty participate in helping make the JLS a success. Both the current Dean of Loyola Law School, Los Angeles, Victor Gold, and the previous Dean, David Burcham (now President of Loyola Marymount University), have been strong supporters of the program from inception. Our co-authors—Jay Dougherty, Allan Ides, Dan Martin, and Dean Gold—have not only regularly participated in the JLS, but shared their expertise in the development of this volume. Tim Oppelt (LLS '07) helped edit several chapters, and our faculty secretaries, Linda Wysocky and Valda Hahn, have been stalwart assistants for many years.

And to all journalists who strive to find meaningful stories about the legal system, and who diligently work to explain the justice system to the public: we thank you.

John Nockleby,
Laurie Levenson and
Karl Manheim
Loyola Law School, Los Angeles
February, 2014

1 Introduction

John T. Nockleby
Professor of Law and Director, Civil Justice
Program, Loyola Law School, Los Angeles

On the night of March 3, 1991, the Los Angeles police and California high-way patrol officers stopped a speeding automobile driven by an African American, Rodney King. When King, who had been drinking but was unarmed, failed to comply with the officers' commands to lay prone the officers beat him more than 50 times with their metal batons and kicked him several times while several other officers watched and a police helicop-ter spotlighted the scene from overhead. Eighty-one seconds of the beating was captured on videotape by an amateur photographer, George Holliday.

The Holliday videotape was played and replayed thousands of times on local and national television. Most people who saw the tape thought the po-lice used excessive force when subduing King. Later, as the officers returned to their stations, they sent text-messages from their in-car computers. The officer in charge at the scene, Sergeant Stacey Koon, typed messages that read: "U[nit] just had a big time use of force. Tased and beat the suspect of CHP pursuit big time." Another officer, Laurence Powell, reported the incident on his computer: "Ooops" and "I haven't beaten anyone this bad in a long time."

The beating led to separate state and federal criminal prosecutions of four police officers, and, much later, a civil trial in which the jury awarded King $3.8 million for his injuries. More importantly, the acquittal of the of-ficers in the 1992 state trial set off one of the most serious riots in American history, resulting in 54 deaths, over 2,000 injured, and nearly a billion dol-lars of property damage. The 1992 Los Angeles riots and the various trials that bracketed them rank as some of the most newsworthy events of the late 20th century.

If a reporter is assigned to cover such events, is there useful background information in law that would assist her? For example, how much force may an officer use when subduing a suspect? If a person is found "not guilty" of a crime in state court, may he be prosecuted a second time in federal court? Isn't the same evidence presented at both trials? And, what is the relation-ship between criminal trial and civil lawsuits involving the same events? Could a person be found "not guilty" of a crime, yet later found "liable" for the same behavior in a civil case? What must a person like Rodney King prove in order to win his civil case? These are some of the questions this book is designed to answer.

The American legal system is complex. Part of the complexity stems from the fact we have parallel court systems, federal and state. So, there are federal crimes and state crimes; federal statutes and state statutes; federal rules and state rules of procedure; a Constitution for the United States that establishes the governing structure of the national government and guarantees a number of individual rights; but also separate state-by-state constitutions that establish the governing structures within each state and that often guarantee individual rights in addition to those established by the U.S. Constitution.

In fact, most of "our law" continues to be developed at the state level, and not the national level. This causes enormous confusion for the citizenry, and even for beginning lawyers. When someone asks a lawyer "what is the law" on a particular question, the answer often hinges on whether the question is one of criminal law or civil law, or invokes federal or state law; but also in which state the questioner resides.

Moreover, the United States has many law-making bodies. Every county, every municipality, every burg exercises jurisdiction over some bailiwick; federal and state agencies step in to regulate matters in ways that may conflict with state and local laws; and often it's challenging to figure out which of several overlapping governing authorities control the outcome of a particular legal question. Zoning is often decided at the local level, but many state constitutions authorize state officials to override powers exercised at the local level. Oftentimes "what is the law" depends on which of potentially conflicting rules controls in a given situation. Sorting out those conflicts is an important part of the lawyer's job.

Because the interplay among different institutional actors, jurisdictions, and sources of law is often brought into discussions about the justice system, the rest of this introduction addresses the following structural tensions within the system:

1   State law vs. federal law
2   State courts vs. federal courts
3   Criminal law vs. civil law
4   Common law (judge-made law) vs. statutory law
5   Judicial independence and judicial accountability
6   Judicial role vs. jury role

State Law vs. Federal Law

The Rodney King beating led the local district attorney to seek indictments against officers Laurence Powell, Timothy Wind, Theodore Briseno, and Sergeant Stacey Koon, the supervising officer. All four were charged under state law with "assault by force likely to produce great bodily injury and a deadly weapon" and with assault "under color of authority." Two officers were also charged with filing false reports, and Koon was charged with being an accessory.

At one level, prosecuting the police officers in state court was routine: most violent assaults are state crimes, not federal. The notoriety of the case arose from the videotape that documented what many people already believed—that the Los Angeles Police Department routinely used excessive force, particularly on black men. Yet, most crimes do not arise to the level of federal offenses.

Indeed, most rules of law defining crimes, or governing enforcement of contracts, protection of property, and remedies for personal injury derive from *state law*. This is a central feature of our constitutional structure: many functions of government are decentralized and the powers of the federal government are limited. If Congress enacts legislation that defines certain behavior as a federal offense, or makes certain contractual provisions uniform across state lines, or changes the tort law of states, ordinarily it must justify the enactment on grounds that the problem being regulated affects interstate commerce or is authorized by another provision of the Constitution.

May States Protect Individual Rights beyond Those under U.S. Constitution?

Many state supreme courts have interpreted their constitutions to protect individual rights more extensively than the U.S. Supreme Court has found under the U.S. Constitution. For example, the Montana legislature enacted a statute that permitted only physicians (and not physician assistants, for example) to provide abortions. The U.S. Supreme Court held the statute did not substantially impede a woman's opportunity to obtain an abortion, a fundamental right of decisional privacy protected by its 1972 decision *Roe v. Wade*. However, the Montana Supreme Court later ruled the same statute was unconstitutional under the state constitution. See *Mazurek v. Armstrong*, 520 U.S. 968 (1997); *Armstrong v. Montana*, 989 P.2d 364 (Mont. 2000).

For example, stalking is usually a state offense, but if the behavior crosses state lines, the federal government has the power to criminalize it. Medical malpractice liability is ordinarily a state problem, but Congress may step in if the issue affects interstate provision of medical care. The limited powers of the federal government will be developed further in the constitutional law chapter (see chapter 2).

As these examples suggest, both the federal government and the states create criminal *and* civil wrongs. Stalking is a criminal offense in many states, but in 2006 the federal government enacted a comprehensive statute that criminalized interstate stalking. Similarly, the rules governing medical malpractice liability have customarily been a state law issue, but Congress may enact legislation restricting medical malpractice tort suits if the provisions are consistent with its power under the Commerce Clause.

Since our federal system created overlapping governments with shared responsibilities, the same behavior might violate both federal and state law. For example, the state prosecution of the officers involved in the King beating resulted in an acquittal of the four police defendants, and the federal government subsequently brought federal charges against the same defendants based on the same behavior, but requiring proof of different elements. The federal charges were based on a federal civil rights statute that prohibit officials acting "under color of law" from depriving persons of constitutional rights, rather than felony assault and related charges. In the federal case, Powell, Briseno, and Wind were charged with willful use of unreasonable force in arresting King, and the supervising officer, Stacey Koon, was charged with willfully permitting the other officers to use unreasonable force during the arrest. After a trial in federal court, the jury convicted Koon and Powell but acquitted Wind and Briseno.

In the United States, the *dual sovereignty doctrine* holds that, within certain limits, either a state or the federal government can prosecute a person subsequent to an acquittal by the other sovereign, even though the state or federal violation arises out of the same act and even though the state and federal offences are substantially the same (see Table 1.1). We explore many of these issues in the chapters on criminal law and criminal procedure (chapters 3 and 4).

Table 1.1 Comparing State and Federal Laws

Usually State	Usually Federal	Often Both
Criminal Law	**Criminal Law**	**Criminal Law**
• Murder	• Kidnapping	• Serious deprivation of civil rights
• Rape	• Bank robbery	
• Crimes against property	• Federal income tax evasion	• Fraud (including securities violations)
• Deliberate violations of state safety laws	• Willful antitrust violations	• Stalking
		• Failure to pay taxes
Civil Law	**Civil Law**	**Civil Law**
• Contract law	• Securities violations	• Antitrust
• Real property law		• Consumer fraud
• Tort law (injuries to person or property)	• Consumer protection (e.g., FDA)	• Violations of safety regulations
• Family law	• Enforcing administrative agency orders	• Violations of U.S. Constitution
• Violations of state constitution		

State Courts vs. Federal Courts

The U.S. Constitution establishes the third branch of the federal government—the federal judiciary—and authorizes Congress to establish the jurisdiction of these federal courts. Similarly, the jurisdiction of state courts is established by state constitutions and state legislatures. Each state's constitution follows the tripartite structure embodied in the federal Constitution.

Generally speaking, the jurisdiction of federal and state courts follows from whether the matter is one of federal or state law. Thus, most cases (whether civil or criminal) arising under state law are heard in state court, while most cases arising under federal law are heard in federal court. For example, the prosecution of the officers involved in the King beating for state crimes occurred in state court, while the federal crimes were prosecuted in federal court. In criminal cases, the jurisdiction of a federal or state court extends only to federal or state crimes, respectively. When both jurisdictions provide criminal penalties for the same offense, federal prosecutors will often defer to state officials.

In contrast, these limitations don't apply in the same way for civil cases. Most civil cases, including tort, contract, property, and family cases, arise under state law, and thus are tried in state courts. As a result, state courts handle more than 98 percent of all civil litigation, and federal courts less than 2 percent. Thus, although federal courts capture significant media attention, the workload of state courts is far more substantial.

In any event, on the civil side federal courts are empowered to hear many types of state law claims. For example, for cases in which parties hail from different states and the damages are large, federal courts may hear the state law claims under what is known as *diversity* jurisdiction. When federal courts hear civil state law cases, they are required to apply the law of the state with the most substantial connection to the dispute. Even though the dispute is heard in federal court, the substantive rules that are applied derive from state law. Thus, a breach of contract claim might be litigated in federal court because the parties are from different states and the amount in dispute is large, but the federal court will apply the state law of the particular state with the greatest connection to the dispute. The chapter on civil procedure (chapter 8) explains these rules in greater detail.

Of course, most of the civil disputes federal courts hear arise under federal law. For example, patent cases, disputes involving the federal government, antitrust claims under the Sherman or Clayton acts, enforcement actions by federal administrative agencies, and tax disputes are all examples of civil cases decided by federal courts. An important additional type of dispute heard by federal courts are constitutional claims arising under the U.S. Constitution, and cases arising under several federal civil rights statutes.

One final point about the relationship between federal and state courts is important to remember. Some types of civil claims can only be heard in federal court (e.g., federal tax cases; cases involving enforcement of federal administrative agency orders). Some types of civil claims can only be heard in state courts (e.g., family law issues such as divorce and custody; enforcement of state administrative directives). However, some important types of cases can be heard in either federal or state courts (e.g., some civil rights actions; constitutional claims not involving federal statutes or federal defendants). These limitations will be discussed more fully in the civil procedure chapter (chapter 8).

Criminal Law vs. Civil Law

Due to the widespread media coverage of notorious cases, most people are aware that the government takes charge of investigating and prosecuting crimes. The types of criminal cases that achieve notoriety often involve murder, assaults, kidnappings, and arson. Most citizens are also generally aware of enforcement involving motor vehicles—such as reckless or drunken driving.

What is often confusing is the distinction between criminal law and civil law—and why the distinction is important. The civil justice system involves many different types of controversies including contract, trademark, and other business disputes; property contests; family law matters; and intellectual property conflicts such as patent and copyright. This book includes chapters on contract, patent and copyright law, and torts, all of which involve civil law. Yet, it is possible that some of the conduct that falls under these types of claims might also involve *criminal conduct*. In fact, some civil claims share common roots with criminal law. This is especially true in the branch of civil law known as *torts* (see chapter 5).

A tort is the general label given to a class of civil wrongs for which courts will provide a remedy. Usually, a cause of action for torts does not involve the enforcement of a contract, though oftentimes torts occur under circumstances in which there is some type of contractual or ongoing relationship between the parties. The subjects of typical torts include injuries to one's *person* (such as assault, battery, negligence) or injuries to one's *property* (such as trespass, interference with one's contracts, and nuisance). Torts are *civil* wrongs; in other words, they are suits for which a private party may hail another person or entity into court—usually to obtain monetary damages.

For example, after both sets of criminal proceedings were concluded against the police involved in beating Rodney King, King filed a civil suit alleging that that the police had deprived him of his federal constitutional rights by using unreasonable force against him while arresting him. The civil case raised issues parallel to the federal criminal case, as it was based on the civil version of the federal statute under which the officers had been prosecuted.

The civil suit filed by King also illustrates several features of civil litigation as distinguished from criminal prosecutions. A crime is considered to be an offense against the state, and one that the legislature has decreed may be brought only by the public's agent (e.g., the prosecutor), whereas a civil suit may be brought by anyone who has been injured who can satisfy the requirements of the particular civil wrong. A crime always involves the government as one of the parties. The prosecutor controls the complaint and makes the decision whether to pursue or drop charges. In contrast, a civil plaintiff is in control of the complaint and, independently of any public interest, may pursue or drop the case.

Even though he was the victim of the attack, Rodney King had no control over the prosecution of the criminal charges against the police officers. In fact, the state prosecutors chose not to call him to testify in the first prosecution. If the government had chosen to offer a plea bargain or dismiss the charges, King would have had no legal standing to object.

A second key distinction between civil and criminal cases concerns the potential remedies. A crime may involve punishments or penalties not available to a civil litigant. For example, a criminal battery (sometimes called an aggravated assault) might result in a jail term or fine paid to the state. A tort suit for battery, on the other hand, cannot seek to imprison the defendant, and the remedies typically involve forcing the defendant to pay damages to the plaintiff, to return property to the plaintiff, or sometimes an order (called an *injunction*) to perform some act or to cease harmful behavior.

Thus in the prosecutions against the police officers, the government sought to imprison the defendants. When Rodney King filed his civil suit, he could obtain no such remedy. The most common remedy in a civil case is a requirement that the defendant pay money damages. In fact, after a state court trial on his civil claims, King was awarded damages of $3.8 million.

A third distinction between tort and crime involves the source of the law. Today, for some act to constitute a crime, a legislature must enact a statute describing the behavior that constitutes the crime, and to assign the penalties for its violation. However, the process of defining the behaviors that constitute a tort or other civil case is a more complex process. That is the subject of the next section.

Common Law (Judge-made Law) vs. Statutory Law

All but one (Louisiana) of the 50 states has a system of "common law" adjudication by which the state develops much of its contract, property, and tort law. The common law is a body of law made by *judges* over several centuries. The method of judicial lawmaking that characterizes common law systems grew out of the English system of judging during the medieval period and was exported to lands colonized by England. Thus, the practice of common law adjudication within the 49 states has a pedigree that antedates the adoption of the U.S. Constitution.

Common law systems should be contrasted with the civil law approach used in many European countries (and Louisiana). A civil law system operates under codes of law ordinarily developed by a legislative body. In a civil law system, judges apply and interpret the statutes adopted by the legislative body. In the United States, at one time criminal law was common law, but now is statutory. In addition, much "civil" legislation has also been enacted, and so the determination of what "law" controls a given civil claim often requires understanding the statutes in a given state, as well as how the common law precedent has developed.

An important feature of common law systems, and one that is frequently confusing to nonlawyers and visitors from civil law systems, is that the rules of law are developed in the process of adjudication, and may be announced by judges in the same cases to which they first apply. For example, when a controversy arises under tort law, the dispute is brought before a judge or panel of judges. The judge will then decide which party prevails and why, and will announce her decision in an opinion. Among other matters, the opinion contains a statement of the governing law that was developed *by the judges* either *in that case*, or in an earlier case deemed sufficiently similar in character to be considered controlling. This decision then becomes *precedent* for resolving conflicts that arise in future cases.

The American version of common law adjudication is also based on a system of *stare decisis*, which refers to the idea that judges should respect and follow precedent. The doctrine of *stare decisis* ("let the decision stand") means that (1) judges are required to follow rules developed by higher courts in their jurisdiction; and (2) judges will ordinarily consider themselves bound by previous decisions of the same court in which they sit (including decisions made hundreds of years ago), unless there is a good reason for changing the rules previously developed. Accordingly, the doctrine of *stare decisis* imposes upon judges the obligation to decide future cases in the same way as past cases. In other words, common law judges are bound to decide like cases alike. This does not mean that judges can't or don't change the common law rules; indeed, common law rules in different areas of law go through periodic upheavals.

A Comment on Retaining vs. Overruling Precedent

As one can easily imagine, the conflict over whether to preserve an earlier rule vs. overturning it has many different dimensions. One familiar context in which the issue arises is constitutional adjudication. For example, during hearings over nominations to the Supreme Court (John Roberts and Samuel Alito), many commentators raised questions as to the degree to which either would prove faithful to precedent. It is obvious that if a judge likes the underlying rule set by the precedent, she's more likely to adhere to it. But, in the abstract it's as impossible to ferret out a judge's views on the viability of precedent as much as it is to ferret out her views of rights in the abstract.

A similar set of considerations underlies much constitutional law adjudication. Constitutional adjudication is, after all, merely one type of common law judging.

Whenever arguments over precedents arise, there are generally several standard rhetorical ploys that are generated no matter the underlying controversy. Table 1.2 maps some common rhetorical moves:

Table 1.2 Should a Court Change or Preserve a Judge-made Rule?

Arguments to Preserve the Rule	*Arguments to Overturn the Rule*
• Keep the system stable	• A stable system may be rigid and out of touch with reality
• People have developed patterns of behavior that rely on the rule	• No one should be able to rely on a rule that is not just, or is unworkable
• The rule is long-standing	• When the reasons underlying the rule are no longer valid, the rule should not be upheld

Nonetheless, even if a common law rule is not changed by judges, there may be sufficient criticism of it such that judges limit the *reach* of the rule without overruling it. Several devices are available to judges, and all are regularly employed in every common law system:

- Develop exceptions to the rule. This has the effect of minimizing negative implications of retaining the rule, but the disadvantage of encouraging litigants to "fit" their case into one of the exceptions, or worse, to create a new exception.
- Limit or narrow the scope of the rule (e.g., instead of a rule applying to all vehicles including motorcycles, airplanes, bicycles, trains, scooters, tricycles), narrow its scope so that it applies only to motorized trucks running on diesel pulling four-wheeled trailers.

Can the Legislature Change the Common Law?

If a state's legislature decides to change the state's common law, it is free to do so provided the enactment does not violate the U.S. Constitution, or the constitution of that particular state. Today, many state legislatures are actively involved in forming, restating, or revising their state's rules of law governing tort, property, and contract. A familiar example is the *tort reform* movement launched during the 1980s by tobacco, automobile, and insurance interests to cut back on common law liability rules, or to *cap* damages. As a general matter, the legislature can overrule or change common law decisions. Indeed, today most bodies of state civil law involve a mixture of statutory law and common law.

One final note must be emphasized when addressing legislative power to change state common law. Judges hold a trump card: *judicial review*. Judges have asserted the power under our constitutional system to be the ultimate arbiters of whether executive orders or legislative enactments comply with the U.S. Constitution or state constitutions. Judicial review will be explored in greater detail in the constitutional law chapter (chapter 2).

Judicial Independence and Judicial Accountability

Judicial independence captures the idea that judges who sit in the United States are required to exercise judgment independent of the political branches. An independent judiciary is also linked to the ideal of the *rule of law* in constitutional democracies, meaning that many rights and liberties are secure only because they are enforceable by a judiciary not controlled by other powerful institutions—either public or private.

Judicial independence is secured both through the way the third branch is structured, and through the way in which judicial decision making is shielded from political and other pressures. The tripartite structure of government ensures that, as a formal matter, once in office, judges do not officially "report" to the other branches, and cannot be removed without following a formal procedure. In addition, an independent judiciary is only possible if judges can exercise impartial judgment in fidelity to law without fear of reprisals from the other branches.

Judicial independence does not mean there's no judicial accountability. As always, there are checks. If other bodies dislike judicial interpretations of statutes or the common law, they can change those laws within constitutional bounds. Public criticism of particular decisions is appropriate, so long the criticism doesn't arise to the level of reprisal or threat.

The real tensions lie in two arenas: control of judicial budgets; and control of the jurisdiction of the courts. The budgetary conflicts come down to how much funding is necessary to finance an independent judiciary (i.e., How many judges? How many courtrooms?). If the third branch is not funded adequately, can one say the rule of law is protected? But "how much is enough" is always a contested issue.

Control over the jurisdiction of the courts is much more complex, and seems to the outsider to be technical, but often implicates important justice issues. During the second term of George W. Bush, business interests convinced Congress that class actions in state courts were damaging their interests, and sought to shift such cases to federal courts, which were viewed as more sympathetic to business interests. In response, Congress enacted and President Bush signed the Class Action Fairness Act of 1995. The act allowed "removal" to federal courts many state consumer class actions. We cover these sorts of issues in the chapter on civil procedure (chapter 8).

The press plays an important role in protecting judicial independence, as well as providing a critical means of ensuring judicial accountability. Courts are open; trials are public proceedings. Court decisions are written published for all to read. The coverage and reporting on these proceedings and trials helps ensure that all three branches play by the rules, and are called to account in a very public way if they do not.

The Judge's Role in Civil Litigation (vs. Jury Role)

Let's suppose that a case has been filed in either federal or state court. Within that system, there are two institutional actors, judge and jury. Although there are some differences between federal and state court civil law practice, the following comments apply generally to both.

Stages of Civil Litigation

There are (roughly) six stages of litigation. Many different motions can be filed by either party at any stage of litigation. Motions to preserve evidence prior to suit are rare, but are sometimes available in unusual cases. However, rulings on motions filed at subsequent stages can so channel the litigation that they determine the success or failure of the parties.

The rough stages and possible maneuvers by either party are illustrated in Table 1.3.

Note that this chart does not address class action litigation. The class action device permits the aggregation of similar claims in a single lawsuit. For example, class actions have been used in thousands of civil rights cases to challenge alleged patterns of discrimination; in prison cases to challenge the conditions of confinement; and in consumer cases such as securities class actions. A number of special pretrial proceedings pertain to class actions, such as whether there are common issues across the class; whether notice need be provided to the class, and, if so, how; determinations as to whether the class representatives are adequate and representative; and inquiries into whether the class lawyers are competent and qualified. We analyze class action suits more fully in the civil procedure chapter (chapter 8).

In general, judges have enormous power to control, channel, or dismiss cases before trial. Most lawsuits never get to trial. In fact, the period before trial (generally known as *pretrial*) is often hotly contested, and many lawyers regard this as the period when lawsuits are either won or lost. Even if a case is ultimately *settled*, the value of the settlement (whether $100 million or $1) often hinges on the ability of each side to forcefully articulate their positions during the pretrial proceedings. (It may be helpful to think of pretrial proceedings as a complex process of negotiation.)

Here are some examples of defining moments in pretrial litigation:

- A plaintiff may file 10 separate claims against a single defendant, but a judge may dismiss all but one of the claims at the pretrial stage. The one that remains may not be sufficiently supported in the evidence and be rejected later in the litigation; or perhaps the damages available for the one remaining claim may make continuing the suit economically unviable.

Table 1.3 Types of Motions that can be Filed in Civil Litigation

Stage of Litigation	Purpose	Examples of Possible Motions
Prior to suit	• Investigation; preservation of evidence • Mediation/arbitration	• Motion to preserve evidence in anticipation of litigation (either party) • Motion to force arbitration (either party)
Suit filed	• Complaint (plaintiff) • Answer (defendant)	• Dismissal of complaint (by defendant) • Motion to strike answer or part of answer (by plaintiff)
Pretrial	• Discovery (e.g., depositions of witnesses; production of documents or other evidence; subpoena documents from third party)	• Motion to dismiss one or more claims (by defendant) • Motions to produce documents or evidence (by either party) • Motion for summary judgment (by either party, but usually by defendant) • Motion to sanction other party or other party's lawyer
Trial		• Motion to exclude evidence; restrict evidence or issues; to disqualify (or qualify) an expert • Motion to dismiss (by defendant) • Requests for jury instructions (either party)
Post-trial		• Motion for judgment not withstanding the verdict (usually by defendant) • Motion for new trial (by either party)
Appeals		• Either party may appeal errors of law • Either party may appeal evidentiary rulings • Either party may contend the evidence does not support the jury verdict

- The suit may make a novel claim that has not been previously recognized in the jurisdiction, and the trial judge may dismiss for failure to state a [legally cognizable] claim.
- A defendant may refuse to provide certain documents before trial, contending that they are *privileged*. The decision to order their production (or not) may determine whether a case can be won or lost.
- If there are several defendants in a case (e.g., in a medical malpractice case: a doctor, a hospital, a nurse, and a pharmaceutical manufacturer),

a decision to dismiss one of the parties may make the suit strategically unwinnable. For example, if a judge dismisses a hospital and a managed care provider from a malpractice suit, leaving only the physician as a defendant, the plaintiff may decide the case against the doctor alone cannot be won.

- Even if the plaintiff has a strong case, the defendant may have *defenses* that prevent the case from moving forward.
- A key witness may die, or move abroad, and thus be unavailable to provide critical evidence.

In general, if a party's evidence does not meet at least a minimum standard, the judge is required to dismiss the case. Also, there are many stages before and during trial at which a judge may dismiss a case on a defendant's motion. In other words, if a case is frivolous or makes claims that cannot be established in the evidence, a trial judge is duty bound to dismiss the case before trial.

Trial Roles of Judge and Jury

Assuming that a plaintiff's credible evidence satisfies the minimum standard, the case is permitted to proceed to trial. A trial judge has the responsibility to decide what law governs the case under consideration. The judge is also bound to regulate the flow of information the jury hears. The jury hears the evidence, and is then instructed by the judge as to what is the law. The members of the jury are bound by their oath to follow the law as laid down by the trial judge.

The relationship between the trial judge and the jury is usually defined by their respective roles: the judge determines what law applies to a given controversy and assesses whether the plaintiff's evidence meets the minimum threshold necessary to satisfy the legal standard. Then, the jury decides based on the believable facts, in light of the law, which party should prevail. In criminal proceedings, the government retains the burden of proof. In civil litigation, the plaintiff ordinarily has the burden of proof as to all issues necessary to establish her case.

After trial, each party is free to file post-trial motions. Once again, a losing party may challenge the outcome or move for a new trial. The losing party is also free to appeal. If a jury verdict goes against a plaintiff, it is extremely hard for that plaintiff to prevail on appeal unless the trial judge committed a serious error. This is because the burden of proof ordinarily rests on the plaintiff.

In contrast, a losing defendant may argue on appeal (once again) that the plaintiff's evidence was insufficient to meet the legal standard, that the trial judge made a serious error, or that the jury's damage award was out of line. Either the appellate or the trial judge is free to review the jury's award, and can either reject the decision for the plaintiff or revise (downward) the amount awarded. For example, in cases in which juries award punitive damages, trial and appellate courts frequently reduce the amounts awarded. The plaintiff is usually given a choice: accept the reduced award or face another trial. Most plaintiffs accept the reduced award.

In summary, the American legal system is complex, with many different moving parts. Our goal in this book is to sweep with broad strokes in order to enable a professional journalist or interested citizen to understand the core features of that system.

2 Constitutional Law

Karl M. Manheim
Professor of Law, Loyola Law
School, Los Angeles

Introduction

What Is Constitutional Law?

The United States has a written Constitution that serves as the highest legal authority in our system of government. The Constitution itself, as interpreted by the Supreme Court of the United States, supersedes all other sources of law—statutes, state law, and even international law. Not all democracies have the benefit of written constitutions. Great Britain, for instance, has a number of distinct instruments (starting with the Magna Charta), as well as decisions from monarchial, executive, legislative, and judicial bodies that form its "constitution." But we have a single authoritative document, amended from time to time, that serves as the "supreme law of the land."

Upon adoption in 1789, the Constitution of the United States created the present federal government and delegated power to its various parts. As a rule, the federal government has only those powers stated in the Constitution, which is why it is said that we have a government of limited powers. There is another sense in which federal powers are limited. The Bill of Rights, adopted in 1791, took away some of the powers granted just a few years earlier. State governments, on the other hand, do not derive their powers from the U.S. Constitution, but rather from their respective state constitutions. Similarly, the individual rights found in the federal Constitution did not apply to the states until the Fourteenth Amendment was adopted following the Civil War.

Constitutional law thus consists both of the powers granted to the federal government and the limits on those powers, plus the limits imposed on state and local governments. When official actions at any level of government and by any branch (legislative, executive, or judicial) conflict with the Constitution, they are said to be unconstitutional and invalid.

But who determines whether an official action conflicts with the Constitution? In other words, who interprets it? In perhaps the most important case in American history, *Marbury v. Madison* (1803), the Supreme Court declared that it had this task and power. Yet, there is nothing in the Constitution itself, or in any other foundational document, that gives the Supreme Court the ultimate power to interpret and enforce the Constitution. This power was simply asserted by Chief Justice John Marshall and has stuck ever since. But, from time to time, other branches of government have (briefly) challenged the Supreme Court's authority. One notable case arose in 1957 when Governor Orval Faubus ordered the Arkansas National Guard to surround Little Rock High School and block admission by black pupils in defiance of the Supreme Court's desegregation order in *Brown v. Board of Education* (1954). In response, President Eisenhower ordered the 101st Airborne Division into Little Rock to ensure the students' safety. The Supreme Court followed that action with a unanimous decision in *Cooper v. Aaron* (1958) affirming that the Constitution means what the court says it means, and all organs of government are bound by the court's interpretation. But the fact remains, without "influence over either the purse or the sword," the Supreme Court—and other courts—must rely on the force of their persuasive reasoning, and ultimately on the executive branch to enforce their judgments.

A Brief History of the U.S. Constitution

Constitutional law usually refers to the interpretation and enforcement of what is technically the *second* Constitution of the United States. The first constitution, called the Articles of Confederation, adopted in 1781, was in effect for eight years, until the new federal government was formed in 1789.

This second constitution has survived, with some changes, for over two centuries. This is an immense achievement, especially when compared to another constitution written at about the same time—the French Constitution of 1791, which lasted hardly a year. Our constitution even survived an attempt to replace it in the Southern states. While the Constitution

---

The Articles of Confederation also created a federal government, but one that was mostly impotent. As Alexander Hamilton stated in an effort to encourage adoption of the federal constitution:

To the People of the State of New York: After an unequivocal experience of the inefficiency of the subsisting federal government, you are called upon to deliberate on a new Constitution for the United States of America. The subject speaks its own importance; comprehending in its consequences nothing less than the existence of the Union, the safety and welfare of the parts of which it is composed, the fate of an empire in many respects the most interesting in the world.

Federalist No. 1 (1787)

of the Confederate States of America (1861)—in some ways our *third* constitution—failed, it is instructive to compare our various constitutions for their different visions of government power, states' rights, and individual liberties.

Fifty-five delegates convened in Philadelphia for the federal constitutional convention in May 1787. General George Washington was elected president of the convention, and James Madison was named secretary. By the end of that famously hot summer, most of the delegates had agreed to the final text, and reported it to the Congress. Congress then submitted the proposed constitution to "ratifying conventions" in the 13 states. The two most serious objections raised by the state conventions were: (1) the Constitution transferred too much power from state governments to the new national government; and (2) the Constitution lacked a bill of rights. Despite these concerns, the Constitution was ratified. Some state conventions ratified the document on condition that the first congress propose amendments that would guarantee individual rights, a mechanism for change embodied in Article V of the Constitution. Congress complied, and in 1791 sent 12 proposed amendments to the state legislatures. The 3rd through 12th of these were adopted and renumbered 1 through 10—these became known as the Bill of Rights.

Two more amendments—regarding state immunity from lawsuits and presidential selection—were adopted in the early 19th century, but a major overhaul in constitutional law occurred following the Civil War with the Thirteenth, Fourteenth, and Fifteenth Amendments (adopted in 1865, 1868, and 1870 respectively). Twelve more have been adopted since then at a pace of approximately one every dozen years, most dealing with voting rights and government structure.

Basic Structure of Government in the United States

While designing the structure of the government, the authors of the Constitution wanted to avoid a concentration of power, fearing the tyranny created by such power in Britain. There are two major structural themes organizing governmental power in the United States: **separation of powers** and **federalism**. The former refers to the allocation of powers among three differently constituted branches of the federal government—the executive branch, the legislative branch, and the judicial branch. The latter is a term that represents the allocation of powers between the federal government and the states.

Although the U.S. Constitution creates and empowers the federal government, it has little to say about state governments. State governments are created and structured by the individual constitutions of the states. The U.S. Constitution merely presumes the existence of states, and provides certain guaranties, such as protection against invasion.

Republican ("Representative") Government

The U.S. government functions as a representative democracy, also known as a **republican** government. Citizens have *no way* to directly influence legislation on a national level. There are no national referenda to vote on, no national initiatives, no way for citizens to propose, ratify, or reject constitutional amendments. National lawmaking at every level is based on the decisions of representatives. Some believe this is because the framers of the Constitution were fearful of "direct democracy"—where citizens directly control the legislative process.

Is "republicanism" antidemocratic? In theory, our representatives are accountable to the popular will. In practice, however, it takes a lot to unseat an incumbent. Once in office, elected officials seem more sensitive to their big campaign donors and their own ambitions than to their constituents. Popular movements to rein in the power of our national representatives (e.g., campaign finance reform, term limits) have met with limited or no success. The republican model is firmly entrenched.

The story is different at the state level. Most states have a form of direct democracy. This is where voters can adopt or reject legislation (proposals known as *initiatives* and *referenda*), or even change their state constitutions. In theory, this makes government more accountable to its citizens, but it is not clear whether the changes brought about by direct legislation are positive or negative. In California, for example, initiatives have sought to sanction racial discrimination, deny rights to same-sex couples, and severely limit taxes and spending. Many of these initiatives go awry, with unintended consequences. One such initiative, known as Proposition 13, set limits on increases in property taxes, and has been credited in degrading the California public school system from the nation's best to nearly its worst.

Initiative—A state ballot measure that proposes to enact a statute or constitutional amendment.

Referendum—A popular vote to overturn an act of the legislature.

Most initiatives and referenda are sponsored by interest groups.

The Amendment Process

Thomas Jefferson is credited with introducing the notion that people ought to change their form of government every few years. Unlike the French Republic of 1791, which created a constitution so perfect it did not provide for amendments, the framers of our Constitution recognized the need to correct mistakes and modernize the basic framework from time to time, as the need arises.

Article V states: "The Congress, whenever two-thirds of both Houses shall deem it necessary, shall propose Amendments to this Constitution . . . [which] shall be valid to all Intents and Purposes, as Part of this Constitution, when ratified by the Legislatures of three-fourths of the several States." This is the basic mechanism for amending the Constitution, and it has been followed in every case but 1 of our 27 amendments.

Rather than three-fourths of the state legislatures ratifying proposed amendments, Congress may specify that the amendments be submitted to ratifying "Conventions in three-fourths" of the states. This has occurred only once, with the Twenty-first Amendment (repealing the Eighteenth Amendment and ending "prohibition"). Apparently, the Congress thought the issue too volatile to be voted on by state legislatures.

Article V does provide an alternate mechanism both for proposing and ratifying amendments, which bypasses Congress entirely. The "Legislatures of two-thirds of the several States" can call a "Convention for proposing Amendments." This has never occurred, but almost did in the mid-1980s. Thirty-three states had "called" for a constitutional convention. Most were based on a desire to enact a balanced budget amendment, but some had other purposes (e.g., overturn the Supreme Court decision against prayer in schools). The California legislature was asked to join the call, which would have provided the requisite two-thirds, but declined to do so. An initiative petition was circulated and qualified for the California ballot, which would have enacted legislation calling for a U.S. constitutional convention. In *AFL v. Eu* (1983), the California Supreme Court struck the initiative from the ballot, holding that, under Article V, only state legislatures can issue a call, not the voters exercising legislative power. This was a highly controversial ruling, and may have contributed to the election defeat of three California Supreme Court justices, but it prevented us from having a new constitutional convention.

Federalism—The Role of States in the United States

Government power in the United States is a combination of centralized and decentralized authority. Certain powers are centralized in the federal government, which operates on a national (and international) scale. Other powers are decentralized, and fall under the domain of state and local governments. This division of powers between state governments and the federal government is known as **federalism**. The structure is thought to be the best way to balance the efficiencies of scale and national interests on the one hand, against local diversity and autonomy on the other. While there is general agreement on the basic theory of federalism, there has been significant (and sometimes violent) disagreement on the precise divisions of authority. For instance, should civil rights and environmental quality be left to the states to protect, or should the federal government set policy on a national level?

It is easy to underestimate the importance of federalism in constitutional analysis. First, it isn't a hot-button topic like free speech or abortion rights. Rather, it speaks the language of bureaucracy and political science. Second, the Supreme Court's federalism issues always seem so technical or mired in history that they turn the public (and journalists) off. Finally, why should we care how power is distributed in America when what we really care about is how that power is used—and how it is being abused?

These attitudes miss the mark entirely. Federalism is not only *the most important* topic in constitutional law, but also the most enduring. Our country was founded amid a federalism battle (the *Federalists* supported a strong national government; the *Anti-Federalists* wanted a weak one, and strong states). Four score and seven years later, the nation was torn apart by another federalism battle—the Civil War (often referred to as the War Between the States, but could just as well be called the Great Federalism War)—which was all about States' rights and its implications for slavery. Franklin Roosevelt's New Deal was another federalism struggle. When the Supreme Court refused to approve of his plan to give the federal government power to regulate the economy, FDR attempted to pack the Court in order to dislodge it from its conservative States' rights positions. Finally, many heated constitutional conflicts today concern federalism issues (e.g., federal civil rights laws, state sovereign immunity, and even health insurance). The Supreme Court has probably decided more federalism cases than any other issue in constitutional law.

Modern Issues of Federalism

The three main doctrines of federalism, still hotly debated, are (1) the extent of state vs. federal power; (2) state sovereign immunity; and (3) federal preemption of state law. As has been the case for over 200 years, ideological conservatives tend to prefer strong state power and weak federal power. States are often either less inclined or incapable of regulating such things as civil rights or economic matters. Therefore, if the federal government is kept out of such areas (in favor of states), then these areas are less apt to be regulated at all. Even where the federal government has power to regulate an area (e.g., disability rights), it may be unable to apply its laws to states if the latter have "immunity" from federal regulation.

Once in a while, states do enact progressive social or economic regulations. Conservatives' tool for dealing with environmental protection laws, labor rights, and other social welfare laws enacted on the state level is to argue the opposite of states' rights, namely, that state laws on such matters are preempted by federal law. Consistency is not only the hobgoblin of little minds but also the pariah of states' rightists. Thus, it is not uncommon to see the same people arguing for states' rights in some areas and federal preemption of state laws in others.

The Tenth Amendment—States' Rights

The powers not delegated to the United States by the Constitution, nor prohibited by it to the States, are reserved to the States respectively, or to the people.

The Tenth Amendment

The Tenth Amendment asserts that any power not given to Congress is a power belonging to state governments. The language of the Tenth Amendment has, over the years, been subject to no less than three interpretations, all tending to diminish federal power.

Doctrine of Enumerated Powers

Article I, section 8 of the Constitution gives to Congress broad powers over such things as interstate commerce, intellectual property, and military affairs. It has long been argued that Congress' powers are limited to this "enumeration," and that forays into areas beyond the list invades the reserved powers of the states. The earliest use of the Tenth Amendment was to reinforce this notion of a limited federal government. But, if you read the amendment carefully, you will see that it does not limit Congress' powers.

As federal power expanded in the late 19th century, due both to Union victory in the Civil War and to rapid industrialization, a conservative Supreme Court decided the best way to limit the federal government was through aggressive use of the Tenth Amendment and strict limits on enumerated powers such as the commerce power. In cases between the 1880s and 1936, the Supreme Court held that Congress could regulate only "interstate" matters; it lacked power to regulate mining, agriculture, manufacture, employment, or anything else "inherently local in character." For example, Congress could not regulate child labor, or even prohibit interstate shipment of articles made by children, since labor was inherently local.

In its most radical decision during this period (called *the era of Dual Federalism*), *United States v. E. C. Knight Co.* (1895), the court held the Sherman Antitrust Act unconstitutional when applied to the American Sugar Refining Co. That company controlled over 90 percent of the production, refinement, distribution, and sale of sugar in America. Yet, since each element of the integrated enterprise was "local in character," regulation was beyond Congress' power. And, of course, states could not regulate most of these elements either, since that would involve the extension of state laws beyond their borders. The Supreme Court went to great lengths to engrain laissez-faire economic theory into the Constitution.

The Era of Dual Federalism formally came to an end in 1941 (after Roosevelt's court-packing plan) with *Darby v. United States*. That case upheld Congress' power to regulate labor conditions, despite the argument that all labor and employment contracts were performed locally, because of their ultimate overall impact on the national economy. A strict demarcation between local and national economic issues may have made sense back in 1787, when the U.S. economy was mostly agrarian and transportation between markets was difficult (indeed, this was the argument of the Antifederalists in their tracts *Letters from the Federal Farmer* [1787–1788]). But such a distinction became sheer formalism once national markets formed. Today, it is difficult for us to conceive of anything that is purely local in character.

Apparently, it is not difficult for the Supreme Court. In a revival of Dual Federalism, the court has declared education and gun possession to be local concerns. In *Lopez v. United States* (1995), the court invalidated the Gun-Free School Zones Act, which made it a crime to possess a gun on or within 1,000 feet of school grounds. The *sale* of guns could be regulated at the national level, because "economic transactions" implicated national markets, but mere *possession* did not. Nor did it matter that guns had a profound effect on students' ability to learn. The relationship between guns in classrooms and the debilitating effect that it had on America's economic health was too attenuated to permit federal regulation. Since education was quintessentially a local concern (never mind the billions of dollars of federal funding), only states could regulate these matters.

On similar reasoning, in *United States v. Morrison* (2000), the Supreme Court held that parts of the Violence Against Women Act exceeded Congress' commerce power. As with gun possession, gender-related violence did not substantially affect interstate commerce. However, medical marijuana that is grown in one's own house for personal consumption *does* affect interstate commerce, despite the fact that it is neither sold nor transported. Thus, the federal Controlled Substances Act was held valid when applied to prohibit this type of marijuana use in *Gonzales v. Raich* (2005). What is nice about the Tenth Amendment and states' rights generally is that the nature of the right can morph into any desired shape.

President Obama's signature legislative achievement, the Patient Protection and Affordable Care Act of 2010, came under sustained attack by conservatives and states' rightists. Among their criticisms was that the act's central feature—the requirement that individuals have or buy health insurance—had nothing to do with interstate commerce and thus exceeded Congress' enumerated powers. The government's counterposition was that the uninsured have "a substantial and deleterious effect" on the national economy, costing governments and individuals with insurance (who wind up subsidizing the uninsured) hundreds of billions of dollars per year. Moreover, those without insurance are, in essence, self-insuring against the risk of future loss. Taken together, health care and its financing is the largest sector of the U.S. economy. Therefore, the insurance mandate was well within Congress's power to regulate the national economy.

In *National Federation of Independent Business v. Sebelius* (2012), five members of the Supreme Court took the states' rights position, holding that an individual's decision to forego health insurance was not itself a species of commerce, and thus could not be regulated by Congress. Justice Roberts's opinion speculated that if Congress could require individuals to buy insurance, as a means of protecting other economic activity, it could also force them to "eat a balanced diet." This is a classic "slippery slope" argument (cannot let Congress do one thing because it can then do just about anything—it is impossible to draw lines). But, of course, that is silly. The connection between the 50 million uninsured Americans and the $2.7 trillion per year health care market is infinitely stronger than that between eating broccoli and the agricultural commodities market.

It is hard to avoid the conclusion that the decision in *Sebelius* was a political one, not a constitutional one. This is reinforced by the ultimate holding in the case, where Justice Roberts switched his vote, joining the 4 moderates, to uphold the act on the theory that the individual mandate was within Congress' enumerated power to tax.

Federal Regulation of States

A second interpretation of the Tenth Amendment emerged when Warren Burger was chief justice in the 1970s. In *National League of Cities v. Usery* (1976), a closely divided court held that, although Congress had power to regulate wages and labor conditions, it could not exercise that power against the states themselves. Private employers had to comply with the Fair Labor Standards Act, but state and local governments (who, by the way, are collectively the largest employer in the country) could not be subject to the same laws, lest their "state sovereignty" be compromised. *Usery* reflected a conservative vision of sovereignty in America; states were the true sovereigns, not the people nor Congress. This is an accurate description of power under the Articles of Confederation (1781), where each state retained its "sovereign" rights, but it neglects the fact that sovereignty passed to the *United States of America* with ratification of the Constitution.

The holding of *Usery* lasted less than a decade. It was explicitly overruled in *Garcia v. San Antonio Municipal Transit Authority* (1985), another close decision. Justice Blackmun reversed his vote noting that state sovereignty, whatever that entailed, was protected through the structural composition of Congress (made up of the states) rather than through judicial decree. If the states did not like Congress imposing a particular obligation on them, they had a simple expedient: oppose the law. States can be subject to federal regulation only if a majority of their representatives in both houses of Congress agree. This is especially true of the Senate, where each state has equal suffrage. No bill becomes law unless a majority of states, through their senators, agree. However, this theory works only if legislation pending in Congress is explicit in its application to the states. Thus, in *Gregory v. Ashcroft* (1991), the court held that federal law does not bind the states (even where private parties engaged in similar activities are) unless a clear statement to that effect appears in the law.

Commandeering the States

The third interpretation of the Tenth Amendment builds on the first two. Even where Congress has power to regulate a particular area (first interpretation), and even where states must comply (second interpretation), Congress cannot "commandeer" state executive or legislative powers. In other words, Congress cannot draft state agents or bodies to enforce federal law. The "anti-commandeering" doctrine was announced in *New York v. United States* (1992) and *Printz v. United States* (1997). The former invalidated the Low-Level Radioactive Waste Policy Amendments Act of 1985 (LLRWPA), which required states to take responsibility for the disposal of most radioactive wastes generated within their borders. Congress clearly had power to regulate this area (nuclear power), and it could apply its regulations to states to the extent they were themselves generating nuclear waste (e.g., state power utilities, nuclear medicine at state hospitals). Thus, the first and second meanings of the Tenth Amendment were satisfied. But, Congress could not require states to enforce federal policy against third parties. The LLRWPA did that, unconstitutionally, by requiring states to regulate disposal. Such "commandeering" of state lawmaking powers denigrated state sovereignty and treated them merely as instruments of the federal government. The court reached a similar conclusion with regards to the Brady Act in *Printz*. That law required local police to do background checks on applicants for handgun ownership. Congress could delegate that power to a federal agency, but could not commandeer state and local officials to implement federal law.

This third interpretation of the Tenth Amendment is potentially the most serious when it comes to Congress' ability to regulate vast areas of modern life. Fortunately, Congress has found a nice end run around *New York* and *Printz*. Rather than *force* states to implement federal law, Congress can *buy* their cooperation. Thus, in setting a national highway speed limit or drinking age, Congress could do one of two things. It either could create a federal highway patrol, which would enforce federal law on the nation's highways, or it could provide federal highway funding to states *on the condition* that states set and enforce their own speed and age limits. Both of these options are constitutional (although the first is impracticable).[1] What Congress cannot do is set federal speed and age limits and require state police to enforce them.

The Three Lives of the Tenth Amendment

The Tenth Amendment is probably the Constitution's most litigated provision. It basically reaffirms the doctrine of enumerated power—that Congress has only those powers delegated to it by the Constitution. Any residual power resides in the states. In this respect, the Tenth Amendment "states but a truism," as the Supreme Court declared near the end of Dual Federalism. It does not answer the question of whether Congress has a particular power; it merely tells us the consequence of that query.

Recently, states' rights federalism has seen resurgence among conservative justices. For a time, the court held that the Tenth Amendment had a second meaning—Congress could not regulate states themselves, even when they were engaged in activities that, when engaged in by private parties (e.g., employment), were subject to federal regulation. This second interpretation gave way, but a third version has replaced it. Congress now violates the Tenth Amendment when it "commandeers" a state if it requires it or state officials to enforce federal policies against private parties. Unlike the original and second interpretations, this version is alive and well.

The Eleventh Amendment—State Sovereign Immunity

The judicial power of the United States shall not be construed to extend to any suit in law or equity, commenced or prosecuted against one of the United States by citizens of another State or by citizens or subjects of any foreign state.

The Eleventh Amendment

One of the first cases decided by the Supreme Court involved a Revolutionary War debt owed by Georgia to a citizen from another state, on which it defaulted. The creditor sued and prevailed in federal court, despite Georgia's claim that it enjoyed sovereign immunity from suit, especially in courts of a foreign sovereign (the United States). The Supreme Court rejected the defense, noting that states, in entering the Union, surrendered whatever sovereign immunity they enjoyed prior to adoption of the Constitution (*Chisholm v. Georgia* [1793]). Georgia responded by passing a law making compliance with the Supreme Court's judgment punishable by death "without benefit of clergy." The Eleventh Amendment quickly followed.

The Eleventh Amendment is the other of the twin pillars of state sovereignty embodied in the Constitution. What it adds to the Tenth Amendment is that even where Congress has enumerated power and can regulate states themselves (e.g., employment discrimination), private parties cannot sue states to enforce federal law. In other words, states are required to obey federal law, but no state or federal court can tell them to do so.

There are several notable exceptions to the Eleventh Amendment. First, it does not apply to suits against states brought either by the federal government or by other states. Second, states can waive their immunity. A state would waive its immunity, for instance, when borrowing money (the situation in *Chisholm*), since investors are unlikely to lend money without legal recourse in the event of breach. Third, Congress may abrogate state sovereign immunity when it passes laws enforcing the Fourteenth Amendment (due process and equal protection), but not when it exercises its other powers. This is partially because the Fourteenth Amendment was enacted later; thus, it was meant as a limitation on sovereign immunity. Fourth, the Eleventh Amendment does not apply to political subdivisions of states, such as cities, counties, and special districts. Therefore, a critical distinction arises between state agencies (e.g., California Highway Patrol) and local entities (e.g., Los Angeles Police Department). The former enjoy immunity; the latter do not. Whether a particular entity is an arm of the state (entitled to immunity), or a political subdivision (not entitled), is determined by how the state structures its own functions. Thus, while school districts in most states are considered local entities, in California they are considered to be state agencies (due to state funding in the wake of Proposition 13), and thus immune to suit.[2]

The final exception to Eleventh Amendment immunity is under a legal fiction known as the *stripping doctrine*, announced in *Ex Parte Young* (1908). When a state officer allegedly violates federal law, she is said to be acting outside her authority ("stripped" of her official state status), since a state *would never* authorize its officers to violate federal law. This is a neat trick. Instead of suing a state or state agency, one can simply sue the state official (e.g., governor, attorney general) who enforces an unconstitutional state law. The court extended the stripping doctrine in *Virginia Office for Protection and Advocacy v. Stewart* (2011), by holding that the doctrine of *Ex Parte Young* also allows a federal court to hear a lawsuit for prospective relief against state officials brought by another agency of the same state. However, there is a limitation to the stripping doctrine, namely that it allows for equitable relief only (injunction), and

---

Legal Fiction—Suppositions of fact taken to be true by courts, but which are not necessarily true. A conventional idea, only indirectly based on facts, respected for the sake of facilitating procedure.

not damages. That is because any money judgment would be paid from the state's treasury; the fiction of not suing the state simply does not extend that far.

The stripping doctrine is the most widely used means to circumvent the effects of the Eleventh Amendment even though damages and other monetary relief are not available. Sometimes one cannot avoid suing the state itself, such as when it holds legal title to disputed land or when a state agency infringes on a patent. Thus, "abrogation" by Congress is the only way to fully avoid the Eleventh Amendment.

Initially, the Supreme Court held that Congress could abrogate state sovereign immunity wherever the states had ceded power; namely whenever Congress validly exercised one of its enumerated powers. But, in *Seminole Tribe of Florida v. Florida* (1996), the court held that powers delegated to the federal government before the Eleventh Amendment was enacted—all the powers in the original Constitution—were curtailed by the later-enacted Eleventh Amendment when it came to suits against states. Only powers granted to Congress *after* the Eleventh Amendment—principally those contained in the civil rights enforcement clause of the Fourteenth Amendment—could be used to abrogate state sovereign immunity.[3]

This *should* be a minor problem at best. Congress has plenary power "to enforce . . . the provisions" of the Fourteenth Amendment against states. So long as it enacts a law, such as an antidiscrimination law, under its Fourteenth Amendment powers, Congress can authorize private suits against states for money. Therefore, advocates of states' rights have had to circumscribe Congress' civil rights enforcement powers as they endeavor to

---

The King Can Do No Wrong—Sovereign Immunity

At common law, the British King could not be sued in his own courts without consent. Despite the fact that we broke from Britain partly because of the crown's abuse of royal prerogative, the nascent states apparently preserved (or did not explicitly reject) the notion of sovereign immunity. Conservative courts in the late 19th and late 20th centuries declared state sovereign immunity to be a bulwark of American federalism. The Eleventh Amendment is textually very narrow—prohibiting only suits against states in federal court brought by citizens of other states. But the court has greatly expanded the Eleventh Amendment to include suits brought by a state's own citizens and suits brought in state court. As sovereign, the state is immune to suit, even when it acts illegally.

The Eleventh Amendment does not apply when Congress validly uses its Fourteenth Amendment powers to abrogate state sovereignty, or where a state official is sued for violating federal law (stripping doctrine). It also does not apply to cities and counties.

maintain state sovereign immunity. This topic is more fully discussed later in this chapter, but the short of it is, under modern Supreme Court precedent, Congress has little power to regulate civil rights under the Fourteenth Amendment. Thus, this way of avoiding the Eleventh Amendment has not proven very effective.

Constitutional Restrictions on State Power

The principal task of the Constitution of 1787 was to create the federal government and endow it with power. State governments already existed and were governed by their state constitutions. However, the federal Constitution transferred significant powers from states to the national government. States necessarily had to be disempowered in certain respects, lest they obstruct the functioning of the new central government.

The Constitution contains two mechanisms for restricting state power. The first is where the text explicitly or implicitly negates state power in a particular area. For instance, "No state shall enter into any Treaty, Alliance, or Confederation." Those are exclusively matters for the national government. The second way is where a state law conflicts with a federal law on the same subject. In such case, state law is said to be "preempted."

Constitutional Preclusion—Textual Limits on State Power

Article I, Section 10 contains a list of things states may not do. They cannot entreaty with foreign powers, keep troops or warships in peacetime, coin money, grant titles of nobility, lay taxes on imports or exports, or engage in war "unless actually invaded." States are explicitly "precluded" from acting in these specified ways. But states can also be precluded by implication.

Certain powers given to Congress are considered exclusive in that similar powers exercised by states would obstruct the workings of the federal government. For instance, Article I, Section 8, clause 3, known as the commerce clause, gives Congress power to "regulate Commerce with foreign Nations, and among the several States, and with the Indian Tribes." Is this a power Congress enjoys *concurrently* with the states, such that both can legislate on interstate or foreign commerce? Or is it an *exclusive* power, in which case it operates as a divestment of a like power in the states just as readily as had a specific prohibition been stated in Section 10? The answer to both is *yes*—sometimes it is concurrent and sometimes exclusive.

The dormant commerce clause is one of the oldest and most potent Constitutional doctrines. It determines when state regulation of commerce is constitutionally precluded and when it is allowed. If precluded, states may not regulate in an area even if there are no federal laws on the subject. For instance, to protect local agriculture, states may try to prohibit growers in other states from sending their produce to local markets. But the dormant commerce clause prohibits states from enacting barriers to trade and other parochial economic legislation, even where Congress has been completely silent on the issue. Similarly, states may not enact immigration laws because Congress' power over the matter is both plenary and exclusive.

The dormant commerce clause, like other federalism doctrines, is capable of manipulation in the pursuit of economic theories (typically laissez-faire) or to protect powerful interests. Thus, when Arizona enacted a safety law limiting railroad trains to 70 cars in length, Southern Pacific Railroad sued in federal court, claiming the law "burdened interstate commerce." The Supreme Court agreed, holding that the added cost of shipping goods outweighed the safety benefits of shorter trains (*Southern Pacific Railroad Co. v. Arizona* [1945]). The question remains, however: Are federal courts really the right place to make these judgments, balancing profits against health and safety? Is that not the job of legislators—and precisely why we vote for some rather than others?

The balancing test provided by the court (burden on interstate commerce vs. local benefits) has come under severe attack as being wholly inconsistent with the judicial mission. And while the Supreme Court has not decided such a balancing case in two decades, lower courts continue to strike state laws regulating economic matters on the ground that they too severely burden interstate commerce. This is judicial activism in action.

The dormant commerce clause doctrine also bars states from discriminating against interstate commerce. Thus, a state may not levy higher taxes or more burdensome regulations on out-of-state businesses than it imposes on local ones. However, the clause applies only to exercises of a state's sovereign powers (e.g., taxation, regulation). If a state enters the marketplace as a participant, the state's actions are treated the same as those of a private party, and therefore exempt from dormant commerce clause restraints. This exception is known as the Market Participant Doctrine, whereby a state may be able to justify conduct that would otherwise violate the dormant commerce clause by showing that the state was acting as a market participant.

The framework for the Market Participant Doctrine was announced in *Hughes v. Alexandria Scrap Corp.* (1976), where a Virginia corporate scrap processor sued Maryland state officials claiming that the state of Maryland was discriminating by preferring resident-based auto-processors and junkyards to out of state companies. The court held that the state of Maryland could prefer in-state processors because, just like a private party, it had the right to choose its own business partners. The doctrine applies only where a state *actually* participates in commercial activities. Where it regulates them instead (say, had Maryland given a tax break to local companies), the doctrine does not apply and the state is subject to the dormant commerce clause.

The most recent Market Participant case involved the state of Kentucky, which issues government bonds and exempts the interest on these bonds from state income tax (as is the practice in all 50 states). Taxing is a sovereign function and ordinarily not eligible for Market Participant exception from the dormant commerce clause. However, the court ruled that preferential tax treatment of its own government bonds was part of the market activity of selling bonds. Therefore, Kentucky was a market participant and not subject to the dormant commerce clause (*Department of Revenue of Ky. v. Davis* [2008]).

Constitutional Preclusion

The Constitution by its own force precludes states from acting in certain ways. Some prohibitions are explicit, such as those listed in Article I, Section 10, or in the Fourteenth Amendment. Others are implied, such as the dormant commerce clause. In either case, the limits are judicially defined and enforced. In this respect, the Constitution is "self executing." It does not need any implementing legislation from Congress to act as a restraint on state power. Individuals (or businesses) can sue directly under these constitutional provisions. Of course, if they sue states they must be careful to use the stripping doctrine, and they cannot obtain damages.

The Supremacy Clause—Preempting State Law

This Constitution, and the laws of the United States which shall be made in pursuance thereof, and all treaties made, or which shall be made, under the authority of the United States, shall be the supreme law of the land; and the judges in every State shall be bound thereby, anything in the Constitution or laws of any State to the contrary notwithstanding.

Article VI, Section 2.

The supremacy clause is the other side of federalism. State laws must yield to the federal Constitution and to "the laws of the United States" (and treaties). When state and federal laws conflict, the latter controls (or "preempts") the former. While the basic principle of preemption is settled, major disputes arise over when state and federal laws actually conflict; in the absence of conflict, both sets of laws should be given concurrent effect. Thus, federal labor laws and state laws on wrongful discharge can often coexist; and employers would be subject to both.

There are two basic types of preemption: "express" and "implied." If a federal statute clearly indicates that Congress does not want state laws on the same subject, then state laws are expressly preempted. The Employment Retirement Income Security Act (ERISA) provides an example

(29 U.S.C. § 1144[a]): "Except as provided in subsection (b) of this section, the provisions of this title and title IV shall supersede any and all State laws insofar as they may now or hereafter relate to any employee benefit plan." Even where Congress states its intent to preempt state laws, it is not always clear how broad the preemptive scope is. With ERISA, for example, it has taken more than a decade of Supreme Court decisions to define what "relate to" means.

Where Congress fails to clearly articulate its preemptive intent, state law may still be preempted if it would interfere with federal regulatory objectives. There are two forms of "implied preemption." "Conflict preemption" arises where an individual or business is subject to inconsistent state and federal laws. If it is literally impossible to comply with both laws, and one must give way, federal law will prevail. For instance, federal law requires automobile manufacturers to install a third brake light on the back of cars above or below the rear window. A state law forbidding such lights (on the ground they are more of a distraction than a safety benefit) will be preempted even if Congress never said anything to that effect. Clearly the two laws cannot coexist; it is presumed Congress would want its law to be obeyed. Recently, the Supreme Court has held that although agency regulations can preempt state laws, preemption is disfavored unless Congress expressly authorizes the agency to preempt state law (*Wyeth v. Levine* [2009]).

State law will also conflict with federal law if it "stands as an obstacle to the full accomplishment of Congress' objectives." For example, state workplace safety standards that are more rigorous than federal Occupational Safety and Health Administration (OSHA) standards are not in actual conflict with them (an employer can comply with both), yet might nonetheless disrupt the balance Congress has reached between worker safety and economic productivity.

Occasionally, Congress has enacted such comprehensive and pervasive regulations in an area (e.g., nuclear power) that state laws are preempted even where they are entirely consistent with federal law. Even an identical state law—word for word the same as federal law—will be preempted under the theory that Congress has "occupied the field" of regulation. In essence, state laws are preempted by occupation when Congress wants all enforcement and interpretation to occur in a federal agency or in a federal court.

"Laws" include not only statutes passed by Congress, but also rules and regulations of federal agencies (see below) and common law as created by federal courts (e.g., the "exclusionary rule"). It is interesting to see federalism at work, not to protect states' rights, but to displace them. Often, the same justices who vigorously defend state sovereignty by limiting the reach of federal law are quick to find preemption of state laws they dislike.

Preemption—The Supremacy Clause in Action

When state law cannot peaceably coexist with federal law, it is said to be preempted. This occurs because Congress (acting within its power) either explicitly or implicitly forecloses state law on a subject. Express preemption is easy in theory, but can be difficult to apply in practice. Even where express preemption is present in a federal statute, the scope of preemption must be determined. For instance, federal law requires health warnings on cigarette packages and expressly forbids state labeling laws. Can a smoker (or her estate) sue a tobacco company under state tort law for failure to warn of hazards, or is that state law expressly preempted?

Implied preemption comes in three flavors: (1) conflict preemption by physical incompatibility; (2) conflict preemption by frustration of purpose; and (3) field preemption where Congress fully occupies an entire field of regulation.

Preemption arises only when Congress has actually legislated on a subject. In contrast, constitutional preclusion occurs when Congress is silent. Plaintiffs challenging a state law might argue in the alternative: (1) state law is preempted by federal law; or (2) if federal law doesn't cover the situation, state law is nonetheless precluded. For instance, automakers challenging a state smog law might argue that it is preempted by federal environmental standards or, if not, burdens interstate commerce, and is thus precluded by the dormant commerce clause.

Separation of Powers—Struggle between the Three Federal Branches

Whatever else one might say about the U.S. Constitution, it is at least well organized. Article I establishes the Congress and vests it with legislative powers; Article II vests the executive power in a President; and Article III creates the Supreme Court (and authorizes "inferior" federal courts) and gives it judicial power. Thus, while the term *separation of powers* never appears in the Constitution, it is apparent from the structure of the federal government that powers are distributed between three separate and distinctly constituted branches of government.

Separation of Powers at the Constitutional Convention

The delegates to the federal convention were influenced by Montesquieu's theory of divided government, in which the powers of law creation, execution, and application were separated amongst different departments. Madison wrote in Federalist 47:

"No political truth is certainly of greater intrinsic value or is stamped with the authority of more enlightened patrons of liberty than this: the accumulation of all powers legislative, executive and judiciary in the same hands, whether of one, a few or many, and whether hereditary, self appointed, or elective, may justly be pronounced the very definition of tyranny."

Although the drafters were in agreement on the basic principle of separation, compromise was needed over which branch got what power. The delegates ultimately chose to give Congress the power to declare war, rather than the president, because the executive would be too prone to use it. In early drafts, the Senate was to appoint members of the Supreme Court. But the Senate was seen as too powerful, and in the last days of the convention, the power of judicial appointment was transferred to the president.

There are three ways in which the implicit but vital constitutional principle of separation of powers can be violated: (1) one branch of the federal government "usurps" power that the Constitution vests in another branch; (2) one branch "interferes" with another branch's exercise of its Constitutional functions; and (3) a branch performs functions assigned to it, but in an incompatible manner (e.g., action by a single house of Congress, or bicameral action that compromises judicial independence).

Despite these common themes, separation of powers analysis must proceed by department because, as it turns out, the Supreme Court is more forgiving of usurpation and interference by the executive branch than by the other branches.

The Power of Congress

All legislative Powers herein granted shall be vested in a Congress of the United States, which shall consist of a Senate and House of Representatives.

Article I, Section 1.

It would oversimplify the separation of powers doctrine to say that only Congress may legislate and Congress may do nothing but legislate. That idealized vision of government functions may have had some credibility in the 18th century, but in a modern industrial state one cannot realistically expect 435 representatives and 100 senators to deliberate every rule and policy matter no matter how detailed or intricate. Accordingly, Congress routinely delegates its lawmaking function to specialized administrative agencies located in the executive branch. Yet, the Supreme Court has been fairly rigid in constraining Congress' action and the scope of its powers.

Beyond Legislating

What else can Congress do besides pass laws? Legislating includes related functions such as investigating and setting the framework for agencies Congress creates. Committee hearings are both ubiquitous and occasionally legendary, as were the Army-McCarthy hearings in the early 1950s. Incident to its investigative powers, Congress may issue subpoenas, hold witnesses in contempt, and refer matters for prosecution. In performing the legislative function and related activities, members of Congress enjoy absolute immunity from civil suit and some immunity from criminal prosecution—as specified in Article I, Section 6.

Congress' other significant powers include:

- *Appropriations*: Congress has "the power of the purse," and it can use it to effectuate policy even where it does not have direct regulatory power. It could, for instance, de-fund executive departments that are frustrating Congress' will, or impose conditions on grant recipients of federal funds. Congressional opposition to a president's policies, for example, could be expressed by limits imposed on appropriations (e.g., prohibiting use of federal funds to transfer Guantanamo prisoners).
- *Jurisdiction of federal courts*: The Constitution creates only one federal court (the Supreme Court) but authorizes Congress to create "inferior" courts. In doing so, Congress gets to specify the extent of their powers, so long as it does not violate separation of powers by interfering with judicial functions. Thus, when Congress passed a special bill directing federal courts to "Grant Relief to the Parents of Terri Schiavo," some judges held this attempt to control the judiciary unconstitutional.
- *Declaration of war*: The interplay between Congress and the president in matters of war and foreign affairs has been at the forefront of separation of powers doctrine. Most of this will be discussed under the section on executive power, but Congress has, from time to time, asserted itself on matters of war policy. The War Powers Resolution (WPR;1973), for example, purports to limit the instances in which the president can commit troops without congressional assent. No president, from Nixon forward, however, has complied with the WPR, or conceded its validity.
- *Impeachment*: This is the process for removing "civil Officers of the United States," to wit: members of the executive and judicial branches.

(Interestingly, members of Congress are not "officers of the United States" and therefore cannot be impeached—they can, however, be excluded or expelled by their respective houses). The House impeaches (indictment by majority vote) and the Senate "tries all Impeachments" (conviction by two-thirds). Roughly a dozen federal judges have been impeached and convicted over the years. Two presidents have been impeached (Andrew Johnson and Bill Clinton), but neither were convicted.

The Senate has some powers not shared with the House. These involve matters of state—ratification of treaties—and confirmation of judicial and executive nominees; the former requiring two-thirds vote, the latter a simple majority. These powers operate in one direction only; the Senate cannot unratify (or abrogate) a treaty, nor can it remove a previously confirmed officer, except via the impeachment process. Only the president may cancel an international obligation or remove an officer.

Bicameralism and Presentment

One of the greatest limitations on congressional power is that, ordinarily, the concurrence of both houses is required to accomplish anything of substance. Other than those powers given uniquely to the Senate, "every Order, Resolution, or Vote to which the Concurrence of the Senate and House . . . may be necessary" (namely all legislation) must be *bicameral* (pass through *both* houses) and it must be "*presented* to the President."

Bicameralism and presentment (B&P) problems arise in the following circumstances:

- *Legislative veto*: Once Congress creates and endows a federal agency (e.g., the EPA), it cannot reject actions taken by that agency, even where the agency flouts the law. Problems can arise if different parties control Congress and the White House. Unauthorized agency action can be corrected either by Congress with new legislation (requiring B&P), or by courts upon review by an aggrieved party. Congress can put agency heads on the hot seat during oversight hearings, or it can de-fund an agency (occasionally threatened, so far never implemented). But direct administration of government functions is beyond congressional power.
- *Line-item veto*: In the 1990s Congress attempted to give the president veto power over particular expenditures in the federal budget, similar to the power most state governors enjoy. Previously, the president had to sign or veto the entirety of an appropriations bill, leading both to political compromise and horse-trading (contributing to the explosion in earmarks—formally called *plus-ups*, but colloquially called *pork*). When it became apparent that Congress had little self-restraint when

spending other people's money, it passed the buck to the president. The Supreme Court barred the line-item veto in *Clinton v. City of New York* (1998), because the maneuver resulted in a different appropriation than Congress had passed, effectively bypassing bicameralism.

Congress—The Most Dangerous Branch

The framers thought legislative power was the greatest threat to liberty and autonomy. Accordingly, in vesting that power in the new government, they bifurcated it in two distinctly constituted houses. The House of Representatives was to be the people's legislature, elected by direct popular vote. The Senate could be counted on to moderate popular passions because it was selected by state legislatures (the Seventeenth Amendment changed that in 1913). The Supreme Court strictly enforces this division through B&P. The design is apparently successful because it has been copied elsewhere. Nebraska is the only state with a unicameral legislature. Most modern democracies have bicameral legislatures, including the European Union with a popularly elected Parliament and a co-legislative Council, comprised of ministers from member states.

Executive Power

The executive Power shall be vested in a President of the United States of America.

Article II, Section 1.

There are only two nationally elected offices in the United States. And one of them—the vice president—is often ceremonial, except for presiding over and casting tie-breaking votes in the Senate. The president is, theoretically, the embodiment of national will.[4] As a result, power tends to concentrate in this office, despite the misgivings of Montesquieu and the framers.

The Constitution is fairly explicit on the powers of the president. These fall into three main categories: (1) military; (2) foreign affairs; and (3) executive or administrative.

War and Treaty Powers

There are two important limitations on this power. First, it is an executive, not a policy-making, power. That means, for the most part, the president cannot initiate war; he can only conduct one after it has been declared by Congress. There is an important and widely used exception to this division of authority. If the United States is invaded or otherwise attacked, very little policy deliberation is necessary in the decision whether to defend the country. Thus, it has long been understood to be part of the president's "inherent" powers to defend the nation. No declaration by Congress is necessary to state the obvious—the United States is at war when under attack.

The President shall be Commander in Chief of the Army and Navy [and] of the Militia of the several States, when called into the actual Service of the United States.

Article II, Section 2

Since the United States "never engages in offensive war," only defensive war, it would seem that participation by Congress is always beside the point. That has been the position of every president since our last declaration of war, on December 8, 1941. Military operations that could become expensive, however, will require appropriations by Congress at some point. Perhaps that is why both presidents George H. W. Bush and George W. Bush sought congressional approval for their respective Iraq wars. The former, at least, claimed he did not need to (and might have launched Operation Desert Storm anyway had the very close vote in the House gone the other way).

The War Powers Resolution, passed over President Nixon's veto in 1974, limits the president's authority to commit U.S. forces to hostilities without congressional authorization. However, neither President Nixon, nor any president since, has accepted the limitations on his war-making powers imposed by the War Powers Resolution. Even where a president concedes Congress' proper role in military funding, the political pressure on Congress to support our troops on the battlefield makes it unlikely that Congress can exert much policy influence on presidential war plans.

The second limitation on the president's war power is that he is Commander in Chief of the armed forces, not of the nation. In one of its most important separation of powers decisions, *Youngstown Sheet & Tube Co. v. Sawyer* (1952), the Supreme Court invalidated President Truman's seizure of the steel mills during the Korean War, despite Truman's claim that a labor strike threatened to cut off the supply of munitions and armaments to our fighting forces. Seizure, at least away from the field of battle, was a policy matter for Congress, not a strategic one for military commanders.

Applying *Youngstown* to the current debate over presidential power, it would appear that secret executive orders directing spying on American citizens, secret prisons, torture and detention without trial, and a host of other civil liberties violations, are also a violation of basic separation of powers principles.

> [The President] shall have Power, by and with the Advice and Consent of the Senate to make Treaties [and to] appoint Ambassadors."
>
> _____
>
> Article II, Section 2

> He shall receive Ambassadors and other public Ministers.
>
> _____
>
> Article II, Section 3

These powers make the president "head of state" in foreign affairs. But, what should be an important limitation on the treaty-making power of the president—the need for advice and consent by the Senate—has not been enforced by the Supreme Court. In the last few decades the president has been able to usurp this shared power through the use of executive or executive-congressional agreements. These are quasi-treaties, negotiated and signed only by the president. But they have only state-to-state[5] significance; they cannot create binding obligations within the United States. Executive-congressional agreements are similar to treaties but can have domestic effect upon passage of implementing legislation by Congress in the ordinary fashion (B&P), rather than by a two-thirds vote of the Senate. Many of our most important international obligations have taken the executive-congressional route, rather than formal treaty. These include NAFTA and our membership in the World Trade Organization (WTO).

Recently, the Supreme Court has held that even treaties are presumptively binding only among nations. Where the textual provisions of a treaty fail to indicate that the president *and* Senate intended for the agreement to have domestic effect, it is a non-self-executing treaty. Therefore, the treaty is not binding upon individuals, businesses or even U.S. states until the treaties provisions are enacted into law by Congress (*Medellin v. Texas* [2008]). In that case, the Supreme Court held that Texas was not bound by the Vienna Convention on Consular Relations to notify consular officials that nationals of their countries were being held on criminal charges. The court also held that Texas need not obey an order of the International Court of Justice (ICJ or "World Court") not to execute a Mexican national, since the treaty establishing the ICJ (the United Nations Charter) was not binding as domestic law. Finally, in *Medellin*, the U.S. Supreme Court held that President Bush's order that Texas comply with the ICJ decision was similarly not binding because the president could not unilaterally convert a non-self-executing treaty into domestic law. It would require an act of Congress to do so.

Executive Orders

The most frequently litigated separation of powers issue is when the executive branch performs legislative functions. In some respect, this is inevitable in a modern administrative state, where agencies (for example the FCC, FDA, and others) engage in "quasi-legislating" as part of their mission. Indeed, Congress often delegates rule-making power to agencies, invoking the agency's purported technical expertise, so they (Congress) can implement congressional policies.

Another form of legislating outside of Congress occurs when the president issues executive orders, often concerning controversial issues. President Truman seized the Youngstown steel mills by way of executive order. Another example is President Bush's *Military Order of Nov. 13, 2001*, concerning the "Detention, Treatment, and Trial of Certain Non-Citizens in the War Against Terrorism." This order has been the subject of several Supreme Court decisions, including *Hamdi v. Rumsfeld* (2004) and *Hamdan v. Rumsfeld* (2006).[6]

The constitutionality of executive orders (and similar action of a legislative character) is assessed under a test devised by Justice Jackson in *Youngstown*. Jackson saw presidential action as falling into one of three "zones."

- In *Zone 1* are those actions taken pursuant to power delegated to the president by Congress. When the president acts here, he is exercising both his and Congress' power (i.e., the maximum power possessed by the United States as a whole). No separation of powers problems arise.
- *Zone 2* consists of those presidential actions for which no congressional approval or disapproval exists. In the face of congressional silence, the president may need to act alone, or may need to wait for Congress. Which of those apply may turn on "imponderables" such as the urgency of presidential action and the damage done to constitutional rights and structure. Jackson referred to this as the "zone of twilight." Rod Serling must have been paying attention.
- *Zone 3* is where the president acts in defiance of Congress. This was the situation in *Youngstown*, where Congress had denied Truman the power to intervene in labor disputes. He did so anyway. Jackson held that the president could lawfully act in a Zone 3 situation only where the power is the president's alone, such that congressional disapproval is irrelevant.

Privileges and Immunities

The Constitution immunizes federal officers in a variety of situations. Members of Congress have "legislative immunity," meaning they cannot be held civilly accountable for statements made as part of the lawmaking process.

Judges have life tenure and salary protection. Finally, the president has a temporary immunity, while in office, from civil and criminal prosecution. In addition to these constitutional immunities, the Supreme Court has created several others as part of its common law powers. These common law rules, like all others, can be overruled by Congress. But, constitutional immunities are beyond congressional encroachment.

The president has absolute office immunity for all acts undertaken while president. The immunity is *absolute* in that it attaches automatically upon being sued, and no proof of malevolence or bad faith (e.g., firing a whistle-blower) will erode the immunity. It applies to all actions arguably taken as part of the *office* of president. In contrast, other governmental immunities are either qualified or functional, or both. A *qualified* immunity attaches only to acts undertaken in good faith.

For instance, the Supreme Court held that Attorney General Ashcroft acted in good faith when he authorized the arrest and detention of Abdullah al-Kidd as a material witness in the terrorism trial of Sami Omar al-Hussayen. The court stated that the attorney general acted on the basis of a valid warrant and therefore enjoyed qualified immunity, regardless of al-Kidd's allegation that the attorney general misused the material witness statute to hold suspected terrorists when the government lacked enough evidence to detain them (*Ashcroft v. al-Kidd* [2011]).

Functional immunity applies to specified functions of the office. Members of Congress and judges have absolute immunity, but only for acts within their legislative and judicial functions. A judge is not immune if she discriminates in hiring a law clerk, since hiring is an executive matter, not judicial.

In addition to immunity from suit, the president also enjoys *executive privilege*. That means the president cannot be compelled to testify or provide evidence. Unlike some immunities, which are stated in the text of the Constitution, privilege is an outgrowth of general separation of powers principles. Inquiry by Congress or the courts into core executive matters might interfere with the president's discretion or ability to obtain necessary advice. This was President Nixon's argument in the Watergate investigation. He asserted executive privilege in his refusal to turn over the tapes he had recorded in the Oval Office. In *United States v. Nixon* (1974), the Supreme Court affirmed the basic principles of executive privilege, but found the privilege qualified rather than absolute. That meant, in that case, that denying the tapes to the special prosecutor would be justified only if disclosing them would compromise national security or interfere with legitimate executive functions. The court gave Nixon the opportunity to make such a showing. He resigned rather than try.

The Supreme Court expanded the use of executive privilege in *Cheney v. District Court* (2004). The court suggested the vice president might also have a privilege based on separation of powers. Accordingly, he could resist turning over records of his Energy Policy Task Force that would, it was alleged, show undue influence by the oil industry in setting national energy policies. Expansion of executive privilege is part of the Unitary Executive strategy because it facilitates presidential control of the administrative state.

The Judicial Branch

> The judicial Power of the United States, shall be vested in one supreme Court, and in such inferior Courts as the Congress may from time to time ordain and establish.
>
> ———————
>
> Article III, Section 1

Courts make policy as part of their common law function (crafting rules of decision and rights to relief). Just as federalism works at the legislative level, by delegating only specific powers to Congress and leaving the rest with the states, it also works at the judicial level. Had the Constitution created an entire body of lower ("inferior") courts, it would have transferred much of the common law function from state to federal realms. By leaving that question to Congress, states were given protection from this form of usurpation; their representatives would have to agree to create other federal courts. Moreover, Congress' power to create, or not create, lower courts means that Congress also specifies their jurisdiction (extent of power). Congress has a like power over the Supreme Court's appellate (but not its original) jurisdiction. Can Congress create courts without the power to hear habeas corpus or deny that power to the Supreme Court? The only cases on this, so far, stem from the Civil War and are somewhat inconclusive. *Ex Parte McCardle* (1868) held that Congress could repeal a particular habeas route, so long as others remained open. *Ex Parte Milligan* (1866) held that habeas must be available to American citizens, even during wartime, at least while civilian courts were functioning.

The issue has recently been reexamined within the framework of the War on Terror. In *Hamdan v. Rubsfeld* (2005) the Supreme Court denied the government's motion to dismiss the case under a provision of the Detainee Treatment Act of 2005, which generally deprived any court, justice, or judge of jurisdiction to consider a habeas corpus application filed by or on behalf of an alien detained at Guantanamo Bay. *Boumediene v. Bush* (2007) held that detainees were not barred from seeking habeas merely because they had been held at Guantanamo Bay or designated as enemy combatants.

Given its control over jurisdiction, can Congress specify that federal courts exercise their power in a particular way? In *United States v. Klein*

(1871), the Supreme Court held unconstitutional a statute directing courts how to treat the effect of presidential pardons. This interfered not only with the judicial function, but also the president's power to issue pardons.

The consensus on congressional control of federal jurisdiction is that Congress has broad power in this area, with three exceptions: (1) Congress may not itself decide cases (or *usurp* the judicial power); (2) it may not *interfere* with the judicial power, either by preventing courts from exercising their essential function of judicial review or by depriving judgments of finality; and (3) it may not *compromise* judicial independence by impressing nonjudicial functions on judges. Note: a president's assertion of executive privilege to protect the sanctity of executive functions also interferes with a court's ability to perform its function (i.e., adjudicate cases). Treating executive privilege as qualified rather than absolute is an effort to balance these separation of powers concern.

Due Process and the Protection of Individual Rights

As reported by the convention on September 17, 1787, the Constitution did not include many guarantees of individual rights. There were a few (e.g., no ex post facto law or suspension of writ of habeas corpus; see, Article I, Section 9), but the grand ones (e.g., freedom of speech, due process) were absent. Roger Sherman, delegate from Connecticut, said that since the state declarations of rights were not repealed by the Constitution, they would be sufficient to protect the people. The Congress, he said, "may be safely trusted." Elbridge Gerry of Massachusetts moved to include a bill of rights. On roll call, not a single state delegation voted for Gerry's motion. Two days later, Gerry proposed adding a declaration that "the liberty of the press should be inviolably preserved." If he could not get a full bill of rights, he would settle for just one. Sherman again answered: "It is unnecessary. The power of Congress does not extend to the press." On the roll call, only one state, Maryland, voted *aye*.

Madison believed that the real danger to liberty lay not simply in "big government," but in big government that was improperly constituted. If the powers of each branch were properly checked—as he believed they were—a bill of rights was superfluous. Some weeks later, when Madison wrote Thomas Jefferson in Paris and informed him that the convention had rejected a bill of rights, Jefferson reacted by return mail with fury: "A bill of rights is what the people are entitled to against every government on earth, general or particular, and what no just government should refuse or rest on inference."[7]

As it turned out, the exclusion of a bill of rights was the convention's worst political blunder, and it would come back to haunt the Federalists during ratification. Many state ratifying conventions demanded, as a condition of their assent to the new government, that Congress add a Bill of Rights.

The first Congress did so and submitted 12 proposed "amendments" to the states for ratification in 1791.

The first and second proposed amendments (involving apportionment and compensation of representatives) did not garner the required three-fourths of the states.[8] But amendments 3 through 12 were ratified and renumbered 1 through 10. The first 8 of these guarantee certain rights against the federal government. The Ninth Amendment presents a bit of a quandary:

The enumeration in the Constitution of certain rights shall not be construed to deny or disparage others retained by the people.

Does this language give courts license to create "unenumerated" rights at will, such as the "right" of employers to pay their employees substandard wages (cf. *Lochner v. New York* [1905])? Unenumerated rights (i.e., those rights not derived from the Constitution itself) were popular during the so-called *Lochner* era—a period of conservative judicial activism. Even liberal justices have occasionally resorted to the Ninth Amendment to justify creating rights (e.g., "right to privacy"; [cf. *Griswold v. Connecticut* (1965), right to use contraceptives]). The better view of the Ninth Amendment is not that it allows courts to create new rights, but that it is a rule of constitutional interpretation; namely the rights that are mentioned (e.g., speech, press) ought to be expansively construed.

Incorporation

Although the Bill of Rights created a set of substantive rights, in *Barron v. Baltimore* (1833), the Supreme Court ruled that it did not apply to the states; it was a restriction only on federal power. For protection against state abuses, citizens had to look to their own state constitutions. Moreover, it was the state ratifying conventions that demanded a Bill of Rights. They likely did not intend to restrict their own power in doing so; rather, they were fearful of the federal government.

But state constitutions did not always provide meaningful protection, as was amply demonstrated by the Southern states. One of the purposes of the Fourteenth Amendment following the Civil War was to interpose federal authority between states and their citizens, to protect the latter. Indeed, the chief architect of the Fourteenth Amendment, Senator John Bingham of Ohio, argued that the main purpose of the privileges or immunities clause was to overrule *Barron* and make the Bill of Rights applicable to the states. After all, what are the "privileges" and "immunities" of U.S. citizens, if not the rights contained in the Bill of Rights?

> No State shall make or enforce any law which shall abridge the privileges or immunities of citizens of the United States; nor shall any State deprive any person of life, liberty or property without due process . . .
>
> ─────────────
>
> Fourteenth Amendment, Section 1, Clauses 2, 3

The conservative postwar Supreme Court disagreed and interpreted the privileges or immunities clause to be almost meaningless (*Slaughterhouse Cases* [1873]).[9] A new argument emerged afterwards—that it was the due process clause that "incorporated" guarantees of the Bill of Rights and made them applicable to the states. Some justices argued for "total incorporation," meaning that the entirety of the Bill of Rights should apply to the states.

The "total incorporation" position never caught on. Most justices, instead, thought that the due process clause, in its protection of "liberty" operated to "selectively incorporate" some of the Bill of Rights, but not all. Under this approach, the First, Second, Fourth, Fifth (mostly), Sixth, and Eighth Amendments have been held to apply to the states, although not necessarily in exactly the same way they apply to the federal government. The Third, parts of the Fifth, and the Seventh Amendments have not been incorporated. That means, for instance, that a state is not under a federal constitutional obligation to provide jury trials in civil cases. Most do, but as a consequence of state law, not because they are required to do so by the federal Constitution.

A variety of formulations have been used over the years to determine whether a particular right found in the Bill of Rights was a component of due process liberty and was thus "incorporated" and made applicable to the states. Some of the tests were fairly restrictive—such as whether a particular right was "essential to a scheme of ordered liberty." Rights of criminal defendants (e.g., Fifth Amendment privilege against self-incrimination) often failed this test and did not get incorporated until much later. Other tests were even more malleable, such as whether a particular state practice "offended canons of decency and fairness of English-speaking peoples." In practice, most of the tests for selective incorporation worked to protect states' rights against judicial interference.

Incorporation doctrine received some clarity in *McDonald v. Chicago* (2010), albeit in a highly controversial fashion. In *District of Columbia v. Heller* (2008), the Supreme Court ruled that the Second Amendment protected an individual right of gun ownership for self-defense, and not just the right of state militias to be armed for the "security of a free State." But Heller involved the direct application of the Second Amendment to the federal government, of which Washington DC is a part. Whether the

Second Amendment should be incorporated was a different question; one resolved by the 5–4 split in *McDonald*. In writing for the majority, Justice Alito adopted the following test for incorporation—whether a right contained in the Bill of Rights was "deeply rooted in this Nation's history and tradition." The majority answered that question in the affirmative, despite the fact that the court had rejected finding a Second Amendment right to individual gun ownership during the previous two centuries.

Incorporation

Most of the individual liberties found in the Bill of Rights have been incorporated through the Fourteenth Amendment due process clause to apply to the states. Thus, when a state law abridges freedom of speech, it violates the First Amendment via the Fourteenth. Some justices reject incorporation. They feel that although the Fourteenth Amendment creates rights against state abuses, principally through non-interpretivist definition of the term *liberty*, these are fewer and not necessarily the same as those found in the Bill of Rights. Some argue for *dis-incorporation* (returning to the days of *Barron*) in furtherance of states' rights federalism, especially in criminal cases.

Standards of Review

If a right is found in the Bill of Rights (through one of the prevailing theories of interpretation) and is incorporated through the Fourteenth Amendment, or otherwise considered part of due process liberty, then that right is **fundamental** for constitutional purposes. Fundamental rights are not absolute. For instance, the rights of free speech and press, which are about as important as they come, will give way to compelling state interests to protect troops in battle and other national security interests. There are judicially created exceptions to every fundamental right, circumstances where the balance shifts from individual rights to state interests. Fortunately, these are rare and hard for a state to establish. But the Constitution contains no absolute rights.

When a state deprives a person of a fundamental right, the state action is subject to the most exacting judicial review—**strict scrutiny**. The standard for strict scrutiny is that a law must be narrowly tailored to meet a compelling government interest. The general interpretation by courts is that narrowly tailored means that the statute must be the least burdensome or least discriminatory manner in which that government's goal can be achieved. If the state law fails this standard, it is unconstitutional. If the law survives strict scrutiny, it is constitutional.

When a claimed right is not found in the Constitution, or not incorporated, it is a nonfundamental ordinary right. Ordinary rights, when deprived, trigger a low level of scrutiny called **rational basis**. Under this standard of review, the state need only show that it is acting rationally and not arbitrarily. States act rationally (even if they do not know it at the time) because a law subject to rational basis review will be upheld if "any conceivable set of facts" (not necessarily those the legislature actually considered) would show a rational basis for the state's action.

Generally courts use either strict scrutiny or rational basis as their standards of review. However in some cases courts rely on a standard of intermediate or mid-level scrutiny. This level of scrutiny is most commonly seen in cases involving gender discrimination. Under this standard courts will look at whether a statute is substantially related to an *important* government interest (the interest need not be compelling). Although mid-level scrutiny can also be exacting, some laws survive, such as naturalization laws that distinguish between American citizen mothers and fathers (*Nguyen v. INS* [2001]).

Because laws subject to strict scrutiny are presumptively unconstitutional, and laws subject to rational basis review are presumptively constitutional, often the only real issue in a case is what standard of review to apply. Once that is known, for all intents and purposes, the case is over.

Standards of Review

Strict scrutiny applies to the deprivation of fundamental (constitutional) rights. Rational basis applies to all nonfundamental (ordinary) rights. Under either test, a court will examine the state's *ends* and *means*.

Strict scrutiny requires that the state prove the following: (1) it has a compelling interest at stake (compelling *ends*); and (2) this particular law or state action is not narrowly tailored to achieve that compelling interest; in other words, whether the *ends* can be achieved by a *means* any less burdensome on the claimant's fundamental right. This is a very difficult standard of review to meet. A law can fail strict scrutiny review either because the state's *ends* are not compelling, or its *means* are not necessary, or both.

Under rational basis review, the state's *ends* need only be legitimate (in contrast to compelling) and its *means* rationally related to those *ends*. Since most state objectives are legitimate (only those specifically prohibited would fail), and most mechanisms (*means*) devised to achieve those goals are rational (only truly counterproductive laws would fail), this is a very easy standard of review to meet.

In some cases the court applies a midlevel standard of review (important *ends* and substantially related *means*), but strict scrutiny and rational basis are the most common.

The Right of Privacy

The word *privacy* appears nowhere in the text of the Constitution, but most justices have found the concept implicit in light of the specific rights that are mentioned. The leading case on privacy is *Griswold v. Connecticut* (1965), which invalidated a state law making it illegal to use contraceptives. Justice Douglas found the right of privacy in the **penumbras** (outer boundaries) of the Bill of Rights, namely as a logical extension of the First Amendment (rights of free speech, assembly, and religion), the Third Amendment (prohibitions on quartering soldiers in private homes), the Fourth Amendment (prohibitions on unreasonable searches and seizures), and the Fifth Amendment (the right against self-incrimination). Taken together, these rights create a **zone of privacy**, especially within the sanctity of one's home, where the prohibition on the use of contraceptives would have to be enforced.

Other justices (in *Griswold* and elsewhere) have found the right of privacy in the Fifth and Fourteenth Amendments' protection of **liberty**. Sourcing privacy in the due process clause gives the court much greater flexibility than having it tied to specific textual rights. Flexibility is not always good in constitutional law, as it allows the personal preferences of judges to creep into the analysis. For example, privacy *qua* liberty did not include sexual intimacy in *Bowers v. Hardwick* (1986), but did some years later in *Lawrence v. Texas* (2003). The due process clause had not changed; the justices had.

Despite the analytical superiority of the *Griswold* framework (broadly reading the Bill of Rights to find underlying principles), the court now mostly uses the due process clause as the basis for the right of privacy, by defining *liberty* to include certain human interests (e.g., procreation), but not others (e.g., rights of biological parents to have access to children).

There are two forms of the *right of privacy*. The one most easily tied to the Bill of Rights is privacy from **government snooping** (i.e., physical privacy of persons, places, and things). This form has its closest expression in the Fourth Amendment's prohibition on unreasonable searches and seizures. Privacy from government snooping applies to interception of phone calls, e-mail, banking information, and other communications and personal data. It would also apply, for example, to collection and use of DNA or medical information.[10]

The second, and more controversial, right invoked under the banner of "privacy" is **personal autonomy**—the right to do with one's body what one chooses and to make life choices free from government interference. Physician-assisted suicide, consumption of marijuana, unpopular sexual practices and lifestyles, and so on would rise to the level of constitutional rights under this approach. Several important rights, such as abortion, were based on the notion of privacy *qua* personal autonomy (since abortions are performed in public establishments, such as clinics and doctor's offices, it is hard to argue the first form of privacy—freedom from government snooping). The personal autonomy form of privacy is more likely found under liberty in the due process clause, which is why that approach has gained popularity on the court.

Family Rights

Abortion Rights

In *Roe v. Wade* (1973), the Supreme Court found that the right of privacy (*qua* personal autonomy) included a woman's right to terminate an unwanted pregnancy. The court rejected the notion that a fetus was a "life" entitled to its own protection under the Fourteenth Amendment. It had not been treated as such at common law, in most states, nor by the medical profession. Religious teaching that life begins at conception could not be codified into state law without violating the establishment clause.

Although a fetus was not a life, the state did have a compelling interest in protecting the "potentiality of life." Thus, as pregnancy progressed and a fetus approached viability outside the womb, the state's interest grew stronger. The point of intersection, where the state's interest outweighed the woman's, was at the beginning of the third trimester. After that point, the state could prohibit abortion. During the second trimester, the state had another compelling interest—the health of the mother—that allowed it to regulate how abortion services were provided, but not to outlaw the procedure.

Roe was revamped in *Planned Parenthood v. Casey* (1992), which rejected the trimester approach, but retained the basic right to have an abortion. States can now prohibit abortion once "viability" outside the womb is reached, so long as the law contains an exception when necessary to protect the life or health of the mother. *Casey* also introduced the concept of "undue burdens" (discussed below), which permits states to obstruct and discourage abortions, so long as they do not outright ban them.

In *Stenberg v. Carhart* (2000), the court invalidated a Nebraska law outlawing so-called partial-birth abortion (in medical terms, "intact dilation and extraction"). Nebraska justified banning these particular previability abortions because they were "brutal and gruesome." This reasoning seemed to treat the fetus as a living feeling being, which had been rejected in *Roe*. Plus, there was no health exception, as required by *Casey*.

Stenberg was a 5–4 decision, with Justice Kennedy voting to uphold the law and Justice O'Connor voting to invalidate it. Now that Justice O'Connor has been replaced by Justice Alito, we have already seen a shift in the court's understanding of abortion rights. In an opinion by Justice Kennedy, the court held that the Partial-Birth Abortion Act of 2003 (18 U.S.C.S. § 1531), which prohibited "knowingly perform[ing] a partial-birth abortion . . . that is [not] necessary to save the life of a mother" did not facially violate the Constitution. The court held that the act did not prohibit the most common abortion procedures used in the first trimester of pregnancy or the usual second-trimester procedure of "dilation and evacuation" (D&E). Thus, the act did not impose an undue burden on a woman's right to an abortion (*Gonzales v. Carhart* [2006]).

As of 2012 there appeared to be four votes to overturn *Roe* (Roberts, Scalia, Thomas, and Alito). Justice Kennedy remains the swing justice here, as in many areas. While unwilling to reject abortion rights entirely, he has been voting to restrict them.

Procreation and Parental Rights

The notion of fundamental rights under the Constitution proceeded on two tracks in the early 20th century. The first involved economic liberties (of capital not labor). These are discussed in detail later in the chapter (see Economic Rights and the Origin of Substantive Due Process section). The second track involved the type of privacy issues we have become familiar with (personal autonomy). It started with the rights of parents to rear their children without state interference. In *Meyer v. Nebraska* (1923), the court invalidated a law prohibiting the teaching of German, and in *Pierce v. Society of Sisters* (1925), the court invalidated an Oregon law that prohibited private schools. The right to raise one's children quickly gave rise to the right to have children. In *Skinner v. Oklahoma* (1942), the court invalidated a law requiring the sterilization of repeat felons, noting "marriage and procreation are fundamental to the very existence and survival of the race." *Skinner* also illustrates how the court's rights jurisprudence can be influenced by external events. Earlier, in *Buck v. Bell* (1927), the court upheld a state eugenics law sterilizing a "feeble-minded" woman. Justice Holmes infamously stated that "[t]hree generations of imbeciles are enough." But then eugenics got a bad name in Nazi Germany. In *Skinner* the court not only repudiated its embarrassing precedent, it set a new course for finding substantive fundamental rights under the due process clause.

The line from *Meyer* and *Pierce*, through *Skinner*, to *Griswold* and *Roe* should be clear enough. They each involve **parenting** decisions. While parents generally have the "fundamental right to make decisions concerning the care, custody, and control of their children," the court still decides on an issue-by-issue basis how expansive parental rights are. Even where a fundamental right is found, states often have "compelling" reasons to abridge them, especially where necessary to protect children.

In *Michael H v. Gerald D* (1989), the Supreme Court declared that "biological" parents had no parental rights against "legal" parents. In that California case, a married woman had an extramarital affair, leading to the birth of a daughter. Under state law, a married woman's husband was conclusively the "father" of the child (unless he was impotent). California law saw the actual father as a stranger, and denied him the right to see his daughter. In a decision that hallmarked his approach to fundamental rights, Justice Scalia wrote that because, at the time of adoption of the Constitution, adulterous fathers had no common law rights in their offspring, they had none under the Constitution either.[11]

Scalia's strict "originalist" approach to constitutional interpretation was subsequently rejected by a majority of the Court, but *Michael H* has not been overruled. The case highlights a common criticism of originalism. The common law rule made sense in the 18th century, when proof of parentage was difficult to obtain and being born out of wedlock carried legal disabilities and the opprobrium *bastard*. But the rule hardly makes sense today, with the availability of conclusive DNA evidence of paternity (e.g., the 98.07% probability in *Michael H*) and discrimination against nonmarital children no longer permitted. But intervening technologies and social standards have no retroactive effect on what the framers of the Constitution intended. To Justice Scalia, it is the latter that controls how the Constitution should be interpreted today.

As *Michael H* indicates, fundamental parenting rights are generally limited to legal parents. Thus, in *Troxel v. Granville* (2000), the court held that grandparents have no constitutionally based visitation rights over the objections of parents. And, of course, even the fundamental right of a parent can be overcome by a compelling state interest (e.g., for child welfare purposes).

Marriage, Divorce, and Sexual Intimacy

Marriage is closely related to procreation and parental rights, and was therefore an early candidate for constitutional protection. It originated in *Loving v. Virginia* (1967), an equal protection case.[12] The liberty basis for marriage obviously has a long pedigree, but it is a good place to discuss the nonabsolute nature of our fundamental rights.

Clearly, the state has strong interests in regulating marriage. That is why you must obtain a marriage license. State interests include birth defects (closely related individuals cannot marry), protection of children (minimum age requirements), and spousal welfare (prohibitions on polygamy and polyandry). The invalidated Virginia law was called the "Racial Integrity Act," often referred to as a racial purity law (enforced by antimiscegenation laws) was invalidated in *Loving*.

How about preserving the sanctity of marriage by limiting it to heterosexual couples? If the fundamental right at stake is the **"right to marry"** *vel non*, than any restriction would have to pass through strict scrutiny. It is far from clear that perpetuating religious and cultural mores about homosexuals would be compelling. However, if the right involved is the "right of heterosexual couples to marry," then a ban on gay marriage simply does not infringe on any fundamental right, and need only survive rational basis review. This also highlights the need to describe the fundamental right at stake with a fair degree of care. How specific should the right be characterized?

Originalists (such as Scalia) would describe the right at the most specific level known at common law. The right of marriage, circa 1787, probably extended only to free adult persons of the same race but opposite sex. Virginia's racial purity law might survive under that reasoning, as would surely a law barring gay marriage. But it is hard, on a principled basis, to claim that marriage is fundamental for some persons and wholly unprotected for others. Accordingly, at least some justices would find that gays have the same fundamental right to marry as anyone else.

States have lead the charge here, both in legislation and judicial decision. The first clear case was *Goodridge v. Department of Public Health* (Mass. 2003), where the Massachusetts Supreme Judicial Court found a right of same-sex marriage in their state constitution. The California Supreme Court followed suit in *In re Marriage Cases* (Cal. 2008). However, the state constitution was amended by Proposition 8 to overturn that decision and deny recognition to same-sex marriages. The California Supreme Court upheld Proposition 8 on state constitutional grounds in *Strauss v. Horton* (Cal. 2009). The proposition was then challenged in federal court on due process and equal protection grounds. In *Perry v. Schwarzenegger* (2010), the district court agreed with both claims, finding that gays had a fundamental right to marry and that they were a "suspect class" for equal protection purposes (see Section 5). The Ninth Circuit affirmed that decision in 2012, but on narrower grounds (*Perry v. Brown* [Ninth Cir. 2012]). The case may be destined for the Supreme Court.

Divorce is the flip side of marriage. It too is fundamental, meaning that state restrictions on its exercise are subject to strict scrutiny. Most state laws imposing predicates for divorce such as abuse, infidelity, and impotence have given way to no-fault divorce laws. In *Boddie v. Connecticut* (1971), the court struck down a state law imposing court fees on divorce petitions as interfering with the right of indigent persons to obtain a divorce. But in *Sosna v. Iowa* (1975), the court upheld a state residency requirement for divorces, finding that the state had a compelling interest not to become the nation's divorce mill.

The last major right in this category is sexual intimacy. This includes how and with whom one has sex. While the missionary position may be preferred by missionaries, can they enforce their sexual preferences on the rest of society? Many state legislatures thought so, and prohibited sodomy and other "crimes against nature." While the court has not ruled directly on this issue, its overturning of a law banning homosexual sodomy in *Lawrence v. Texas* (2003) suggests that states have little if any authority to regulate our sexual practices.

The same applies to our sexual partners. States seem to want to know with whom we are having sex. Can they prohibit sex outside of marriage or with persons of the same sex? *Lawrence v. Texas* (2003) answers the latter explicitly (gays have a right of sexual intimacy) and the former implicitly (recognizing "an emerging awareness that liberty gives substantial protection to adult persons in deciding how to conduct their private lives in matters pertaining to sex").

Family and Sex Rights

Family rights were among the earliest fundamental rights protected under the due process clause. The rights to marry, divorce, have children (or not), and raise them free from state interference, are all fundamental. Similarly, matters of sexual intimacy (choice of sex partners and perhaps sexual practices) are now seen as components of due process liberty. The state may regulate these matters only in pursuit of compelling state interests.

What constitutes a compelling state interest? Proselytizing religious views or outdated morals no longer works. Simply because a practice was banned in Elizabethan times does not mean it can be today. But compelling interests do arise occasionally, for example, protection of children, genetic defects, and abuse of the special privileges associated with marriage (*see Reynolds v. United States* [1878]; upholding bigamy statute).

Where a state successfully shows a compelling interest, it must pursue that interest through narrowly tailored means. For instance, in *Zablocki v. Redhail* (1978), Wisconsin had a compelling interest in child welfare. But it could not advance that interest by denying remarriage to a person simply because he was in arrears on child support payments. The state law failed strict scrutiny of *means*.

The Right to Die

When the Constitution was adopted in 1787, suicide was illegal at common law and remains so today in most states. It is also illegal to assist someone committing suicide. What is the state's interest in preserving someone's life over his or her objection? Centuries ago, the king needed a large and stable constituency to pay taxes and provide soldiers for national defense. Suicide was an affront to the king's sovereignty over his subjects. Accordingly, originalists do not find suicide to be a constitutionally protected right.

But what if a person is suffering from a terminal illness, or in a persistent vegetative state (PVS)? The Supreme Court has recognized a limited right in such cases, but made some strange law in the process.

In *Cruzan v. Director, Missouri Department of Health* (1990), the court held that Nancy Cruzan, in PVS following an auto accident, had the right to resist forced feeding, hydration, respiration, and other unwanted medical care. The court based its holding on the common law tort of battery. Essentially, forced treatment was a form of unwanted touching, which people had a right to resist at common law. Finding a fundamental right here meant that Missouri had to show a compelling interest and least restrictive means in its efforts to continue Cruzan's life-sustaining treatment. Since Cruzan was in PVS, the state's interest was in assuring that she did, in fact, oppose the medical treatment. The Supreme Court upheld the state requirement of clear evidence of the patient's desires. Following *Cruzan*, many states promoted the use of advanced care directives (or **living wills**) to remove any doubts in cases where patients are unable to express their desires.

Not only patients on life support but also those with painful terminal illnesses may want to end their lives. This presents the case of **doctor-assisted suicide** or, as some call it, *death with dignity* or *compassionate dying*. Yet, there is no escaping the fact that ending someone's life when it is presently functioning, whatever the merits of the individual case, is a form of euthanasia. This raises many of the same historical images as eugenics and other forms of population control. And, some of the most notable proponents of this right (Jack Kevorkian comes to mind) do not instill confidence that doctor-assisted suicide can be responsibly practiced.

In *Washington v. Glucksberg* (1997), the Supreme Court held there was no constitutional right to end one's own life. The court distinguished between the right to refuse medical service and the right to assisted suicide. While the right to refuse care was fundamental due to the long-standing common law battery principles of refusing unwanted touching, assisted suicide had no basis upon which it was practiced in the history and tradition of the country. While individual cases of terminal suffering might turn out differently, the claimed right was too broad to be recognized as fundamental, and too likely to be abused (say, for financial or emotional reasons). While a state is free to allow assisted suicide (as Oregon does), it can instead prohibit it if it chooses.

Positive Rights

Thus far, every fundamental right we have discussed has been a **negative right**, which means there are things the state cannot do *to* you (e.g., cannot prohibit abortion, gay sex). A negative right means you want the state to stay out of your way. **Positive rights**, in contrast, are things you demand the state do *for* you (i.e., the state must provide some type of benefit). Positive rights usually involve demands on the state treasury. Rights to free public education, medical care, welfare assistance, housing, and so forth are all considered positive rights. But, as a general rule, there are no positive rights in the federal Constitution. None.

Education, Health Care, and Government Benefits

States are under no federal constitutional obligation to provide **public education,** or to provide any particular quality if they voluntarily create public schools (*San Antonio Indep. Sch. Dist. v. Rodriguez* [1973]). There are two major ways around this startling proposition. First, most state constitutions require a system of public schools. So, many cases alleging inadequate education (e.g., because of inadequate funding) are filed in state court under state law. Second, while states need not provide any positive rights, if they voluntarily do so, they cannot discriminate in the enjoyment of the right. Thus, providing a free public education to some, but not others, can violate the equal protection clause even though the due process clause does not require this (or any other) positive right. Discrimination in the enjoyment of fundamental rights is discussed in the Fundamental Equal Protection Rights section, below.

Medical care is another positive right that states are not required to offer (even when it is urgent, emergency, or life-saving care). The basic proposition is that the state does not deprive liberty by withholding assistance. Thus, in *Harris v. McRae* (1980), the court upheld the Hyde Amendment, which prohibited the use of federal Medicaid funds to pay for abortions, including medically necessary ones.

Because government assistance is not a fundamental right, state denials are subject only to rational basis review. The legitimate state interest in the Hyde Amendment was promoting childbirth. Conceivably, a state law denying assistance could fail rational basis, but that is unlikely. For instance, a California law denying prenatal medical care to undocumented pregnant mothers was upheld by a state court in *Crespin v. Coye* (1994), even though the evidence showed that every dollar the state saved in withholding prenatal care would cost the state $3 in postnatal care once the babies (now U.S. citizens) were born.

We have already seen one exception to the rule against positive rights, in the case of discriminatory treatment. Another exception arises when the state creates a **special relationship** with the person claiming state benefits. Thus, inmates in state custody have a right to food, clothing, and medical care. Since the state has deprived inmates of the ability to care for themselves, the state must assume that responsibility. Children in a state's child welfare system (e.g., foster care) are also entitled to positive rights.

In *Brown v. Plata* (2011), the Supreme Court found that because of overcrowding in prisons, inmates with serious mental illness were not receiving minimal, adequate care. The court ordered the state of California to reduce its prison population to 137.5 percent of design capacity because crowding was the primary cause for the inadequate medical care. It is interesting to note that in the dissenting opinion, Justice Scalia (joined by Justice Thomas) admonished the majority for affirming "what is perhaps the most radical injunction issued by a court in our Nation's history: an order requiring California to release the staggering number of 46,000 convicted criminals." Justice Alito (joined by Chief Justice Roberts) filed a separate dissenting opinion in which he wrote that the "Constitution does not give federal judges the authority to run state penal systems." Evidently, five justices disagreed; not only do federal courts have the authority, they have the obligation to oversee state prisons if state officials are incapable of complying with the Constitution.

Government Protection

One of the most important positive rights that states usually provide is **police protection**. But since there is no federal constitutional obligation that they do so, it is not a violation of due process for them to provide inadequate protection. In other words, the state's failure to protect is not a constitutional problem. *Town of Castle Rock, Colorado v. Gonzales* (2005) illustrates this point in a tragic way. Jessica Gonzales obtained a restraining order against her estranged husband. A state court ordered the Castle Rock Police Department to keep the husband away from Jessica and her three children. Yet, they refused to enforce the order even after she notified them that her husband had taken the kids. The husband eventually killed all three children and took his own life. In her suit against the city, the Supreme Court held Gonzales had no protectable due process rights.[13]

Economic Rights and the Origin of Substantive Due Process

The first uses of the due process clause to protect individual rights were in the economic arena. In the late 19th century, a very conservative Supreme Court ruled that states could not legislate on economic matters because doing so violated "liberty of contract." Under this laissez-faire theory, competent adults had the right to enter into any economic relationship they wished, free from state interference. Thus, it was an employee's right to work for substandard wages, for long hours, or in dangerous working conditions. State efforts to protect worker safety, health, or labor conditions were forms of economic protectionism. These served no broad public interest, only the private interests of workers. And it violated their (and their employers') liberty rights.

The milestone case in "economic substantive due process" is *Lochner v. New York* (1905). The state had capped the number of hours that bakers could work in a day and in a week. Joseph Lochner sued—for his employees, of course, who supposedly wanted to work more than 10 hours a day. The court found that bread baked in the 12th hour of a baker's shift was no less healthful than bread baked early in the shift, so it could not be said the law promoted public health and safety. As for promoting worker rights, it was simply beyond the legislature's power to enact such special interest laws.

The *Lochner* era, as the period from 1883 to 1937 came to be known, is now seen as a highly illegitimate exercise of judicial power. In the guise of protecting individual rights, the court championed the cause of big business and capital. Worse yet, it made up the rights as it went along. *Liberty* mostly meant the right to make money free from government interference. Many

Economic Liberties—Birth, Death, Revival

The first use of the due process clause was to protect the economic interests of business and capital. Early on, corporations were deemed "persons," and thus entitled to protection under the Fourteenth Amendment. Under the rubric of "economic substantive due process" the court closely scrutinized all economic regulations and approved very few. Thus, while labor laws were generally unconstitutional (see *Lochner*), those protecting women often fared better. See *Muller v. Oregon* (1908; holding that women needed state protection, the court found that "the physical well-being of woman becomes an object of public interest").

As Justice Black noted in *Ferguson v. Skrupa* (1963), "the doctrine that prevailed in *Lochner*. . .—that due process authorizes courts to hold laws unconstitutional when they believe the legislature has acted unwisely—has long since been discarded. We have returned to the original constitutional proposition that courts do not substitute their social and economic beliefs for the judgment of legislative bodies, who are elected to pass laws. . . Whether the legislature takes for its textbook Adam Smith, Herbert Spencer, Lord Keynes, or some other is no concern of ours." I wonder if that same reasoning would hold if a state adopted Karl Marx for its economic textbook.

Still, economic regulation is an area of extreme deference to legislatures. Justice Stone said it best in *United States v. Carolene Products Co.* (1938); such a law will be sustained if "any state of facts either known or which could reasonably be assumed affords support for it."

Economic due process has seen a minor revival recently. In *BMW of North America, Inc. v. Gore* (1996) and *State Farm Mutual Automobile Insurance Co. v. Campbell* (2003), the court struck down large punitive damage awards in tort cases as violating the companies' due process rights. It remains to be seen just how far the current Supreme Court is willing to revive *Lochner*.

opponents of fundamental rights jurisprudence today see little difference between the substantive due process methodologies of the *Lochner* era and the current court's acceptance of abortion and sexual rights. Of course, there is a difference—economic rights and economic policy are quintessentially legislative in character. The very purpose of representative government is to balance competing economic interests. On the other hand, rights of privacy and personal autonomy ought not be subject to popular vote. What I do in my bedroom is not a matter of concern for my neighbors; how high I build my house is.

Deprivations and Undue Burdens

States may not deprive any person of life, liberty, or property. If state action does not rise to the level of a deprivation, then the due process clause is not implicated. One way to think of the nonrecognition of positive rights is that in failing to provide benefits or to protect, the state is not depriving you; it is just not assisting you.

The Supreme Court has held that only **intentional acts** constitute deprivations. In other words, there can be no negligent violation of due process. Otherwise, every tort (such as an auto accident) committed by a state officer would be transformed into a constitutional violation. Intentional torts (e.g., police beatings), however, do count. That is why due process cases are sometimes referred to as **constitutional torts**.

The requirement of *deprivation* has spawned a whole new doctrine when it comes to abortion rights. Ordinarily, a law restricting or regulating the exercise of a constitutional right is subject to *strict scrutiny*. As applied to a law requiring a pregnant woman to receive counseling and wait 24 hours before having an abortion, a court would ordinarily ask whether this law was necessary to serve a compelling state interest. Under that approach, the law would likely fail (deterring abortion is not a compelling state interest). But *Planned Parenthood v. Casey* (1992) provided a different approach entirely.

Under *Casey*, a court makes a preliminary inquiry into the state law being challenged. Does it impose an "undue burden" on a woman's exercise of her fundamental right? If her rights are not burdened (i.e., not deprived), then due process is not implicated.

Undue Burdens

Only those laws that "unduly burden" a woman's ability to exercise her constitutional right to terminate a pregnancy will be subject to strict scrutiny. This approach requires a threshold question: does a state restriction rise to the level of an undue burden? If so, the law is subject to strict scrutiny. If not, it is subject only to a rational basis standard of review. One would apply this threshold analysis to waiting periods, parental consent, and spousal notification requirements, and so forth.

How does the court know whether a particular restriction is a *permissible* or an *undue* burden? Justice O'Connor stated that the distinction turned on whether the law's "purpose or effect is to place substantial obstacles in the path of a woman seeking an abortion." So, a "substantial obstacle" constitutes an "undue burden." That does not move the analysis very far. How does the court know whether a 24-hour waiting period (or any other restriction) imposes a substantial obstacle?

The court never gives us a metric by which to answer this threshold question. At best, it seems, a restriction is permissible (not an undue burden) where a justice, in her own subjective judgment, would not be deterred by it. In this manner, counseling and 24-hour waiting periods, while inconvenient, do not ultimately affect the ability to have an abortion (for most women, anyway), while a spousal notification requirement could. Similarly, a parental consent requirement is an acceptable burden if there is a judicial bypass mechanism in special cases (e.g., abuse). Again, if a restriction falls short of becoming an undue burden, it is subject only to rational basis review.

Procedural Due Process

Thus far in this chapter, we have talked only about the *substantive* protection afforded by the due process clause. But there is no escaping the fact that the clause uses the term *process*, thereby suggesting that states must follow certain procedural regularities when it comes to affecting a persons' life, liberty, and property. This requirement traces back all the way to the **Magna Carta** (1215), which enjoined the king to observe the "law of the land." One way to think about the difference between the procedural and substantive components of due process is that the former specifies *how* the state affects your rights, while the latter looks at *when* it can do so.

Each branch of government must observe procedural due process, and the term has different meanings in different contexts. The legislative branch would violate procedural due process if it passed secret laws or met in the middle of the night. This is not a significant problem these days; although one might argue that legislative indenture to lobbyists comes perilously close to violating our right to transparent government.

The judicial branch must also observe procedural due process. Many of the criminal rights provisions in the Fourth, Fifth, and Sixth Amendments go to the issue of fair trials. This was once an active area of Supreme Court jurisprudence, and it still arises in habeas corpus cases where a federal court will look into whether a state trial was fair. But not much is happening on this front these days; most of the rules are settled by now.

Most of the action in procedural due process involves the executive branch of government. This is where general laws are applied to individuals and the risk of arbitrary action is greatest. If the Social Security Administration were to reduce or deny your benefits, the DMV were to cancel your drivers' license, the zoning board were to deny your remodel plans, and so forth, you would want an opportunity to contest that decision. In each of these administrative actions, you would be entitled to notice and an opportunity to be heard (usually) before your rights are denied.

Procedural due process is concerned with the nature and timing of individual participation in government decisions affecting them. When and how much "process is due" under procedural due process is governed by *Mathews v. Eldridge* (1976). This case set a flexible standard to match the timing and formality of individual hearings to the nature of the respective interests involved. You may be entitled to an independent review *before* state-promised medical benefits are withdrawn, but you are not entitled to an on-the-spot trial before the state trooper takes your license for suspicion of driving under the influence. Sometimes the hearing can come *later*.

What sort of life, liberty, and property rights trigger entitlement to procedural due process? When it comes to substantive due process, only constitutional (or fundamental) rights merit protection. In addition to these, nonfundamental **state-created rights** also cannot be deprived without procedural due process. For instance, states are under no obligation to provide free education. But if a state agrees to do so, and then claims you do not qualify (perhaps saying you are not a resident), you would be entitled to a procedural due process hearing to contest that individualized administrative decision. Many ordinary rights (e.g., reputation) get procedural protection, even though they lack substantive protection. And, as the example in the Procedural Due Process box shows, positive rights can be protected under procedural due process.

Procedural Due Process

When a state intentionally denies constitutional rights or state-created rights through administrative or executive action, it must observe procedural due process (PDP). This usually means giving the person notice of the reasons for deprivation and an opportunity to contest them. Serious deprivations (e.g., involuntary civil commitment) will require elaborate and timely procedures. Less serious deprivations (e.g., reduction in benefits) may be accomplished with less formal procedures, including, sometimes, those that occur after the deprivation has begun.

Whether a state has created a liberty or property interest protected by PDP requires a close examination of state law, or of whatever action is claimed to have created the right. If a state hires an employee with an expectation of continued employment, then termination of the employee may require a PDP hearing.

Not all deprivations of life, liberty, or property are unconstitutional, only those lacking due process. Thus, if a state satisfies PDP in deprivation of a right, it is entirely constitutional. This might not be known until after a state-provided procedure is completed. Thus, PDP cases often have an *exhaustion requirement*, meaning that an aggrieved person must pursue her state administrative remedies before filing suit.

Equal Protection of the Laws

Liberté, égalité, fraternité was the motto of the French Revolution, and embodied in the French Constitution of 1789, but the ideal of equality did not find its way into the American Constitution until nearly 70 years later. Indeed, our founding vision of "life, liberty and the pursuit of happiness" was notably devoid of an equality principle. There was some homage to equality in the original Constitution[14] and in some early case law, but it was not until the Fourteenth Amendment (1868) that general notions of equality were enshrined in constitutional text.

Nor shall any State . . . deny any person within its jurisdiction the equal protection of the laws.

———————

Fourteenth Amendment (1868)

As with other constitutional provisions, the language of the equal protection clause must be parsed and interpreted.

- *Any State*: Only "state action" can trigger the commands of the equal protection clause (and constitutional rights generally). While the state action doctrine is complicated enough that it receives its own subsection (below), the basic principle is simple: only states, state entities, and state officers need obey the Fourteenth Amendment. Private parties—you and me (unless you write for a government publication or I teach at a state university)—are not covered; we cannot violate the equal protection clause.

- *Deny*: What does it mean to deny someone a right? If public schools wind up segregated because of racial housing patterns, and schools in affluent white areas are newer, have better teachers and facilities, and spend more per pupil than schools in minority neighborhoods, there is surely inequality in many measurements of educational opportunity. But, as it turns out, this is not due to any intentional denial of equality by the state, and therefore does not violate the equal protection clause. Again, this issue is complicated enough to warrant its own section below.

- *Any Person*: Corporations are persons too, so they enjoy the benefit of the equal protection clause.[15] The Constitution is full of surprises.

- *Within Its Jurisdiction*: Nonresidents and aliens are subject to state jurisdiction (criminal laws, etc.) just as state citizens are, so they are entitled to equal protection. So too are illegal aliens. Recall that the status of newly freed slaves was often disputed by the Southern states, so everyone needed protection, not just state citizens.

- *Equal Protection of the Laws*: It is hard to be a textualist when interpreting this language since its meaning is not self-evident. For instance, does a law separating the races for purposes of public accommodation, education, or marriage, but that imposes the same penalty on whites as on blacks for violation, equally apply the law to both? The Supreme Court thought so for nearly a hundred years after the equal protection clause was enacted. Today, that is a preposterous proposition.

Before we get into the thick of discussing the equality principle, an initial observation should be made. As interpreted by the court, the clause guarantees *treatment as an equal*, but not *equality of treatment*. In other words, everyone should be treated the same by law (irrespective of their characteristics or status), but everyone does not need to wind up with the same basket of benefits: equal protection is a procedural guarantee (same treatment) but not a substantive guarantee (same results). So, referring to an earlier example, when schools in black parts of town are nothing more than glorified jails, while schools in white parts of town actually provide an education, we have substantive (outcome) inequality, but that is not unconstitutional. It would violate equal protection only if pupils were treated differently (e.g., sent to good or poor schools) because of some personal characteristic (e.g., skin color).

Standards of Review

Any unequal treatment by a state will trigger the equal protection clause. Yet, people are being treated unequally all the time. High-income folks are subject to higher tax rates than low-income earners (and people who inherit their fortunes may pay no tax at all). People who drive too fast get speeding tickets; those who drive within the speed limit do not. Obviously, government could not function very well if every instance of unequal treatment was considered unconstitutional.

The Supreme Court has divided equal protection cases into two broad categories (and several more subcategories). Most instances of unequal treatment (such as the examples above) are subject to **rational basis review**. This is the same rational basis test we saw under the due process clause. It is very hard for a state law to fail this highly deferential standard of review. In contrast, some instances of inequality trigger a much closer examination by the court known as **strict scrutiny**—again similar to due process analysis. Strict scrutiny is usually fatal to the challenged law.

In *United States v. Carolene Products* (1938), footnote 4,[16] Justice Harlan Stone provided the basis for the different degrees of scrutiny:

> There may be narrower scope for operation of the presumption of constitutionality when legislation appears on its face to be within a specific prohibition of the Constitution . . .
>
> [It may be that] similar considerations enter into the review of statutes directed at particular religious, or national, or racial minorities; whether prejudice against discrete and insular minorities may be a special condition, which tends seriously to curtail the operation of those political processes ordinarily to be relied upon to protect minorities, and which may call for a correspondingly more searching judicial inquiry.

This distinction is still used and forms the basic rule. Discrimination against discrete and insular minorities, and discrimination in the exercise of fundamental rights, both trigger strict scrutiny. Most every other type of discrimination is subject only to rational basis review.

Standards of Review

In determining whether state action is constitutional, a court will examine both the state's goals (its *ends*) and the mechanism (*means*) it adopts to achieve them. When subject to **strict scrutiny**, the *ends* must be **compelling** and the *means* must be **necessary** to get there. Very few state objectives are ever considered compelling. Even when one is found, discriminatory *means* are seldom necessary.

Rational basis requires only **legitimate** *ends* and **rational** *means*. Most state goals are legitimate. A discriminatory classification will be found irrational only if arbitrary (e.g., only redheads may be considered for a state job) or counterproductive.

Fundamental Equal Protection Rights

The concept of fundamental rights is usually associated with due process. If a state denies someone the right to marry, for instance, that would be a deprivation of liberty. Occasionally, the state's interference with a fundamental right does not rise to the level of a deprivation, and thus does not violate due process. Consider the various ways the state does regulate marriage (e.g., licensing, blood tests, bigamy). These survive due process analysis because whatever burdens it imposes are not seen as deprivations. Still, if burdens are applied in a discriminatory manner (e.g., only some persons must meet the burden, not others), we not only have an equal protection problem, but one that will trigger strict scrutiny.

Whenever a right that has been found to be fundamental for due process purposes is denied, burdened, or enjoyed on a discriminatory basis, that unequal treatment is subject to strict scrutiny under the equal protection clause. But the **fundamental rights strand** of equal protection goes further than that. The court has found some rights fundamental only for equal protection purposes. In other words, discriminatory treatment of that right will trigger equal protection strict scrutiny, even though even-handed denial is subject only to rational basis review under the due process clause.[17] The two most important equal protection fundamental rights are the right to vote and the right to travel interstate.

Voting Rights

The right to vote in state elections is not guaranteed in the Constitution, even though the Constitution assumes that states will have electoral systems. Even the right to vote in federal elections is indirect. For instance, in selecting representatives to the House, "the electors in each state shall have the qualifications requisite for electors of the most numerous branch of the state legislature" (Article I, Section 2). U.S. senators were not popularly elected until the Seventeenth Amendment. Voting for president and vice president is still left up to the states. The Fourteenth Amendment even let states deny voting rights and simply reduced a state's representation in Congress proportionately.

Still, more amendments to the Constitution (nine) deal with electoral issues and voting rights than any other single subject. Some explicitly prohibit discrimination in voting: the Fifteenth Amendment (no discrimination on account of race), the Nineteenth Amendment (no discrimination on account of sex), and the Twenty-fourth Amendment (no discrimination on account of age). Taken together, the original Constitution and the many amendments on this topic have been interpreted to suggest that the right to vote is fundamental for equal protection purposes. This means that a state does not have to allow any citizens to vote for particular offices or issues (no due process violation), but does have to allow all citizens to vote if it allows any (or else it will violate equal protection).

States have discriminated against people in the exercise of their fundamental equal protection right to vote in several ways.

- *Denial*: States have allowed some people to vote while denying others. For instance, New York allowed only property owners and parents with kids in the public schools to vote in school board elections. This scheme failed strict scrutiny review in *Kramer v. Union Free School District* (1969).
- *Burden*: States have imposed prerequisites to voting (e.g., literacy tests and poll taxes). The burdens were themselves uniform (everyone had to overcome the same burden in order to vote), but produced disparate outcomes (poor and uneducated citizens could not satisfy the burden and therefore could not vote).
- *Dilution*: States have afforded greater weight to some votes than to others; this is tantamount to giving some voters more votes than others. For instance, Tennessee gave each county one seat in the state senate. As a result, small rural counties had, collectively, the same voting strength as populous urban counties (i.e., a voter in a county of 1,000 people had 100 times the voting power as one living in a county of 100,000 people). This was declared unconstitutional in *Baker v. Carr* (1962).
- *Counting*: It would surely violate equal protection for a state to count some people's votes and not others. That is not much different than denying some the right to vote in the first place. But sometimes whether one's vote is counted or not depends on the electoral machinery. Every voting system, whether it is paper ballots, voting machines, or touch screen electronic voting, is prone to error. Votes may be missed or rejected as invalid for any number of reasons (e.g., incompletely detached chads on punch cards). The equal protection problem arises when a

state uses one type of machinery in some parts of the state and another type (with different error rates) in another part of the state. Whether your vote gets counted may depend, to some degree, on where you live. The Supreme Court has been willing to accept differential error rates (even, say, where minority areas use machines with a 1% error rate while white areas have newer equipment with a 0.1% error rate). But, in *Bush v. Gore* (2000), it held that recount procedures that allowed different standards to discern a voter's intent was a denial of equal protection.[18]

- *Voter Identification*: Voter ID laws suppress voting by vulnerable populations (the disabled, elderly, poor, new citizens). Earlier cases held that certain voter qualifications and poll taxes impermissibly burdened voting rights; however, the court declined to expand those principles in *Crawford v. Marion County Election Bd.* (2008). The court concluded that an Indiana law requiring voters to produce a government-issued photo ID when they vote in person was justified by the legitimate state interests in preventing voter fraud. Because the burden on voting rights was not severe enough to trigger heightened scrutiny, the state needed only a rational basis to sustain its voter ID law. The interest in detecting and deterring voter fraud (even if none has occurred) and promoting voter confidence were strong enough to justify this burden on the right to vote.

As demonstrated, the fundamental rights strand of equal protection is triggered in a variety of ways. Outright denial of a fundamental right is not necessary; discriminatory burdens also trigger strict scrutiny. But the court must first agree that a significant burden exists. This emulates the undue burden analysis of substantive due process: whether a burden is substantial enough is itself a highly manipulable factor.

Right to Travel

The right to travel throughout the United States, free from state regulation, was first articulated by Justice Bushrod Washington in *Corfield v. Coryell* (1823; recognizing the "right of a citizen of one state to pass through, or to reside in any other state, for purposes of trade, agriculture, professional pursuits, or otherwise"). At the time of the holding, the right was seen as one of the "privileges and immunities" of state citizens. More recent decisions have refined the right into at least two groupings: (1) where states actually impede ingress or egress from a state (e.g., taxing or prohibiting interstate travel); and (2) where they impose penalties on interstate migration. The latter is now treated as a burden on the fundamental equal protection right to travel. Most often, the penalties take the form of denied benefits during a waiting period after moving into a state.

States have imposed "durational residency requirements" on new residents (those exercising their fundamental equal protection right of interstate migration) in a variety of areas. Waiting periods for exercising the right to vote (*Dunn v. Blumstein* [1972]), exercising the right to run for office (*Bullock v. Carter* [1972]), receiving welfare benefits (*Shapiro v. Thompson* [1969]), receiving indigent medical care (*Memorial Hospital v. Maricopa County* [1974]), and so on have all been struck down as burdening the equal protection right to travel. The burden arises because a resident of one state, enjoying such benefits there, risks losing them at least temporarily when moving to another state.

Durational residency requirements are not always subject to strict scrutiny. It depends on whether the requirements are imposed on new state residents or imposed to determine whether a person is, in fact, a state resident. States must treat all their residents the same, both long timers and recent arrivals (*Saenz v. Roe* [1999]). But, it need not extend the same benefits to nonresidents as it does to residents. How is a state to know whether someone within its borders is a resident or not? Objective indicators, such as a drivers' license, utility bill, and so forth, can help. But these can be easy to obtain, even where a person has not formally taken up residency.

This problem arises most often with respect to portable benefits. People might feign residency simply to take advantage of the state's beneficence, without ever intending to become permanent members of the state's economic or political community. Out-of-staters might "move into" a state with liberal divorce laws simply to obtain a divorce, and then "move back." Accordingly, a one-year residency requirement for obtaining a divorce was upheld in (*Sosna v. Iowa* [1975]). Or a high-school graduate from New

---

Equal Protection Fundamental Rights

Unequal allocation, denial, or other disparate treatment of equal protection fundamental rights triggers strict scrutiny. Equal protection fundamental rights are found in one of two ways: (1) rights that are fundamental for due process purposes are automatically fundamental for equal protection purposes; (2) even where a right is not fundamental under due process, it still can be under equal protection. The court uses the same basic methodologies and theories of interpretation in finding equal protection rights as it does for due process, except it is marginally more generous. One reason is that finding an equal protection violation still leaves a state with an option; it can either remove the burden or extend it. For instance, after the *Kramer* case, New York could have either let nonproperty owners vote for school board, or denied everyone (i.e., have an appointed board). Since voting (at least in local elections) is not a due process fundamental right, it can be denied uniformly. But, as an equal protection fundamental right, it cannot be denied selectively.

Jersey might "move to" California just to attend UCLA at subsidized tuition rates. Because these benefits (divorce decree, college degree) are portable (remain with you after you end your "residency"), there is a greater risk the individual was never a genuine resident. States can impose **bona fide residency requirements**, including the presumption of certain duration before residency attaches. There is less of a risk with temporary benefits (those that expire when you leave the state, such as welfare payments), so residency requirements are more suspect in such cases.

Protected (Suspect) Classes

The classic equal protection case involves discrimination against people because of their traits or characteristics, rather than because they are exercising a fundamental right. Indeed, the whole idea of strict scrutiny originated with racial classifications. As Justice Black stated in *Korematsu v. United States* (1944), "all legal restrictions which curtail the civil rights of a single racial group are immediately suspect."[19] Thus, if the court finds that a statute discriminates against a suspect class, it will apply strict scrutiny.

Race, Ethnicity, and Religion

Race is the prototypical suspect classification. This flows from Justice Stone's formulation in *United States v. Carolene Products* (1938), along with religious, national, and other "discrete and insular minorities." Here too, the basic proposition is simple—unequal treatment on account of race or similar classification is inherently suspect. There are two areas of difficulty: (1) what classifications are suspect; and (2) when is discrimination based on race, rather than on some nonsuspect characteristic such as wealth (which has been used as a proxy for race). The second question is deferred to later, while the former is addressed in this section.

The whole idea behind "suspect classes" is that people should not be treated differently due to traits beyond their control. Under liberal theory, people should reap the benefits of their own effort and industry and suffer the consequences of their own failings. Thus, it seldom raises equal protection problems to treat people differently based on their actions. Felons go to jail, not because of who they are, but because of what they do. Status crimes, on the other hand, are vestiges of our illiberal past. Punishment for *using* drugs is different than punishment for *being* an addict.

For the most part, people's racial, ethnic, and religious identities are established at birth; they have no (or little) control over them. To treat them differently based on birth characteristics, rather than their own behaviors, is manifestly unfair. This is especially true if their group constitutes a political minority, such that they do not really have an opportunity to correct abusive laws through the electoral process. If one is a member of a *discrete* (readily

Affirmative Action

One particular form of racial discrimination merits special discussion. Does discrimination *in favor of* racial minorities, rather than *against* them, trigger the same standard of review. The Supreme Court has said yes, even though there is no comparable history of invidious discrimination against whites (and therefore no need for the protection of strict scrutiny). Although whites are just as discrete and insular as blacks, they have neither lacked effective access to political remedies nor the means to correct legislative abuses, as have racial minorities. Applying the standard test for suspect classes—is the class is "saddled with such disabilities, or subjected to such a history of purposeful unequal treatment, or relegated to such a position of political powerlessness as to command extraordinary protection from the majoritarian political process"—would not yield strict scrutiny. But it applies here too.

The rule is sometimes based on Justice Harlan's statement in *Plessy v. Ferguson* (1896) that our constitution is "colorblind." Of course, this was a hortatory statement, as constitutional law has been anything but colorblind for most of our history.

Some affirmative action programs may be old-fashioned racial politics, but most attempt to rectify racial imbalances of one sort of another. Unless one believes that blacks are innately inferior to whites, there must be some external cause for their significantly lower numbers in elite colleges, high-paying jobs, and positions of power. If that cause, either now or in the recent past, was state-sanctioned discrimination, then a narrowly tailored affirmative action program to rectify the discrimination will survive strict scrutiny. But private discrimination is neither unconstitutional nor a valid basis for remedial laws. The state cannot use affirmative action to correct private biases.

One area where the court does allow affirmative action without a showing of prior state discrimination is in college admissions. The court has accepted "educational diversity" as a compelling state interest (in part due to the competing constitutional right of academic freedom). Using race as a so-called soft factor in admissions (i.e., goals are ok, quotas are not) survives strict scrutiny of *means* as well as *ends*.

identifiable) and *insular* (limited opportunity to leave) minority group, and discriminated against on that ground, strict scrutiny applies.

Sex, Alienage, and Birth Status

In some respects, discrimination against women has been more enduring than racial discrimination. For instance, blacks got the right to vote in 1870; women did not until 1920. Classifications based on sex also meet the **indicia of suspectness**: (1) the sex trait is immutable; (2) there is a history of invidious discrimination; (3) they are based on negative stereotype; and (4) differential treatment is grossly unfair and seldom if ever justified by legitimate state interests.

But, there is a problem with the fourth index of suspectness in this case: sometimes a person's sex *is* relevant to legitimate state interests. For instance, paternity can be a lot harder to establish than maternity, so perhaps the law can take that into account. Unlike with racial and other suspect classifications, there are germane differences between the sexes. For this reason, the court has declared sex to be a **quasi-suspect class**. Discrimination (either against women or against men) is subject to a **midlevel** standard of review.

A similar analysis applies to alienage and birth status (marital status of one's parents). Discrimination against (legal) aliens or against illegitimate children, such as in employment or inheritance, respectively, is subject to midlevel review.

Midlevel review means that the state's *ends* must be **important** and its *means* **substantially related** to them. We have now seen three groupings of state interests: (1) *legitimate* (easy to meet); (2) *important* (hard to meet); and (3) *compelling* (super-hard to meet). We have also seen three corresponding relational tests for the closeness of *means* to *ends*: (1) *rationally related*; (2) *substantially related*; and (3) *necessary*. Midlevel scrutiny lies somewhere between rational basis (state almost always wins) and strict scrutiny (state almost always loses). It is sometimes called **intermediate scrutiny**.

Applying midlevel review to quasi-suspect classifications, the Supreme Court usually invalidates them, but occasionally upholds them. It has done so with statutory rape laws (*Michael M v. Superior Court of Sonoma County* [1981]; upholding the law only to men) and citizenship of foreign-born non-marital children (*Nguyen v. I.N.S.* [2001]; holding that if the unmarried mother is not a U.S. citizen, the citizen father must "legitimate" the child within a certain time).

Sexual Orientation and "Almost" Suspect Classes

Gays and lesbians are not a suspect class or a quasi-suspect class. The court has not even entertained the issue. But it has applied a form of heightened review to state laws discriminating against them. In *Romer v. Evans* (1996), the court invalidated a Colorado constitutional amendment that forbade cities from including sexual orientation in their antibias laws. Nominally subjecting the law to mere rational basis review (no suspect class and no fundamental right involved), Justice Kennedy found the state law was motivated by hostility to gays and lesbians, rather than a legitimate interest.

One important feature of rational basis review is that the court will accept any proffered justification for the law, even if it was not the actual one considered at the time of adoption. Any *conceivable* rational basis will suffice. But, the court was not deferential in the Colorado case, instead looking behind the state's rationalizations to find the true purpose in enacting the law. This is a hallmark of heightened judicial review. So, commentators view *Romer* as a case of **rational basis with bite**. Due to this lack of deference, rational basis with bite is closer to strict scrutiny than it is to rational basis.

A similar result was obtained in *Plyler v. Doe* (1982), a case challenging Texas's exclusion of "illegal" alien children from public schools. Although illegal aliens are hardly a suspect class, and education has not been found to be a fundamental right, the disadvantaged class was nearly suspect (the children were in the United States at no fault of their own) and the right involved was *close* to being fundamental (education is vital for the "preservation of a democratic system of government"). Applying rational basis with bite, the court found that the state's proffered interest (conservation of scarce state resources) was legitimate, but that the *means* (denying education) was irrational. Condemning kids to a lifetime of illiteracy would damage the state's economy, not save it.

State Action Requirement

State schools that discriminate in admissions, employment, and so forth, are subject to the equal protection clause, but private schools are not. This sharp distinction is due to a limitation in the equal protection clause itself, which says "no state shall . . ." Of course, private discrimination may be contrary to state law, or even federal statutes, but not the equal protection clause. Not only is private discrimination entirely outside the scope of equal protection, a state that refuses to use its own laws to prohibit private discrimination has not *denied* anyone of equal protection. Bottom line: private discrimination and a state's tolerance of it are both entirely constitutional. That is why Congress passed its own civil rights legislation in the 1960s.

The rule is simple enough—private discrimination is not unconstitutional. But what if the private school in the above example receives some, most, or all of its funding from public sources? What if public officials sit on the private school board, or regulate its activities, or even sanction its discriminatory policies? Is the school still private?

The State Action Doctrine is a set of elaborate rules attempting to preserve the distinction between public and private realms of action. There are four basic ways private actors can assume an aura of "stateness" and be subject to constitutional constraint.

1 *Sovereign Function*: A private entity that performs a function that is normally an exclusive state prerogative will be treated as if it were a state. Examples include privately owned "company towns," political parties, and private prisons.
2 *Delegation*: Where the state delegates state power to private parties (e.g., the sheriff assembling a *posse* to catch the bad guys), those persons

are literally exercising state power even if they are private in all other respects.

3   *Nexus*: If there is a sufficiently close and strong relationship between the state and the private party, they may be seen as engaging in joint action. That was the case in *Burton v. Wilmington Parking Authority* (1961), where the privately owned Eagle Coffee Shop refused to serve blacks. Because the store was in a public building and paying rent to a public entity, they had a "symbiotic relationship." This category hardly ever applies anymore. State funding, licensing, or general regulation of private business is not enough of a nexus to qualify.

4   *Endorsement*: The state may endorse or sanction private discrimination in such a way as to add its imprimatur to the action. Thus, a state court that enforces a racially restrictive covenant in housing satisfies state action.

This last category is tricky. Not all state enforcement of private rights leads to state action. If I summon the police to remove an unwanted guest from my house, there is no state action even if my decision is racially based. There is a difference between neutral state enforcement (lending no aura of state endorsement of the underlying private action) and discretionary state endorsement, where the state must agree with the private action before enforcing it. That was the case in *Shelley v. Kraemer* (1948), in which Missouri courts enforced land covenants only if consistent with public policy. When they enforced a restrictive covenant, they were signaling approval of the discrimination, and they were enforcing them against third parties (to invalidate a sale between willing buyer and seller)—something that only the state could do.

The State Action Doctrine is highly controversial, especially in this day of privatizing government functions. Land use regulations enacted by a home-owner's association may be functionally equivalent to zoning, but they are not subject to the Constitution.

De Facto vs. *De Jure* Discrimination

In *Brown v. Board of Education* (1954), the Supreme Court held that segregation in public schools violated the equal protection clause. But the public schools are just as segregated today (perhaps more so) than in 1954. The difference is that today's segregated schools got that way through private discrimination (e.g., "redlining" by housing lenders). Even where that private discrimination is tacitly sanctioned by the state (usually through state inaction), it is considered *de facto* and not covered by the equal protection clause. Only *de jure* (official) discrimination is subject to equal protection review.

The Requirement of Purpose

By many metrics, racial minorities underperform in relation to their white counterparts. This is often true in standardized testing. Where such tests are used to distribute benefits (public employment, admission to state college, etc), minorities may be severely disadvantaged. A case in point is Test 21, the standardized U.S. civil service exam that was administered to applicants for the Washington D.C. police department. Blacks failed the test four times as often as whites. Yet, in *Washington v. Davis* (1976), the Supreme Court held that any disparity was not the result of intentional racial discrimination. Perhaps it was due to blacks' inferior public education (D.C. schools were officially segregated until the 1970s), private biases, or social differences. Unless plaintiffs could prove the police department's intent to discriminate on the basis of race, only rational basis review would apply.

Proving discriminatory intent is usually very hard. It must be done in one of three ways:

1 *Facial Racial Discrimination*: If a law discriminates on its face (where it specifies differential treatment on racial grounds), intent is *per se* proven. This is a rare occurrence (usually poor drafting).
2 *Extrinsic Evidence*: A law that is neutral on its face, but producing discriminatory results (e.g., Test 21) can be found intentionally discriminatory if outside evidence is found showing the law was written in such a way as to produce those results. This happened in *Rogers v. Lodge* (1982), in which historical records showed that the list of felonies meriting disenfranchisement under Alabama law was chosen as it was specifically because blacks were more likely to commit those crimes. "Smoking guns" like that also happen rarely.
3 *Gross Statistical Disparity*: Suppose the fire department sets a minimum height requirement of 5'10" for firefighters. Such a law facially discriminates, but on nonsuspect lines. Height discrimination receives only rational basis review. But the disparate impact against women is great; very few will qualify. If the disparity is large enough, it may raise an inference that the criterion was established precisely *because* it would exclude women. Grossly uneven outcomes for a quasi or suspect class will shift the burden of proof to the state to offer a plausible nondiscriminatory explanation for the disparity. If the state cannot show why a height of 5'10" is a bona fide occupational qualification, a court could find intentional discrimination.

Retrenching Equal Protection

Plaintiffs in equal protection cases bear the burden of proof on most elements of the case. They must prove that any discrimination was intentionally along suspect class or fundamental rights lines (and committed by a state actor).

Only where heightened review is found applicable will the burden shift to the state. The requirement of intent (coupled with the state action doctrine) operates to transmute most instances of illegal *de jure* discrimination into constitutionally acceptable *de facto* discrimination. These recent developments have greatly reduced the force of the equal protection clause.

The First Amendment

Congress shall make no law respecting an establishment of religion, or prohibiting the free exercise thereof; of abridging the freedom of speech, or of the press; or the right of the people peaceably to assemble, and to petition the Government for a redress of grievances.

First Amendment

Background

Johannes Gutenberg has been described as the most influential person of the second millennium, and perhaps the most dangerous. His invention of moveable type so threatened the English crown and church's monopolies on public discourse that they responded with draconian measures. Sedition was punished by the Court of Star Chamber (1487–1641). The Licensing Act (1557) granted a royal monopoly to the Stationers Company; all others were prohibited from publishing. When in 1663 John Twyn published a book critical of the king, he was drawn and quartered.

Some of these laws were exported to the colonies. John Peter Zenger was tried in 1735 for seditious libel of the governor of New York. His lawyer, Alexander Hamilton, argued that Zenger's statements were true. The judge rejected the claim that truth could be a defense, but the jury acquitted Zenger anyway.

These precedents were fresh in the minds of the first Congress when it proposed the First Amendment. Britain wasn't impressed. Shortly after the amendment's adoption, the crown tried Thomas Paine *in abstentia* for publishing *The Rights of Man*, which remonstrated against hereditary government. Also unimpressed, seemingly, was Congress a few years after it proposed the First Amendment. The Alien and Sedition Acts (1798) prohibited "false, scandalous and malicious writings," although they did allow truth as a defense. Used mostly for political witch-hunts, by Federalists against Republicans, the constitutionality of the act was never adjudicated. Upon assuming office, Jefferson pardoned all those convicted under the law.

Not only did the First Amendment get off to a rocky start, it has often provided sparse protection since. From prosecutions of "sympathetic" Southern publishers during the Civil War, to those of socialists and pacifists during World War I, to communists during the McCarthy era, the ideals of free speech and free press have been elusive. Even today, the command that "Congress shall make *no law*" abridging religion, speech, and the press has often been interpreted to mean *some laws*, so long as Congress has a good enough reason to do so. The court has achieved this re-write through the use of complex doctrine and linguistic theory.

Unprotected and Lesser-Protected Speech

Using both originalist and dynamic interpretivist approaches, the court has excluded some categories of speech altogether from the ambit of First Amendment protection. These include forms of speech that were probably not within the framers' concept, such as obscenity and libel. Speech that fails to serve any of the underlying purposes of the First Amendment is similarly unprotected.

Categories of Unprotected Speech

The following types of speech have been "categorically excluded" from First Amendment protection; regulation of such speech is subject only to rational basis review.

- *Obscenity*: Obscenity is a particularly graphic and offensive form of pornography. The test for obscenity was established in *Miller v. California*: (1) appeals to a prurient interest in sex; (2) portrays sex in a particularly offensive way (e.g., hard core); and, (3) taken as a whole, lacks serious scientific, literary, or political value.

- *Solicitation of a Crime*: Solicitation is part of the criminal act itself; such acts are not constitutionally protected simply because communication is involved. Previously, mere advocacy of dangerous ideas (e.g., protesting war, teaching communism) could be prohibited. That doctrine was overturned in the 1960s.

- *Incitement to Violence and True Threats*: An exhortation to others to engage in acts of violence is unprotected if it is (1) specific, (2) imminent, and (3) physically proximate; specific threats are also unprotected.

- *Fighting Words*: Epithets that are likely to cause a reasonable person to respond with a breach of the peace are part of the unlawful act itself (similar to incitement).

- *Serious Threats to National Security*: In *Near v. Minnesota* (1931), the court held that publishing the locations and sailing times of our troop ships was unprotected speech. Since *Near*, the "troop-ship" exception has been much discussed but seldom invoked. In *New York Times v. United States*, the court rejected Nixon administration efforts to suppress *The Pentagon Papers* because it was unable to show how publication would directly threaten American troops. But in 1979, a district court enjoined *Progressive Magazine* from publishing the article "The H-Bomb Secret: How We Got It, Why We're Telling It." This seems to be the only known case to trigger the *Near* exception.

The Supreme Court has resisted efforts to expand the categories of unprotected speech. In *United States v. Stevens* (2010), the court invalidated a federal statute that banned the creation, sale, and possession of videos depicting animal cruelty ("crush videos"). While the underlying acts could be punished (they aren't speech), depictions of them were protected even if done for profit. In *Snyder v. Phelps* (2011), members of the Westboro Baptist church demonstrated outside the funeral of Marine Lance Corporal Matthew Snyder, who had been killed in action in Iraq. The protestors believed that American casualties were God's wrath for our immoral ways. Their signs—"Thank God for Dead Soldiers," "Thank God for 9/11," "Thank God for IEDs," and "God Hates You"—intentionally caused Snyder's family severe emotional distress. Yet, the court ruled that speech on political or social matters, or other matters of public concern, was protected no matter how revolting it may be.

The court has also found that some categories of speech, while serving some of the values underlying the First Amendment, are deserving of lesser protection. This is often because important countervailing interests are at stake.

Lesser Protected Speech

- *Libel of Private Persons*: In *New York Times v. Sullivan* (1964), the court held that libel of public officials or public figures (e.g., celebrities) was fully protected speech. Only actual malice or careless disregard for the truth could justify the chilling effect that a libel case would have on free speech. But libel of private persons is different. Where the defamed individual has not voluntarily injected herself into the limelight, or lacks access to the press for rebuttal, then her rights of privacy and reputation are infringed. Libel of private persons is less protected because damages may be awarded for false speech; yet receives some protection because punitive damages can be awarded only for malicious libel.

- *Commercial Speech*: Advertising and other speech that proposes a commercial transaction has First Amendment value, especially to the listener (smart shopping). But since the profit motive underlies such speech, it is not as easily chilled (deterred) as traditional forms of speech. Thus, while commercial speech is protected, some doctrines (e.g., overbreadth) do not apply.

- *Adult and Indecent Speech*: Soft core pornography is protected (contrast hard core—that which meets the *Miller* test), but to a lesser extent.
  - *Broadcast Indecency*: Because of the uninvited and pervasive nature of radio waves, the Federal Communications Commission (FCC) can regulate broadcast decency, at least during prime time when children are apt to be listening. This power does not extend to subscription services (cable, satellite), telephone communications, or to the Internet.

   ○ *Child Pornography*: There are two dimensions to "kiddie porn." The first is use of children in the production of pornography. The state has a compelling interest in protecting children against exploitation and can regulate this aspect. The second is adult porn that is accessible to children. The state has a compelling interest here too, but cannot regulate in such as way as to unnecessarily infringe adults' right of access. Two attempts to ban Internet sex sites have been rejected by the court.

   ○ *Adult Zoning*: Because of the "secondary effects" of adult entertainment (congestion, crime, neighborhood deterioration), the court has upheld zoning laws that confine adult theaters to certain parts of town.

Time, Place, and Manner Regulations

Every speech act consists of both communication and action. A protest march down Fifth Avenue is part speech and part traffic. Government can regulate the traffic part (nonspeech elements) without having to survive strict scrutiny, so long as it is not targeting the speech (i.e., discriminating based on the speech content of the march) or unduly burdening it. The time, place, and manner (TPM) test is used to determine whether a regulation is directed at the communication (anti-speech) or the noncommunicative action components (nonspeech).

A TPM regulation must: (1) be content neutral (apply to all marches, all billboards, etc.); (2) be narrowly tailored to serve a significant state interest; and (3) leave open alternative avenues of communication. The first part of the TPM test serves a "switching function" to determine whether strict scrutiny applies (the rule for content-based regulation) or intermediate scrutiny applies (the rule for content-neutral regulations). If the latter, then a narrowly tailored statute used to promote important ends (parts 2 and 3) will suffice. The last part of the test assures that the impact on speech (even if a content-neutral regulation) isn't too severe. In practice, the midlevel scrutiny for content-neutral TPM regulations is fairly low level. Most such laws are upheld.

Speech in Public Places

The TPM test applies to speech occurring in a "traditional public forum." The state *can* impose content distinctions for speech occurring on other public property. For instance, in an elementary school, military base, courthouse, city council chambers, and so forth, speech can be restricted to certain topics, or denied altogether. Nonpublic fora are simply inappropriate places for general speech to occur.

Public Forum Doctrine

The court has created a four-part construct for publicly owned property:

- *Traditional Public Forum*: Sidewalks, streets, parks, and those public ways that have historically been used for public speech purposes. In the public forum, government may impose only reasonable TPM regulations. It cannot deny speech access.
- *Nonpublic Forum*: All other public property (public buildings, police cars, municipally owned transit) that is not traditionally dedicated for public speech purposes. Of course, speech occurs here, but it is either government speech (see below) or invited speech. The public has no right of speech access to nonpublic fora. The TPM doctrine is inapplicable here.
- *Limited Public Forum*: Government may intentionally open up a non-public forum for designated public speech purposes (e.g., public hearings at city hall). When it does so, it may discriminate as to *subject matter*, but not as to *viewpoint*. For instance, it may take commercial advertising in a public transit system, but not political advertisements, or vice versa, but it cannot rent space in the school auditorium for Democratic rallies, yet deny it for Republican rallies.
- *Selective Access Public Forum*: In *Forbes v. Arkansas Public Broadcasting* (1998), the court upheld a public station's decision to invite only some candidates to a televised debate, holding that when the state opens up a nonpublic forum (public TV qualifies as that, since the speech occurring there is usually government speech) it can do so on a selective basis. This adds a new wrinkle to the Limited Public Forum doctrine, since it suggests that government can discriminate based on who the speaker is. This is very dangerous to free speech principles.

Speech in Private Places

As the history of the First Amendment indicates, most government regulation has been of private speech occurring on private property (books, newspapers, theaters). The public forum doctrine does not apply here, but the TPM doctrine does. In short, government can impose only content-neutral, TPM criteria.

Examples of this include commercial signs, billboards, and advertising. The state may regulate size, placement, and so forth, for aesthetic and public safety purposes. But as soon as it starts regulating content (no cigarette advertisements on billboards) then the appropriate level of scrutiny would apply (e.g., midlevel for commercial speech).

Symbolic Speech

In classical terms, speech is either oral or written. But human forms of communication aren't so narrow; they include dance, body language, flag burning, and a limitless array of action that conveys meaning to others. A silent vigil (with its powerful message) merits the full protection of the First Amendment. It is symbolic speech.

Burning the American flag is speech, but it is also action. And it can be a dangerous action under the wrong conditions. A law that prohibits setting fire in a public place may be directed to public safety concerns, rather than meant to suppress speech. In *United States v. O'Brien* (1968), the court provided a four-part test to determine if regulation of symbolic speech was antispeech (designed to suppress certain content), and thus subject to strict (or intermediate) scrutiny, or nonspeech (content-neutral), and thus reviewed by a lower standard. O'Brien was convicted of a federal crime of defacing his draft card, which he burned during a Vietnam War protest.

The O'Brien Test

1   Does government have the power to regulate the conduct? (Yes, regulating the draft was within Congress's power.)
2   Does the regulation advance an important government interest? (Yes, draft cards help determine eligibility, and the draft was vital for national security.)
3   Is that interest unrelated to the suppression of speech? (This element performs a "switching function"—if the state's interest is to suppress speech, immediately exit the O'Brien test and head directly to strict (or intermediate) scrutiny. The court answered yes in O'Brien; another example of a good test being misapplied in the very case that announced it. The federal law had been enacted in response to Vietnam War protests, so it was hard to see a purpose other than to stifle a potent form of protest; but the court did.)
4   Is the incidental effect on speech no greater than necessary? (Yes, O'Brien could protest the war in countless other ways; burning his draft card may have added force to his speech, but wasn't indispensable.)

Nearly any action can be deemed symbolic speech. When I drive down the highway at 100 miles/hour, what I'm really doing is communicating to my terrified fellow drivers how cool I am and how fast my car is. But speed limit (and most other) laws easily pass the O'Brien test, so they would be subject to a rather low level of judicial review.

Government Speech

I'm not sure how this happened, but governments have the right to speak too. And they don't need to be even-handed or unbiased in their views. Legislation, foreign policies, taxes, and so forth, all express a particular viewpoint. Government need not give equal time to opposing views. Why? Because we can vote the rascals out of office if we disagree with what they are saying.

But governments are constructed entities; for the most part they must act and speak through human beings. This does not pose a conceptual problem when the human is a government officer (e.g., president or governor), but sometimes he or she is just an employee or a contractor. In *Rust v. Sullivan* (1991), the court held that federal health funding regulations prohibiting doctors who receive federal funds from discussing abortion options with pregnant patients did not abridge the free speech rights of the doctors. In providing family counseling, the doctors were speaking for and on behalf of the government (which could advance a particular viewpoint; namely preference for child birth and adoption over abortion). Doctors could express their own views, just not within the federal program where they had contracted to promote the government's purpose.

Not all government funding of private parties gives rise to government speech. It depends on whether the government is prescribing the message, or facilitating the private party's own speech. For instance, in the public schools, government prescribes the curriculum and teachers are selected for their ability to communicate it well. But at the university level, faculty are customarily hired to provide their own views and expertise within a topic area; thus giving rise to the First Amendment doctrine of *academic freedom*, even in public universities.

This point was illustrated in *Velasquez v. Legal Services Corporation* (2001). Although the federal government provides funding for indigent legal services, it could hardly prescribe what legal arguments a lawyer can make on behalf of her client. Thus a restriction on Legal Services Corporation funding, prohibiting legal aid lawyers from challenging certain laws, was an unconstitutional restriction on the lawyers' (and clients') speech.

Commercial Speech

Until *Virginia Board of Pharmacy v. Va. Consumer Council* (1976), commercial speech was unprotected. That meant states could regulate or prohibit speech on commercial matters without any First Amendment implications. But *Virginia Board* held such speech contributed to the marketplace of ideas and was protected, at least in part. Commercial speech (such as advertising drug prices) could be regulated only for false and misleading content or if it proposed illegal transactions. In later years, the level of protection for commercial speech, while nominally still mid-level, has in fact been elevated.

In *Brown v. Entertainment Merchants Ass'n* (2010), the Supreme Court invalidated a California law that prohibited the sale of violent video games to minors. Despite the violence, "video games communicate ideas—and even social messages—through many familiar literary devices (such as characters, dialogue, plot, and music) and through features distinctive to the medium (such as the player's interaction with the virtual world)." What is interesting about *Brown* is that the vendors asserted not their own speech rights, but those of minors who wanted to buy the games without parental consent. Thus, in the struggle between parents and the commercial world over what children are exposed to, the court seems to favor the latter.

In *Sorrell v. IMS Health* (2011), the court invalidated a Vermont law that restricted the sale, disclosure, and use of pharmacy records that revealed doctors' prescription practices. Pharmaceutical marketers wanted that information so they could tailor their sales pitches to doctors (a practice known as *detailing*). The Supreme Court held that the marketer's First Amendment rights trumped the privacy interests of doctors and patients. Justice Kennedy's opinion suggests that commercial speech is now entitled to full First Amendment protection.

Corporate "personhood" has been a contentious issue ever since artificial entities were found to be "persons" protected by the Fourteenth Amendment. They seem to have nearly the same breadth of constitutional rights as citizens do (while they cannot literally vote, they can influence elections through campaign spending and activities). Yet, in *FCC v. AT&T* (2011) the court held that corporations do not have a right of personal privacy that would protect them from the disclosure of public records submitted to federal agencies. However, this was a case of statutory construction, not constitutional interpretation, so the alignment of the justices was different. Had AT&T been found to enjoy "personal privacy" under the statute, it probably would have doomed a whole range of consumer protection and business regulatory laws.

Campaign Speech

Because campaign spending is viewed as a means of expressing political support and communicating ideas, this activity is granted First Amendment protection. Laws that burden political speech are subject to strict scrutiny. In *Buckley v. Valeo* (1976), the court noted that contribution and expenditure limitations "operate in an area of the most fundamental First Amendment activities" in that "[d]iscussion of public issues and debate on the qualifications of candidates are integral to the operation of the system of government established by our Constitution." The First Amendment also

80 Karl M. Manheim

protects the right of candidates to spend as much of their own money on their own campaigns as they choose. In *Davis v. Federal Election Comm'n* (2008), the court invalidated the "millionaires' amendment" to federal election law. That provision allotted additional public funds to candidates who agreed to limit their own fundraising when opponents spent over a threshold amount. Justice Alito stated that Congress has no interest, let alone a compelling one, in leveling the playing field in elections.

In one of the most important political speech cases ever decided, *Citizens United v. Federal Election Comm'n* (2010) gave corporations unprecedented power to influence the outcome of elections. The case elevated corporate interests to equal the political rights of citizens. Citizens United (a nonprofit corporation) produced the film *Hillary: The Movie*, which challenged the qualifications of Senator Hillary Rodham Clinton for president. The FEC ruled that the Bipartisan Campaign Reform Act (BCRA) prohibits corporations and labor unions from using their general funds to spend on "electioneering communications" that directly advocate the election or defeat of a candidate. Corporations can establish political action committees (PACs) for election advocacy, but cannot use general treasury funds for such purposes.

By a 5–4 vote along ideological lines, the majority held that corporate funding of independent political broadcasts in candidate elections cannot be limited. The court went on to state that political speech is indispensable to a democracy, which is no less true because the speech comes from a corporation. Corporations may not be able to vote themselves, but they now have the right to basically buy votes.

In *Arizona Free Enterprise Club's Freedom Club PAC v. Bennett* (2010), the court held that Arizona's matching funds scheme violated the First Amendment. The Arizona Clean Elections Act provided public subsidies to candidates who "opt-in" by agreeing not to raise more than a certain dollar amount or amount per donor. The act was designed to avoid political corruption (and passed in response to several notable instances of election buying). It also worked to (partially) level the playing field of candidates who opt-in, and are thereby restricted in their expenditures and are grossly outspent by privately financed opponents. Thus, along the lines of *Citizens United*, the Supreme Court found this law unconstitutional. Leveling the playing field in elections is constitutionally prohibited.

Privacy, Technology, and Propriety Rights

We've examined privacy through the lens of substantive due process, but it's most closely related to the rights of speech, religious conscience, and assembly protected by the First Amendment. As technology advances, threats to privacy and confidentiality in our personal communications grow even more pronounced. This emerging area of law is well beyond the scope of this chapter, but setting up a framework for analysis helps complete our discussion of free speech.

Surveillance and Access to Data

Government collects data from us all the time, from the vitals of birth to the circumstances of death. Most data collection is for legitimate public health or public safety purposes. But some information is specially protected by the Fourth Amendment (search and seizure)[20] and the Fifth Amendment (self-incrimination).[21] Thus, interception of our phone and e-mail conversations by federal agencies, tracking our Internet activity, thermal imaging of actions inside our homes, and other surveillance activities, all give rise to Fourth Amendment concerns. They also implicate the First Amendment; at least to the extent that government surveillance chills our speech.

The infamous, and now abandoned, Office of Total Information Awareness, run by John Poindexter, is an example of government information gathering run amok. From National Security Agency (NSA) "wiretaps" of Internet traffic (using the Echelon devices NSA installed on the servers of Internet service providers [ISPs]), to interception of tens of millions of wireline and wireless phone calls each hour, the prospect of Big Brother grows real. Surely, the right of free speech includes the right of private speech. Perhaps.

Beyond that, for what purposes can government use the information (legally and illegally obtained) it has about us? When private phone companies release our phone records to snoopers, or insurance companies, medical offices, or employers disclose our health and personnel records, there may be serious violations of federal or state privacy laws, but no constitutional problems. On the other hand, government databases (those birth and death records, plus a wide array of other information) are subject to constitutional command. If the state of California collects DNA samples from every arrestee, whether charged or not, and retains it even if he is acquitted, it has the genetic information not just of the arrestee, but also his parents, siblings, and children. It will be interesting to see how the First Amendment develops in the context of emerging technological threats to privacy and personality.

Neighboring Rights (Copyright; Right of Publicity)

A copyright gives its owner the exclusive right to use, display, perform, recite, and reproduce the copyrighted work, as well as to make derivative works. In short, a copyrighted work is removed from the public domain; no one else may communicate that particular expression. One remedy for infringement of copyright is an injunction; a classic case of prior restraint. How does this square with the First Amendment?

The Supreme Court has had little difficulty reconciling copyright with free speech. First, a copyrighted work is someone else's speech, not yours. Second, a judge-made exception (codified at 17 U.S.C. §107) allows for "fair use" of a copyrighted work ("for purposes such as criticism, comment, news reporting, teaching, scholarship, or research"). Finally, it is only a particular expression, not the underlying ideas or facts, that can be copyrighted. Thus, there is little ultimate impact on the "marketplace of ideas."

A problem similar to copyright occurs where one person exploits another's public persona without permission. Thus, using pictures of Brittney Spears to sell products or websites is not only an invasion of her right to privacy, but also her *right to publicity* (profit from her own fame). This is not a right found in the federal Constitution, but some state laws provide such rights. As with copyright, one does not have a free speech right to use another's proprietary assets, including her personality.

Free Press

The right of free speech is surely enjoyed by the fourth estate, as it is by others. But does the First Amendment's free press clause provide any additional protection? The general answer is no; the press (however defined) does not enjoy rights beyond those provided under free speech, despite special mention in our charter of liberties. That said, some speech rights (e.g., prior restraints) are most often invoked by the press, but their application does not depend upon any special status of the claimant. Rather, rights that would be unique to the press—reporter's privilege and access to government information—have yet to be identified by the Supreme Court.

Reporter's Privilege

As the recent jailing of *New York Times* reporter Judith Miller amply demonstrated, there is no constitutional right to withhold confidential information, other than as federal and state law provides as testimonial privileges. In other words, the free press clause is not violated no matter what impact loss of confidentiality would have on the press' ability to gather and report matters of public importance (especially that relating to government wrongdoing). Any relief on this front must be obtained from Congress, where draft shield laws have languished for years, or from the states. Most states do provide a reporter's privilege (in state cases); but there is no federal law.

Some have argued that any such privilege should differentiate the classic case where a reporter obtains information *about* wrongdoing, or another subject of investigation, from the Miller case where providing the information *is itself* the crime (outing a covert agent). In the former, the press is performing its idealized function of preserving a free state; while in the latter, the information exchange between source and reporter is not one that serves underlying First Amendment values.

Right of Access

Democracies die behind closed doors. Yet, the court has declined to create a right of access to government information and proceedings. In *Houchins v. KQED* (1977), the court rejected a First Amendment right of press access to investigate prison conditions. Nor does the press have a constitutional right to other government information. The Freedom of Information Act (FOIA) is a statutory right. When FOIA exemptions are challenged on First Amendment grounds, the press usually loses.

One exception is found in criminal trials. In *Richmond Newspapers v. Virginia* (1979), the court declared a limited right of access if "the place and process have traditionally been open to the press and general public." The limited right (note, it is not unique to the press) was gingerly extended to deportation hearings by the Sixth Circuit after the government, citing the Patriot Act, tried to close them. Access can be restricted when necessary to protect other constitutional rights (*Stewart v. Nebraska Press Ass'n* [1975; balancing rights of free press vs. those of fair trial]). It remains to be seen whether other proceedings (e.g., combatant status tribunals at Guantanamo) will be closed to the press.

Prior Restraints

Under the British crown, control of the press was accomplished mainly through licensing laws. Licenses, of course, were awarded only for approved content. This practice was fresh in the minds of the framers when the press clause was drafted. Thus, any scheme of prepublication review by the state is especially disfavored.

An injunction against publication, or other speech, is the classic prior restraint. Only grave and specific threats to national security will justify an injunction (*New York Times v. United States* [1970]). It is far better to punish speech after the fact, in those rare cases where regulation will survive the appropriate level of scrutiny. The reasons are two-fold: (1) *ex post* punishment is determined by a jury (which presumably acts to constrain state abuses), whereas *ex ante* restriction is determined solely by a judge; and (2) prior restraint forecloses any beneficial impact of the speech. It is forever lost.

Many forms of speech still require licensing (e.g., a parade permit). But, there, licensing goes not to the content of speech (if it does, it is invalid), but to the nonspeech elements (traffic control). Still any prerequisite to engaging in speech must be as short as administratively practicable.

Religious Rights (Separation of Church and State)

Congress shall make no law respecting an establishment of religion, or prohibiting the free exercise thereof.

First Amendment

Under the crown, the established English church dominated politics, often with arbitrary ecclesiastical rule. By the time of ratification of the Constitution, most states had disestablished their official churches while still encouraging the private practice of religion as essential to the peoples' welfare. Still, the debate over state endorsement of religion was intense. Among the more famous polemics was Madison's *Memorial and Remonstrance* (1785) against Virginia's religious tax levy. This was followed by the Religious Freedom Act (1786), sponsored by Jefferson, which severed all links between church and state in Virginia.

While many of the framers supported separation of church and state, they often did so for different reasons. Roger Williams, an evangelical, felt separation was necessary to protect the church from corrupting political influences. Jefferson argued that separation was necessary to protect secular interests. And Madison felt that both church and state benefited from the decentralization of power that resulted from separation. To him, religion was simply one of many factions competing for power.

Many of the framers were deists who rejected Christian orthodoxy and the divinity of Christ. Jefferson even wrote his own version of the bible, subtitled *The Life and Morals of Jesus of Nazareth*, which contradicted prevailing dogma. Until recently, a copy of the *Jefferson Bible* was given to every entering member of Congress.

The original constitution contained only one reference to religion. Article VI, clause 3 states: "no religious test shall ever be required as a qualification to any office or public trust under the United States." This reflects the separatist intentions of key framers. But the state ratifying conventions wanted more. Accordingly, the First Amendment added additional protections.

Prior to adoption of the Fourteenth Amendment, the establishment and free exercise clauses did not apply to the states.[22] Religious conflict prevailed in some states. In New York and Pennsylvania, Protestants demanded that the King James version of the bible be the standard instructional text for the common schools. Catholics demanded the Douai version, plus state funding. The conflict grew violent, and dozens were killed in the Battle of

Philadelphia and elsewhere during the so-called bible wars of 1844. The American Republican Party (aka Know Nothing party) wanted laws guaranteeing the supremacy of Protestant values in schools and denying state funding to Catholic schools.

The Blaine Amendment (1874) would have added a specific prohibition to the Constitution against public funding of religious schools. It was understood that it would bar aid only to private Catholic schools while permitting continued Protestant control of public schools. It failed in Congress, but was adopted by 34 states as amendments to their own constitutions. Some states went even further, prohibiting (parochial) private schools, thereby ensuring that children were exposed to Protestant instruction. Those laws were invalidated in *Pierce v. Society of Sisters* (1925).

Establishment Clause

Early Supreme Court cases on the establishment clause followed Jefferson's notion of strict separation of church and state. In *Everson v. Board of Ed* (1947), the court declared: "The First Amendment has erected a wall between church and state. That wall must be kept high and impregnable." The test under this doctrine was described in *Lemon v. Kurtzman* (1971):

1　A law must have a valid secular *purpose*;
2　The primary *effect* of the law must be secular (neither to advance nor inhibit religion);
3　The law must not foster *excessive entanglement* between government and religion.

As the court grew more conservative in the 1970s, the *Lemon* test drew its detractors. Another test, based on government *neutrality* began to gain favor. Under this test, a law is invalid if it favors one religion over another ("sect preference") or religion over secularism. It must minimize state encouragement or discouragement of belief and observance. A still more favorable approach (from the standpoint of religion) has recently emerged, called the *accommodation test*. Under this test, government can recognize the role of religion in society and accommodate its presence. It prohibits only the literal establishment of a state religion or the coercion of religious participation. At the extreme, coercion means only religious taxes or penalties for nonbelief.

Because of their variation, these three tests (separation, neutrality, and accommodation) reflect profound disagreement on the court. Some justices adhere to the view of the United States as a secular country, while others prefer the ideal of religious pluralism. As with political pluralism, the majority is usually entitled to get its way.

The *Lemon* test was recently used to invalidate a display of the 10 Commandments inside a county courthouse (*McCreary v. ACLU* [2005; lacked a secular purpose]). In a companion case, *Van Orden v. Perry* (2005), the accommodation test was used by a four-member plurality to uphold a similar display at the Texas state capitol because it was accompanied by other historical texts. The concurrence cited state neutrality.

Religion in Public Schools

These programs violate the establishment clause:

- Prayer in the classroom. Even where nondenominational, prayer as part of the curriculum has a subtle coercive effect.
- Moment of silence in the classroom (at least if intended to replace prayer).
- Prayer at graduation ceremonies (probably other school functions a well).
- Ban on teaching evolution.
- Teaching creation science or intelligent design.
- State funding of parochial schools or teacher salaries, either directly or through tuition tax credits.

These programs do not violate the establishment clause:

- Providing buses or textbooks for parochial school students.
- Tax credits for school expenses (at least if not limited to religious schools).

The common theme of the above is that state aid to pupils attending religious schools is ok, but aid to the schools themselves is not. Nor can public school curricula contain religious elements. The rule is different at state colleges, where indoctrination of students isn't as likely. Indeed, where state schools fund student organizations, they cannot discriminate against religious clubs (based on the clubs' free speech rights).

Tax expenditures for religious purposes have been a contentious issue ever since Madison's *Memorial and Remonstrance* in 1785 (opposing Virginia's religion tax). Every once in a while the struggle turns violent, as with the bible wars of the 1830s and the Philadelphia riots in 1843. But, lately at least, war is waged in the courts. The Warren court relaxed standing requirements so that taxpayers could challenge illegal expenditures for religious purposes (*Flast v. Cohen* [1968]), but the Rehnquist court began retrenching (*Valley Forge Christian College v. Americans United for Separation of Church and State* [1982; taxpayers could not challenge U.S. Army gift of property to religious school]).

The Roberts court has continued the trend of allowing taxes in aid of religion. In *Arizona Christian School Tuition Org. v. Winn* (2011), taxpayers challenged a tuition tax credit for donations to scholarship organizations that fund religious instruction. They alleged the tax credit violated the establishment clause because it effectively funneled money to private religious schools. The court, in a 5–4 decision, held that tax credits, while having the same economic effect as expenditures, represent a taxpayer's own spending rather than the state's.

The establishment clause has shrunk considerably in reach. Under a developing theory known as *accommodation*, government may recognize and aid religion so long as it does not effectively coerce people's religious beliefs. Jefferson and Madison would be chagrined.

Free Exercise Clause

The free exercise clause protects religious beliefs as well as religious practices. The former is about as close to an absolute right as found in the Constitution. The state may not compel or regulate beliefs. But religious practices are similar to symbolic speech; they contain expressive and non-expressive components. A bigamy law, for instance, regulates conduct quite apart from any exercise of religious beliefs. Such a law was upheld in *Reynolds v. United States* (1878).

Sherbert v. Verner (1961) set the test for the free exercise clause. As long as a law served a purpose unrelated to religion, it would be subject to an *ad hoc* balancing test: does the state's interest outweigh the burden on religious practices? In *Braunfeld v. Brown* (1961), a Sunday closing law was upheld as serving a state purpose other than fostering of religion. But, in *Sherbert*, a law denying unemployment insurance to sabbatarians (whose faith would not let them work on Saturdays) was held too burdensome in light of the state's exemption for Sunday worshipers.

Sherbert was overruled in *Employment Division v. Smith* (1990). Smith was denied unemployment insurance for having used peyote as part of a religious ritual. Justice Scalia wrote that a law of general application (one not triggered solely by religious practices) did not implicate the free exercise clause; hence no balancing of state and private interests was necessary. Since *Smith* uses a rational basis standard of review, only the most egregious interferences with religious practices will be held invalid. But they occur. For instance, in *Church of the Lukumi Babalu v. Hialeah* (1993), the court struck a local ordinance prohibiting the ritual killing of animals, but not other rendering (such as for consumption, experimentation, or humanitarian reasons). Because the law targeted a practice only when part of religious exercise, strict scrutiny was appropriate. Most recently, a Washington law denying scholarships to students enrolled in religion-degree programs (as well as vocational programs) was upheld as not targeting religious practices (*Locke v. Davey* [2004]). Lack of funding was not a burden on free exercise. The law might have failed equal protection if it singled out particular religions or religion in general, but it did not.

Regulating Religion

"The free exercise clause embraces two concepts—freedom to believe and freedom to act. The first is absolute, but in the nature of things, the second cannot be. Conduct remains subject to regulation" (*Cantwell v. Conn.* [1940]).

Under the modern *Smith* test, a law regulating religious acts will be upheld if it serves a purpose unrelated to religion (compare *O'Brien* test). Even serious burdens of free exercise are ok so long as non-religious actions of the same type are also affected.

Free exercise claims also fare poorly in military context. The clause does not require religious exemptions from the draft (*Gillette v. United States* [1971]). Nor does it require military authorities to permit the wearing of yarmulkes (*Goldman v. Weinberger* [1986]).

Congress reacted angrily to *Smith*, and passed the Religious Freedom Restoration Act of 1993 (RiFRA). RiFRA provided a statutory right to be free from laws burdening religion, whatever their purpose or application. In *Boerne v. City of Flores* (1997), lower courts held that a local zoning law violated RiFRA because it disallowed church expansion. The Supreme Court reversed, holding that RiFRA was unconstitutional—it exceeded Congress' power. Since a nontargeted burden on religion did not infringe the First Amendment (or Fourteenth), Congress lacked power to make it into a civil rights violation.

However, relying on the spending clause (Article I, §8) rather than its civil rights enforcement power (Fourteenth Amendment, §5), Congress was able to pass the Religious Land Use and Institutionalized Persons Act (RLUIPA).[23] The Act was upheld in *Cutter v. Wilkinson* (2005), despite the claim that it provided a special benefit for religion. Applying its new establishment clause test, the court held that Congress could accommodate religious needs even if other constitutional rights were not protected.

Economic Rights

The historian Charles Beard argued that the Constitution was written by and for men of property.[24] While that view is not widely shared, it is unmistakable that several key provisions of the Constitution protect property interests, and that protection has received high status at various times. This section provides a short survey of relevant provisions.

Due Process

As discussed earlier, the due process clause was invoked early on to protect economic rights such as "liberty of contract." While economic substantive due process has been overruled—indeed discredited—vestiges remain. This is seen mainly with price control (rate regulation). Procedural due process provides a second means of protection for property.

Price Control

Governments regulate prices in a variety of contexts, at both the wholesale and retail levels. This ranges from public utilities (e.g., electric rates) to housing (e.g., rent control) to royalties (e.g., compulsory copyright licenses). Nearly every effort to regulate prices has been challenged by those whose property is regulated. Early cases relied on economic substantive due process, but as that waned, later cases used a hybrid notion of *confiscation*.

Nebbia v. New York (1934) was decided near the end of the *Lochner* era. There, the court upheld a law setting minimum prices for milk: "Price control, like any other form of regulation, is unconstitutional only if arbitrary, discriminatory, or demonstrably irrelevant to the policy the Legislature is free to adopt." In *Federal Power Comm'n v. Natural Gas Pipeline Co.* (1942), the court held a rate would be too low if it is "so unjust as to destroy the value of [the] property for all the purposes for which it was acquired," and in so doing "practically deprive[s] the owner of property without due process of law." In other words, government-fixed rates that are so low as to "confiscate" property are unconstitutional.

It would be nice if there were a formula for the quantitative analysis that the doctrine necessarily demands. Several formulations have been tried by the court (e.g., market rates of return), but none were very satisfactory. Today, all the court requires is that a rate be within the "zone of reasonableness." The lower end of that is synonymous with a "taking" of property (see Fifth Amendment—The Just Compensation Clause, below). It does not mean that rates have to return a profit. But if, say, an electric utility company is not permitted to charge enough to pay for the cost of generation and providing service, then such low rates would be counterproductive and outside the zone of reasonableness.

Procedural Fairness

The preferred mechanism for dealing with government acts affecting property rights is by demanding procedural fairness. This is true not only in rate regulation, where substantive standards have given way to the right to be heard, but with other interests in property. The due process clause includes a procedural component, which is triggered whenever a protected "life, liberty or property interest" is adversely affected. Unfortunately, the Constitution does not define *property*, and the court no longer engrafts "natural rights" theories (e.g., Locke's labor theory of property) onto that term. Rather, whether a property interest exists, and its contours, are determined by positive law based on a reasonable expectation of protection that has been given by the state or federal government (*Roth v. Bd. of Regents* [1972]).

Once a property right is found (nearly all forms of capital investment satisfy the *Roth* standard), any significant impairment of the right must satisfy procedural due process. That means open meetings, fair hearings, and the like. This is why rate-setting bodies, such as public utility commissions, engage in elaborate investigations and public input before acting.

The Contracts Clause

No state shall . . . pass any . . . Law impairing the Obligation of Contracts.

Article I, 10, clause 1

The contracts clause was once a formidable impediment to state economic regulation. But several prerequisites for invoking the clause severely limit its reach today. First, the clause applies only to state regulation of contracts. Federal laws are not subject to the clause (but still have to observe due process constraints). Second, the clause applies only to contracts in existence on the date a challenged law is enacted. Otherwise, anyone could enter into a contract term forbidden by law and then challenge the law as an impairment. Thus, if a state were to limit mortgage interest rates, holders of existing mortgages might have a claim, but parties to future mortgages would be well aware of the rate restrictions when they chose to enter into the contract.

Beyond these formal limitations on the clause, the Supreme Court's test for when an impairment occurs is very deferential to state regulation. Economic regulations will not trigger contracts clause scrutiny unless they are specifically aimed at existing contracts. Thus, a law regulating prices generally will not trigger the clause merely because some parties had previously set prices by contract (*Exxon Corp. v. Eagerton* [1983]). But a law that affects only existing contracts does trigger the clause. A three-part test applies in that case:

1   Is there a substantial impairment of contractual obligations? Here the court distinguishes between obligations and remedies. For instance, in *Home Building & Loan Ass'n v. Blaisdell* (1934), the court upheld the Minnesota mortgage moratorium law, which gave homeowners additional time to redeem properties in default. The law affected the banks' remedies (when it could foreclose) but not the homeowners' obligation to pay the mortgage. It would be interesting to see how a state law reducing defaulting homeowners' mortgage payments (e.g., "mark to market") would fare under *Blaisdell*. A federal mortgage relief law would not be subject to the contracts clause.
2   What is the strength of the public interest behind the impairment? The greater the impairment, the more important the public interest must be. This creates a sliding scale standard of review. For instance, addressing the housing crisis may be a strong state interest, but cancelling underwater mortgages would be a substantial impairment.
3   Is adjusting the contracting parties' rights reasonable and appropriate in light of the identified public purpose? This is where the public and private interests are balanced. In *U.S. Trust v. New Jersey* (1977), the court ruled that diversion of bridge and tunnel toll revenue by the Port Authority of New York and New Jersey, to pay for acquisition of a trans–Hudson River rail line, was not an interest sufficient to offset the bond holders' contract guaranty of dedicated tolls. *U.S. Trust* is best understood as raising the standard of review when a government entity adjusts its own contracts (less deference to the state is warranted) than when adjusting private contracts.

In addition to these three inquiries, the court weighs other factors, such as whether the contract was entered into against a regime of heavy state regulation. In that case, the parties may have expected further regulation such that, when it comes, it does not materially affect their contract rights. As a result of the triggering elements and generally deferential standard of review, the contracts clause provides little relief these days to economic players, at least in regulated industries.

Fifth Amendment—The Just Compensation Clause

Nor shall private property be taken for public use, without just compensation.

The Fifth Amendment

The Fifth Amendment protects property twice; first in the due process clause, and again in the just compensation (or "takings") clause. This signifies either obsession on the part of the framers with property rights, or their view that two different forms of government action can affect property. Probably the latter. In addition to the police power (the power to regulate) governments have long enjoyed the power of eminent domain—the power to condemn private property and put it to public use. Until the *Lochner* era of economic substantive due process, the due process and takings clauses were mostly confined to these respective forms of government action.

At the very least, the takings clause says that whenever government exercises its power of eminent domain (to literally "take" private property), it must pay "just compensation," usually measured as fair market value. In a typical eminent domain case government first offers to simply buy the property. This is usually in connection with some public works project, such as redevelopment. A holdout landowner may not want to sell, or may want to extract surplus value (an enhanced price due to the pending project). If no agreement is reached, the government "condemns" the land and lets a court decide fair value, often based on battling expert appraisal testimony.

Public Use Requirement

Property rights advocates have long resisted the use of eminent domain, especially when the resulting "public use" isn't ownership by the government (say, for a park), but another private owner. The Supreme Court has affirmed three times that it is up to the legislature to decide what constitutes a "public use," not the courts. In *Berman v. Parker* (1954), the court upheld the use of eminent domain for redevelopment projects. In *Hawaii Housing Auth. v. Midkiff* (1984), the court upheld a Hawaii plan that broke up large land holdings and re-vested them in individual owners. Most recently, in *Kelo v. City of New London* (2005), the court again upheld the use of eminent domain for redevelopment. General benefits a community obtained from economic growth were sufficient to satisfy the "public use" requirement

Kelo was a close decision (5–4). Many observers thought that an activist court would come down on the side of property rights. But, substituting a court's judgment for that of the legislature, in determining what types of "uses" provided public benefit, would return us to the *Lochner* era, when courts made economic and social policy.

Possessory Takings

Sometimes government "takes" property without going through the formality or expense of condemning it. Indeed, if it can acquire property for free through regulatory or other action, why bother with eminent domain? The court recognized that the police power might be used as an end-run around the just compensation requirement.

In *Pumpelly v. Green Bay Co.* (1871), a dam erected on Fox River caused the submersion of private upstream lands, essentially wiping them out. In effect, the state had "taken" the land for the public use of erecting a dam. It was immaterial to the constitutional requirement for compensation that the state had not acted in eminent domain. In such cases, rather than the state seeking formal transfer of title (and paying for it), the owner must bring suit to recover compensation for her lost property. This is called *inverse condemnation*.

In short, when government permanently occupies private property (or authorizes another to do so) it has, for all intents and purposes, "taken" that property as if by condemnation. It does not matter why the state has done so, or how much property it has taken. A possessory taking, even for the noblest of purposes, or the smallest slice of property, will obligate the state to pay just compensation.

Regulatory Takings

The equivalence of permanent physical occupation and eminent domain is a logical one. But during the *Lochner* era, the court extended the takings clause to cover ordinary economic regulation. If government action affected the value of property (as all regulation does), it could be invalidated under the takings clause. This theory was announced in *Pennsylvania Coal v. Mahon* (1922), which invalidated a Pennsylvania law requiring mining companies to leave enough underground coal in place to avoid subsistence (sinking) of surface dwellings. Justice Holmes reasoned that "while property may be regulated to a certain extent, if regulation goes too far it will be recognized as a taking." And requiring mining companies to suffer diminution in the value of their mineral interests simply went "too far."

The notion that economic regulation might be subject to the strict commands of the takings clause proved to be a potent tool for property rights advocates. Economic theories were developed to test when regulation went "too far." Regulation of utility rates, for instance, would be unconstitutional if the utility's earnings were below market rates. By the end of the *Lochner* era, the court realized it had to back off the takings clause just as it had done with economic substantive due process. Today, the concept of *regulatory takings* still exists, but the severity of interference with property rights (and values) must approximate that of possessory takings; in other words, total diminution in value (from the property owner's perspective; see *Agins v. Tiburon* [1980]).

Judicial Review

One of the most remarkable features of the American system of government is the independence of our judiciary. This third branch of government keeps the other two honest, or at least faithful to the Constitution. They do this by exercising a power known as *judicial review*. We take it for granted that courts can invalidate unconstitutional actions of the two political branches—legislative and executive—and of the states. But it wasn't always the case. In fact, the Constitution itself is silent on who has final interpretive authority. But in *Marbury v. Madison* (1803), the court declared itself the final word on constitutional meaning (and it has remained that way ever since).

The significant power of judicial review has a corollary—restraint in its exercise. One of the hardest parts of any constitutional case is convincing a court that it should actually hear the dispute, rather than let other bodies (e.g., state courts, agencies) resolve it. In fact, the Supreme Court has erected an entire body of law that governs when federal courts can hear cases. The several "justiciability" doctrines determine if a federal court has jurisdiction (power to hear and decide a case). They apply only to federal courts; state court jurisdiction is determined by their own state constitutions. They often have justiciability requirements of their own, but they are seldom as restrictive as the federal rules. Justiciability doctrines are complex and controversial. Sometimes they are used to keep disfavored cases or disfavored litigants out of federal court. In this section, we'll take a brief tour through the doctrines. But, first we'll look at another level of complexity; the fact that we have two parallel judicial systems.

Our Dual Judicial System—The Role of State Courts

Federalism is a principal feature of American government. The federal government exercises only those powers specified in the Constitution (the doctrine of "enumerated power").[25] One manifestation of federalism is that state governments operate under structures that look very much like the federal system. Every state has legislative, executive, and judicial branches. In some ways, the court systems of the 50 states compete with federal courts for business, and certainly for authority. Because state and federal courts have similar and often overlapping jurisdictions, it is important to know how they interrelate.

Two important principles describe the business and jurisdiction of state and federal courts. First, state courts have *general jurisdiction*. This means they can hear most types of cases, including those based on federal law. Indeed, they must hear federal cases and federal defenses (e.g., Fourth Amendment defenses in criminal cases). The only exception is where Congress vests exclusive jurisdiction in federal courts (e.g., federal crimes and some civil matters—antitrust, patent). Otherwise, someone raising a federal issue has a choice of filing in either state or federal court.

The other basic principle is that federal courts have *limited jurisdiction*. This fits in with the notion that the federal government as a whole has limited (enumerated) power. Article III of the Constitution both creates the federal courts and defines their power. In contrast to states' general jurisdiction, there are only nine types of cases that federal courts may hear. The two most often invoked are *federal question* and *diversity*. The former refers to any case "arising under the Constitution or laws of the United States." Most constitutional claims fit in here. The latter refers to cases between citizens of different states, even ordinary tort cases (e.g., auto accident between California and Nevada residents). The purpose of this was to avoid state biases in their own courts. Other cases that federal courts can hear include admiralty, diplomatic, and cases against the United States.

Ordinarily, a case that starts in one system cannot get into the other. However, there are exceptions. The most notable exception is that the U.S. Supreme Court has final review over federal issues in state cases. Another exception is habeas corpus, where a lower federal court can review whether a state defendant has received a fair trial. Beyond these constitutional issues, rules of venue and choice of law have also developed that determine where a case can be heard and under whose laws.

Jurisdiction, Venue, and Choice of Law

Because jurisdiction is synonymous with power, and both state and federal courts jealously guard their own, complex rules have developed for determining which court has authority over a particular case. Similar conflicts increasingly arise in international disputes, partly as a consequence of globalization, However, the fact that a case involves international law or litigants does not change the normal rules of state or federal jurisdiction (even treaties can be litigated in state court). Also, there is no appeal from the U.S. Supreme Court to any international tribunal. This is unlike the situation in some other countries where parties may appeal a decision of a national court to an international one (e.g., the European Court of Justice or the Inter-American Court of Human Rights).

Justiciability—Standing, Mootness, and Political Questions

In some states, the legislature can ask the courts for advice on pending laws. This is thought to help assure that only constitutional laws are enacted. The downside is that judicial advice is necessarily given in the abstract, without the benefit of specific facts and specific litigants. It also permits the political branches to "pass the buck" on controversial legislation to the nonpolitical branch—the courts.

The Massachusetts legislature, for example, can seek advice from that state's supreme judicial court. It did so recently on the question of gay marriage. The "opinion of the Justices" (it is not a decision in the classic sense) set off a nationwide controversy that some believe played a role in the presidential election of 2004.

In contrast, the U.S. Supreme Court cannot give advice. It can only decide cases and controversies; in other words, those legal issues that have already resulted in actual disputes between people who are directly affected.

Standing

The case and controversy limitation on federal judicial power gives rise to several justiciability doctrines, the most important of which is standing. To establish standing, a federal plaintiff must meet the following four requirements:

1   *Suffered a "discrete and palpable" injury.* The harm complained of must be particular to plaintiff or a definable group, rather than general to a large population. For "generalized grievances" (harms that are general to a large population), claimants must pursue political remedies (i.e., seek redress from the legislature). Moreover, the injury cannot be too abstract, but instead must be "legally cognizable." Not all harms qualify (e.g., stigmatic injuries to racial minorities).

2   *The harm must have been "caused" by defendant's purported illegal activity.* Even if defendant violated the law, the link between that violation and plaintiff's injury may be too tenuous. For instance, when the IRS illegally granted tax relief to discriminatory private schools, the court was unconvinced that the IRS's action contributed to "white flight," thus causing plaintiff's injury—the re-segregation of her public school. But when Congress limited the liability of nuclear power operators in the event of future catastrophic accident, the court did find a connection between that action and injury to neighboring residents (a decrease in their property values). This standing element is highly manipulable.

3   *The harm must be "remediable."* Unless a court is able to give a meaningful remedy against defendant, it cannot redress plaintiff's harm. In such case, the court isn't deciding a case; it is merely rendering an advisory opinion.

4   *Plaintiff must assert her own legal rights.* One may suffer a discrete injury due to the infringement of someone else's rights. *Warth v. Seldin* (1975) held that such third-party (or *jus tertii*) standing was not usually permitted. In *Warth*, an exclusionary zoning law of the city of Pennfield, New York, operated to exclude low-income residents. The law may have been enacted to obstruct black residents of neighboring Rochester from moving into town. When white residents of Pennfield challenged the law, the Supreme Court held they had suffered a discrete injury in fact (inability to live in an integrated community). However, the white residents were not themselves the victims of the city's

discriminatory practices. Instead, they were asserting the equal protection rights of the blacks who had been denied entry. The rule against *jus tertii* standing has been imposed by the court as a matter of "prudential self restraint"—to avoid unnecessary friction with other branches. Approved instances of *jus tertii* standing include some First Amendment claims and where a close relationship exists between claimant and right holder (e.g., parent/child, doctor/patient). Furthermore, an association can sue on behalf of its members if at least one of its members can meet the standing requirement and if the issue is germane to the purposes of the organization.

Standing is usually determined shortly after a case is filed, long before discovery and trial. Therefore, plaintiff's factual allegations must be accepted as true on any motion to dismiss. This works in theory, but not always in practice. For instance, in the IRS case mentioned above, plaintiff was not allowed to proffer expert economic testimony showing how white flight was facilitated by the beneficial tax status of private schools.

Ripeness and Mootness

A case must be "live" at all stages of litigation. If it is filed prematurely (i.e., before the harm has actually occurred), it may be speculative either as to whether the harm will occur or, if it does, what its precise contours will be. Challenging a law before it is implemented is an example of an unripe case. Many controversial issues (e.g., contraception, sexual practices) have been kept out of federal court on this basis. For suits filed before an injury actually occurs, there must be a strong likelihood that it will occur, and little benefit in waiting (i.e., the facts are already known and are unlikely to change).

The flip side of ripeness is *mootness*. A case may become stale after it is filed. For example, the defendant may have died, or stopped its illegal conduct, or provided plaintiff with the relief she sought. Some claims cannot be adjudicated before it is too late to render meaningful relief (e.g., election disputes and abortion challenges, by their very nature, become moot before they can be decided) and so a strict rule would prevent such cases from ever being decided by a federal court. The Supreme Court has created an exception to mootness, known as "capable of repetition yet evading review," to allow for jurisdiction in such cases.

Strangely, a case can be unripe and moot simultaneously. In *Lyons v. Los Angeles* (1983), Lyons, a black man, sought an injunction against the Los Angeles Police Department's routine use of excessive force—the carthoid chokehold. He nearly died in the hands of police. While his past injury was compensable by monetary damages, an injunction against future use of the chokehold would not provide him any remedy (he was no longer being

choked when the case was filed). Thus, that claim was moot. When he asserted the likelihood that he would be stopped and illegally choked again
(the LAPD has had that reputation of using excessive force against blacks),
the court deemed that claim speculative (i.e., unripe). Between the time of
Lyons's injury and the Supreme Court decision in his case dozens of blacks
died from chokeholds, yet none were able to present a justiciable case for an
injunction against the illegal practice.

Political Question

Some constitutional claims are simply inappropriate for judicial inquiry, as
the Constitution itself vests final decision-making authority with one of the
political branches. Can a federal court declare that a state lacks a "republican form of government" for some defect in its political composition or
procedures? In *Luther v. Bordon*, the court held that Article IV is merely a direction to the federal political branches to "guarantee" states republican government, not a judicially enforceable command. Therefore, injured parties
must seek redress from the political branches in these cases, not the courts.

Another example is impeachment. What does it mean for the Senate to
"try all impeachments"? Can it delegate that task to a committee? In *Nixon v.
United States*, Judge Walter Nixon was impeached for corruption, but the
Senate Judiciary Committee conducted the trial. The full Senate never heard
the testimony; it convicted Nixon solely on the committee's recommendation. Whether this violated the impeachments clause, the court said, was a
matter for the Senate to decide, not the court.

In *Vieth v. Jubilirer* (2004), four members of the court thought that partisan gerrymandering was a political question. There, Tom Delay had engineered the redistricting of Texas's congressional districts with the effect
of reducing the number of Democratic leaning districts and increasing the
number of Republican districts. Years earlier in *Reynolds v. Sims* (1964),
the court concluded that redistricting was not a political question, partly
because the injured parties had no recourse to a remedy at the political level
(that was precisely their claim). Thus, *Vieth* may signal an expansion of the
political question doctrine to deny justiciability in politically charged cases.

Jurisdiction Stripping—Congress's Control over Courts

Federal courts can also be precluded from deciding cases due to Congress's
control over their jurisdiction. Article III authorizes Congress to create
lower federal courts. The greater includes the lesser, so Congress can create
lower courts but decline to vest them with full jurisdiction allowed by the
Constitution. Jurisdiction once granted can also be withdrawn (stripped), so
long as it is not done in a manner that violates separation of powers principles (e.g., to prevent federal courts from performing their essential function

of deciding constitutional questions). Congress also can determine the appellate jurisdiction of the Supreme Court (but not its original jurisdiction).

The Detainee Treatment Act of 2005 is an example of jurisdiction stripping. It prohibits federal courts (both lower courts and the Supreme Court) from hearing petitions for habeas corpus from persons detained at Guantanamo. This isn't the first time Congress has tried to keep habeas cases out of court. They did so after the Civil War to keep the Supreme Court from reviewing the Reconstruction Acts (see *Ex parte McCardle* [1869]). And the recently introduced (and misnamed) Constitution Restoration Act would prohibit federal courts from hearing any challenge to government action "acknowledg[ing] God as the sovereign source of law, liberty, or government."

Abstention

Even where a federal court has jurisdiction to hear a case, it may decline to do so for reasons of *comity*. This is the respect that courts of one sovereign show to those of another. As applied to our federal system, it means that cases already pending in state court cannot ordinarily be adjudicated in federal court. See *Ex Parte Young* (1908). Also, cases properly in federal court, but which have a potentially dispositive state law element, can be referred to state court for resolution. See *Railroad Com'n v. Pullman* (1941).

There are several complex abstention doctrines. They typically operate to deny federal jurisdiction in favor of state courts. This wouldn't be so problematic if state courts were as vigilant as federal courts in enforcing federal rights. But state judges are usually elected, and subject to majoritarian political pressures. And while the U.S. Supreme Court can review state court decisions (at least the federal issues in state cases), the court's docket is typically about 80 cases a year. So the vast majority of cases in which abstention applies never receive federal court review.

These jurisdiction-limiting devices (justiciability, stripping, abstention) produce outcomes without a decision on the merits. Because they are often technical in nature, they can slip beneath the radar and escape the headlines. Yet, they are as important as any substantive decision. Indeed, they often have broader effect, since they categorically exclude entire classes of cases or claimants from federal court.

Notes

1 In *Sebelius*, the Supreme Court invalidated part of the Medicare expansion in the Affordable Care Act, holding that withholding all federal Medicare funding from noncompliant states *coerced* them into enforcing federal law, rather than simply giving states the option.
2 The Eleventh Amendment is the only constitutional provision that distinguishes between states and their political subdivisions. All other constitutional provisions apply equally to lesser levels of state government.

3 The Supreme Court crafted an exception to this rule in *Central Virginia Community College v. Katz* (2006), in which it ruled that, for historical reasons, Congress may abrogate sovereign immunity when it passes laws under the Bankruptcy Clause (Art. I, § 8, ¶ 4).

4 Except, sometimes, the Supreme Court chooses the president. For instance, the Great Compromise of 1877, brokered by five Supreme Court justices, resulted in Rutherford B. Hayes (R) being declared president despite Samuel J. Tilden (D) having apparently won both the popular and electoral votes. Fortunately, the Supreme Court learned its lesson and has not meddled in presidential politics since then. Ok, maybe once.

5 *State*, in international law terms, denotes a sovereign nation.

6 A military order is a form of executive order.

7 Thomas Jefferson, December 20, 1787. Cited in Julian P. Boyd et al. (eds.), *The Papers of Thomas Jefferson* (Princeton University Press, 1950.)

8 The original Second Amendment was ratified in 1992, some 201 years late. It is now the Twenty-seventh Amendment. It delays until the next election any pay increase Congress votes for itself.

9 No new rights were found protected by the privileges or immunities clause until *Saenz v. Roe* (1999) (the right of interstate migration and the right to be treated equal to other state citizens).

10 In *Whalen v. Roe* (1977), the court assumed that individuals have a constitutional right to "information privacy," but held it not violated by a New York law requiring physicians to report certain prescription information to state agencies. However, in *NASA v. Nelson* (2011), Justice Scalia challenged that assumption, arguing there was no right to information privacy in the Constitution.

11 Justice Scalia's approach shows the importance of defining the right at stake. In *Michael H*, Scalia defined the right as the right of an adulterous father rather than that of a biological father.

12 Fundamental rights are protected by the equal protection clause as well as the due process clause. The difference is whether the right is denied to all or just to some. The fundamental rights strand of equal protection is discussed in Section V.

13 *Town of Castle Rock* reached the Supreme Court as a procedural due process case (see below); any claim to a positive right, even under a theory of special relationship, was dismissed along the way.

14 See, for example, Article I, Section 2 ("Representative and direct taxes shall be apportioned among the several states which may be included within this Union, according to their respective numbers"). In some cases, statements of equality were decidedly *unequal*, for example, Article I, Section 3 (each state given equal suffrage in the Senate).

15 See *Santa Clara County v. Southern Pac Ry. Co.* (1886), in which the chief justice admonished: "The court does not wish to hear argument on the question whether the provision in the Fourteenth Amendment applies to these corporations. We are all of [the] opinion that it does."

16 Footnote 4 is considered the most important footnote in constitutional law. It even has its own entry in Wikipedia.

17 Sometimes a right is first found fundamental for equal protection purposes, and later for due process purposes. See, for example, *Loving v. Virginia* (1967; anti-miscegenation statute violated the equal protection right to marry).

18 The Florida Supreme Court had ordered county officials to manually recount votes and scrutinize those that had been rejected by counting machines. Although the goal was uniform throughout the state (discern the voter's intent), the state court did not articulate a fixed test for doing so. This allowed election officials, for instance, to declare a vote cast based on a three-sided chad in some

counties and a dimpled chad in others. The case has been uniformly criticized as establishing equal protection rules that greatly deviated from previous doctrine. For instance, there was no showing of any intent to discriminate, or that discriminatory treatment would in fact result. Since the results from all counties were to be reviewed by a single judge, it would seem that any ensuing disparities could have been corrected at that time. Perhaps because of the unprincipled ruling in the case, the court has confined the holding to that case only; admonishing that it cannot be applied elsewhere.

19 While the notion of applying strict scrutiny to suspect classifications originated with *Korematsu*, it was not applied there, where the internment of Japanese-Americans was upheld. Sometimes you have to pay more attention to what the court does than what it says.

20 The Fourth Amendment provides "the right of the people to be secure in their persons, houses, papers and effects, against unreasonable searches and seizures shall not be violated, and no warrants shall issue without probable cause." In a recent decision, *United States v. Jones* (2012), the Supreme Court unanimously held that the government's installation of a global positioning system (GPS) tracking device on a vehicle, and constant monitoring of a suspect's movements, constituted a search within the meaning of the Fourth Amendment. Writing for the majority, Justice Scalia unsurprisingly applied an originalist approach arguing that a vehicle is an "effect" as the term is used in the amendment, thus it would have been considered a search at the time the amendment was adopted. Justice Alito wrote separately to argue that the Fourth Amendment applied wherever an individual had a "reasonable expectation of privacy." He expressed additional concern over emerging technological threats to privacy in an era where physical intrusion is unnecessary to carry out many forms of surveillance. Justice Sotomayor concurred with both Scalia and Alito, creating what may be the court's first 5–5 decision.

21 Law enforcement and intelligence agencies are often stymied in their efforts to investigate and surveil by the use of encrypted communications and password-protected data. At least one court has held that individuals have a Fifth Amendment right to refuse government demands to supply decryption keys or passwords (*In re Grand Jury Subpoena*, 11th Cir. 2012).

22 Some argue that the clauses were intended to leave the states free to establish their own official religions, and barred federal interference so as to protect states, not individuals. Thus, it never should have been "incorporated" through the 14th and applied to the states.

23 Section 3 of RLUIPA, 42 U.S.C. § 2000cc-1(a)(1)-(2), provides in part: "No government shall impose a substantial burden on the religious exercise of a person residing in or confined to an institution," unless the burden furthers "a compelling governmental interest," and does so by "the least restrictive means."

24 See Beard, *An Economic Interpretation of the Constitution of the United States* (Transaction Publishers, 1913).

25 The basic principle of federalism is that all powers not delegated to the federal government by the Constitution remain with the states.

3 Criminal Law

Laurie L. Levenson
Professor of Law and David W. Burcham
Chair in Ethical Advocacy, Loyola Law
School, Los Angeles

Introduction

Criminal justice issues are a media favorite. From street crime to white-collar offenses, crimes make their way into the news. There are a wide variety of crimes, and each jurisdiction (state and federal) has its own codes defining what constitutes a criminal offense. Accordingly, it is crucial to consult an expert who is versed in the law of the jurisdiction. Nonetheless, there are certain things that all criminal laws have in common.

First, crimes generally carry the possibility of imprisonment. This differentiates crimes from civil cases, like torts and contract disputes. Whereas civil cases carry the possibility of court order or money damages, criminal defendants face the possibility of loss of liberty and being stigmatized as a criminal.

Second, crimes are offenses against society. Therefore, there really aren't any victimless crimes, even though people often refer to euthanasia, prostitution, and drug use under that label. The fact that society has designated an activity as a crime means that society finds the defendant's conduct morally wrong, dangerous, or both. For that reason, local cases are labeled *State versus*, *Commonwealth versus*, or *People versus*, and federal cases are *United States versus*.

Third, we define crimes by their **elements**. Elements are what the prosecution must prove beyond a reasonable doubt to convict a defendant. Generally, crimes require both (1) **a criminal act** and (2) **criminal intent**.

Criminal Acts

The most basic element of a crime is the requirement that there must be an act. When discussing this element, lawyers will occasionally use the Latin *actus reus*. A criminal act can be a **positive act** (e.g., punching someone) or **a failure to act** when there is a duty to do so. The act or omission must be **voluntary**, which, in legal terms, simply means that the person's brain was engaged with his body. For example, if a person has a convulsion and strikes another person, he is not guilty. In the famous case of Black Panther Huey Newton, the defendant argued that he was not guilty of murdering a police officer because he shot his gun when he had a convulsion after being shot himself. Similarly, in some jurisdictions, if a person is asleep or blacks-out and commits a crime, the defendant is not guilty. However, it is still considered to be a voluntary act, if the defendant knew he might become unconscious and hurt someone. Therefore, if an epileptic drives a car and suffers a blackout, he is responsible if he knew he was subject to blackouts. If a person is coerced by threats into committing a crime, that defendant acts voluntarily but may have the separate defense of duress, which is discussed below.

In America, unlike in some European countries, there is no general duty to be a Good Samaritan. Therefore, it is not a crime to stand by as another person is harmed. Two famous cases demonstrate this: the Kitty Genovese case in New York, in which a woman was stabbed to death while neighbors peeked out of their curtains but did not call for help, and the Jeremy Strohmeyer case, in which Strohmeyer's friend David Cash watched while Strohmeyer sexually assaulted and killed a young girl in a Las Vegas casino bathroom. Despite the general rule, there are some limited situations in which a person has a duty to help, especially if he can do so without harm to himself. Generally, a person has a duty to help if: (1) the defendant has a special status relationship with the victim (e.g., a parent to a child, or a captain to his passenger); (2) a statute creates a duty to help, report, or act (e.g., tax reporting statutes or statutes requiring teachers and doctors to report crimes); (3) a contractual duty exists (e.g., babysitters or life-guards); or (4) a person assumes the care of another. Most recently, some jurisdictions have passed laws that require priests to report incidents of child molestation that come to their attention.

Criminal Intent

The second basic element of a crime is the mental state of the defendant when committing the crime. Just as with the criminal act, lawyers sometimes use Latin, *means rea*, to refer to criminal intent. Different crimes require different levels of intent. Serious crimes usually require that the defendant had the intent to cause a harmful result. This is known as **specific intent** and includes when a defendant acts purposely or knowingly to cause harm. A good example with the crime of "assault with intent to kill." The defendant is not guilty of this crime unless he has the purpose to kill. Lesser crimes, such as simple assault, only require **general intent**, which includes reckless and sometimes grossly negligent behavior.

On very rare occasions, the law does not require that the defendant have any criminal intent. These violations are called **strict liability offenses**, and they punish a defendant who accidentally commits a crime. Some examples are speeding in a car or mislabeling pharmaceutical drugs. It does not matter what explanations defendants have for these acts; they are automatically guilty. Generally, because the punishment for these crimes is very low and the possible harm to society is high, a defendant is punished just for committing the act. Strict liability crimes are also known as *public welfare offenses.*

Analyzing Crimes

When examining a possible crime and attempting to define that crime, it is best to look at the source of criminal law and the definitions given by the courts. The easiest way to find the requirements for a crime is to look at the applicable statute, or possibly the jury instructions given by local courts. In its jury instructions, the court tells the jury what must be proved to have a crime. In federal courts, proposed jury instructions are often filed by the parties before trial. Another good place to look for the so-called black letter law is the prosecution's trial memorandum.

It is important to be careful when reading criminal statutes. They are often convoluted and written in legal shorthand. For example, a statute may state that "a defendant who murders is guilty of a crime." To understand what *murder* is, you must know the common law definition of that term. That is where jury instructions or cases become helpful.

Further, when looking at a crime, it is important to know that crimes come in different levels of severity. More serious crimes are called **felonies.** In most jurisdictions, a felony is a crime that carries a penalty of more than one year in prison. **Misdemeanors** carry a lesser penalty, and criminal *violations* may only subject the defendant to minimum jail time or fines.

Overview of the Criminal Justice System

The next chapter discusses in detail how a case proceeds through the investigative and prosecution phases. However, it is helpful to know from the start what generally happens in the criminal justice system and who the players are.

The Players

The **defendant** is the person charged with a crime. Corporations and other artificial legal entities may be charged with crimes. Of course, they cannot be put in jail, but they can face other consequences, like fines and probation. If a person has not yet been charged but is suspected of committing a crime, that person may be the target or subject of an investigation. These terms are used loosely, although a **target** is ordinarily thought of as the person the government is focusing on charging; a **subject** is someone who may possibly be charged, but is not the primary focus of the government's investigation. **Suspect** refers to anyone alleged or believed to have committed a crime.

The **victim** is the person harmed by a crime. For certain crimes, like rape, the victim is frequently referred to as the *prosecutrix*. Recent statutes have given victims more of a say in the courtroom. However, it is the prosecution who has the final word as to whether to prosecute a case and how it will be prosecuted.

Law enforcement officers investigate crimes and apprehend suspects. There are many different law enforcement agencies. Most state crimes are investigated by the local police or troopers. Prosecution offices, such as those of an attorney general or district attorney, may also have their own investigators. Federal authorities rely on a whole panoply of law enforcement agencies, including the Federal Bureau of Investigation (FBI; everything from bank robbery to fraud to terrorism), Secret Service (counterfeiting cases), Immigration and Customs Enforcement (ICE; immigration offenses), Drug Enforcement Administration (DEA), Alcohol, Tobacco and Firearms (ATF; arson, gun violations), Internal Revenue Service (IRS; tax violations), and so forth.

Defense counsel represent the defendant. Defendants charged with crimes where they might face prison have a constitutional right to have a lawyer. If a defendant cannot afford a lawyer, a public defender or lawyer from the indigent panel is appointed. To get an appointed lawyer, a defendant must complete a financial affidavit. These affidavits are generally not available to the press. Ethically, the duty of defense attorneys is to represent their clients within the boundaries of the law. The ethical duties of attorneys are discussed more thoroughly in chapter 10. Also, the protections that apply to attorney-client relationships are discussed in chapter 10. In general, though with a few exceptions, the attorney-client privilege protects confidential communications, written and oral, between lawyer and client.

The **prosecutor** represents the people and bears some special responsibilities in the quest to seek justice. Thus, unlike the defense lawyer, a prosecutor must provide to his opponent all exculpatory information that may assist the defendant, as well as information that could be used to impeach the prosecutor's witnesses.

The Criminal Process

The best way to understand the criminal justice process is to understand that less than 2 percent of all criminal acts are actually prosecuted at trial. **Discretion** is built into every stage of the criminal justice process. Police officers have the discretion of whether to arrest an individual. Prosecutions have the discretion of whether to file charges. Judges have discretion in deciding defendants' motions. Jurors have discretion in deciding whether to convict, even if they are persuaded the defendant is guilty. Thus, it is misleading to think of a "typical" criminal case. Discretion is built into the criminal justice system, in part, to tailor justice to each case.

Timeline of the Typical Criminal Process:

The typical criminal process follows a relatively predictable pattern:

COMMISSION OF THE CRIME→
ARREST→
FORMAL FILING OF CHARGES→
PLEAS AND PLEA BARGAINING→
TRIAL→

- Prosecutor has burden of proving defendant's guilt.
- Defendant has the right to testify, but cannot be compelled to do so.

CLOSING ARGUMENT→

- Prosecutor goes first and last.
- Both sides must stick to the evidence presented at trial.

JURY DELIBERATIONS→

- A juror has two choices: guilty or not guilty.
- Jurors cannot be asked to explain the verdict.
- If they cannot agree on a decision, then a hung jury may result—a state can retry generally and then the case returns to the beginning of the timeline.
- If there is a mistrial because of a disruption in the proceedings, the case can be retried.

RELEASE OR SENTENCING

In the typical case, a defendant is **arrested** after committing a crime. A defendant may be arrested before or after formal charges are filed. Once the defendant is arrested, the prosecutor decides what charges to file. In many state courts, such as California, the prosecutor will file charges, and the court will hold a **preliminary hearing** to determine whether there is enough evidence to proceed with those charges. In federal courts, the **grand jury** ordinarily decides whether there is enough probable cause for the charges. If there is, an indictment is returned.

The filing of formal charges triggers many of the defendant's rights, including the right to counsel and the right to a speedy trial. Before trial, a defendant is entitled to discovery and may file pretrial motions, including motions to suppress evidence illegally obtained by the police. It is also standard for the parties to engage in **plea bargaining**. If a defendant enters a **guilty plea** or **nolo contendere plea,** there is no trial. The difference between a guilty plea and a nolo contendere plea is that a guilty plea is an admission of guilt that can be used in related civil proceedings to hold the defendant automatically liable. If the defendant enters a nolo contendere plea, the victim must prove a case of liability in the civil matter.

If a defendant does not plead guilty or nolo contendere, the defendant may have a court or jury trial. In order for there to be a **court (or Bench) trial**, both sides must agree to waive a jury trial. In a court trial, the judge decides whether there is enough evidence to prove beyond a reasonable doubt that the defendant is guilty—there is no jury. In a jury trial, juries of 6–12 persons make that determination. It is not constitutionally required that there be 12 jurors or that their verdicts be unanimous, although that is the practice in many states.

At trial, the prosecutor has the burden of proving a defendant's guilt. The defense has no obligation to present evidence, and some of the most effective defense attorneys win their cases through skillful cross-examination of the government's witnesses, poking holes in the government's case. At the end of the prosecution's case, the defense typically makes a motion for a not guilty verdict by the court due to lack of evidence. It is extremely rare for such a motion to be granted. Ordinarily, judges would prefer for juries to decide the case.

A defendant has the right to testify, but cannot be compelled to do so. The defense has the right to present witnesses, including so-called hostile witnesses who might work for or otherwise align themselves with the prosecution.

In closing argument, the prosecutor goes first and last because the prosecutor bears the burden of proof. Both sides are supposed to stick to the record (i.e., evidence presented at trial) in making their arguments, but some courts are more lax than others in allowing the lawyers to draw inferences from that evidence. Certain arguments are off limits, such as asking jurors to put themselves in the victim's shoes or religious arguments citing the Bible.

In the United States, unlike in some other countries, jurors only have two choices—**guilty or not guilty**. They do not have the option of finding that the case was "not proved." Thus, if a defendant is found not guilty in the United States, it does not mean that the defendant was innocent of the charges, in that the defendant had nothing to do with the crime. Rather, it means that the prosecution did not prove the case beyond a reasonable doubt. In some jurisdictions, there is a procedure by which a defendant can seek a juridical finding of "innocence" to clarify the record.

Because we do not ask jurors to explain their verdicts, they have a power referred to as **jury nullification**. Jurors can return a not guilty verdict even if they believe the defendant broke the law. Jurors may do this because they disagree with the law, because they sympathize with the defendant, or for political reasons. Thus, the law is "nullified" by the jury in that case.

If jurors cannot agree on a verdict, a **hung jury** may result, ending the case undecided. The prosecution generally has the right to retry a case if there has been a hung jury, although states can limit the number of times a defendant is retried. If something happens during trial, such as a witness becoming ill or some disruption in the proceedings, that interrupts the proceedings enough, the judge can declare a **mistrial**. In the event of a mistrial, the case can generally be retried. However, if the government intentionally caused the mistrial, double jeopardy may bar retrial.

Once a defendant has been convicted, the matter is scheduled for **sentencing**. There are different types of sentencing systems. In federal court, there are guidelines for sentencing that look to the nature of the defendant's crime and the defendant's criminal history. Other jurisdictions have completely discretionary sentencing or mandatory sentences.

Homicide Law

There are many different types of crimes, but homicides capture most of the media's attention. In legal terms, **homicide** is the **killing of another human being**. There are different types of homicide, ranging from first-degree murder to negligent homicide. Each jurisdiction can determine how to categorize its homicides. Ordinarily, the more intentional the killing is, the higher the degree of homicide. Thus, even though a person may negligently kill 20 other people, that defendant's crime may be of a lesser degree than a defendant who intentionally kills one other person. This section will review the differences between murder and manslaughter and general issues that arise in homicide cases.

Causation

All homicides require that the prosecution prove that the defendant *caused* the death of another human being. In criminal cases, causation is usually not much of an issue. For example, if a defendant shoots another person and that person bleeds to death, the defendant has caused the victim's death.

In oddball cases, causation may become a sticky issue. For example, what if a defendant hits a victim with his car? The victim is injured but can survive with a blood transfusion. However, the victim refuses the transfusion because of religious beliefs. Even though the defense will claim that the victim's actions were the real cause of the death, the law ordinarily would not find the victim's decision to be a **superseding, intervening act** that breaks the chain of causation.

Ultimately, it is up to the jury to determine whether the defendant was the cause of the victim's death. Jurors are asked to look at two separate issues to determine causation and to hold the defendant responsible. The first is whether, somewhere in the course of events, the defendant did something to put the victim at risk of losing his or her life. If so, the defendant's action was the **actual cause** of death. The second is whether the defendant's actions were close enough of a cause to be counted as having caused the harm.

In other words, if enough has occurred in between the defendant's action and the harm caused, it would be unfair to say that the defendant's action was really the cause. This closeness of causation is called **proximate cause.** Rarely are jurors' decisions on causation overturned.

In a rare case, a defendant may claim not to be the cause of the victim's death because the defendant's actions only injured the victim, but another person actually caused the death. For example, suppose one defendant stabs a victim, but the victim is shot before bleeding to death. Jurisdictions take different approaches to such a scenario. In some jurisdictions, both defendants are considered guilty of murder. In other jurisdictions, the first defendant is considered guilty of attempted murder, and the second defendant is considered guilty of murder.

It can also take a long time for some victims to die. If an injured victim is placed on life support and the family decides to end life support, the family's decision does not break the chain of causation. The defendant is still considered the cause of the death.

In some jurisdictions, though, there is a **"year and a day" rule** governing causation. Under this rule, a victim must die within a year and a day of the defendant's harmful acts in order for the defendant to be responsible for the death. Many jurisdictions have abandoned this rule and let jurors decide in each case whether the defendant's actions were a sufficient cause to hold the defendant responsible for the death.

Human Being

Occasionally, defendants will be charged with **killing a fetus.** This issue becomes confusing for the public because the killing of fetuses is permitted under abortion law. Each jurisdiction decides whether and under what circumstances killing a fetus is murder. Thus, a defendant who kills another person's fetus may be guilty of murder, even if that fetus was not viable.

Murder vs. Manslaughter

Different jurisdictions categorize their killings in different ways. The movement to categorize homicides by their severity arose when all homicides—intentional or accidental—were punishable by death. To try to tailor the punishment to the crime, jurisdictions set forth standards to categorize homicides by their severity.

Murder

Murder is considered the most serious type of homicide. There are different levels of murders (first degree, second degree, etc.). The classic definition of murder is "an unlawful killing of another human being with malice." Malice is a tricky word to define. It does not necessarily mean that the defendant acted with spite in killing the victim. Rather, **malice** typically includes:

- Acting with the intent to kill;
- Acting with the intent to cause serious bodily harm; or
- Acting with conscious disregard to another.

Motive vs. Intent

It should be noted that bad motive is not a requirement to prove murder. Motive is used to prove intent, but the good or bad motive of the defendant ordinarily figures into sentencing and not into whether the defendant is guilty of murder. Thus, a defendant who engages in a mercy killing may face the same charges as a defendant who kills the victim to obtain the victim's insurance proceeds.

Thus, a defendant who shoots to maim a victim, but ends up killing him, has acted with malice. A defendant who drives his car down a sidewalk, realizing that he might kill, but not necessarily intending to kill other people, acts with malice. In old legal terms, the defendant has acted with a **depraved and wanton heart**, that is, with malice.

In many jurisdictions, **first-degree murder** covers the killing of certain types of victims (such as law enforcement officers) and **premeditated** killings. The definition of **premeditation** can vary slightly among jurisdictions. However, it is commonly thought of as a defendant who kills the victim after cool reflection. In many jurisdictions, premeditation can be formed in a manner of seconds, or even between the first and second shot at the victim. Premeditation requires the defendant to consider the consequences of the acts at hand and proceed with the intent to kill the victim. To prove premeditation, prosecutors typically introduce a **motive** for the killing, **planning**, and the **manner** in which the victim is killed. A classic situation would be a defendant who lays in wait and ambushes his victim.

Second-degree murder, sometimes referred to as *general murder*, is often a catch-all for all intentional killings in which there has not been enough cool reflection to hold the defendant responsible for first-degree murder. It also covers the reckless killings where the defendants **consciously disregard** the risk their actions pose to other person's lives. In some jurisdictions, this type of malice is referred to as **implied malice**.

Here are some examples of classic reckless murders:

- Throwing steak knives at friend to scare them;
- Driving a car in a manner where you are fairly sure you could injure or kill someone; or

- Keeping a pit bull even after you have been warned that the dog is going to kill someone one day.

Even though these different levels of murder require prosecutors to prove different facts, prosecutors are not required to designate the degree of murder when they initially charge a defendant. Thus, at the beginning of a case, it will not always be apparent what level of murder the defendant faces.

The penalty for a murder conviction varies by jurisdiction. In those jurisdictions that have the death penalty, only first-degree murders with special circumstances (as explained later in this chapter) qualify for capital punishment.

Manslaughter

There are two basic types of manslaughters, although different jurisdictions give them different names. First, the term *manslaughter* (or **voluntary manslaughter**) is often used to designate intentional killings committed in the **heat of passion**. For example, if a defendant finds his wife in bed with another man, explodes in anger, and kills them, he might claim heat of passion and face a manslaughter, not murder, conviction. Originally, the heat-of-passion doctrine was limited to only those situations where the defendant personally witnessed a spouse engaged in an adulterous act or was faced with an assault situation. However, many jurisdictions have expanded the doctrine to any situation where: (1) the defendant was actually provoked, (2) the defendant did not have time to cool off, and (3) a reasonable person would have been provoked. A few jurisdictions, such as New York, apply manslaughter whenever the defendant was experiencing an **extreme emotional disturbance**. There need not be a specific provocative act. Even with the relaxation of the heat-of-passion doctrine, however, words alone are almost never considered to be a sufficient provocative act to justify killing.

More recently, heat of passion has been applied in battered spouse cases. However, courts often struggle with whose perspective should be used to decide whether a reasonable person would have been provoked. For example, how should cooling time be determined if the abuser is sleeping? Or is there adequate provocation if the beating occurred one hour prior to the killing? Traditionally, defendants argue that the reasonable person should be someone in the defendant's situation, such as the battered spouse. Prosecutors argue that the defendant's particular emotional state should not be considered in the decision.

Manslaughter is also sometimes used in cases where a defendant argues **imperfect self-defense**. For example, Erik and Lyle Menendez tried to argue that they killed their parents out of self-defense. Although it was a long shot to win a full acquittal, if they had convinced the jury that they honestly feared their parents, even though a reasonable person would not have, they would have qualified for a partial defense and found their crime dropped from murder to manslaughter.

The second use of the term *manslaughter* is to designate negligent killings. A **negligent killing** is when a person *should have realized* that his or her acts were putting another person at risk. The law often labels such killings as **involuntary manslaughter**. The negligence required for a criminal conviction is greater than that required for civil liability. Typically, involuntary manslaughter covers situations of "clueless defendants," such as:

- Parents who leave young children to suffocate in a hot car;
- Nightclub fires where patrons are killed; or
- Fatal work-site accidents that occurred because of unsafe conditions.

If a "reasonable person" would have known better, the defendant may be guilty of manslaughter or negligent homicide.

Like the punishment for murder, the punishment for manslaughter varies by jurisdiction. Typically, it is substantially less than the punishment for murder and can even be as low as probation in some jurisdictions.

Felony-Murder and Misdemeanor-Manslaughter (Unlawful Act Doctrine)

In some jurisdictions, the controversial doctrine of **felony-murder** still exists in the law. The felony-murder doctrine makes defendant *automatically* guilty of murder if they cause a death while committing a felony, even if the death itself is accidental. Consider, for example, defendants who rob a bank. Although the defendants may not intend to kill anyone, if their announcement that they are robbing the bank results in a patron having a heart attack, the defendants are automatically guilty of murder. Moreover, if one defendant is working with other robbers, each defendant is guilty of any murders the other accomplices may commit.

The Brandon Hein Case

The felony murder rule reaches killings performed by accomplices in felonies, as well as those performed by the defendant. In California, Brandon Hein was convicted and given life imprisonment without possibility of parole for his part in the 1995 stabbing murder of 16-year-old Jimmy Farris, the son of an LAPD police officer. The four people present when the murder took place—Hein, two other youths, and the actual killer—were convicted under the felony murder rule because the murder was committed during the course of an attempted robbery. The four were attempting to steal marijuana from Farris's friend Michael McLoren. The case attracted international attention as some felt Hein's involvement justified the sentence, while others that the life sentence was cruel and motivated by partisan politics.

Prosecutors often use the felony-murder doctrine as a short-cut to prove murder. Just as with different degrees of murder, they can argue it as an alternative theory for murder. For example, assume the defendants set a fire in which a victim is killed. It is no use for the defendants to argue that they only intended to commit arson, not murder. Under the felony-murder doctrine, the defendants are automatically guilty of murder.

The felony-murder is most commonly applied to dangerous felonies, such as robbery, burglary, rape, arson, and kidnapping. Many jurisdictions have rejected the doctrine or use it only as a presumption that the defendant acted with malice. A defendant can receive the death penalty for a felony-murder if there is evidence that the defendant had substantial participation in the felony and acted with conscious disregard of the victim's safety.

Recently, the felony-murder doctrine has been used in gang prosecutions. For example, if gang members get in a gunfight with police and an innocent person is killed, the prosecution may argue felony-murder. In some jurisdictions, such as California, a related doctrine called the **provocative act doctrine** is used for these situations.

The **misdemeanor-manslaughter doctrine** (also known as the *unlawful act doctrine*) works the same way for nonfelony cases as the felony-murder doctrine works for felony cases. If a death occurs during the commission of a misdemeanor or nonfelony, the defendant is automatically guilty of manslaughter. For example, if a fire breaks out in an apartment complex where the defendant is guilty of unsafe housing violations, prosecutors can argue the defendant is automatically guilty of manslaughter for any deaths that occur.

Death Penalty Cases

The death penalty currently exists in 33 states. In 1972, the Supreme Court held that the death penalty is constitutional if it is imposed with fair procedures. However, the court has struck the death penalty down as unconstitutional if applied to mentally retarded defendants or minors. There is no firm rule as to what makes a defendant mentally retarded, although the current guidelines focus on defendants whose IQs are under 70. A minor is a defendant who commits a capital offense before the age of 18. It is also unconstitutional to execute an insane person, including a person who becomes insane while awaiting execution. However, prisons may administer medication to make a defendant sane enough to be executed.

Only the worst of the worst are supposed to receive the death penalty. Thus, death penalty cases require that the prosecution prove the defendant is guilty of a death-qualified offense (e.g., murder with special circumstances) and that aggravating factors regarding the crime and the defendant's background outweigh mitigating factors. Death penalty cases are, therefore, bifurcated proceedings. First, there is the **guilt phase** in which jurors determine whether the defendant committed the charged offense. If the jurors find the defendant guilty of a special circumstances murder, then there is a

penalty phase. In this phase, the prosecution presents aggravating evidence regarding the crime and the defendant's background (such as continuing dangerousness), and the defense presents mitigating evidence regarding the defendant (such as the defendant's mental state, family background, etc.). In the penalty phase, it is common for family members of the victim to testify as to *victim impact evidence*, that is, how the crime affected the victim's family.

The death penalty requires a unanimous verdict by the jurors that the defendant deserves the death penalty. If there is not a unanimous verdict, the defendant commonly receives life without the possibility of parole.

If the defendant receives the death penalty, there are lengthy appellate and collateral challenge procedures that frequently delay the defendant's actual execution. Direct appeals challenge errors in the defendant's trial. However, **habeas corpus petitions,** filed in state or federal court, challenge the constitutionality of the proceedings. Such challenges often include questioning whether the defendant received ineffective assistance of counsel. Additional evidence may be presented during these proceedings, unlike in a normal appeals process. In a typical habeas process, every action by defense counsel is scrutinized. As a result, it is not uncommon for a defendant not to be executed until 15 years or more after the commission of a crime.

As an additional route to escape from the death penalty, condemned inmates may seek **clemency** from their state's governor, or, in the federal system, from the president of the United States. No set standards control governors' decisions. Governor, like the sovereigns of old, have complete discretion in whether to grant clemency.

Other Crimes of Violence

Other than homicide, there are many types of crimes of violence that a defendant may commit. Each one has its own elements that set forth what the prosecution must prove to convict the defendant. Because of the plethora of crimes, and the differences from jurisdiction to jurisdiction, this book cannot possibly lay out every crime. However, this section gives a brief description of those crimes more prevalent, both in the legal system and in the popular media.

Assault

Assault is a physical attack on a victim. It can range from punching a victim to assault with a deadly weapon. We even have some pre-assault crimes, such as stalking or criminal harassment. However, because of constitutional concerns over a defendant's freedoms of speech and movement, stalking ordinarily requires repeated threatening acts and a clear showing of the defendant's intent to harm the victim.

Kidnapping

Kidnapping is the abduction of a person by force, fraud, or instilling fear. Kidnapping can range from simple kidnapping to aggravated kidnappings, such as kidnapping committed with the purpose of committing a more serious offense, like murder or rape.

Robbery

Robbery is the taking of property from another person by the use of force or fear. For example, if a person puts a gun in your face and asks for your wallet, that is robbery. The word *robbery* is frequently misused by the public and press. It is often reported that a person's car or home was "robbed" while that person was away. Technically, it would not be robbery, but more likely larceny or burglary that was committed because no force can be used against a victim who is not present.

Mayhem

For mayhem, think Mike Tyson. *Mayhem* is the intentional disfiguring of another person. It includes cutting off or biting off another person's body part.

Arson

Arson is the intentional burning of a structure. There are often degrees of arson, depending on the structure that is destroyed and whether there are any occupants. Arsons are also committed as a means of insurance fraud. In that case, the defendant is guilty of both arson and the crime of fraud.

Sexual Offenses

The most commonly known sexual offense is **rape**. At common law, rape was defined as "sexual intercourse with an unmarried woman without consent and by force, intimidation, or fraud." In many jurisdictions, it also required resistance by the woman. However, times have changed. No longer is resistance by the woman required, and no longer is rape limited to sexual assaults on females. Rather, there is a wide range of sexual offenses prohibited by statute.

It is interesting to note that the traditional definition of rape is not as broad as just "sex without consent." Because there was a concern that women would fabricate the charge, it also required proof of force, intimidation, or fraud. Fraud must be more than a man promising fidelity or other misleading promises; it has to be the type of fraud where the woman literally does not understand that she will be having sex with the man.

As a number of high-profile cases, such as Kobe Bryant's case, have demonstrated, one of the most controversial types of sexual offense is **acquaintance rape**. To prove rape, prosecutors must prove that the defendant knew that the victim was not consenting. Proving this to the satisfaction of a jury can often be difficult if the evidence in the case comes down to a swearing contest between the victim and the defendant. To prove lack of consent, prosecutors frequently rely upon evidence of injury to the victim.

Rape is one of the most unreported crimes, with estimates that less than 20 percent of all rapes are reported. One of the reasons for underreporting is that the crime traditionally carried a stigma for the woman and the woman felt that she was being put on trial. To limit the attack on women and the claim that they "asked for it" by being too promiscuous, legislatures, including Congress, have enacted **Rape Shield Laws**. Under these laws, the sexual background of a woman is inadmissible, except under limited circumstances. Those circumstances include: (1) when the woman previously had sex with the defendant and the defense is claiming consent; (2) when the woman had sex with other men and the issue is who penetrated the woman; and (3) when there is a constitutional requirement that the evidence be admitted.

There is also another interesting evidentiary rule that applies in rape cases. Ordinarily, propensity evidence is not admissible in criminal cases to show that because the defendant committed a crime before, he must have committed the same crime again. However, in sex crimes, such "propensity evidence" of a former sex crime is admissible.

Statutory rape prohibits sex with a minor. It is irrelevant whether the defendant believed the minor consented or was old enough to consent. Statutory rape is a classic strict liability offense where the defendant is guilty once he does the act. In some jurisdictions, there is a so-called young lover defense to statutory rape. Under those laws, if the minor is almost an adult and is not much younger than the defendant, there may be a defense to statutory rape.

Child pornography is a crime prosecuted by both state and federal officials. It is not illegal to possess adult pornography; however, child pornography is prohibited. Pornography is defined as obscene depictions, or in other words, "sexual matters that, taken as a whole, appeal to the prurient interest of the average person when applying contemporary standards."

Finally, there are laws that prohibit **prostitution** and solicitation of prostitutes. The police may use decoys to apprehend prostitutes and their Johns. Although entrapment is frequently raised as a defense, it is rarely successful so long as the prosecution proves that the defendant intended to commit the crime and the police simply provided an opportunity for the defendant to do so.

Solicitation, Attempt, and Conspiracy

Efforts to commit a crime, even if not successful, may be crimes in themselves. These are referred to as **inchoate crimes**. The three main inchoate crimes are solicitation, attempt, and conspiracy. When referring to these crimes, we often refer to the *incomplete crime* also—for example, attempted murder, or conspiracy to commit robbery.

Solicitation is a request or proposal to commit a crime. A defendant can commit this offense with mere words, so long as the defendant seriously wants to commit a crime. It makes no difference whether the person solicited agrees to commit the crime. A solicitation is complete once the request is made. However, a defendant cannot commit both solicitation for a crime and the crime itself. If the defendant solicits a crime and the crime is committed, the defendant is guilty of the completed crime. The solicitation charge **merges** into the completed offense (also known as the *substantive offense*).

Attempt is a more serious crime than solicitation. An attempt is an effort **beyond mere preparation** by the defendant to commit a crime. Courts often refer to a defendant coming within *dangerous proximity* or taking a *substantial step* toward completing a crime. There is no set line for how far a defendant must go to be guilty of attempt. The jury will make that decision. In most jurisdictions, a defendant can get around a charge of attempt even after beginning to commit the crime if the defendant's change of mind qualifies for the defense of withdrawal or abandonment. However, those defenses don't work if the defendant is just waiting for a better opportunity to commit the crime. The defendant must show a genuine abandonment of the plan, which is shown in different ways in various jurisdictions. As with solicitation, if a defendant attempts to commit a crime and is successful, the attempt charges merges with the completed crime, and the defendant is only guilty of the completed crime.

Conspiracy is an agreement between two or more persons to commit a crime. The existence of this crime allows law enforcement to apprehend defendants at the earliest stages of their criminal planning. It is irrelevant whether a crime is actually committed; it is sufficient if a defendant agrees with another to commit a crime. For the purposes of a conspiracy charge, there does not need to be an *express* agreement to commit a crime. Rather, concerted action by the defendants may show a functional agreement to commit a crime. A mere wink or smile may show intent to agree. Also, the co-conspirators do not have to all join the conspiracy at the same time, or even know all of the other co-conspirators.

In some jurisdictions, prosecutors must prove that there was an **overt act** committed in furtherance of the conspiracy for the defendants to have committed a crime. An overt act is any act (legal or illegal) committed by any co-conspirator that shows the conspiracy is getting off the ground. Prosecutors will often provide a long list of overt acts in an indictment in order to provide jurors with a step-by-step account of how they believe the conspiracy occurred.

Conspiracy is sometimes referred to as the *darling of the prosecution* because it provides so many advantages to prosecutors. It is a separate crime from any crime that may be completed—unlike solicitation or attempt, it does not merge with the completed crime. Thus, a defendant who conspires to commit a crime and commits it is guilty of both offenses. In addition to giving prosecutors an additional charge against defendants, conspiracy offers **evidentiary advantages** to the prosecution. Prosecutors may use co-conspirators' statements against fellow conspirators at trial. Ordinarily, such statements might be hearsay and unable to be used at trial, but the law of evidence contains a special exception for co-conspirator statements. Also, conspiracies, by their nature, can occur in many places, thus allowing prosecutors to have their choice of location to bring the criminal action.

Perhaps the greatest advantage for prosecutors in bringing a conspiracy charge is that each conspirator is responsible for the acts of the other conspirators. Defendants are automatically liable for any crime committed in furtherance of the conspiracy, regardless of whether the individual defendant participated in it or even knew about it. This is known as **co-conspirator liability**. For example, A, B, and C conspire to rob a bank. If only B shows up and actually robs the bank, A and C are still guilty of the robbery. Moreover, if B steals a car to use in the robbery, A and C are guilty of the car theft even though they didn't know that B was going to steal the car.

Prosecutors love conspiracies because they give the prosecution an opportunity to **put pressure on the smaller players** to cooperate against the bigger targets. Typically, the prosecution will work from the outside in (or bottom up), squeezing the minor defendants to cooperate against more major defendants.

Conspiracy charges are popular for a wide range of criminal activities, from gang conduct to white-collar crimes. In some jurisdictions, there are special conspiracy-like charges that have been tailored to gang or organized crime activities. The Racketeering and Interstate Corruption Act (RICO) of 1974 allows prosecutors to tie together multiple conspiracies by charging participation in a criminal enterprise and a pattern of racketeering activities. This statute has been used for everything from the mafia to prison gangs to corrupt political offices. Judges generally do not like RICO charges because the law in the area is confusing and the cases can become quite cumbersome.

Some states have passed RICO-like statutes to deal with organized gang activities. It is not a crime to be a member of a gang; however, it may be a crime to be an active participant in a group that commits gang activities.

Accomplice Liability

In addition to co-conspirator liability, a person may be guilty of criminal acts committed by another person by being an accomplice. Another term for an accomplice is an *aider and abettor*. To be an accomplice, a defendant must do something to help the crime succeed with the purpose for the crime to succeed. It is even possible to be an accomplice to an attempt. To be guilty as an accomplice, it is usually insufficient that the defendant had some sense that a crime was occurring; rather, the defendant must have the purpose for the crime to succeed. For example, assume that you are a mattress salesman and Heidi Fleiss, the notorious Hollywood Madam, enters your store to buy a mattress. If you sell her a mattress with the inkling that she may use it for prostitution, that still does not make you an accomplice to the prostitution.

In order to prove accomplice liability, prosecutors must often prove that the defendant had a **stake in the criminal venture**. The more of a stake that the defendant has in a criminal venture, the more likely it is that the defendant had the purpose for the crime to succeed.

One of the mistakes that reporters make is to report that the defendant is "guilty of being an accomplice." There is no separate crime of being an accomplice. Rather, accomplice liability is the theory by which a defendant who intentionally participates in a crime is guilty of the crime that was committed—the same crime as the person who actually performed the act. Historically, different types of participation in a crime were called different things, with participants being labeled as *principals*, *accessories before the act*, or *accessories after the fact*. Today, differences in participation are usually sorted out at the time of sentencing.

The only category that is still treated differently is **accessory after the fact**. An accessory after the fact does not know of a crime until after it occurs and then the accessory helps cover up the crime or helps its participants elude apprehension. The punishment for being an accessory after the fact is typically more lenient than the punishment for being guilty of the substantive crime.

Theft Crimes

We all know what *theft* means. It is the taking of property without the owner's permission. However, the law distinguishes between different types of theft to create a wide variety of theft crimes. These range from petty theft to grand larceny. In legal terminology, **theft** and **larceny** mean the same thing—the taking of another person's property without permission and with the intent to permanently deprive that person of his or her property. If a defendant can convince the jury that he only intended to borrow an item, the defendant may be guilty of the crime of trespass, but not theft.

What happens, though, when the owner of the property allows the defendant to possess the property, but the defendant later decides to use it for personal purposes? When the defendant converts ownership of the item from the owner without permission, this is called **embezzlement,** and is a type of theft. The classic example is the bank teller who has been given a customer's money to hold for safekeeping. If the bank teller then spends the money for his own purposes, the teller is guilty of embezzlement.

Other times, a victim is deprived of property by some sort of scheme designed to trick people into giving up their property. Such a scheme is called **fraud.** Fraud may be committed in an infinite number of ways. The heart of the charge is a misrepresentation by the defendant. In other words, look for the defendant's lies. To determine who committed a fraud, follow the money. Prosecutors generally assume that the person who benefited from a fraud is responsible for the fraud. As an additional twist, if a defendant uses the mail or wires to commit the fraud, even if for limited purposes such as mailing confirmations of transactions, the defendant is guilty of mail or wire fraud.

One of the most prevalent types of theft crime is **burglary.** Burglary is entering into a building with the intent to commit a crime inside. If the defendant commits theft once inside, he is actually guilty of two crimes—both the burglary (which is complete once there is the illegal entry) and the theft. However, even if the defendant is not successful at committing a crime once inside the building, the defendant is still guilty of burglary. Burglars may have the intent to steal or the intent to commit other crimes after illegally entering or staying inside a building. Thus, a defendant who enters a home with the intent to rape or murder someone inside is also guilty of burglary.

White-collar Crimes

We live in the era of white-collar crime. The basic phrase **white-collar crime** was coined by a sociology professor in the 1940s. As the phrase suggests, defendants who commit white-collar crimes are often educated professionals. Moreover, the type of crime that they commit does not involve violence, but rather the taking of money. In addition to mail and wire fraud described above, white-collar crime can include securities fraud, tax fraud, bank fraud, computer fraud, extortion, perjury, obstruction of justice, and political corruption.

It is not difficult to recall any number of famous white-collar criminals of recent history, including Ken Lay and his co-defendants in the Enron case, Michael Milken and Ivan Boesky, Charles Keating, Dennis Kozlowski, John and Timothy Rigas, Jack Abramoff, Leona Helmsley, and Martha Stewart. The most successful prosecutions try to simplify the case for the jury so that jurors can understand the basic lies that the defendants used to dupe others (including the government) and succeed in their scheme.

White-collar Crime

Law enforcement officials often give their own pet names to many types of fraud. For example, a *boiler room case* refers to telemarketing schemes in which misrepresentations are used to defraud naive investors. If the defendant had the intent to defraud the investor, it is not a defense that the investor was ignorant or greedy. A defendant can also be guilty of scheming to defraud an entity of the loyal services of one of its employees. These are known as *schemes to defraud a victim of intangible rights.*

Securities fraud cases are particularly complex. There are both criminal and civil laws that prohibit **insider trading**. Insider trading is the use of confidential information by corporate insiders—people with more information than the normal participant in the market—to trade securities. In order to maintain public confidence in the trading markets, securities laws are designed to prevent insiders from taking advantage of their special information. At the heart of Martha Stewart's case, although she was never charged with it, was the theory that she sold her stock when she received insider information that it would be taking a fall.

Another common white-collar crime is **tax fraud**. Tax frauds can range from misdemeanor failure to file a tax return to felony tax evasion. Law enforcement will frequently use tax charges to apprehend defendants suspected of engaging in other illegal behavior. Think Al Capone! The advantage of using tax charges is that defendants must report all income, even if it is illegally obtained, and tax investigators are known for being particularly good at conducting financial investigations.

In the 1980s, when the savings and loan (S&L) industry deregulated, a slew of major **bank frauds** were committed, resulting in bank failures. By misreporting institutional assets and liabilities, bank insiders were able to inflate S&L accounts. When regulators finally learned of the scheme, the S&L's assets had been drained off by the defendants through personal loans or bonuses, and the institutions were left in the red.

Insurance and real estate fraud are also perennially popular white-collar crimes. Fake accident schemes are one way to commit insurance fraud; worker's compensation fraud may also be committed by those who fake injuries seeking to recover insurance. Real estate frauds often involve the artificial inflation of property values by corrupt appraisers or the use of straw buyers. The defendants then obtain financing based upon the false value of the property and walk away from their obligation, leaving the financial institution holding property not worth its alleged secured value.

White-collar crime can even include **piracy crimes**, such as **copyright and trademark violations**. Because of federal law enforcement's limited resources, copyright and trademark violations are often left to the civil justice system. However, if the violations are particularly egregious, these violations can also be charged as federal crimes.

Political corruption crimes are also considered white-collar crimes. They range from **bribery** (the giving of something in value in exchange for an official act) to violation of **campaign finance laws**. Because of the complexity of the campaign finance laws, it is often difficult to make a conviction stick. The best evidence that prosecutors can get for all white-collar crimes is often from the cover-up. If defendants try to conceal their activities, it is pretty good evidence that they knew their activities were wrong.

Cover-up crimes include **perjury, false statements,** and **obstruction of justice.** Perjury is knowingly providing false testimony under oath with regard to a material matter in an official proceeding. Perjury may occur at trial, in pretrial hearings, or in the grand jury. It may be verbal or written. The issue is frequently whether the statement was really false or whether the defendant knew it was false. Perjury can be a difficult charge to prove because defendants can often successfully argue innocent mistaken recollection.

It is a separate federal crime to make a **false statement to a federal official** even if it is not under oath. This is frequently referred to as a *section 1001* violation because it is charged under Title 18, United States Code, § 1001. Because so many people try to mislead investigators, false statement charges are the bread and butter of federal cases.

Obstruction of justice may occur in a variety of ways. It can range from trying to convince a witness not to testify to destroying subpoenaed documents. The Arthur Anderson prosecution is a classic example of an obstruction of justice case that spelled the death penalty for that corporate defendant. Obstruction of justice may also be very useful evidence that the defendant has committed a crime that he wants to hide from the authorities.

Computer crimes are also considered to be white-collar crimes. Computer crimes range from intentionally accessing computers without authorization (i.e., hacking) to spreading computer viruses. The primary statute that is used is 18 U.S.C. § 1030. Computers may also be used to commit other crimes, such as fraud.

The **primary federal investigative agencies** for white-collar crimes are the Federal Bureau of Investigation (FBI), Postal Authorities, the Treasury Department, and the Secret Service. In addition to being charged with protecting federal officials, the Secret Service takes the lead in investigating counterfeiting cases.

As with other types of crimes, **corporations** as well as individuals can be guilty of white-collar crimes. In proving that the corporation is guilty, prosecutors can use the collective knowledge of those in the corporation to show criminal intent. The negative publicity from a charge against a corporation may itself have serious consequences for the corporate entity. If there is a conviction, the corporation can be placed on probation, ordered to pay fines, and debarred from government contracts. When crimes take place in a corporate setting, both the individuals of a corporation and the corporate entity itself can be charged with a criminal activity.

When multiple defendants are charged in white-collar crimes, they often form **joint defense agreements.** These agreements are designed to keep confidential the sharing of information among the defendants. Prosecutors love to break up cooperation among defendants by offering a defendant a deal to testify against other fellow defendants. Those who cooperate early often get the best deal, creating a rush to the prosecutor's door. Negotiations for agreements often occur even before formal charges are filed. This is known as *pre-indictment negotiations.* Prosecutors will want an explanation of how the defendant can help the prosecution's case. To ensure such negotiations are not used against the defendant in case an agreement is not reached, defense lawyers will seek immunity prohibiting the prosecutors from using the information in any prosecution against that defendant. These are sometimes known as *Queen for a Day* agreements.

Many criminal defense lawyers specialize in either white-collar crime or other types of crimes. It is not surprising to find that some of the top white-collar criminal defense lawyers are former prosecutors. They understand how the prosecution works and use their relationships with former colleagues to negotiate the best deals for their clients.

Although white-collar crimes traditionally have been punished less severely than other crimes, sanctions were stepped up under the Federal Sentencing Guidelines. White-collar criminals can receive anything from probation to 30 years in prison for their offenses, depending on the nature of the offense, the amount of the financial loss, the defendant's level of participation, and the defendant's criminal background.

Narcotics Offenses

Jurisdiction over Drug Crimes

Unlike many other types of crimes, both state and federal courts have jurisdiction over drug crimes. Although a state can legalize the use of certain drugs (for example, marijuana) under state law, defendants can still be prosecuted by federal authorities if those drugs are listed as *controlled substances* and prohibited by federal law.

In the 1980s, the government announced its war on drugs. Now, it is estimated that more than 50 percent of all inmates in America's prisons are serving time for drug convictions. The war on drugs has had a disproportionate impact on minorities. Currently, one out of every three young African American men is a defendant in the criminal justice system, and more young black men go to prison than to college.

Narcotics offenses range from simple possession of a drug to manufacturing and distribution. The key issue in drug cases is ordinarily whether the defendant knowingly possessed an illegal substance. Special legal doctrines have been created for those defendants who play dumb and claim that they did not know they were transporting narcotics. The **deliberate ignorance doctrine** (also known as the *Jewell Doctrine* or *Ostrich Defense*) holds that if defendants strongly suspect they are dealing with a drug and deliberately avoid confirming their suspicions, that is enough to prove that the defendants knowingly possessed the drug.

Many drug offenses carry **enhancement penalties**, especially if they occur near schools or if the defendant possesses a firearm. Additionally, drug convictions trigger forfeiture laws. Not only is the contraband subject to **forfeiture**, but so also are the automobiles used to transport it and the homes used to store it. Even attorney fees are subject to forfeiture if the government can trace them to illegal proceeds.

Disparities in the drug laws have prompted claims that the system is **racially biased**. For example, under the Federal Sentencing Guidelines, the punishment for crack cocaine (a drug used predominantly by minority defendants) is higher than that for powder cocaine (a drug favored by white, upper-class defendants). Despite the controversy, Congress has not eliminated the disparity.

The most prevalent drug in the United States is alcohol. Since Prohibition laws were repealed, states have permitted the possession and consumption of alcohol by adults, though certain restrictions still apply to certain activities when using alcohol. For example, as is commonly known, driving a vehicle while under the influence of alcohol (DWI or DUI) is illegal. When stopped for suspicion of DUI, a driver must agree to take a blood-alcohol test or face revocation of his or her license. Three types of tests are standard: breathalyzer, blood test, or urine test. Each jurisdiction may establish what concentration of blood-alcohol supports a DUI conviction. The amount usually ranges between 0.08–0.10 percent.

If a defendant kills a person while driving under the influence of alcohol, **homicide charges** may be filed. If the defendant previously had been warned about the consequences of drunk driving or had prior arrests for the offense, a murder charge may be filed. Otherwise, the charge is usually some type of manslaughter. In some jurisdictions, special vehicular manslaughter statutes have been enacted to make the punishment for vehicular manslaughter as high as that for murder if the death results from drunk driving.

Civil Rights Violations

Cases like the Rodney King beating trial, described in the introduction to this book, or the assault on Abner Louima have drawn attention to the use of federal civil rights statutes to prosecute police misconduct. Police beating cases may be prosecuted in state courts under assault and murder statutes, or in federal court under the federal civil rights statutes, 18 U.S.C. § 241 and § 242.

It is a crime for an official "acting under color of state law" to deny persons of their constitutional rights. The civil rights statutes can also be used to prosecute private individuals who deny persons of their civil rights because a racial, ethnic, or religious animus. No racial motive for police misconduct is required for it to be a federal crime.

Because police are allowed to use force in their duties, the key issues in civil rights cases are whether the police exceeded the lawful use of force and whether they acted willfully in violating the defendant's rights. In other words, it is not enough to show that there was a police beating. The prosecutors must prove that the force was excessive and that the officer knew it was excessive at the time.

Terrorism Crimes

Many statutes can be used to prosecute terrorism crimes. Alternatively, terrorist suspects may be treated as enemy combatants and be detained without being charged with a crime. The most popular statute used to prosecute suspected terrorists is 18 U.S.C. § 2339B, which prohibits all forms of material support for terrorist organizations. This is the statute that was used to prosecute John Walker Lindh, the American Taliban supporter.

Common Defenses to Crimes

Apart from the crimes themselves, another component of the criminal justice system are the ways that defendants can defend against allegations of criminal misconduct. The most common defense to criminal charges is that the prosecution did not prove its case. Indeed, the burden is on the prosecution to prove all elements of a crime **beyond a reasonable doubt**. A defendant is under no obligation to present evidence, and some of the finest defense lawyers win their cases through cross-examination of the government's witnesses.

However, even if the prosecution presents evidence that a defendant appears to have committed a crime (i.e., a prima facie case), the defense has the opportunity to offer a justification or excuse for that offense. Such excuses are called *affirmative defenses.*

The most common affirmative defenses are discussed in this section. They include alibi, self-defense, necessity, duress / coercion, intoxication, insanity, diminished capacity, entrapment, mistake of law and mistake of fact, and consent.

Alibi

Evidence that defendants were not present at the time of the alleged crime and that the defendants have people who will vouch for their whereabouts is generally called an **alibi**. An alibi defense can be presented through a defendant's testimony or those of alibi witnesses. To avoid too many surprises at trial and give each side an opportunity to check witnesses' stories, a defendant must give notice to the prosecution of any planned alibi defense. Prosecutors must also give notice the defendant, but of the witnesses they will call to rebut the alibi.

Self-defense

People have the right to use self-defense to protect themselves from harm. However, the right of self-defense is not a green light for vigilantism. Accordingly, strict requirements are typically put on a claim of self-defense.

First, to argue self-defense, defendants must show that they **honestly felt threatened**. However, a defendant's claim is not enough. It is also important that a **reasonable person in the defendant's situation would have felt threatened**. Without this requirement, hot heads could use self-defense as an excuse to assault others. In some jurisdictions, if a defendant has an honest but unreasonable fear of the attacker, the defendant may be able to get a reduced charge of manslaughter.

Second, the threat must be **immediate**. The law generally does not allow preemptive strikes. Thus, an inmate who fears that he will be assaulted by his cellmate cannot just rub him out and claim self-defense.

Third, self-defense must be **proportional**. In order to use deadly force in self-defense, the defendant must face deadly force. Many jurisdictions also allow lethal force when the defendant faces a person trying to commit a serious crime on the defendant, such as rape or robbery. If the defendant only faces a minor threat, the defendant may only respond with minor force.

Fourth, the defendant **cannot start the fight**. If the defendant is the initial aggressor, the defendant cannot later claim self-defense when the victim tries to protect himself and responds with violence against the defendant.

Finally, in some jurisdictions, the defendant may have a **duty to retreat** before using deadly force. This duty is only triggered if the defendant can do so safely, and the rule generally does not apply when people use self-defense in their own homes. Under the so-called Castle Rule, in your own home, you have the right to stand your ground.

Battered Spouses

Battered spouses and children traditionally have had a difficult time claiming self-defense because they often kill when their abusers are asleep. This issue is similar to that discussed above with murder and manslaughter. Although these defendants feel constant fear, they have a hard time convincing jurors that they honestly and reasonably feared their victim while he slept. Jurors also don't understand why the defendant doesn't just leave to avoid the abuse. In order to persuade jurors that the defendant had a sincere and reasonable fear (for a person in her situation) of the attacker, and why the defendant did not feel that retreating was a viable option, defendants in battered spouses and children cases often call expert witnesses to explain to the jury the psychological attributes of someone subjected to abuse, often called *battered women's syndrome*.

Defense of Others

Jurisdictions take two different approaches to the issue of whether it is justified to use force in defense of another person. In some jurisdictions, the defendant can use force if the person the defendant is defending would have been able to use force. However, this defense would not cover situations when the defendant comes across a person being beaten and mistakenly believes that the person had the right to engage in self-defense when, in fact, the person was being subdued by an undercover police officer. Therefore, other jurisdictions have adopted a rule that defense of another person is justified when a reasonable person would have believed that the person being assaulted was entitled to engage in self-defense.

Defense of Property

The general rule is that **lethal force may not be used to protect property**. Property is not as valuable as life, even a thief's life. Accordingly, a person cannot set up a spring gun or post a killer dog to kill a person trying to steal personal possessions. A defendant who is at home can use self-defense against a burglar because it is quite likely that the defendant faces physical harm. However, lethal force cannot be used just to safeguard's one's possessions.

Law Enforcement Defense

Police may use lethal force to apprehend a dangerous felon, but may not use it to stop a person who does not pose a risk to the public. Of course, so long as the police reasonably believe the suspect is a threat, lethal force is permitted, even if the police turn out to be wrong.

Necessity

In rare situations, a defendant may claim that he is not guilty of a crime because the act was performed out of necessity. Self-defense is actually a type of necessity defense—the killing was "necessary" to protect the defendant's life.

However, necessity defenses apply in other situations as well. For example, if a hurricane strikes leaving people stranded and without supplies, they can steal a boat to escape or food to survive. A necessity defense does not justify wholesale looting, as seen in New Orleans after Hurricane Katrina. However, it can be used on a limited basis.

The necessity defense is frequently invoked by defendants engaged in **civil disobedience**. For example, protestors who destroy government property to protest the war may argue that they are compelled to engage in illegal conduct to preserve lives. Most frequently, the necessity defense will fail in these situations because the defendants cannot meet its strict requirements.

First, to argue necessity, the defendant must have **faced a choice of evils**. Economic necessity alone does not justify commission of a crime. Defendants cannot steal because they were fired from their jobs.

Second, there must **be no apparent alternatives**. Here is where the protestors fail. They have the alternative of using legal methods, such as elections and petitioning the government to change the policies regarding the war.

Additionally, the defendant **must face an immediate threat, choose the lesser harm, and not personally create the necessity**. Thus, hikers could not break into a cabin to escape an approaching storm when they had hiked up the mountain knowing they might need immediate shelter.

Most recently, the necessity defense has been raised by inmates who flee institutions to avoid prison rapes or assaults. Because they have the alternative of going to prison officials for relief, their defense usually fails. Moreover, the Supreme Court added a special requirement for these cases that defendants surrender themselves as soon as they are free of the prison environment.

The necessity defense has also been used unsuccessfully by abortion protestors. Even though protestors may believe that they are saving lives by sacrificing that of an abortion doctor, the necessity defense is not a defense to murder.

Duress / Coercion

The duress defense, also known as *coercion*, provides a defense for defendants who are **forced under the threat of immediate grave bodily harm or death to commit a crime**. The type of threat must be one that would cause an ordinary person to yield, and duress is not defense to killing another person. Duress is also not a defense if the defendant created the situation of being threatened. For example, gang members cannot claim duress if they join a gang and then are threatened with harm if they don't commit a robbery on behalf of the gang.

Patty Hearst tried a type of duress defense when she was charged with participating in a bank robbery with the Symbionese Liberation Army. She claimed that her captors had brainwashed her and forced her to participate in the robbery. However, her defense failed when jurors rejected her story.

Intoxication

There are two types of intoxication defenses: **involuntary intoxication** and **voluntary intoxication**. **Involuntary intoxication** is when a person is coerced into taking an intoxicant, doesn't know that she has ingested an intoxicant, or has a pathological response to a substance that causes the defendant to be unexpectedly intoxicated, such as if the defendant became high from taking a baby aspirin. Involuntary intoxication is generally a defense to a crime.

However, a **voluntary intoxication** defense is much more limited. The Supreme Court has held that there is no constitutional requirement that courts recognize a voluntary intoxication defense. When it is allowed, it generally only applies to drop a serious charge to a lesser charge because the defendant was too intoxicated to form the level of intent required by the initial charge. For example, if a defendant was too intoxicated to premeditate a murder, he may be not guilty of first-degree murder, but rather second-degree murder.

Voluntary intoxication is not a defense to most crimes because they only require general intent (i.e., enough thought by the defendant that he or she knew what his or her actions were). Where a voluntary intoxication defense does apply, a defendant must demonstrate more than the fact that he took some "liquid courage"; he must show "prostration of his faculties."

Insanity

Insanity is one of the more controversial defenses. There is a misperception by the public that guilty defendants easily escape punishment by arguing insanity. The truth is quite different. Less than 2 percent of all defendants who claim insanity are acquitted. Moreover, a defendant who is found not guilty on the basis of insanity is ordinarily subject to involuntary commitment. Thus, the defendant will be in custody, but at a mental health facility instead of a prison.

An **insanity** defense is distinct from an **incompetency** defense. **Incompetency** focuses on whether the defendant has the mental ability to stand trial. In order to be competent to stand trial, the defendant must understand the nature of the proceedings and be able to assist the defense counsel. This threshold for competency is called the *Dusky standard.*

Insanity focuses on a separate issue. The question with insanity is whether the defendant acted with a rational mind at the *time of the crime* (not the time of trial). There are several different tests for insanity that are used by different jurisdictions. The most popular of them determines that a defendant is legally insane if at the time of the commission of the offense the defendant was acting under a defect or disease of the mind, such that the defendant did not know *either* the *nature and quality* of the acts *or* that the *acts were wrong*. For example, a defendant doesn't know the nature and quality of actions if the defendant is so completely hallucinatory that he doesn't realize that he is cutting open a person's head, but instead believes he is opening a melon. A defendant may also be insane under this test if, because of a verifiable mental disease or defect, the defendant doesn't realize that society considers certain actions to be wrong.

This test for insanity, called the *M'Naghten test*, is considered the most conservative standard for assessing insanity. It doesn't work for a defendant who expresses regret over decisions. Thus, Texas mother Andrea Yates originally had a difficult time of arguing insanity after drowning her young children because she called the police right after the drowning to report that she had done something wrong. This call reflected that she knew the nature of her acts and that they were wrong.

Insanity cases often become a battle of experts. The defense needs an expert who will testify that the defendant had a verifiable mental disease or defect. A wide range of conditions qualify as mental diseases or defects. Psychosis is the classic example, but defendants also seek to admit evidence of mental illnesses such as PTSD (posttraumatic stress syndrome) or other syndromes. Judges are constantly asked to determine whether newly named syndromes, such as the Compulsive Gambling Syndrome or PMS, qualify as mental diseases or defects. If a defendant pleads insanity, the government is entitled to have its own expert examine the defendant.

Some jurisdictions have relaxed their insanity tests. For example, many jurisdictions recognize the **Deific Command Exception**. Under this exception, a defendant may know what he is doing and know it is wrong according to society's laws, but he still feels compelled to do it because he believes he has been commanded to do so by God or some Supreme Being. For this exception to work, the defendant must convince the jury that he believed he was hearing voices directly from the divine. Merely having odd religious beliefs is not enough.

Some jurisdictions also use an **irresistible impulse** test for insanity. Under this test, an accused is legally insane if the defendant, because of a mental disease or defect, is unable to stop from committing the crime. It is often called the *policeman at the elbow test* because a defendant who meets this standard could not stop from committing the crime, even if a policeman were standing right there.

Finally, some jurisdictions have relaxed the insanity standard to accommodate diseases such as schizophrenia where the defendant may not have total impairment, but is sufficiently impaired so as to lack **substantial** capacity to appreciate the wrongfulness of the criminal conduct. This is the most lenient of the standards to determine whether a defendant is entitled to an insanity defense.

Diminished Capacity

Insanity is not the only type of mental defense that may be presented in a criminal trial. Insanity is an all or nothing proposition. A defendant who is insane is not guilty of the crime. However, a defendant may have some mental impairment without being insane. Rather, something about the defendant's brain prevents the defendant from forming the intent necessary to be guilty of committing the crime. In these situations, defendants attempt to use the **diminished capacity** defense if it is available in their jurisdictions.

For example, defendants may claim that because of a chemical disorder, their brains could not form the premeditation to kill and, therefore, they should be guilty of a lesser homicide. This is precisely what was argued in the infamous San Francisco Twinkie Defense case. Dan White shot the gay mayor and supervisor of San Francisco and then claimed he was not guilty of murder because he had eaten too many Twinkies, altering his blood chemistry and making it impossible for him to act in a premeditated manner. The jury bought the defense, and White was only convicted of manslaughter. The outrage over this case led many jurisdictions, including California, to abolish the diminished capacity defense. Now, in order to call an expert, the defendant must be arguing a full insanity defense.

Entrapment

If a defendant is caught red-handed, what defense is most likely to come up? If you answered entrapment, you are correct. Entrapment is a defense where the defendant essentially claims, "The government made me do it." It is crucial for this defense that the defendant was led into committing a crime by a government agent or informant. A defendant cannot claim entrapment just because a friend or colleague provides enticement to commit a crime.

The DeLorean Case

In the summer of 1982, innovative carmaker John Z. DeLorean received a phone call from James Hoffman, a former drug smuggler turned FBI informant. DeLorean met with Hoffman to discuss an investment opportunity to help save his company. Over the course of the next three months, Hoffman slowly explained his intricate plan involving cocaine smugglers, a bank for laundering money, and the specifics of how much money DeLorean would be required to front money to procure the deal. DeLorean went along with these discussions, planning to trade DMC stock for the seed money for the drug deal. It was clear that DeLorean believed he was being brought into a drug deal because he wrote a letter to his attorney and sealed it, with instructions to open it only if he did not return. The letter explained that he feared for his family's safety if he tried to back out of the deal. Nonetheless, DeLorean was charged with trafficking in cocaine by the government.

DeLorean's attorney stated in *Time* magazine (March 19, 1984), "This [was] a fictitious crime. Without the government, there would be no crime." The DeLorean defense team had no need to call a single witness—they successfully argued that the police had asked him to supply the money to buy the cocaine. DeLorean was found not guilty due to entrapment on August 16, 1984.

In late 1982, DeLorean's legal troubles were satirized in the comic strip *Doonesbury*, in which the character of Uncle Duke travels to Hollywood to become a film producer and make a movie based on DeLorean's life story. In an ironic twist, Duke, in an attempt to raise the money needed to buy the rights to the story, sets up a cocaine deal and is arrested by undercover government agents.

In **federal court**, it is relatively easy for the government to refute a claim of entrapment. All it must show is that the defendant was **predisposed** to commit a crime and that the government simply offered him the opportunity to do so. The prosecution can use all types of evidence about the defendant's background to show that he was predisposed to commit the crime.

In some state courts, the entrapment standard is more favorable to the defendant. It is a more **objective standard** that doesn't focus on the defendant's criminal background. The question is **whether the government's conduct would have likely induced a law-abiding person to commit the crime.** If so, then the claim of entrapment can prevail.

John DeLorean was successful in raising an entrapment defense when he was caught kissing kilograms of cocaine. His lawyer, Howard Weitzman, hit on the perfect note when he constantly argued to the jury, "What if the government had just let him alone?" Washington, D.C., mayor Marion Barry had less successful in arguing entrapment because the evidence showed that he had used drugs many times before his current illegal actions. Using this other evidence, the government was able to show Barry was predisposed to commit the crime.

Mistake of Law and Mistake of Fact

The common saying among lawyers is that "mistake of law is not a defense, but mistake of fact is." This means that a defendant cannot escape responsibility due to ignorance of the law. "**Ignorance or mistake of the law is no defense.**" A defendant could not argue, "Gee, I never knew it was against the law to kill my neighbor." Nor does a misreading or misunderstanding of the law by the defendant make the defendant's actions permissible—it does not matter that the defendant believed the action to be law abiding. Clearly, if mistake of law were a defense, every defendant would claim it.

Only under limited circumstances is mistake of law a defense. For example, if the government tells people it is okay to engage in certain practices and then changes its mind after the defendant's acts, it cannot retroactively hold the defendant responsible for that act. Additionally, if the government never publishes a law, the defendant may argue ignorance of the law. Finally, some crimes actually require that the defendant know what the law is and intentionally violate it to be guilty of a crime. For example, it is a crime to "knowingly use food stamps in an unauthorized manner." If the defendant doesn't know that the use of food stamps is unauthorized, the defendant is not guilty of the crime.

Disagreement with the law is also not a defense, even if the defendant's disagreement is sincere. Therefore, tax protestors are guilty of evading income tax so long as they are aware that there is a legal duty to file. The fact that they disagree with the law provides no defense.

On the other hand, a defendant may be able to escape criminal liability if the defendant was mistaken about some key fact that would make his conduct criminal. A classic example is a defendant who mistakenly picked up another person's purse, believing it was hers. She made a mistake of fact. Because the definition of stealing is "knowingly taking the property *of another person*," the defendant is not guilty of the crime because of her mistake of fact (i.e., she didn't know that she had someone else's handbag).

Consent

Generally, consent is not a defense to criminal actions, particularly violent crimes. The reasoning behind this is that a person's body belongs to society, and a person is not free to give other people permission to injure or terminate it. The big exception is rape. Because rape is defined, in part, by having sexual intercourse without the consent of the victim, consent is a defense and is often a major issue in many sexual assault cases. A case can be the defendant's word against the victim's. There is no problem with a swearing contest so long as the jurors can decide whom they believe. Moreover, there are some situations where the law presumes the victim is incapable of giving consent, such as when the victim is underage, mentally disabled, or intoxicated.

Sentencing

For defendants and victims, the most important part of the criminal justice process is probably sentencing. Once a defendant is found guilty of a crime, the key question is what consequences there are to that conviction.

We punish crimes in several ways—imprisonment, fines, probation, and community service. Before we discuss how the sentencing procedures work, it is important to consider what the purposes of punishment are.

Purposes of Punishment

There are at least four purposes of punishment. First, we punish defendants because they need to make amends for the harm they have caused. Known as **retribution**, this purpose of punishment focuses on holding the defendant responsible for criminal actions. It is the "eye for an eye, tooth for a tooth" purpose of punishment. Of course, the theory does not work as described—a defendant cannot always repair the damage done, we do not have forms of punishment that mirror their crimes, and the state, not the victim, is striking back at the defendant. Thus, while we punish defendants because they "deserve it," criminal punishment does not take the form one would imagine retribution might. Imprisonment and fines are the most common types of punishment imposed.

Second, we punish defendants so that we can **deter** future bad conduct by that defendant and others. The goal is to make the costs of committing crime greater than the benefits. The problem with this theory is that criminals do not necessarily rationally evaluate their decisions before committing a crime. Therefore, they are not deterred, even though they know they may face serious consequences.

Third, we punish defendants so that they won't be able to hurt others. This is known as **incapacitation**. Of course, unless defendants are executed, it is impossible to completely prevent them from committing future crimes, even if they are in prison. However, prisons are designed to protect the public from dangerous criminals.

Fourth, we punish defendants so as to change their ways. **Rehabilitation** of defendants is not in vogue much right now, but historically it was an important consideration in sentencing.

Sentencing Procedures

There are different approaches to sentencing. In some jurisdictions, great discretion is given to the judges to select a sentence so long as it is within the statutory maximum. This is known as **indeterminate sentencing**. Other jurisdictions take a much more restrictive approach to sentencing by having mandatory sentences or sentencing guidelines. This is known as **determinate sentencing**. The federal courts currently have an Advisory Guideline system in which the courts initially consult the U.S. Sentencing Guidelines for their recommendation of a sentence and then make their own decision as to what sentence is appropriate.

Ordinarily, before a defendant is sentenced, the court will order a **presentence report**. This report gives the court information regarding the defendant's background and the circumstances of the crime. The prosecutor and defense will be given an opportunity to submit their own sentencing information. At the time of sentencing, the defendant has the right to speak (also known as *the right of allocution*), but is not required to speak, to the court. In many jurisdictions, victims or their representatives also have the right to address the court at sentencing.

When the court imposes a sentence, it may either order the immediate remand of a defendant into custody or stay its order. The court's sentencing order is known as the **final judgment** in the case.

A defendant sentenced to less than a year in custody is often sent to the local jail to serve his time. Jails also hold the pretrial prisoners. If the defendant is given a felony sentence, he is sent to a prison. There are different levels of prison, ranging from minimum security to supermax prisons, like those in Pelican Bay and Florence, Colorado.

If a defendant is given probation, it may be supervised or unsupervised and may come with conditions, like required community service. Other conditions on probation may be imposed so long as they have a reasonable relationship to defendant's conviction or rehabilitation.

Parole (or supervised release) is the transition time after a defendant serves his prison term, but before the defendant is cleared of the criminal justice system. The federal system no longer has a parole board, but many states still do.

In addition to being ordered to pay fines, defendants may also be ordered to pay restitution to the victims. Fines are paid to the government treasury; restitution is paid to the victims.

Constitutional Limitations on Sentencing

The Eighth Amendment prohibits "cruel and unusual punishment." The Supreme Court has interpreted this amendment to mean that sentences **should not be disproportionate** to the crime committed. To make this determination, there is a three-factor test: (1) How grave was the crime?; (2) How does the sentence match up with sentences for different crimes in the same jurisdiction?; and (3) How does the sentence match up with the same crime in different jurisdictions?

Although the courts should theoretically apply these factors, in practice nearly all sentences are considered constitutional. For example, the Supreme Court has held that life sentences for first-time drug offenders or three-strikers with petty convictions are constitutional.

The Constitution also requires "truth in sentencing." In 2000, the Supreme Court held in *Apprendi v. New Jersey* that when a judge imposes a sentence beyond the presumptive maximum sentence, the judge can consider only those facts a jury found proved beyond a reasonable doubt. This comes into play, for example, with aggravated crimes or additional jail time for weapons offenses—if the jury did not determine that the defendant possessed a gun while selling drugs, the judge cannot use weapons possession to impose a higher sentence.

Juvenile Justice System

Juveniles who commit crimes are treated differently in the juvenile justice system. Although some juveniles (e.g., over the age of 16) may be certified to be tried as adults, most juveniles are prosecuted through juvenile delinquency proceedings. They are not entitled to the same procedures as adults and their sentences are ordinarily much shorter.

The juvenile court is considered a civil, rather than criminal, forum in most jurisdictions, even though it decides whether minors have committed crimes. There is neither a finding of "guilt" nor any "conviction" within the meaning of adult criminal laws. Minors are "committed" to a Youth Authority, rather than being sentenced to jail or prison.

The procedures regarding juvenile cases are explained in more detail in the chapter on criminal procedure (chapter 4).

4 Criminal Procedure

Laurie L. Levenson
Professor of Law and David W. Burcham
Chair in Ethical Advocacy, Loyola Law
School, Los Angeles

Introduction

The topic of criminal procedure covers both the rules governing police officers' conduct in conducting investigations and the procedures used when a case progresses through the criminal justice system. Most of the rules in this area come from the Constitution (specifically, the Bill of Rights), court decisions, and the governing rules of procedure. In most jurisdictions, such as California, the rules governing police conduct are essentially the same as those for the federal courts. However, states have the option of adopting rules that are more protective of defendants' criminal rights.

Purpose of Criminal Procedure

The first question that is often asked is why should people accused of doing terrible things have all these rights? After all, these rights may make it more difficult to convict them and protect the public. The answer is simple: in America, and under our Constitution, we believe that the individual should have protections from the power of the state. Criminal procedure rules perform essentially two functions: (1) they make it more likely that we will get the right result and convict only guilty individuals; and (2) they ensure that people going through the process feel like they have been treated fairly.

Standing and State Action

Several technical rules govern the area of criminal procedure. First, only defendants whose rights have actually been violated have the right to challenge the police's behavior. This is called **standing**. For example, if the police illegally search A's house, but find evidence that can be used against B, B cannot challenge the search because his constitutional rights were not violated. Second, the Constitution only applies to actions by government officials. Thus there must be **state action** in order for there to be relief. For example, if your neighbor illegally breaks into your home and turns over evidence to the police, there is no state action. Therefore, even though your neighbor should not have entered without your permission, the evidence would still be admissible.

Enforcement of Criminal Procedure Rights—The Exclusionary Rule

The main mechanism we use to enforce a defendant's constitutional rights is the **exclusionary rule**. The rule provides that if a police officer obtains evidence in an illegal manner, that evidence is inadmissible in the trial against the defendant. The rule may apply to the **fruit of the poisonous tree**, namely evidence that is the byproduct of an illegal search or seizure. However, the exclusionary rule does not apply to excluding people. Thus, even if the police learn of a suspect through illegal procedures, that person may still be subject to prosecution if there is lawfully obtained evidence supporting the charge.

The exclusionary rule is controversial because it may allow guilty individuals to go free in order to deter the police from violating people's constitutional rights. Over the years, the Supreme Court has carved **exceptions to the exclusionary rule**. Thus, illegally seized evidence can be used to **impeach** a witness, if it would have been **inevitably discovered** through lawful means or there is an **independent lawful source** for obtaining that evidence. Moreover, if the police use a warrant to search for and seize evidence, even if that warrant has an error, the exclusionary rule will not apply so long as the officers acted in **good faith** that it was a valid warrant. The **good faith exception** generally does not apply to warrantless searches, although the Supreme Court has recently held that an officer's good faith reliance on earlier Supreme Court decisions allowing car searches incident to arrest exempts the search from the exclusionary rule. The Supreme Court has also held that an unintentional error in the police database for warrants does not require suppression of a warrant that has been recalled.

Suppression Motions and Hearings

Defendants are required to file motions before trial challenging the alleged illegal seizure of evidence. These early motions allow the court to rule on the admissibility of the evidence before jeopardy attaches, and allow the prosecution to appeal the trial court's ruling if it does suppress any evidence. If the court denies a motion to suppress, the defense must wait until after a conviction to contest the court's ruling.

In a motion to suppress, the defendant will identify any illegal searches or confessions. He may also argue that a warrant was based upon false information and call for a **Franks hearing** to determine whether an officer made false statements in support of a warrant. Ordinarily, a suppression motion will be accompanied by declarations or other statements establishing the basis for the motion. The government will file a response to the motion and the court will hold a hearing. At the hearing, it is customary for the declarants to be subject to cross-examination and for the court to hear legal arguments. For journalists, suppression hearings are an excellent opportunity to learn the specifics of a case and the evidence that the prosecution plans to use in its case.

Procedurally, suppression hearings are often heard at the same time as a preliminary hearing in a case. However, such as in federal court, they may also be heard independent of any other court procedure.

Investigative Criminal Procedure

Investigative criminal procedure refers to the rules governing searches, seizures, and electronic investigation of defendants. These rules are based primarily on the Fourth and Fifth Amendments of the Constitution.

The Fourth Amendment provides: "The right of the people to be secure in their persons, houses, papers, and effects, against unreasonable searches and seizures, shall not be violated, and no Warrants shall issue, but upon probable cause, supported by Oath or affirmation, and particularly describing the place to be searched and persons or things to be seized."

The Fifth Amendment provides: "No person . . . shall be compelled in any criminal case to be a witness against himself."

The challenge for the courts has been to identify how these general rights translate into specific rules for the police. In doing so, courts are constantly trying to balance the rights of the defendant against the interests of society in securing its safety and apprehending criminal suspects.

Searches

The Fourth Amendment prohibits unreasonable searches and seizures. Ordinarily, it is expected that the police will have **probable cause** and a **lawful warrant** before conducting a search. **Probable cause** is a showing of suspicion that demonstrates reason to believe that evidence of a crime will be discovered where a search is being conducted. See full discussion of probable cause and the rules for a lawful warrant later in this chapter.

What Is a Search?

There are many exceptions to the warrant rule. Moreover, not all police investigative work constitutes a search for criminal procedure purposes. That is because the Fourth Amendment only protects areas where people have a **legitimate expectation of privacy**. This may be a home or a car, but it may also be a person's body or a phone booth. A person also has a reasonable expectation of privacy in the curtilage of one's home, such as in a backyard that is fenced off from public access.

The first question in any criminal procedure case is whether the defendant had a legitimate expectation of privacy in the area that was searched. If the defendant did, the Fourth Amendment applies. If either the defendant did not expect privacy, or a reasonable person would not have expected privacy, than the police conduct does not constitute a search that is governed by the Fourth Amendment.

Because there must be a legitimate expectation of privacy in the area searched, some inspections by the police **are not considered searches** at all and do not require a warrant or probable cause. The most common examples are:

1 Searches of open fields
2 Searches of trash containers
3 Searches and eavesdropping in public areas
4 Canine sniffs
5 Requests for bank records
6 Observations of evidence in plain view
7 Aerial-surveillance of property[1]
8 Observations made by technology that is commonly available to the public, such as observations made using a flashlight, telephonic lens, or even binoculars[2]

If police obtain evidence in these manners, the evidence is not subject to challenge under the Fourth Amendment.

One of the hottest issues in criminal procedure is whether use of high-technology police surveillance constitutes a search. Previously, the Supreme Court had held that police surveillance of suspects on the open roads was not a search because the suspects had no reasonable expectation of privacy. However, the Supreme Court has recently struck down the use of GPS devices that have been surreptitiously affixed to a suspect's car to conduct such surveillance.[3] The Supreme Court applied the law of trespass—a theory previously abandoned by the Supreme Court—to determine that the police action was a search. The Supreme Court has not yet decided whether electronic surveillance that does not require a physical trespass will be considered a search, although that day is no doubt coming soon.

Probable Cause

If the defendant had a reasonable expectation of privacy in the area searched, the police must have had probable cause to search the area. There is no precise formula for probable cause. Rather, it refers to enough particularized facts so that a reasonable person would believe that there is a **fair probability** that criminal activity has occurred and that evidence of that criminal activity will be obtained from the search. Thus, police need more than a hunch before they can conduct a search. They must identify specific facts that led them to believe there has been criminal activity.

The courts give great deference to the police in determining probable cause. The court will look to the **totality of the circumstances** to determine whether there was evidence of criminal activity. Moreover, the courts defer to the expertise of police officers in analyzing the nature of suspicious activity. In determining probable cause, the police are entitled to rely on their own observations, as well as the observations of others. They may use reliable informants, their personal knowledge, and any corroboration they obtain.

Warrant Requirements

As the Fourth Amendment discusses, generally the police should obtain a warrant before conducting a search or seizure. A warrant is a document issued by a judicial officer (ordinarily a magistrate or commissioner) that authorized the police to conduct a search or seizure.

The requirements for a lawful warrant include: (1) it is issued by a neutral and detached magistrate, (2) it is based upon probable cause, (3) it describes with particularity the place to be searched, and (4) it describes with particularity the things to be seized. To obtain a warrant, police officers usually submit an affidavit to the court with the information they claim supports probable cause. The cover sheet is ordinarily the warrant itself that identifies the place to be searched and items to be taken. Most frequently, the affidavit is attached to the warrant and can provide a tremendous amount of information regarding the nature of the investigation. In emergency circumstances, police may apply for warrants telephonically, although they must also eventually prepare a written copy of the information submitted to the court.

Judges do not expect warrants or their supporting affidavits to be perfect. If an officer makes a mistake in his factual representations to the court, the warrant will still stand so long as the mistake was not intentional or reckless, or there is sufficient probable cause without the misrepresentation. Similarly, if the police list the wrong address on the warrant, the warrant may still survive if the description given of the search location provides enough specificity.

A warrant can call for the seizure of almost any type of physical evidence. It need not be just contraband. It can include any evidence of a crime, ranging from documents to computers and bedposts. Also, a warrant can be issued against a nonsuspect, so long as there is probable cause to believe that evidence of a crime will be found.

Execution of Search Warrants

Once police officers obtain a search warrant, they should execute it within a reasonable period of time or the probable cause for the warrant can become stale. Most jurisdictions require that a warrant be executed within 10 days of its issuance. A court can extend that time, but if there is no extension, 10 days is the limit.

Generally, warrants must be executed during the day time (6:00 a.m.–10:00 p.m.), but a judge may expressly authorize a nighttime warrant. When executing a warrant, police are required to **knock and announce** their presence before entering the building to do a search. However, in exigent circumstances, such as when the officer's safety may be at risk, the police may dispense with the knock-and-announce requirement. Moreover, the Supreme Court has recently held that a violation of the knock-and-announce requirement does not require suppression of evidence. The officers need only give the occupant a reasonable time (as little as 15 seconds) to respond and then they may forcibly enter the premises.

If no one is present, officers may execute a warrant and leave notice that there has been a search. However, under the so-called sneak-and-peek provisions of Federal Rule of Criminal Procedure 41, officers can conduct surreptitious entries and not leave notice that they have conducted a search.

Once inside, officers may search all areas authorized by the search, including areas like closets, drawers, attics, and compartments where evidence may be concealed. They may also temporarily detain occupants of a premise while they conduct the search. The Supreme Court held in *Wilson v. Layne*, 526 U.S. 603 (1999), that it is unconstitutional for police to invite members of the media to observe execution of a warrant inside a home.

In conducting the search, officers may stay as long as reasonably necessary to complete the search. Once the search is concluded, officers must return the warrant to the magistrate with an inventory of the items that were seized.

Under many state laws, searches of attorney offices and medical facilities require the use of a special master. A special master is appointed by the court to ensure that confidential information is not read by the investigating officers until it is reviewed by the court for attorney-client and patient-physician privileges.

If a warrant is used for a search, the presumption is that the search was constitutionally valid and the defendant has the burden of proving the search violated his rights. By contrast, if a search is warrantless, the prosecution has the burden of proving a valid exception to the warrant rule.

Exceptions to Warrant Rule

It is likely that more searches are conducted without a warrant than with a warrant because there are so many exceptions to the warrant rule. These exceptions have developed because in deciding whether a search is unreasonable, as prohibited by the Fourth Amendment, the courts balance the defendant's right of privacy with other needs of society and law enforcement.

PLAIN VIEW AND PLAIN TOUCH

The plain view exception allows officers to seize evidence they see in plain view while they are legally present in a place. For example, assume that police officers have a warrant to enter a house to search for narcotics. While they are in the house, they see a gun on the counter. They may seize the gun even without a warrant for it.

Officers are not allowed to manipulate objects to put an item in plain view. Thus, police officers cannot look under a stereo to check the serial numbers to see if it is stolen. The contraband nature of the evidence must be apparent without the necessity of a further search.

Likewise, officers may seize evidence that by plain touch they determine to be evidence of a crime or contraband. For example, assume that a person has been stopped for a pat-down search for weapons. While doing the pat-down, the officer touches an object that definitely feels like a cellophane baggie of narcotics. The officer may seize that baggie. However, if the officer needs to squeeze and manipulate the object to determine it is contraband, it may not be seized.

SEARCH INCIDENT TO ARREST

Police are entitled to conduct a full search of an individual and his belongings when that individual has been lawfully arrested. They may also conduct a search of areas within the so-called grab area of the suspect at the time of the arrest, including the passenger compartment of the car, so long as the police are: (1) searching for evidence of the crime of arrest; or (2) the suspect is not yet in the back of the patrol car. This exception applies even if the defendant is arrested shortly after he has exited his car.

AUTOMOBILE SEARCHES

Because of the mobility of cars, officers may conduct a full search of a car (passenger compartment and trunk) if there is probable cause to believe that the car is carrying contraband. In conducting this search, police may look into containers found in the car, as well as into the items of passengers of the car.

INVENTORY SEARCHES

If there is a standard procedure to inventory the contents of a seized car, police may use evidence they find during that inventory, even if there was no warrant for their collection. Because the inventory is technically not designed to discover evidence but to safeguard the contents of the car, it is not subject to the warrant requirement.

CONSENT SEARCHES

The police do not need a warrant to conduct a search if they have valid consent. Consent must be voluntary and voluntariness is determined by a totality of the circumstances. The court will look to many factors to determine voluntariness. For example, the use or threat to use force can invalidate consent. Consent is also invalid if officers lie and state that they already have a warrant. However, telling a suspect that the officers plan to get a warrant and will likely obtain one does not make consent involuntary. Moreover, officers don't have to warn a suspect that he has the right to refuse consent. Consent is still valid even if the suspect thought he didn't have a choice, so long as the police do not coerce the consent.

In some situations, a third party may consent to a search if that third party has authority to consent to a search of the location. Authority may be actual or apparent. For example, a girlfriend could tell officers that she lives with the suspect, has joint control over the premises, and authorizes the search. Likewise, spouses can generally give consent for jointly occupied residences. However, if the co-occupant is present and denies a request, the officers need to get a warrant.

A person may revoke his consent after the police begin a search, but the manner in which that revocation is done may give officers reason to believe there are exigent circumstances for a search.

EXIGENT CIRCUMSTANCES

When there is an emergency situation, such as hot pursuit of a suspect or concerns that evidence will be destroyed, police officers may conduct a search and seizure without first obtaining a warrant. For example, if officers respond to a crime scene and are told that a robbery suspect has fled into a nearby house, officers may enter that house without obtaining a warrant.

Moreover, even in the absence of exigent circumstances, officers can secure a home while a warrant is obtained. Securing a home may include barring individuals from entering or leaving the dwelling and doing a cursory inspection to ensure that evidence is not being destroyed.

BORDER SEARCHES

Government officials do not need a warrant to conduct searches at international borders. So long as the search is routine and not unduly intrusive (e.g., x-raying an individual), officials can conduct the search without a warrant or even probable cause.

ROADBLOCKS

Police may conduct temporary roadblocks without a warrant so long as the focus is on public safety, not investigation of criminal behavior. Thus, sobriety checkpoints are permitted as well as checkpoints to locate witnesses to a recent crime. However, officers cannot set up checkpoints to find persons carrying narcotics in order to prosecute them for narcotics offenses.

SCHOOL SEARCHES

The Supreme Court held in *New Jersey v. T.L.O.*, 469 U.S. 325 (1985) that students have lesser expectations of privacy. Thus, school officials may conduct warrantless searches of students' handbags and backpacks with only reasonable suspicion of illegal activity. However, if the search is particularly intrusive, such as a strip search of a student, a higher level of suspicion may be required.

School officials may also conduct suspicionless drug-testing of high school students who participate in extracurricular activities. There is no need to show any reasonable suspicion that the individual student who is tested has been involved in any illegal activity.

Because private schools are not governed by the Fourth Amendment, officials at those schools may conduct even intrusive searches without violating the Constitution.

EMPLOYER INSPECTIONS

In a private company, employers may search the workspaces of employees without triggering the Fourth Amendment. However, if there is a search of the office of a government employee, the same balancing that occurs for school searches is employed. The employee's reasonable expectation of privacy in his or her workspace is balanced against the government's need to conduct a search. Accordingly, the files, correspondence, and computers of government employees may be searched without a warrant.

Drug testing of government employees is considered a search under the Fourth Amendment. However, there may be special needs for such testing, such as preventing accidents by government officials using drugs. Where there is a safety interest in testing, there is no need for individualized suspicion and the government may have a mandatory drug-testing program.

If drug-testing is being used primarily to collect evidence of a crime, then it is not considered a special needs search, and both probable cause and a warrant are required.

PAROLEE AND PROBATIONER SEARCHES

Police need no suspicion to search a probationer or parolee. All that they need to know is that the person they are searching is on parole or probation. Additionally, law enforcement cannot conduct such searches simply to harass the individual, or in an arbitrary manner.

SECURITY SEARCHES AT AIRPORTS, COURTHOUSES, PRISONS, AND SO FORTH

Security searches are considered special needs searches and may be conducted without specific suspicion of criminal activity. The purpose of these inspections is to protect the public's safety, not to collect evidence of a crime. Accordingly, there is no requirement of particularized suspicion or a warrant.

COMMUNITY SAFETY EXCEPTION

Police are allowed to conduct a search when its purpose is not to collect evidence of a crime, but to respond to an immediate issue of community safety. For example, if the police respond to a bank robbery and catch the robbers, but cannot locate the loaded gun used in the robbery, they may conduct an immediate search of the vicinity so that the gun will not fall into a child's hands.

ADMINISTRATIVE INSPECTIONS

Law enforcement may also conduct routine administrative searches pursuant to statutes that authorize such searches. For example, building inspectors are often authorized to conduct routine searches of buildings. The purpose of these searches is to determine whether there has been compliance with applicable codes. Sometimes administrative warrants are required for such searches, sometimes they are not. So long as officers are complying with the statutory scheme for such searches, the search is permissible. Common administrative inspections include inspections by fire marshals, food inspectors, child welfare officials, and immigration officials looking for illegal laborers.

TRASH AND ABANDONED PROPERTY

There is no expectation of privacy in one's trash. Accordingly, police may search a person's trash. They may also search properties that have been abandoned by individuals.

JAIL SEARCHES

Jail officials may conduct strip searches of any suspects arrested and booked into the jail, regardless of how minor the offense.

Temporary Stops ("Terry Stops" or "Stop and Frisk")

Ordinarily, probable cause is needed for a full arrest and search of an individual. However, an individual may be temporarily detained and a pat-down search conducted with less than probable cause. Pursuant to the Supreme Court's landmark decision in *Terry v. Ohio*, 392 U.S. 1 (1968), police officers may stop and frisk an individual when they have **reasonable suspicion** to believe that crime is afoot and that the suspect may be armed and dangerous.

REASONABLE SUSPICION

Reasonable suspicion is not precisely defined by the courts. However, the best understanding is that a totality of the circumstances would lead a reasonable police officer to believe the suspect is involved in a crime, and articulable, individualized reasons support this belief. Judges generally give great deference to police officers in deciding whether there is reasonable suspicion. Realizing how quickly matters occur on the streets, the courts are reluctant to second-guess the actions of police officers. Courts are becoming more sensitive to the use of profiles in determining when individuals should be detained, especially if the profiles are based upon race. If all the police have is a hunch based upon a person's appearance that he or she is involved in criminal activity, then the police may find it difficult to satisfy the individualized, reasonable suspicion rule. A person's race may be one factor in deciding reasonable suspicion, but not the only factor. Police officers may also use informant's tips to form reasonable suspicion.

DETENTION VS. CONSENSUAL ENCOUNTERS

Detention occurs whenever a reasonable person would not feel free to leave the officer's presence. In such situations, police officers must identify specific facts justifying the detention. However, police officers are allowed to have **consensual encounters** with individuals. For example, no suspicion is needed for a police officer to approach an individual and ask him or her to answer some questions. The suspect is free to walk away. But, if the officer blocks the person's departure, or takes away her airplane tickets so she can't leave, then there may be a detention that requires reasonable suspicion. In determining whether there has been a detention that requires reasonable suspicion, courts consider the following factors: physical obstruction of movement, an officer's show of force, whether the officer retained the person's identification or tickets, threatening tones or coercive orders, the duration of the stop, whether there were coercive surroundings, and whether the police told the individual that he or she was free to leave.

FRISK AND DEMAND FOR IDENTIFICATION

During a Terry Stop, police may demand to see the identification of the person they have detained. They may also ask the individual questions needed to resolve whether there is ongoing illegal activity and whether the suspect poses a danger to the public.

Because the key justification for a frisk is to protect officers against hidden weapons, not to search for evidence, a frisk is less than a full-blown search. Rather, it is a pat-down or customary inspection of the suspect. Officers may pat down the suspect's body. They may also order persons out of a car to conduct a frisk, including any passengers. If officers feel an object during a pat-down that has the size and contours of a weapon, they may seize it, even if it turns out to be something different.

PROTECTIVE SWEEPS

Police officers may also conduct protective sweeps of premises when they arrest someone to ensure that there is no danger to the officers. Thus, if officers arrest someone in his or her home, officers may look in the home to ensure that no one present could endanger the officers while they conduct the arrest.

Wiretapping and Electronic Searches

Because the Fourth Amendment protects expectations of privacy, not physical spaces, wiretapping and other types of electronic surveillance are considered to be searches under the Fourth Amendment. As such, they must ordinarily comply with the Fourth Amendment's requirements of probable cause and a warrant.

Title III of the Omnibus Crime Control and Safe Streets Act now governs the use of electronic surveillance, such as wiretapping. It requires that the police apply to the court for a wiretapping warrant and demonstrate not only probable cause to believe that illegal activities are being conducted, but that traditional investigative techniques are insufficient to discover evidence of that crime. Officers must also take steps to minimize their interception of legitimate conversations and make regular reports to the court of what is being discovered in their intercepts. Wiretaps are labor-intensive and expensive investigative efforts.

Wiretapping for national security purposes is subject to a much lower standard. The Foreign Intelligence Surveillance Act (FISA), as amended by the USA PATRIOT Act of 2001 (renewed in 2006) gives the Foreign Intelligence Surveillance Court (FISC) authority to issue surveillance warrant whenever the attorney general certifies that a purpose of the intercept is national security. There does not need to be traditional probable cause for such intercepts. Rather, the government need only show that intercept will be directed at conversations of foreign agents and is related, in part, to national security. The FISC is appointed by the chief justice of the Supreme Court. It is composed of 11 federal judges from around the country. FISC only hears requests from the government, and there is no notice to the target of an investigation that an application has been submitted to FISC, nor is there a right for a person under surveillance to appeal a FISC order.

Phone records or lists of Internet sites visited by a user do not need a warrant. In cases unrelated to national security, law enforcement may obtain a *pen register* for such records, which is simply an order by the court authorizing the release of such records. For cases involving national security, law enforcement may issue their own national security letters to obtain such records. However, if they wish to view the contents of e-mail conversations, search warrants under Title III or FISA warrants must be obtained.

Roving wiretaps may be issued under either Title III by a federal judge or under the USA Patriot Act by the FISC. A roving wiretap authorizes interception of conversations by certain individuals no matter what phone apparatus they use, rather than simply authorizing the interception of conversations on a particular device.

There is no requirement that officers obtain a warrant before using a beeper or other sensory enhancement device to follow the movements of a suspect. So long as the beeper only traces the suspect's public movements, it does not require a warrant.

Finally, if a conversation is voluntarily recorded by a participant in that conversation, it does not violate the Fourth Amendment and is admissible in federal court. However, many states, including California, have laws prohibiting the clandestine recording of conversations by parties to the conversation, unless done for law enforcement purposes. Such secret wiretapping forms the basis of allegations in the current prosecution of private investigator Anthony Pellicano and the lawyers who utilized his services.

Arrests

The Fourth Amendment also sets the standards for arrests. An arrest occurs whenever a reasonable person would not feel free to leave and the detention is more than temporary. Although handcuffs are often used during arrests, the use of handcuffs alone does not demonstrate that an arrest has occurred. If the handcuffs are removed shortly after the initial encounter, there may not be an arrest. The courts look to the totality of circumstances to determine whether there has been an arrest.

The general rule is that a warrant based upon probable cause is required for an arrest. The warrant must identify the person to be arrested and be supported by an affidavit that articulates probable cause that the individual has been involved in criminal activity. Like search warrants, arrest warrants may be based upon hearsay. Search warrants may identify the arrestee by name, alias, description, or even his or her DNA composition.

Warrantless arrests are permitted in numerous situations. In these situations, officers submit a supporting affidavit and complaint after the arrest to justify their seizure of the defendant.

Warrantless Arrests

No warrant is required when an officer makes a public arrest of a defendant for a crime (felony or misdemeanor) that the officer has witnessed. Moreover, no warrant is required if the police learn from a third party that a suspect has committed a felony. The officers may conduct a public arrest and then submit a post-arrest affidavit of probable cause. Police officers have the authority to arrest individuals for relatively minor violations, including traffic violations, as long as an officer has probable cause to believe that the individual committed the offense in the officer's presence.

In-Home Arrests

In *Payton v. New York*, 445 U.S. 573 (1980), the Supreme Court held that an arrest warrant is required to arrest an individual in his home, absent exigent circumstances, like a hot pursuit. Moreover, if the defendant is going to be arrested in the home of a third party, a search warrant is needed in addition to the arrest warrant. These warrant requirements apply to arrests in rental properties or hotel rooms, so long as the person arrested has rightful possession of the premises. If a person is just temporarily visiting a premise, the warrant requirement may not apply. If an illegal search is conducted of a third party's home to arrest the defendant, only the third party has standing to challenge that search and arrest.

Hot Pursuit Arrests

Warrantless arrests are permitted in homes if the officers are in hot pursuit of a suspect. The hot pursuit exception is based on the fact that the suspect poses a danger to public safety or may destroy evidence if he is not immediately apprehended.

Confessions and Interrogations

A principle tool of law enforcement is interrogation of suspects. Police interrogation is governed by the Fifth Amendment of the Constitution that provides, in pertinent part: "No person . . . shall be compelled in any criminal case to be a witness against himself." The privilege prohibits the government not only from compelling a person to testify in court against himself but also from compelling admissions through interrogation.

Voluntariness Requirement

To satisfy the Fifth Amendment, confessions must be voluntary. Voluntariness is fact-dependent. The court will examine many factors in the case, such as whether police used physical or psychological coercion. Police are allowed to use trickery to obtain a confession, even by lying to the suspect and telling him that a co-defendant has implicated the defendant in a crime. However, police may not use threats of force or actual force to obtain a confession. An involuntary confession cannot be used for any reason in a trial because it is considered to be unreliable.

Miranda Rule

To ensure that confessions are voluntary, the Supreme Court adopted the **Miranda rule** in 1966. Under that rule, a confession during custodial interrogation is inadmissible unless the suspect receives four warnings describing his rights and then gives a knowing, intelligent, and voluntary waiver of these rights. A police officer also must cut off questioning if a suspect invokes his right to silence or his right to consult counsel, even if this invocation follows a waiver of rights.

The Miranda warnings must advise a suspect that: (1) the suspect has the right to remain silent, (2) anything the suspect says can and will be used against the suspect in court, (3) the suspect has the right to consult with counsel, and (4) if the suspect cannot afford a lawyer, a lawyer will be appointed to represent the suspect.

The rationale behind the Miranda rule is that custodial interrogations are inherently coercive and therefore the defendant needs to be advised of his rights before such interrogations occur. If there is a violation of the Miranda rule, the prosecution may not introduce the confession at trial, except as impeachment evidence. Although controversial, the Rehnquist Supreme Court reaffirmed, in *United States v. Dickerson*, 530 U.S. 428 (2000), that Miranda is a constitutionally based rule and therefore could not be overturned by legislation.

Physical evidence discovered through a violation of the Miranda rule is not suppressed, only incriminating statements made by the suspect.

CUSTODIAL QUESTIONING

The Miranda rule only applies if a suspect is questioned while he or she is in custody. If a person is not in custody, no Miranda rights need be given. *Custody* includes either formal arrest or restraint on freedom of movement of the degree associated with arrest. It may occur on a public street or in a stationhouse. If a suspect freely accompanies the police to headquarters for questioning and is not yet under arrest, then the suspect is not in custody and Miranda rights need not be administered. An ordinary traffic stop is not considered to be custodial, and therefore the police can ask the driver questions without first administering Miranda rights.

The test to determine whether a person is in custody for Miranda purposes is whether a reasonable person in the defendant's situation would feel free to leave. This is an objective standard, but the courts will consider the age of the suspect in making the determination.

INTERROGATION

The Miranda rule only applies if a suspect is interrogated. Interrogation includes both direct questioning and words or actions that police should know are likely to elicit an incriminating response from an average suspect. Thus, it includes more than express questioning.

If a suspect makes a voluntary statement not in response to questioning, then the Miranda rule does not apply. Thus, if a suspect blurts out a remark to the police, and the remark is not made in response to questioning, the Miranda rule does not apply.

EXCEPTIONS

The Miranda rule does not apply to **routine booking information** obtained from a suspect. It also does not apply when there are **exigent circumstances** for the police to obtain the information, such as the need to **protect public safety**. For example, if a shooting has just occurred and the police are trying to find the gun that could still be used to hurt others, the officer can ask about the whereabouts of the missing weapon.

MIRANDA WARNINGS

Although most Americans are familiar with the Miranda rule by its recitation during television programs, no script is actually required for administering the Miranda warnings. So long as all four rights are presented to the suspect, and the suspect indicates that he or she understands those rights and voluntarily waives them, there is compliance with the Miranda rule. The Miranda rule does not require that the police advise a suspect that a lawyer is waiting at the stationhouse to speak to him.

WAIVER OF MIRANDA RIGHTS

The burden is on the prosecution to prove that a suspect voluntarily waived his or her Miranda rights. A waiver need not be in writing. It may be oral. The court looks at a totality of the circumstances to determine whether a suspect voluntarily waived his rights, including whether the suspect indicates that he is willing to talk to the police and does not want an attorney. However, a waiver may not be presumed from a suspect's silence after warnings. There must be some evidence in the record that the suspect understood his rights and decided not to exercise them. This evidence may be minimal such as a defendant answering questions after sitting two-and-a-half hours of questioning.

INVOCATION OF MIRANDA RIGHTS

If a suspect invokes his Miranda rights, all questioning must cease. However, there is a difference between a suspect invoking his right to remain silence and a suspect invoking his right to counsel. If a suspect invokes his right to remain silent, the police may approach the suspect later, readminister the Miranda rights, and, if there is valid waiver, obtain a statement from the suspect. By contrast, if a suspect invokes his right to counsel, the police may not reinitiate questioning of the suspect unless the suspect initiates the contact. This is known as the **Edwards rule.**

Additionally, not all statements made by a suspect after he or she is given the Miranda warnings are considered an invocation of the defendant's right to remain silent or right to counsel. If a suspect does not unequivocally invoke his rights, police may continue to ask questions to determine whether the defendant is willing to waive his rights. For example, assume that the suspect is given his Miranda rights and then says, "I probably shouldn't tell you anything. My lawyer would be mad." Courts have held that such remarks need not be construed as an invocation of the right to counsel.

IMPEACHMENT WITH SUSPECT'S SILENCE

Once a suspect is advised of his Miranda rights, he has the right not to answer police questions. Thus, the prosecution may not introduce a suspect's post-Miranda silence as evidence against a defendant, even though one might have expected an innocent person to respond to the remark. For example, assume that a suspect has been advised of his right to remain silent. Then, officers tell the suspect that the DNA indicates he was the killer. The prosecution cannot introduce evidence that the suspect did not contest the accusation when he was confronted by the police officer. However, silence before a suspect is advised of his Miranda rights may be used as impeachment because the suspect has not yet been guaranteed that he has the right to remain silent.

SUBSEQUENT CONFESSIONS

Although the exclusionary rule applies to violations of a suspect's Miranda rights, police can undo the taint from a defective first confession by readministering the Miranda rights and obtaining a lawful confession. So long as the second confession is not directly derived from the first confession, the second administration of the Miranda rights dispels the taint of the first invalid confession. The exception is when the police develop a policy to deliberately fail to advise a suspect of her Miranda rights, obtain a confession, and then give the Miranda rights in order to have the suspect reaffirm her confession. In such situations, the second confession is also invalid.

Invocation of Right to Counsel

The Sixth Amendment guarantees a defendant the right to counsel in all critical stages of a criminal case. Once a defendant invokes his right to counsel, police generally cannot reinitiate contact with the suspect. However, they may question the suspect about unrelated crimes. The Sixth Amendment is offense-specific. Thus, even if the police question a defendant who is represented by counsel about a closely related crime, there is no violation of the Sixth Amendment right to counsel if a lawyer has not yet been appointed to represent the defendant on that charge.

The Massiah Rule

Once a defendant is indicted or counsel is appointed, the police may not deliberately elicit incriminating statements from a defendant, even if the defendant is not in custody. Thus, the police may not use undercover informants to ask questions of a defendant once he is indicted because such activity undermines the right to counsel.

Obtaining Information through Jailhouse Informants

Statements made to jailhouse informants are not covered by the Miranda rule because Miranda only covers police interrogations. However, if a defendant has asked for counsel or already has counsel representing him, police may not use an informant to deliberately elicit information from the suspect. If the defendant volunteers information to the jailhouse informant, such information may be used against the defendant. Therefore, listening post informants may be used by the government in jail, and defense counsel are wise to inform their clients not to speak to anyone in jail about their case. Moreover, if an inmate is not working for the government at the time he elicits a statement from the defendant, then any statement made by the defendant to that inmate may be used.

Demanding Testimony or Production of Evidence from a Defendant

The Fifth Amendment also protects a defendant from incriminating himself in other ways, including by being called as a witness for the prosecution. Accordingly, a defendant has a Fifth Amendment right not to testify in his criminal trial or before the grand jury. A defendant cannot be sanctioned for exercising that right.

No Adverse Inferences in a Criminal Case

No adverse inference may be drawn in a criminal case from the defendant's refusal to testify. It is considered a **Griffin error** for a prosecutor to refer in closing argument to the defendant's failure to testify in the trial. How-ever, if a defendant asserts his Fifth Amendment right, this assertion may be used against him in a civil case. For example, assume that a defendant is charged with fraud and is facing a civil suit for the same activity. The defendant's assertion of his Fifth Amendment right cannot be used to draw a negative inference in his criminal case, but can be used in the companion civil case.

Subpoenas for Evidence

A suspect has the right not to produce evidence against himself; however, the evidence itself is not protected by the Fifth Amendment. Thus, pros-ecutions may use a search warrant to obtain evidence created by the sus-pect, such as a journal or records. Moreover, an attorney or accountant may not claim the privilege for the client. Thus, prosecutors may subpoena a suspect's records from the attorney or accountant without violating the suspect's Fifth Amendment rights. The Fifth Amendment only applies to real persons. A corporation or artificial entity does not have a Fifth Amendment right and a custodian of those companies may be ordered to testify and produce records.

If documents are subpoenaed from a defendant, the defendant has the right to assert the Fifth Amendment as to the production of the documents, but not to the documents themselves because the documents were volun-tarily created. To overcome a defendant's assertion of the privilege in pro-duction of documents, prosecutors may seek immunity so that the fact that the defendant produced the documents will not be used against him at trial. Rather, the prosecution will have to find another way to link the documents to the defendant, such as handwriting exemplars or the testimony of other witnesses.

Only Testimonial Evidence Is Protected

The Fifth Amendment only covers testimonial evidence, not physical evi-dence. Thus, a suspect can be compelled to produce hair samples, blood samples, fingerprints, handwriting exemplars, DNA samples, and other types of physical evidence, even if this evidence may incriminate the defen-dant. Likewise, a suspect in a drunk driving case can be required to undergo sobriety tests without violating the suspect's Fifth Amendment rights.

Special Rules for Police Officers

Under the Supreme Court's decision in *Garrity v. New Jersey*, 385 U.S. 493 (1967), if a police officer is required to provide a statement under threat of administrative action or dismissal, then the statement cannot be

156 Laurie L. Levenson

used against the officer in a subsequent criminal trial. This rule creates special challenges for prosecutors investigating police misconduct cases because law enforcement will often conduct internal investigations prior to the prosecutor's investigation of the case. The officer's statements are protected, as well as any evidence derived from those statements, including statements by other officers who were exposed to the target officer's Garrity statements.

Use Immunity and Transactional Immunity

One way that prosecutors overcome a person's assertion of Fifth Amendment rights is to provide immunity for that person. If the person is immunized from having the statement used against him, he no longer has a Fifth Amendment right to refuse to answer the question or provide the evidence.

There are two types of immunity: use immunity and transactional immunity. **Use immunity** only protects the suspect or witness from having the statement, or any evidence derived from it, used against that person in a criminal trial. Use immunity is often obtained through statutes providing that if a court order compels a person to provide a statement, that statement automatically receives use immunity. Prosecutors may apply to the court for such use immunity in either grand jury or trial proceedings. If use immunity is granted, the person providing the compelled statements may still be prosecuted, but the burden is on the prosecution to demonstrate that their evidence was obtained independent of the immunized information. Prosecutors often use clean and dirty teams when immunized statements are involved in a case. The trial team is considered the clean team and is not exposed to evidence until the dirty team of prosecutors determines that it is not derivative of immunized statements. Even the inadvertent use of immunized information, or evidence obtained therefrom, may be devastating to the prosecution's case. For example, when Ollie North was given immunity by Congress to testify in the Iran-Contra hearings, his immunized testimony tainted any subsequent prosecution witnesses who had watched or otherwise been exposed to North's testimony.

Transactional immunity is broader than use immunity. It protects an individual from prosecution on criminal charges related to his testimony, not just the use of the testimony itself. Transactional immunity may be conveyed by a letter agreement by the prosecution. Thus, it is sometimes called *informal* or *letter immunity*.

Good Faith Basis for Asserting Fifth Amendment Right

Witnesses, as well as suspects, may assert the Fifth Amendment right. However, there must be a good faith basis for believing that the testimony being solicited implicates the witness in a crime. A witness may assert his or her

Fifth Amendment right in a deposition, as well as in a court proceeding. The threat of possible prosecution in a foreign country is not a basis for asserting the Fifth Amendment. The privilege only applies to prosecutions in the United States.

Waiver by Testifying

By testifying regarding a matter, a witness or defendant waives his or her Fifth Amendment right as to all questions regarding that matter. Thus, if a defendant takes the stand to testify, she cannot refuse to answer questions on cross-examination regarding her testimony. If a witness or defendant improperly asserts the Fifth Amendment, all of the witness's testimony may be stricken, as was done in the infamous Patty Hearst bank robbery trial.

Lineups and Identifications

There are also constitutional rules governing the use of lineup and other types of identification evidence in criminal cases. The police cannot use **unduly suggestive** measures to obtain identifications, although such identifications may be admissible if they are otherwise reliable. Additionally, if identification procedures involving the defendant occur post-charges, the defendant may have a right to have his lawyer involved.

Lineups

A lineup occurs when a defendant is required to stand with other individuals to determine whether he can be identified by witnesses in the case. If the lineup occurs before a defendant is arraigned, there is no right to have counsel present at the lineup. However, if the lineup occurs after arraignment, the defendant has a Sixth Amendment right to have counsel present.

Lineups cannot be unduly suggestive. Thus, it would be impermissible to have five short people in a lineup and the defendant as the only tall suspect. If a lineup is unduly suggestive, the court may preclude the prosecution from introducing its results at trial. Moreover, if there is no independent basis for the witness's trial identification of the suspect, that identification may also be excluded.

Photospreads

Another common way of having witnesses identify a suspect is through the use of photospreads. Like lineups, photospreads cannot be unduly suggestive. A defendant does not have a right to have counsel present when a witness is shown a photospread. If a tainted photospread is used, the court may preclude the introduction of its results at trial. Likewise, the witness who was exposed to the tainted photospread may only be allowed to make an in-court identification if there is an independent basis for that identification.

Show-ups

Show-ups are the least reliable type of identification because they occur when the police show the witness the picture of only one person, or drive the witness by one suspect, to determine whether that person committed the crime. Because they are so suggestive, show-ups are usually only permitted when there is an urgent need for the victim or witness to identify the suspect. The court must determine whether the identification is reliable.

Reliability of Identifications

To determine whether an identification is admissible, the court must decide whether the police procedures were so suggestive as to make the resulting identification unreliable. In making this determination, courts consider:

1   The degree of police suggestiveness;
2   the opportunity to view the suspect before the identification;
3   the degree of attention focused on the suspect during the criminal events;
4   the accuracy of a witness's description of the suspect before the identification;
5   the witness's level of certainty;
6   the time between the pre-identification opportunity to view and the identification itself; and
7   other information relating to the witness's certainty over the identification, such as whether the victim had prior contact with the suspect.

It is relatively rare for courts to bar identification evidence. Rather, they tend to permit the evidence to be presented to the jury, but allow defense counsel to argue to the jury the unreliability of the witness's identification.

Problems with Eyewitness Identifications

Recent studies have indicated that eyewitness identifications are often faulty, especially when they involve the identification of a person of a different race. A study by the Innocence Project at Cardozo Law School indicates that 77 percent of all inmates cleared of being wrongfully convicted were convicted based on mistaken eyewitness identification.

To convince jurors that eyewitness testimony is not reliable, some defense lawyers will ask the court's permission to have an eyewitness expert testify. Courts are divided on whether such witnesses should be allowed to testify.[4]

Rules Governing the Adjudicative Process: How a Criminal Case Goes through the Court System

Overview

Although there are slight variations by jurisdiction, there is a general process by which a case proceeds through the criminal justice system. Here is a quick overview of that process. After the overview, each stage of the proceedings will be discussed in more detail.

A criminal case can start in one of two ways: (1) law enforcement officials may suspect that criminal behavior is afoot and begin an investigation that leads to formal charges and an arrest; or (2) law enforcement officials may respond to the commission of a crime, arrest their suspects, and then conduct a full investigation of the case.

Often times, law enforcement officers arrest individuals before they have had time to secure an arrest warrant. In these situations, the officers must file an initial charging document against the defendant, known as the **complaint**. A magistrate judge decides whether there was sufficient **probable cause** to arrest the defendant and to hold him until formal charges can be filed. A defendant must appear before a magistrate within 48 hours of his or her arrest, absent exigent circumstances. At the **initial appearance**, a defendant is informed of the charges against him, assigned counsel, offered the opportunity to argue for pretrial release, and advised of his constitutional rights. Following the initial appearance, prosecutors will seek formal charges against the defendant by use of a grand jury or preliminary hearing.

In the federal system, defendants are formally charged by the grand jury. If the defendant remains in custody, prosecutors have 10 days to conduct a preliminary hearing at which they demonstrate they have sufficient evidence to hold the defendant for trial. However, if prosecutors obtain an **indictment** from the **grand jury** before the 10-day period expires, no preliminary hearing need be conducted. Every defendant charged with a felony in federal court is entitled to an indictment. If a defendant is only charged with a misdemeanor, the prosecutors may file an **information** with the court without proceeding to the grand jury. If a defendant makes bail and is out of custody following his arrest, prosecutors have 20 days to conduct a preliminary hearing or obtain a grand jury indictment.

In state courts, it is more common for a defendant to have a **preliminary hearing** to decide whether there is sufficient evidence to bind over a suspect for trial, although a grand jury may also be used. At the preliminary hearing, the defendant has the right to counsel who can cross-examine the prosecution's witnesses. Sometimes, hearsay may be used in the preliminary hearing. The prosecution need not prove its case beyond a reasonable doubt at this stage. It is sufficient if the prosecution demonstrates probable cause for the charges. In some jurisdictions, motions to suppress evidence are heard at the time of the preliminary hearing.

Once a defendant is formally charged by indictment or bound over after a preliminary hearing, the next step in the process is for the defendant to be **arraigned** on the trial charges. At the arraignment, the court ensures that the defendant has a copy of the indictment or information and asks the defendant to enter an initial plea. It is also common for the court to set a preliminary trial date at the time of the arraignment. Most defendants enter pleas of not guilty at the time of arraignment.

Many things happen between the time of the arraignment and the assigned trial date. First, counsel for either side may file **pretrial motions,** such as motions to suppress evidence that was illegally seized. Defendants may also file a variety of other motions, such as motions to dismiss charges, motions to sever, motions for discovery, and motions in limine to clarify what evidence will be allowed at trial. Importantly, this period of time will also be used for the parties to obtain **discovery.**

A majority of defendants choose to enter **guilty pleas** rather than going to trial. If a defendant chooses to proceed to trial, either side may subpoena witnesses. On rare occasion, the court will also authorize the deposition of witnesses, although witness interviews or grand jury testimony of witnesses are the primary means of obtaining witness statements in federal criminal cases. If a defendant plans to rely on an alibi or mental defense, the defendant is required to provide pretrial notice of these defenses.

Both the prosecution and the defense have a constitutional right to a **jury trial,** although this right may be waived. In federal criminal cases, a jury of 12 persons is selected. The verdict of the jurors must be unanimous. However, the Constitution does not require 12-person juries, nor unanimous verdicts.

The jury is selected through the process of **voir dire.** During voir dire, jurors are questioned regarding their attitudes and backgrounds. If a juror cannot be impartial, the court may excuse the juror **for cause.** Additionally, each side in a federal felony case is entitled to exercise a certain number of **peremptory challenges.**

Once a jury is sworn in, the trial ordinarily begins with opening statements by the lawyers for each side. In a criminal case, the defense may reserve its **opening statement** until after the prosecution's case. The opening statement generally gives the jury a roadmap of what the prosecution or defense expects the evidence will be at trial.

The judge controls the order of testimony and the **presentation of evidence** in a trial. The prosecution begins by presenting evidence against the defendant. The defense has an opportunity to cross-examine any witnesses called by the prosecution. When the prosecutor has rested, the defense may move for a **judgment of acquittal.** The granting of such motions is rare because it requires a finding that no reasonable jury could convict the defendant on the evidence presented.

After the prosecution's presentation, the defense has an opportunity to present evidence and witnesses. When the defense has concluded its presentation, prosecutors may present rebuttal evidence. After all of the evidence has been presented, the defense may move again for a motion of judgment of acquittal. It is then time for the lawyers to give closing argument. In **closing arguments**, the prosecutor has two opportunities to speak to the jury—both as the opening closing argument and in rebuttal. The prosecutor is given this opportunity because the prosecution must prove its case beyond a reasonable doubt. Following closing argument, the court gives the jury its **jury instructions**, and the jury recesses for its deliberations. The jury then returns a **verdict**, if it is able to do so. If the jury cannot reach a verdict, it is declared a hung jury, and a mistrial is ordered.

If a defendant is convicted, he or she is **sentenced**. Different jurisdictions have different sentencing procedures. The two major models are **indeterminate (discretionary) sentencing** in which a wide range of discretion is given to the judge to determine the sentence. The other type of sentencing is **determinate or guideline sentencing**, in which certain findings are used to identify the appropriate sentence.

A defendant has a right to **appeal** his conviction. If the conviction is affirmed, the defendant may **petition for review by writ of certiorari** to the state's supreme court or, in the federal system, to the U.S. Supreme Court. A defendant may also file a motion for collateral review of his conviction. This is known as **petition for writ of habeas corpus** and may only be filed in federal court to attack federal constitutional errors in a conviction. The most common issues raised in such a petition are ineffective assistance of counsel and the prosecution's failure to provide exculpatory evidence.

The rest of this chapter details each of these stages of a criminal case.

Critical Stages of a Criminal Proceeding

Arraignment / First Appearance / Pleas

Ordinarily, the first time a defendant appears in court is at his arraignment following his arrest. At this court appearance, the defendant will be assigned counsel, advised of his rights, advised of the initial charges against him, and given the opportunity to argue for bail. The magistrate will also review whether there was sufficient probable cause for the arrest, although this review is done on the papers submitted by the government and not by listening to witnesses. First appearances are often very brief proceedings and the magistrate who proceeds over them is not likely to be the trial judge.

At an initial appearance or arraignment a defendant may be asked to enter a plea. There are three types of pleas: (1) not guilty, (2) guilty, and (3) nolo contendere. Not guilty does *not* mean "I didn't do it." It simply means, "government, prove your case." A guilty plea is an admission that the defendant committed the crime. Nolo contendere is a no contest plea. A defendant who pleads nolo contendere may be punished the same as a defendant who pleads guilty. However, a guilty plea is an admission that is binding in civil cases and will lead to an automatic judgment against the defendant in a companion civil case. By contrast, a nolo contendere is not an admission for a civil case.

Bail and Pretrial Release

Foremost on defendant's minds from the beginning of a case is bail and pretrial release. Often times, a bail schedule will be in effect when a defendant is arrested and the defendant may post bail according to that schedule. However, if the defendant is in custody at the time of his first appearance, he may argue for bail.

In determining whether to grant bail, the court may consider whether: (1) the defendant is a **flight risk** and (2) if the defendant poses a **danger to the community**. The court will often receive a report from the probation department to assist it in this determination. Many factors may go into the court's decision, including the defendant's prior criminal history, the severity of the charges, the defendant's ties to the community, the defendant's immigration status, the strength of the government's case, and whether the defendant is cooperating with the prosecution.

Judges ordinarily have broad discretion in deciding whether to grant bail and the conditions to be put on a defendant who is released. Those conditions may range from the posting of a monetary bond to home confinement.

If bail is allowed, many different types of bonds may be posted. Some defendants are released on their own recognizance, which means that they promise to return. Other bonds require that money and/or property be posted for the defendant's release. An unsecured bond is a promise by the defendant to pay a certain amount if he violates conditions of his bond, including by not appearing as ordered by the court. A secured bond is one that is supported by a monetary payment.

Defendants who cannot post the full amount of their bonds may often post a 10 percent down payment and post collateral for the remaining portion of the bond. If the defendant appears for all proceedings, the 10 percent is returned with the collateral. Often defendants use a bail bondsman to post their bond. If a bail bondsman posts bond, he will typically charge a nonrefundable 10 percent for the bond and hold security for the rest.

At the end of proceedings, if a defendant has made all of his appearances, bond is exonerated and returned to the person who posted the bond. However, if the defendant fails to appear or violates a condition of release, bond may be forfeited. A bail bondsman has the right to apprehend a person who has skipped bond, although he or she must follow the laws of the jurisdiction (including foreign countries) where he finds his bounty.

Sometimes there are allegations that illegally obtained money is being used to post bail. The court may hold a **Nebbia hearing** to determine the source of money being used to post bond.

A bail hearing is sometimes referred to as a **detention hearing**. A defendant may have such a hearing throughout the criminal process as circumstances change. For some crimes, there is a presumption that a defendant will be detained pretrial, such as narcotics offenses in the federal system. In most states, all but the most serious crimes (e.g., capital offenses) are eligible for bond, although the bond required may be higher than what the defendant can pay.

Occasionally, an individual will be held for trial who is not a suspect at all, but is a **material witness** to the proceedings. Witnesses are held as material witnesses if there is a substantial risk they will not appear at trial. They are also entitled to argue for bail.

In the current war on terrorism, there are many types of detention. Enemy combatants are not handled through the ordinary criminal justice system. Accordingly, even if they are American citizens, they are not entitled to bail. Likewise, defendants held on immigration violations are not subject to these rules.

Formal Charging

PROSECUTORIAL DISCRETION

Prosecutors have great discretion in deciding what charges to file against a defendant. They can decide which defendants to charge, how many charges to bring, whether charges will be brought in federal or state court (assuming there is jurisdiction for both) and when there is more than one applicable statute, whether to charge a more serious or lesser charge. The only requirement is that there is probable cause for the charges. Realistically and ethically, prosecutors should only bring charges if they can prove their case beyond a reasonable doubt. However, the law only requires probable cause (something akin to "more likely than not") for charges to be filed.

Prosecutors have the discretion to combine defendants and crimes in one set of charges. If the joinder of these charges or defendants is unfairly prejudicial, the court may grant a severance.

The prosecution must prosecute a case in the proper venue, or, in other words, where the crime was committed. A defendant may seek change of venue when the defendant cannot receive a fair trial in the venue in which the case was filed.

SELECTIVE AND DISCRIMINATORY PROSECUTION

Prosecutors may not file charges solely based upon a defendant's race, gender, or ethnicity, nor to penalize a defendant for exercising a constitutional right. However, there is no requirement that a prosecutor be an equal opportunity prosecutor. In order for a defendant to prove discriminatory prosecution, the defendant must show more than the fact that the prosecution's charging decisions have a disproportionate impact on one group. They must show that it is the intent of the prosecution to discriminate. This is a very high standard and rarely met.

VINDICTIVE PROSECUTION

Prosecutors can threaten to file more serious charges if a defendant refuses to cooperate or plead guilty. However, they must not increase the charges against a defendant merely because a defendant exercises a constitutional right, such as the right to appeal a conviction. In order to increase the charges against a defendant on retrial, the prosecution will have to show what new information they obtained that would justify the additional or more serious charges.

GRAND JURY AND PRELIMINARY HEARINGS

The initial charges used to arrest and hold a defendant are not necessarily those that the defendant will face at trial. A formal charging procedure will decide those charges. Two mechanisms determine the formal charges for trial: **grand jury** and **preliminary hearing**. The Fifth Amendment guarantees federal criminals the right to a grand jury indictment for felonies. However, this right does not extend to state cases, and state prosecutors commonly file their own charges and proceed by preliminary hearing.

Grand Jury   A grand jury is typically comprised of 23 citizens from the community who decide whether charges should be brought against an individual. There is often no requirement that a grand juror have any background or expertise in the law. In many jurisdictions, grand jurors are chosen randomly from the community. In other jurisdictions, grand jurors are selected by the judges of that jurisdiction. Depending on the type of grand jury, grand jurors may serve from 6 months to 18 months. In many state jurisdictions, there may be only one grand jury for the entire county. When this is the case, the grand jury is unlikely to hear most of the criminal cases. Rather, high-profile cases or cases with political implications may be brought to these grand juries. Accusatory grand juries focus on whether there is probable cause to support criminal charges. Investigative grand jurors are involved in the long-term investigations and regularly subpoena witnesses and documents for the grand jury's review. In the end, an investigative grand jury may or may not indict a case.

In some jurisdictions, there are also civil grand juries whose responsibility is to provide oversight of government agencies. These grand juries do not bring indictments; rather, they issue reports regarding the operation of government departments.

The grand jury has a foreperson, but real control of the grand jury is ordinarily with the prosecutor. Typically, the prosecutor will decide which witnesses will be called to testify before the grand jury, which charges the grand jurors will be asked to indict, and what evidence will be sought by grand jury subpoena. In the federal system, as well as that of many states, the defense is not entitled to be present in the grand jury or present any evidence to it. Rather, in the grand jury, the prosecutor is present with the witness and grand jurors to direct the proceedings. If a witness wishes to consult with his or her lawyer, the witness must request permission to leave the grand jury room for that discussion.

Additionally, a defendant does not have a federal constitutional right to have exculpatory evidence presented to the grand jury. Under federal law, a grand jury may indict based solely on hearsay and may use inadmissible evidence (such as evidence obtained by an illegal search) in making its decision to indict. Some states, such as California, require that there be sufficient non-hearsay and admissible evidence to support an indictment, and that exculpatory evidence be presented to the grand jurors.

It takes a majority of a quorum to indict a case. If the jurors vote in favor of an indictment, they return a true bill. If grand jurors refuse to indict, the prosecution can represent its case to another grand jury or, in state courts, file charges and proceed by preliminary hearing.

Grand jury proceedings are secret. It is ordinarily a crime for a person to contact a grand juror for purposes of obtaining information regarding the discussions of the grand jury. However, witnesses themselves are ordinarily free to discuss their testimony.

Once a case is indicted, grand jury transcripts remain secret in federal cases until the witness testifies in court. In state courts, grand jury transcripts are often released to the public after indictment.

It is very difficult for a defendant to attack a grand jury proceeding. Judges have limited supervisory power over grand juries. It is widely (and accurately) believed that grand juries will usually abide by the prosecutor's wishes. As is popularly said, "a grand jury will indict a ham sandwich."

Preliminary Hearing

An alternative approach to bringing formal charges is by using the preliminary hearing. A preliminary hearing is like a mini-trial. The prosecution presents witnesses and evidence to support its charges against the defendant. Unlike at a trial, the prosecution need only show that there is probable cause for the charges. The decision is made by a judge, not jury.

Different jurisdictions have different rules for their preliminary hearings. In many jurisdictions, the prosecution may present its case through hearsay.

The defense may also present evidence, although this is rarely done. For the defense, the preliminary hearing is advantageous because it provides a preview of the prosecution's case, including the credibility of some prosecution witnesses.

ARRAIGNMENT AFTER FORMAL CHARGES ARE BROUGHT

Once formal charges are filed, the defendant is arraigned on those charges and assigned to a trial court. The trial court will select a trial date and set the timetable for pretrial motions. At the arraignment, the defendant will be advised of the charges against him, be asked to enter an initial plea, and be given an opportunity to argue bail.

Right to Counsel and Right to Self-Representation

Perhaps the most important right that a defendant has is the right to counsel under the Sixth Amendment. The right to counsel was established in the seminal case of *Gideon v. Wainwright*, 372 U.S. 335 (1963). Defendants who can afford counsel have the right to counsel of their choice. Interference with this right may result in automatic reversal of a conviction.

Indigent defendants are also entitled to the assistance of counsel, but they do not have the right to select their appointed lawyer. Typically, defense counsel are appointed from a public defender's office or a panel of counsel available for indigent defendants.

In cases in which the defendant may actually go to jail, the defendant is entitled to counsel. However, in minor cases, where there will not be jail time even if the defendant is convicted, there is no right to counsel. The right to counsel covers all critical stages of a proceeding. Thus, it covers any trial-like event, such as post-indictment lineups, guilty plea negotiations, trial, sentencing and first appeals. It does not ensure a right to counsel for habeas corpus proceedings or petitions for writ of certiorari. Laypersons ordinarily cannot serve as counsel for another defendant, but petitioners for habeas corpus or certiorari may receive the assistance of jailhouse lawyers.

The Constitution only ensures the right to "effective assistance" of counsel. It does not entitle the defendant to a superstar lawyer. In *Strickland v. Washington*, 466 U.S. 668 (1984), the Supreme Court established the standard for determining whether the defendant received ineffective assistance of counsel. To demonstrate ineffective assistance of counsel, a defendant must show: (1) specific errors by counsel that "fell below an objective standard of reasonableness," and (2) prejudice. Prejudice means that "there is a reasonable probability that, but for counsel's unprofessional errors, the result of the proceeding would have been different." The court defined a reasonable probability as "a probability sufficient to undermine confidence in the outcome."

In deciding whether defense counsel made an error in his or her representation, the court must show great deference to the strategic decisions by counsel at the time they were made. Thus, it is not necessarily ineffective assistance of counsel for a lawyer to concede in closing argument that his client murdered the victim because the lawyer's strategy may have been to avoid a stiff penalty for his client by having his client appear ready to accept responsibility for his actions.

Moreover, if the prosecution has a strong case against a defendant, it may not matter that defense counsel made errors. If there is little chance that the defendant would have been acquitted, even fairly serious errors by defense counsel may not be prejudicial. There have been famous cases where defense counsel have slept during trial and the court has been willing to state that the defendant received ineffective assistance of counsel. The reason for such a finding is that it was unlikely that even the most zealous representation of counsel would have made a difference in the verdict.

There a few situations where the court is willing to find per se prejudice and ineffective assistance of counsel: (1) where the government interferes with the defendant's right to counsel, (2) where counsel is denied altogether or given a lawyer who abandons his role altogether, and (3) where defense counsel has an actual conflict of interest at the time of the representation. A conflict of interest can arise when defense counsel represents more than one defendant, especially if the most effective strategy would be to blame the crime on the other co-defendant. Because of this problem, judges have the right to disallow waivers of these conflicts.

It is fairly standard procedure for a defendant to challenge the actions or inaction by his counsel in a habeas corpus proceeding. If the defendant makes such a challenge, he waives attorney-client privilege and the court may hold a hearing to discover why defense counsel made the strategy calls he did.

Recently the Supreme Court has recognized the right to effective assistance of counsel during plea bargaining. Accordingly, if defense counsel gives erroneous advice to the defendant, including failing to inform the defendant that he is subject to deportation, or defense counsel fails to advise the defendant of a plea offer, the defendant may succeed in withdrawing his guilty plea.

Under *Faretta v. California*, 422 U.S. 806 (1975), a defendant also has the right to self-representation. Self-representation requires a knowing waiver of the right to counsel. Thus, the trial judge must warn the defendant of all of the downsides of waiving counsel. A defendant may lose the right of self-representation if he is disruptive and fails to follow court procedure.

Some courts appoint standby counsel to assist pro se defendants. No matter what kind of counsel is appointed, the defendant has the right to make three crucial decisions in a case: (1) whether to plead guilty, (2) whether to testify, and (3) whether to plead insanity.

Discovery

Discovery is a critical stage of a criminal case. In order for counsel to know how to defend a case, he or she must know what evidence the prosecution plans to present. Different jurisdictions have different statutory rules regarding discovery. Under Federal Rule of Criminal Procedure 16, the defendant is entitled to any statements he made to the police, a copy of his prior record, access to the physical evidence, and reports by government experts. The defendant must provide reciprocal evidence of the physical evidence he plans to use and his expert's reports. Witness statements must be provided pursuant to the Jencks Act, 18 U.S.C. § 3500, which states that witness statements must be provided no later than immediately after a witness testifies. It is common practice for prosecutors to advance this timetable by providing witness statements before trial, unless there is a risk that the witness will be intimidated into changing his testimony.

In state courts, the discovery rules may also require that names, addresses, and statements of witnesses be provided by both sides of a proceeding early in the discovery process. For both state and federal courts, there is ordinarily a rule requiring the disclosure of an intent to use an alibi or a mental defense.

In addition to discovery requirements set forth in the rules and statutes, the defendant has a constitutional due process right to discovery of exculpatory evidence and evidence that could be used to impeach the prosecution's witnesses. This is known as the *Brady/Giglio rule*. If the prosecution fails to provide this evidence, the defendant is entitled to a new trial if he can show prejudice because of the government's failure.

Pretrial Motions

A variety of pretrial motions may be filed by the defense and the prosecution. These may include, among others:

- Motion to disqualify the judge
- Motion for a competency hearing
- Motion to dismiss
- Motion to substitute counsel
- Motion to change venue
- Motion to suppress
- Motion for a continuance
- Motion for discovery
- Motion for an informant's identity

It is also standard for the court to hear **motions in limine,** which are designed to get pretrial rulings on what evidence will be permitted in a case.

Typically, if the defendant loses a pretrial motion, he must wait until after a conviction to appeal that ruling. In extenuating circumstances, the defendant may seek a writ from the appellate court reversing the trial court's decision. Prosecutors may file an interlocutory appeal when the court grants a suppression motion. The prosecution may also file an immediate appeal when a case is dismissed before a jury is empanelled.

Plea Bargaining

Plea bargaining is a critical element of the criminal justice system. It is estimated that defendants plead guilty in more than 90 percent of all cases. Although some jurisdictions have resisted plea bargaining, it is fact of life in America. Without it, it is unlikely that the criminal justice system could process the number of cases that it does. For example, in Los Angeles County alone, over 1 million cases each year are filed. There are not enough courtrooms or judges to try all of these cases.

In deciding what type of deal to offer a defendant, prosecutors consider the nature of the charges, the strength of their case, the defendant's role in the crime, the costs of prosecuting the case, including the toll on witnesses and victims, the defendant's criminal history, and the need to enlist the defendant's cooperation in prosecuting other individuals. In federal court, judges do not participate in the plea bargaining negotiations, although they do in some state courts.

Plea bargains are ordinarily not binding on the courts, although judges are eager to resolve cases and most plea bargains are accepted. Strategically, prosecutors like to make deals "from the bottom up," thereby enlisting the cooperation of less culpable defendants to prosecute the major players in a crime.

Guilty Pleas

Most defendants end their cases with guilty pleas, not a trial. A guilty plea is both an admission by the defendant that he or she committed the crime, and a waiver of the defendant's constitutional right to trial. At a guilty plea, the court must ensure that the defendant knowingly and voluntarily waived his or her right. Accordingly, the court will typically advise a defendant at a guilty plea of the rights he is waiving, tell the consequences of pleading guilty (including the maximum possible sentence), inquire as to whether the plea is being coerced in any way, and ask for a factual basis for the plea. The factual basis for the plea may be provided by the defendant, his counsel, or the prosecutor.

Once a defendant pleads guilty, his case is terminated except for sentencing. Unless the defendant specifically reserves the right to do so in a conditional plea, the defendant waives most issues for appeal by pleading guilty.

For example, the defendant waives the right to argue that evidence was illegally obtained in the case.

A defendant may move to withdraw his guilty plea for good cause, but such a motion is rarely granted once it is indicated what sentence the defendant is likely to receive.

Pretrial Publicity, Change of Venue, and Gag Orders

A defendant may seek a change of venue when pretrial publicity has compromised his right to a fair trial. To succeed with such a motion, it is insufficient for the defendant to claim that jurors know about his case. Rather, he must demonstrate that they have formed opinions about the case and can no longer be fair jurors.

A judge may take several other step to protect a defendant's right to a fair trial from prejudicial pretrial publicity, including:

1   Delaying the start of the trial
2   Carefully screening potential jurors
3   Sequestering the jury
4   Instructing jurors to ignore pretrial publicity
5   Imposing gag orders on the participants

A gag order should only be imposed if the threat to a defendant's right to a fair trial outweighs the First Amendment right to speak and report on a case and the least restrictive gag order is imposed.

Speedy Trial Rights

A defendant has a Sixth Amendment right to a speedy and public trial. Charges must be filed against a defendant within the prescribed statute of limitations. The statute of limitations for most federal crimes is five years, but there are exceptions. For example, there is no statute of limitation on murder. Each state sets its own statute of limitation. Constitutionally, the due process clause covers preindictment delay. Delay does not violate due process unless it is made with bad faith and there is prejudice.

After a defendant is charged, the defendant is entitled to a speedy trial. Most jurisdictions have speedy trial acts that govern when a trial must begin. For example, the federal Speedy Trial Act requires that trial begin within 70 days, although there are many exceptions to the rule. Additionally, the Supreme Court set forth a four-part test in *Barker v. Wingo*, 407 U.S. 514 (1972). In determining whether there has been too much delay in starting the trial, the court must consider: (1) the length of the delay, (2) the reason for the delay, (3) whether the defendant asserted his right to a speedy trial, and (4) any prejudice from the delay. Absent any prejudice, it is very difficult to get a court to find a speedy trial violation, especially given that the remedy for such a violation is dismissal of the case with prejudice.

The trial in a case may be delayed for many reasons. Frequently, both sides need additional time to investigate the case, submit pretrial motions, and prepare their witnesses. It is not unusual in a major case for there to be months or even years of delay in getting to trial.

Jury vs. Court Trial

RIGHT TO JURY TRIAL

Under the Sixth Amendment, the defendant is entitled to a jury trial for any serious offense. A serious offense is any crime that is punishable by more than six months in jail, regardless of the punishment the defendant actually receives.

TWELVE-PERSON / UNANIMOUS JURIES NOT CONSTITUTIONALLY REQUIRED

Constitutionally, a defendant is entitled to a jury trial, but the Constitution does not prescribe the number of jurors that are required or whether the verdict must be unanimous. Federal rules require 12-person juries and unanimous verdicts. However, the Supreme Court has upheld as few as 6-person juries and has accepted split 9–3 verdicts.

JURY SELECTION

Jurors are selected from a panel (venire) of jurors. The size of venire depends on how many challenges the court expects to be exercised in a case. Once the venire is questioned in process called **voir dire**, the parties may exercise challenges to select the petite jury that will sit on the case. In reality, the parties do not pick their jurors; rather, they unpick jurors by excusing those jurors who they think will be least favorable to their side.

There are two types of challenges to jurors: (1) challenges for cause, and (2) peremptory challenges. There are unlimited challenges for cause, but they can only be exercised when a juror has demonstrated that he or she is biased and cannot be a fair juror on the case. Each side in a case has a limited number of peremptory challenges. They may be used for any reason, so long as they are not exercised to discriminate against a juror on the basis of race, gender, ethnicity, religion, and, in some jurisdictions, sexual orientation.

If a party (prosecution or defense) demonstrates a pattern of dismissing jurors on the basis of race or gender or other prohibited reasons, the opposing party may raise a **Batson motion** arguing that the challenge should be disallowed. The burden then shifts to the party exercising the peremptory challenge to show a nondiscriminatory reason for the challenge. In the end, the judge decides whether the challenge was proper.

ANONYMOUS JURIES

There has been a recent move to shield juror identities, but the use of anonymous juries remains controversial. Anonymous juries were originally used in organized crime cases as a way to protect jurors from retaliation. Proponents argue that anonymity makes jurors freer to reach a verdict of conscience. Opponents allege that anonymity makes jurors less accountable for their verdicts.

COURT TRIALS

If a defendant wishes to proceed with a court trial, he must waive his right to a jury trial. The prosecution also has the right to a jury trial so it must join in the waiver. A trial by the judge alone is called a *court* or **bench trial**. In addition to deciding what evidence will be admitted and the applicable law, the judge must decide whether the defendant is guilty or not guilty.

DEATH PENALTY CASES

Not every jurisdiction has the death penalty. Where the prosecution is seeking the death penalty, bifurcated proceedings are used. First, the jury is asked to determine whether the defendant is guilty of an offense that makes him eligible for the death penalty. Second, if the defendant is guilty of such an offense (e.g., first-degree murder with special circumstances), then there is a separate penalty phase in which the jury hears aggravating versus mitigating evidence to determine whether it should recommend the death penalty.

To sit on a capital case, jurors must be death-qualified. In other words, they must not have a conscientious objection to the death penalty that prohibits them from ever imposing the death penalty.

Trial Rights

RIGHT TO BE PRESENT AT TRIAL

In addition to the rights already discussed, a defendant has the right to be present at trial and to present evidence in his own defense. If a defendant flees before trial, the defendant should not be tried in absentia. However, if a defendant voluntarily absents himself during trial, the trial may continue.

The defendant has the right to appear in civilian clothing during trial. To the extent possible, security measures should also be shielded from the jury.

RIGHT OF CONFRONTATION

The general rule is that a defendant has the right to face-to-face confrontation of his accuser; namely, the prosecution witnesses. However, in exceptional situations, such as cases involving sexual assaults of children, the court has discretion to allow the child to testify via closed circuit television.

The defendant's right to confront witnesses includes not only the right to cross-examine prosecution witnesses, but also the right not to be tried by hearsay. Under the Supreme Court's key decision in *Crawford v. Washington*, 541 U.S. 36 (2004), testimonial evidence may not be introduced against a defendant unless the defendant had an opportunity to cross-examine the declarant and the declarant is unavailable for trial.

PROOF BEYOND A REASONABLE DOUBT

In a criminal case, the burden is on the prosecution to prove its case beyond a reasonable doubt. There is no precise definition of proof beyond a reasonable doubt, but it is the highest standard of proof used in any case. While no case can be proved beyond all doubt, the reasonable doubt standard requires that the jurors have the level of certainty they would need before making the most important decisions in their lives.

While the burden of proof is always on the prosecution, the defense may have the burden of coming forward with evidence to prove certain affirmative defenses, like duress or insanity.

JURY INSTRUCTIONS

The most critical aspect of a case is often the jury instructions. If the court errs in the jury instructions, the defendant has a basis for appeal. In federal court, proposed jury instructions are filed with the court early in the case and are an excellent source for determining what the prosecution must prove and what the defenses are likely to be.

ORDER OF PRESENTATION

At trial, the presentation to the jury begins with opening statements. The prosecution goes first because it bears the burden of proof. The defense may either give its opening statement at the beginning of the trial or wait until after the government's case and before the defense presents its evidence. Opening statements are supposed to be a roadmap of what each side will present in the case. Smart prosecutors will be upfront with weaknesses in their case so that jurors don't hear them for the first time from the defense.

After opening statements, the prosecution presents its case. Evidence includes witness testimony, physical exhibits, and stipulations. A stipulation is simply an agreement by both parties that something occurred. It may be a written or oral stipulation.

The defense has the opportunity to cross-examine each witness. After cross-examination, the prosecution can ask more questions on redirect.

In some rare cases, the questioning may go back and forth until the court cuts it off.

During the questioning of witnesses, the opposing counsel can object to the nature of the questions. The court rules on these objections. Sustaining the objection means the question was improper. If the court overrules the objection, it can be answered. When the court needs to hear lengthier arguments on objections, it may call the parties to sidebar to discuss the issue. Transcripts of sidebars should be available for the media, even though they involve discussions outside the presence of the jury.

After the prosecution presents all of its evidence, it rests. The defense will typically make a motion for acquittal, arguing insufficient evidence was presented to support a conviction. These motions are routinely denied because the legal standard requires that the court at this point view all of the evidence presented in the light most favorable to the prosecution.

The defense then has the option of presenting its own evidence, but it has no obligation to do so. In a case where the prosecution had problems with its presentation, the defense can simply argue that the prosecution did not prove its case beyond a reasonable doubt.

When the defense does present evidence, it ordinarily saves the defendant as the last witness, if the defendant is going to testify at all. Many factors need to be considered in deciding whether a defendant will testify. These include:

1   How strong was the government's case?
2   Does the defendant have a prior record?
3   Has the defendant made statements that can be used as impeachment?
4   What will defendant's appearance be like on the witness stand?
5   How sympathetic is the defendant?

The defendant traditionally testifies last so that he can hear everyone else's testimony before he takes the witness stand.

When all the evidence has been presented, the parties present closing arguments and the judge instructs the jury. The prosecution speaks twice in closing argument because it has the burden of proof. Prosecutors must be careful not to commit misconduct in their closing argument. Misconduct includes referring to the defendant's failure to testify, arguing evidence not in the record, commenting on evidence excluded by the court, and making religious arguments for conviction.

DELIBERATIONS

Once the jurors retire to deliberate, the only communications with the jurors should be in open court with both parties present. Ex parte communications with jurors are absolutely prohibited. Moreover, if jurors consult outside sources (e.g., the Internet, a newspaper, or even a dictionary) during deliberations, that inquiry may provide a basis for the defendant to attack a conviction. After a verdict, the defendant may submit affidavits by jurors to support a motion for a new trial. Although statements by jurors about their actual deliberations are generally inadmissible, information regarding outside contacts is allowed.

There is no rule as to how long jurors will or should deliberate in a case. Although many people believe that a quick verdict is good for the prosecution, the opposite may be true, as it was in the famous O. J. Simpson case. Jurors get into their own rhythm for a case. It is difficult to know how deliberations are proceeding, unless jurors submit questions during the deliberations. Although it is a bit like reading tea leaves, the questions can sometimes indicate what issues are of concern to the jury.

Occasionally, jurors are dismissed during deliberations. A juror who disagrees with other jurors should not be dismissed, but a jury who refuses to deliberate may be dismissed. Jurors may also be dismissed for violating the court's orders, having failed to reveal pertinent information during the jury selection process, or for illness or personal reasons. If a juror is removed, the rules of the jurisdiction then govern whether an alternate is put in the juror's place or deliberations continue with only 11 jurors, as they do in federal court.

If jurors indicate they cannot reach a decision, the judge has the option of giving an **Allen charge**, which is a jury instruction that encourages jurors to reach a verdict. The judge must be very careful in giving this instruction not to pressure holdout jurors to arbitrarily change their votes.

If the jurors cannot reach a verdict, it is called a **hung jury**, and a mistrial is declared. The case can be retried.

VERDICTS

Jurors generally return **general verdicts** that indicate whether the defendant is guilty or not guilty of an offense. Occasionally, jurors are asked to make specific findings about a case. Those special findings are included on a **special verdict** form.

Jurors have the power to engage in **jury nullification**. Jury nullification is when jurors disregard the law and vote to acquit a defendant who should otherwise be found guilty. Once a defendant is acquitted, the defendant cannot be retried because of double jeopardy rights.

Sentencing

If a defendant is convicted, the court will schedule a future date for sentencing. Prior to sentencing, the court will receive a report from the probation department regarding the defendant, as well as sentencing memoranda from the prosecution and defense. Motions for a new trial are also frequently heard at the sentencing hearing or before that date.

At the time of sentencing, the court must permit the defendant to speak to the court. Depending on the jurisdiction, there may also be an opportunity for victims to address the court. Sentencing systems vary by jurisdiction. If the court is relying on an enhancement to sentence a defendant beyond the ordinary term for his violation, the court must have a jury finding to support the enhancement unless it relates solely to the defendant's prior criminal record.

Many jurisdictions now have three strikes laws that dramatically increase the sentences of repeat offenders. For example, under California law, a defendant subject to punishment under its three strikes law may receive a sentence of 50 years to life imprisonment, even though his last conviction was not a violent offense. The law creates harsh punishment for defendants convicted of enumerated serious offenses, which include narcotics, burglary, and other nonviolent offenses. The judge has the discretion to strike prior offenses to avoid the three-strikes law (in California, these are referred to as *Romero motions*), but there is a tremendous amount of political pressure on the court not to be lenient on these offenders.

A judge does not get to decide where a defendant will serve his prison term. That is a decision for the Bureau of Prisons. The judge can only make a recommendation. The judge may also delay the beginning of the sentence so that the defendant can get his affairs in order.

The potential sentence a defendant faces is set forth in the statutes for that jurisdiction. However, it is important to check with the prosecutors to see how the sentencing laws of the jurisdiction will actually affect the possible sentence in that case. Sentencing laws can be quite complicated, especially if the court has the discretion to run sentences concurrently or consecutively. Moreover, if the jurisdiction has a parole system, the defendant may only serve in jail a fraction of the actual sentence imposed.

A defendant may be ordered to pay a fine and/or restitution as part of his sentence. A fine is paid to the government; restitution is paid to the victims.

Probationary sentences may also be imposed. Judges typically have great discretion in determining the terms of probation. They may include house arrest, community service, or even creative sentences, like reconciliation meetings with the victim. A *split sentence* is a sentence in which the defendant serves a period of time in custody and a period of time on probation. If a defendant violates probation, he is sent to jail to serve a custodial sentence.

A defendant sentenced to a short period of incarceration is typically sent to a local jail. For more serious crimes, a defendant will be sent to a prison somewhere in the jurisdiction's penal system. Defendants convicted of federal crimes can be sent to a federal prison anywhere in the United States. The prisons have different security classifications, ranging from the super-max prison in Florence, Colorado, that holds defendants like Zacharias Moussaoui to Club Feds, which are prison camps for low-security inmates.

After a defendant serves a portion of his sentence, he may become eligible for parole. A paroled defendant remains under the supervision of corrections officials. A violation of parole may result in the defendant returning to prison to serve the remainder of his sentence.

Sentences are lawful if they comply with statutory requirements and are not cruel and unusual. The test for whether a sentence is cruel and unusual is whether the sentence is disproportional. To determine this issue, the court looks at: (1) the gravity of the offense, (2) how the sentence compares to sentences for other crimes in that jurisdiction, and (3) how the sentence compares to sentences for the same crime in other jurisdictions. It is extremely rare for a sentence to be found disproportional.

Appeals

All defendants have the right to an initial appeal after a conviction. An appeal notice ordinarily must be filed within 10 days of a conviction. It may take months or years for an appeal to be heard by the court. It is not unusual for a defendant to seek new counsel to represent him on appeal. Issues for appeal may range from evidentiary rulings in the trial to challenges to the jury instructions. If a defendant claims the evidence was insufficient to support his conviction, the appellate court is required to view all evidence in the light most favorable to the prosecution in making its decision.

On appeal, factual findings by the trial court are reviewed under a clearly erroneous standard. Great deference is given to the trial court's findings since the trial court had the opportunity to assess the credibility of the witnesses. Issues of law receive a de novo review (i.e., are decided with no deference) by the appellate court.

Appellate courts typically sit in three-justice panels to decide appeals. Oral argument for appeals is quite different from arguments at trial. It is much more formal and consists primarily of the appellate justices asking questions after initial arguments by each of the parties.

If a defendant wins on appeal, his conviction is vacated or reversed. Unless the appellate court finds the evidence was insufficient for a conviction (in which case, the defendant is thereby acquitted on that count), the case is sent back (remanded) back to the trial court for a new trial. If a conviction is affirmed, the rulings of the lower court stand.

In rare cases, the initial ruling by the appellate panel will be reheard by a court en banc. The en banc court is the full appellate bench. A defendant may also file a petition for certiorari for review by a state or U.S. Supreme Court. The high court has the discretion to decide whether to hear these cases. Death penalty cases ordinarily have the right of automatic review by the state supreme court.

Habeas Corpus and Collateral Challenges

In addition to appealing a conviction, a defendant might file a collateral challenge to a conviction, claiming a constitutional violation in his case. For example, the defendant may claim that he was denied his Sixth Amendment right because he had ineffective assistance of counsel or that he was denied his right to a fair trial because the prosecution withheld exculpatory evidence.

Defendants frequently file their own habeas petitions because they are not entitled to lawyers once their appeals are completed. These proceedings often get bogged down in procedural rules that set deadlines for the filing of petitions and prohibit the filing of consecutive petitions, except in limited circumstances.

Although it is rare for habeas petitions to be granted, defendants occasionally succeed when DNA testing indicates that the defendant could not have been responsible for the crime. The court sets a very high threshold for showings of actual innocence justifying the grant of a habeas corpus petition.

Double Jeopardy

The Fifth Amendment guarantees that no person shall "be subject for the same offense to be twice put in jeopardy of life or limb." In reality, that means that a defendant cannot be tried twice for the same offense, except under limited circumstances.

The focus of the double jeopardy clause is on trying a defendant twice. Jeopardy does not attach until the jury is sworn or, in a court trial, the first witness is called. Thus, the government can appeal the pretrial dismissal of a case because the defendant has not yet been subject to trial.

There are many exceptions to the double jeopardy rule. Despite the double jeopardy clause, the following is permitted:

- Retrial following a hung jury.
- Retrial after a reversal on appeal.
- Sentencing for multiple offenses related to a single set of facts.
- A government appeal from a court's dismissal of a case.
- A government appeal if a judge grants an acquittal after a jury has convicted.
- Prosecutions by separate sovereigns (i.e., federal prosecution after unsuccessful state prosecutions). This is known as the principle of *dual sovereignty*.
- Successive prosecution for a different crime arising from the same set of facts, so long as the new crime does not have identical elements as the prior offense. This is known as the *Blockburger Rule*.

If a mistrial is ordered at trial, there may or may not be a double jeopardy bar to retrying the case. If the defense caused the mistrial or the mistrial was caused by manifest necessity, then retrial is allowed. However, the prosecution cannot cause a mistrial and then retry the defendant.

Execution and Clemency

Many executions in this country are currently on hold as the courts try to determine whether the method of execution violates the prohibition against cruel and unusual punishment. In addition to challenging his conviction and sentence in court, a defendant may also seek clemency from the governor of his state. Clemency is not a formal legal proceeding. Rather, it is a request for grace. The governor has complete discretion in deciding whether to grant clemency.

Prisoner Rights

Prisoners have limited rights in custody. If they feel their rights have been violated, they bring civil suits under 18 U.S.C. § 1983 challenging the conditions of their imprisonment. To show their treatment is cruel and unusual, an inmate must show that the prison officials have acted with deliberate indifference with respect to the conditions of confinement. Thus, it is insufficient to show that the inmate received poor health care or faced unsafe conditions in confinement. The inmate must show that the prison officials were on notice of the problem and deliberately ignored the problem.

Conclusion

As emphasized throughout this chapter, each jurisdiction may set its own rules regarding the procedure for handling criminal cases. So long as these procedures comply with minimum federal constitutional principles, they are permitted.

Notes

1 So far, the lowest level of aerial surveillance that the Supreme Court has authorized was 400 feet by a low-flying helicopter. See *Florida v. Riley*, 488 U.S. 445 (1989). It is an open question whether drones that fly directly into someone's yard would be permitted.
2 In *Kyllo v. United States*, 533 U.S. 27 (2001), the U.S. Supreme Court held that new technology, such as thermal imaging devices, could not be used to search a house if it could reveal intimate details about the conduct of individuals in the home. However, Justice Scalia noted that this limitation would not apply once technology was in common usage.
3 *United States v. Jones*, 132 S. Ct. 945, 181 L. Ed. 2d 911 (2012).

4 For more information regarding the problems with eyewitness identifications, see "Cover Story: Eyewitness Identification Evidence," *Science and Reform*, 29 Champion 12 (Nat'l Assoc. of Criminal Defense Lawyers 2005); Symposium: Reforming Eyewitness Identification: Convicting the Guilty, Protecting the Innocent, 4 *Cardozo Pub. L. Pol'y & Ethics J*. 233 (2006); Henry Weinstein, Commission Urges Changes in Use of Eyewitness Identifications, *L.A. Times*, 14 Apr. 2006, p. B3; Anne Constable, Eyewitness Identification Has Shortcomings, Some Say. *Santa Fe New Mexican*, 8 Dec. 2002, p. A1.

5 Torts

John T. Nockleby
Professor of Law and Director of the Civil
Justice Program, Loyola Law School,
Los Angeles

The civil justice system involves many different types of claims, including cases as diverse as divorce, contracts, and zoning. Cases might be profoundly important, such as constitutional disputes between states, or involve local small claims between two strangers, such as routine fender benders. One type of civil suit involves tort claims. Because tort suits are often covered in the media, and regulate a wide range of conduct, this chapter will outline some of the most common tort disputes that arise.

What Is a Tort? General Definition

Tort is a French word meaning "wrong." Torts consist of injuries to person or property usually not involving enforcement of a contract. Tort law is enforced through lawsuits brought by individuals or entities who believe they've suffered injury. In contrast to crimes, which are brought by government prosecutors, the rights protected by tort law must be enforced by the individual person or entity. Ordinarily the state is not a party except when the state itself brings a lawsuit to enforce tort rights.

Tort law arose as judge-made law. As described in the introduction (chapter 1), tort law is part of the common law system in which judges make the law. Judges have historically determined what behaviors constitute those wrongs that are subject to redress. Apart from a few special situations, tort law is also a matter of state law, not federal law. State legislatures of course may change the common law consistent with individual state constitutions, or adopt new torts or modify ancient ones, but in the United States, state courts continue to modify their state's tort law in accordance with judicial judgment.

Many torts have ancient roots in the English common law, going back hundreds of years. However, judges have historically been willing to transform tort law—sometimes dramatically—if they are persuaded that changed conditions or a different policy judgment requires it.

The fact that courts create new rights, destroy others, or modify existing rights and duties is not unusual. But, it is important to recognize that if a state

News Flash! Judges Destroy Ancient Rights!

Action for Seduction had Roots in 14th Century; "Civilization Threatened" if Men Can't Legally Control Wives, Daughters, Group Asserts; Southern High Courts Fight Trend

At common law, a father could bring a suit for seduction against a male who had sexual relations with his daughter. Even if the woman was an adult, her seduction was regarded as an injury to the father. The action derived from the early common law action of enticement. Suits for seduction were very common in the latter party of the 19th century.

Two other judge-created torts, alienation of affections and criminal conversation, gave husbands the right to sue an interloper for inducing his wife's affections (*alienation*), or engaging in sexual intercourse (*criminal conversation*). During the 20th century, courts gradually eliminated these torts. By 1995, 42 of the 51 U.S. jurisdictions had abolished the causes of action either by judicial decree or legislation. Those that retained the torts (e.g., North Carolina, Utah) typically extended the rights to wives whose husbands had been enticed by other women.

high court makes such changes, it is necessarily changing the understandings that were in place up until that moment.

The array of torts is extensive: negligence claims to defamation to toxic torts to product defects. Although the precise contours of each tort may differ, they may generally be classed into three categories: intentional torts; negligence; and strict liability. Neither of the latter two torts requires proof of intent, and thus are known as *unintentional torts*.

New Yak Observer "all da newz all da time!"

Extra! Extra! Judges Create New Tort!

New Action Permits Recovery for Intentionally Causing "Emotional Distress;" Bullies Associations and Collection Agencies Fight New Tort; Practical Jokers Fearful

Courts today recognize different torts that permit recovery for mental distress. Prior to the 1930's, it was difficult for someone to bring a separate suit for emotional distress. It was possible to recover for emotional injury only if one sought emotional distress damages associated with another tort such as battery or trespass. Over a period of many years most state courts recognized a new tort, called "intentional infliction of emotional distress," although the exact contours of the tort remain controversial. In more recent years the state courts have also allowed recovery for negligently-inflicted emotional distress.

Intentional torts, as the name implies, require some proof of intentional interference with another's rights in person or property. Intentional torts include most types of fraud, battery, intentional infliction of emotional distress, much defamation, and certain business torts such as unfair competition and interference with others' contracts.

Both negligence and strict liability torts involve claims that someone interfered with another's rights, but did so unintentionally. The most common tort, negligence, covers most unintentional harms. As the name implies, under this tort one is liable to another for causing harms only if one has acted negligently, which in legal parlance means exposing others to unreasonable risks. In contrast, the strict liability torts require proof that someone caused another harm, but do not require a showing that the actor behaved unreasonably. The most common strict liability torts involve hazardous materials or products.

Types of Torts (illustrations)

Intentional torts

Battery
Assault
Interference with another's contract
Fraud and misrepresentation
Trespass to chattels (personal property)
Invasion of Privacy
Intentional Infliction of emotional distress

Unintentional Torts

Negligence, including Wrongful death
Strict Liability for abnormally dangerous activities

Mixed doctrines (sometimes require proof of intent; sometimes can be unintentional)

Trespass to land
Nuisance
Unfair competition
Product disparagement
Defamation
Products liability

Intentional Torts

By definition, intentional torts require proof that the defendant acted intentionally. This is easier to state in theory than to establish in practice. The eminent legal scholar and (eventual) Supreme Court Justice Oliver Wendell Holmes famously said that even a dog understands the difference between being kicked and being stumbled over.

Because the legal system tends to treat intentionally causing injury more seriously than injuries negligently or unintentionally caused, it is frequently important to differentiate intentional torts from unintentional torts. In theory, drawing the distinction shouldn't be too difficult.

For example, suppose you knock someone off a barstool when you pass by in a crowded bar, and the person suffers serious injury. Are you liable? Lawyers will ask whether you tried to kick the stool (intentional, battery); ignored the fact that the stool was unstable when you rushed past (unintentional, negligence); or merely brushed up against the stool as you passed by (no liability because neither intentional nor done negligently).

The more difficult cases of intent involve behaviors that are intentional in some respect, but not necessarily in the respect that the legal system requires. Does a factory that knows its smoke is harmful commit a battery when it

---

Examples of Intentional Torts & Defenses to Them

I   Intentional Torts (partial list)

Injuries to person

    A   Battery and assault
    B   Intentional infliction of emotional distress
    C   Invasion of privacy

Injuries to property

    D   Trespass to land
    E   Trespass to chattels (personal property)

Injuries to economic relationships

    F   Fraud and misrepresentation
    G   Unfair competition
    H   Inducing breach of contract

II   Defenses to Intentional Torts

    A   Consent
    B   Self-defense
    C   Defense of property
    D   Privilege of necessity

continues to produce the smoke despite knowing the harmful effects on its neighbors' lungs? Does a pharmaceutical manufacturer that hides dangerous side effects of a particular drug commit a battery when it continues to sell its drug into the market without warning of the danger? If I blow cigarette smoke, knowing you are sensitive to the smoke, have I acted intentionally?

While not fully settled, many courts have distinguished among intentional acts based on the likelihood of injury to a specific person or small group of known individuals. So, if a manufacturer knowingly sells a contaminated product likely to injure others, that would satisfy the requirements of an intentional tort. On the other hand, if a manufacturer fails to give prompt notice of a *risk* of injury that doesn't create a substantial likelihood of harm to occur to a specific person or small group of persons, that has been typically treated as an unintentional act.

In contrast, the smoker's liability is complicated by another doctrine—courts often must draw lines between behavior that is socially acceptable and that which is not (see Battery and Assault).

Battery and Assault

A *battery* is a harmful or offensive intentional touching of another outside the bounds of pleasantry without consent. Some cases are easy: everyone understands a punch in the nose or an unwanted sexual pawing. However, several issues make this tort more problematic.

Consider how the tort law treats unwanted touchings by children. In one famous case, a 5-year-old boy pulled a chair away in which his aunt was about to sit. The court said the kid (not his parents) was liable since he understood when he grabbed the chair that his aunt would likely hit the ground. In another case, an 11 year old who reached across the aisle during school and touched or kicked another kid on the shin was held liable for thousands of dollars of damage when the kick exacerbated a pre-existing injury. In neither of these cases was it considered relevant that the kid was not actually trying to harm another person. The courts held that so long as each kid knew that *some* harmful or offensive contact was likely to result, that was enough.

Another issue that arises concerns the issue of socially acceptable or "consented" touchings. You have a right not to be touched in your person, but standing on a crowded bus or subway creates inevitable jostling that courts say is expectable. Even though cigarette smoke is known to be harmful, some courts have determined that in a crowded world, some contacts with your body are inevitable. Unsurprisingly, courts located in states in which tobacco is an important product are more likely to find that inhaling second-hand smoke is a risk that people must endure merely by living in a modern society.

Like battery, the tort of assault is an intentional tort. However, whereas battery requires some contact with the person, assault requires only that the plaintiff apprehend an imminent harmful or offensive contact. Thus, throwing a bat at the plaintiff but missing is an assault if the plaintiff anticipated she was about to be hit. Threatening another with a punch might be an assault if the actor threatens immediate violence; telephoning a threat is not an assault (though it might be a different tort).

Another common issue that arises concerns the often violent contact that occurs in the sporting context. Periodically one hears reports that a football team set out to physically disable another player. Can such conduct constitute battery? In general, the answer is no, provided that the contact occurred during the ordinary course of play. It's only if the behavior is so outside ordinary play, and arises to the level of recklessness toward the safety of another player, that courts have created a small window of redress.

Intentional Infliction of Emotional Distress

In the classic formulation, a plaintiff claiming intentional infliction of emotional distress must establish four requirements: (1) the defendant acted intentionally or recklessly; (2) the defendant's conduct was extreme and outrageous; and this conduct (3) caused (4) plaintiff severe emotional distress. Anyone who's ever been in love, been called terrible names, or had a job involving a nasty supervisor has probably experienced emotional distress as a result of another's behavior. Courts have wrestled with the challenge of defining outrageous behavior in a way that targets the worst behaviors without sweeping up all uncivil behavior.

For example, the vagueness of the outrageousness standard opens the door to widely differing interpretations of acceptable social behavior. It also calls into question whether there is a single standard of outrageousness, or whether the standard is likely to shift from one setting to another. Many courts and commentators have worried about the vagueness of the standard, and some have attempted to identify common factors. Frequent contexts in which the tort has been invoked include serious threats of violence; repetitious collection efforts by bill collectors; blackmail; threats to embarrass; or threats that target particularly vulnerable members of the society such as children and pregnant women.

Defamation

What Is Defamation?

Defamation is a false statement of fact about another person, communicated to a third party, that negatively affects the individual's reputation in the community. Lawyers are frequently asked about slurs (such as *a**hole*, *fatso*), but these words, although hurtful, are not verifiable as statements of "fact," so cannot be the subject of defamatory actions. Nor can words not reasonably taken as true (such as calling a woman a *b**ch*; or words obviously understood as satire or hyperbole) be made the subject of a defamation action. Nonetheless, words such as *slut*, perhaps also intended as slurs, carry meanings that are verifiable and thus can be defamatory.

The tort action for defamation is centuries-old, yet has seen substantial modification in recent years because many communications that under the old common law were punishable as defamatory are today protected under the First Amendment. As a result, some of the special rules governing defamation are hoary; and some are of very recent origin.

In classical terms, defamation was either oral (*slander*) or written (*libel*), so special rules developed depending on whether the communication was one or the other. Today, the distinction persists, but most courts are likely to limit slander to spoken words not recorded, while defamation includes not only published words, but spoken words on radio or television, at least where the words are recorded in some fashion.

Some words have historically been regarded as so damaging that they are regarded as per se defamatory, which essentially results in a lessoning of the plaintiff's burden of proof. These categories include: allegations that someone carries a loathsome disease (such as an STD); that someone has engaged in sexual impropriety (e.g., adultery); someone has committed a serious crime; or attacks that challenges a person's competence in their profession. Such charges are assumed to undermine a person's character.

Many people assume that opinion is also protected speech, since one can in good faith hold an opinion even if it is factually false (e.g., "I believe the world is flat"). But this is not the case: someone can incorporate a falsehood into a statement of opinion, such as "I believe Tom Smith slept with his neighbor's wife." In such mixed fact-and-opinion statements, courts attempt to discern whether the author is actually asserting the underlying falsehood.

If the person about whom the alleged defamation has been made is either a public official or a public figure, special rules apply. The terms *public official* and *public figure* are terms of art. Public official generally means a person in government who exercises power (e.g., an elected official or an appointed bureaucrat, and possibly a police officer; but not a secretary). A public figure in turn is either is either well-known in the society (e.g., movie stars; television hosts; high officials in corporate America like Warren Buffet or Bill Gates), or private citizens who have become active in some dispute (and are therefore "limited" public figures as to that dispute).

In a series of important First Amendment cases beginning in 1964, the U.S. Supreme Court held that states could not simply follow the centuries-old common law when it came to defamation of such persons. Instead, public officials and public figures had to prove that the defamatory statement was made either with knowledge of the falsehood or with reckless disregard for whether it was false. This heightened standard of proof meant that if a reporter merely failed to check a quote, or even if they were negligent in reporting a story, they could not be held liable for defamation.

Furthermore, suppose the person claiming defamation is a private person (not a public figure or a public official). As to this group, there's a further test. If the underlying matter is of importance to the public (in technical terms, "a matter of public concern"), then the person claiming defamation must prove that the publisher was at fault when the defamatory content was published. However, if the underlying matter is not of public concern, the state may impose liability without fault.

Defenses to Defamation Suits

Even if someone has written words that defame another, there are some important defenses. Truth is always a defense to a defamation suit. Allegations made in open court, whether by lawyers, judges, or witnesses, are absolutely privileged, as are defamatory statements made by a legislator on the floor of the chamber. Further, when petitioning the government, people are privileged to make false claims.

Moreover, high government officials are privileged to defame people when exercising the power vested in them. The idea behind this latter defense is not to absolve government officials per se, but rather to acknowledge that if an official could be sued every time she spoke she would have no time for anything other than defending lawsuits. In addition, there's an implicit recognition that press reports will often pressure government officials to correct their errors.

In addition to these defenses, there are some important limited or qualified privileges. The most important among the qualified privileges include the common interest privilege; and the privilege of fair comment. The common interest privilege allows those who are in a group (e.g., a condominium association; or a private citizens organization) to make defamatory comments about a matter of common concern to other members of the group so long at the speaker isn't reckless with the truth. The fair comment privilege protects reviewers (such as restaurant or hotel reviewers) who make erroneous statements in good faith.

Invasion of Privacy

The word *privacy* encompasses many meanings. Many journalists are familiar with the constitutional right of privacy represented by the contraception and abortion decisions, for example. These rights involve *decisional* privacy.

In contrast to decisional privacy cases, the privacy *torts* address the extent to which one may control *information* about oneself. Typically, privacy torts involve *intrusion* into another's affairs, or *misuse* or *disclosure* of private information about someone to other people.

Three interrelated themes characterize the privacy torts. First, the doctrines reflect a deep-seated conflict between public and private information. If tort law protects private but not public information from disclosure, the tort law signifies the values the line protects. If some event occurs in a public space, may anyone capture that information and redistribute it without penalty? And, if so, how do we define public spaces?

The answer to these questions at one time was relatively clear: conduct that occurs in a public space can be recorded and replayed by others without running afoul of the privacy torts. But many recent technologies have called this generalization into question. For example, suppose I record your conversation from 50 feet away using a directional mike, or use infrared technologies to "see" into your home. Or suppose I purchase from your cell phone provider GPS tracking information that shows where your phone has traveled over the last six months. Newer technologies are challenging old privacy canards, and no definitive answer to these or similar questions can be stated with confidence.

Second, the privacy torts reflect a continuing tension between the desire to promote the free flow of information (sometimes represented by the imperative of the First Amendment rights of free speech and press), as against the interest in not having debilitating or embarrassing information about oneself "proclaimed from the house-tops," as a famous article by Samuel Warren and Louis Brandeis article described it in 1890.[1]

The problem of spreading harmful information is not new. The eavesdropper, or a person who literally stood outside dwellings, has been roundly castigated for centuries. But if information is truly private, may the information be distributed under the protection of the First Amendment?

In a series of cases extending back 30 years, the U.S. Supreme Court has found that the First Amendment restricts what states may define as private under state tort law or state statutory law. In one case, a state forbade publication of a rape victim's name, but the police mistakenly posted the victim's name on a wall accessible to journalists, and one paper published the name. The court said that the government could not punish the paper since the government itself had released the name.

Third, as technology has developed more prying mechanisms, privacy concerns have become much more pronounced. Intrusions obtained using familiar (to us) technologies such as wiretapping and surreptitious photography were the grist of 20th-century privacy cases. The 21st century is more likely to see increasing privacy claims based on abuse of databases, infrared imagers, and Radio-Frequency Identification (RFID) chips.

Two privacy torts arise with some frequency: the intrusion tort; and the so-called publicity tort. The intrusion tort requires the plaintiff to prove three things:

1 intentional intrusion, physically or otherwise,
2 intrusion was upon the solitude or seclusion of another or his private affairs or concerns, and
3 proof that the intrusion would be highly offensive to a reasonable person.

Intrusion can be accomplished in a variety of forms. Tapping phones, rummaging in another's private papers, placing cameras in private spaces (such as dressing areas), are all examples. When the intrusion tort was found inadequate to protect people from "close following" or stalking, however, several legislatures enacted anti-stalking statutes.

Many difficult privacy intrusion cases arise that challenge the line between public and private. For example, in 1964, a newspaper photographer positioned himself outside a local fairgrounds fun house where jets of air blew from below. He snapped a shot of a 44-year-old married woman whose dress had been lifted by the blown air, exposing her lower body including her panties. The Alabama Supreme Court held this was an invasion of privacy and upheld an award of $4,166 to her. It's not clear that the case would be decided the same way today, or considered as shocking in a different jurisdiction, for the idea of privacy shifts with the culture.

In another case arising in California, the plaintiff was severely injured in an automobile collision. A local television station, developing a story on emergency rescues, miked the emergency nurse and had a camera operator follow the nurse as she spoke to the patient who was still trapped in the car, and then after she was lifted onto a helicopter ambulance. The station sought the permission of the private ambulance company (but not the victim) to record the conversation. The California Supreme Court held that a jury could conclude that placing a mike on the nurse and recording the nurse's communications to the victim and other rescuers, and filming in the air ambulance, would be "highly offensive to a reasonable person" and thus triggered the intrusion tort.

One of the most significant issues raising privacy concerns today is the accumulation of vast amounts of data about millions of citizens in private databanks. Many databases are maintained by local, state, and federal governments. Banks, insurance companies, credit card companies, and other commercial enterprises also sell data. The digitalization of information has created a fearsome capacity to store, search, and interlink all these databases. Most importantly, programmers can generate algorithms that can connect seemingly unrelated databits about individuals, and thereby develop comprehensive psychographic profiles of people—encompassing characteristics such as opinions, attitudes, beliefs, and lifestyles.

Early cases challenging retention of transactional data by credit card companies on privacy grounds have been unsuccessful. In a 1995 case against American Express, an Illinois appellate court concluded that retaining transactional data and compiling and selling lists of customers based upon that data did not constitute an intrusion.

Although the intrusion tort is useful in protecting against certain types of privacy invasions (e.g., snooping into the remote desk of one's neighbor while on a social call), much privacy law involving communications and data is now addressed by federal and state statutes. The patchwork of state and federal statutes includes: federal laws such as the Electronic Communications Privacy Act; the Computer Fraud and Abuse Act; the Privacy Protection Act; the Privacy Act; the Fair Credit Reporting Act; plus a wide variety of state statutes.

A second privacy tort, giving publicity to private affairs, is also invoked with some frequency. Once again, the dividing line between public and private is often at issue. In addition, because these cases often target publications, the First Amendment is frequently invoked as a defense. The tort gives a cause of action if all four elements are satisfied:

1   The defendant gave publicity to a matter.
2   The matter concerned the private life of another.
3   The publicity would be highly offensive to a reasonable person.
4   The matter is not of legitimate public concern.

A number of high profile suits have been filed against media outlets stemming from investigative journalism, but many of these cases have protected *publication* of the private information, provided the investigators did not violate law in obtaining the information (or otherwise commit violations of the intrusion tort). For example, the Supreme Court has held that broadcasting the contents of an illegally intercepted cellular telephone conversation about a public issue was protected under the First Amendment where the broadcaster had nothing to do with the interception and received the tape from an anonymous mailer.

Similarly, in *Desnick v. American Broadcasting Co.*, television journalists sent testers posing as patients into several offices of an ophthalmic surgeon to determine whether unnecessary surgeries were being performed. Equipped with concealed cameras, the testers secretly videotaped two doctors examining them. Although remanding to determine whether the ensuing broadcast was defamatory, the court held that the means the testers used to gain entry into the offices and to make surreptitious recordings did not violate the examining physicians' rights to privacy.

Trespass to Land; Nuisance; Trespass to Chattels (Personal Property); and Conversion

The trespass tort protects a lawful occupier of land from physical intrusions onto the land, while the conversion and trespass to chattels torts guard against interferences with personal possessions. Trespass to land is an intentional tort, but the only intent required is intent to enter the property. So, a person who unwittingly enters another's land may be liable for a technical trespass.

Trespass to chattels requires intentional interference with possession, such as where a defendant damages the property or temporarily takes property from the plaintiff. Conversion is a more serious interference with personal

192 *John T. Nockleby*

property. If your neighbor borrows your roto-tiller for a weekend without your permission, it's a trespass to chattels. If he keeps it for a year, it's a conversion.

A more challenging property tort is nuisance. Nuisance is defined as an unreasonable and substantial interference with the use and/or enjoyment of land, such as where a defendant's factory produces unhealthy fumes over plaintiff's land. Two questions in nuisance cases arise regularly. First, how much interference will trigger the tort? And second, how does a court balance competing and inconsistent uses of property? Both of these questions focus on how courts will balance legal and often socially useful but competing and inconsistent uses of neighboring land.

As to the first, courts have been unwilling to permit de minimus interferences to trigger the tort. For example, if your neighbor keeps horses (within the zoning law) whose smell wafts through your yard, you will ordinarily have no suit unless the smell is profoundly disruptive. In contrast, air pollution created many dilemmas for 20th-century courts. In one view of property, *any* interference with another's use or enjoyment of his land should be enjoined. But courts quickly realized that such an approach would stifle development (*progress* in the 19th-century vocabulary), so quickly relaxed the standards to require substantial interference.

A related question asks how courts should balance uses that are incompatible with each other. Consider how courts should balance competing interests in sunlight. Can I build my high-rise even though it casts a shadow over your swimming pool? Or suppose suburban sprawl creeps closer to cattle feedlots and the suburbanites complain about the smell. These cases explicitly invoke public policy, often in ways that advantage the more powerful economic interest in the community.

In the Boomer case, decided in 1970 by the highest court of New York, a $45 million cement factory that employed hundreds belched smoke and fumes over a wide swath, creating unhealthy conditions. The neighbors sued to prevent further damage to their land. The court declared the factory a nuisance, but held that the neighbors would not be permitted to shut it down despite the ongoing nature of the harm to their land. Instead, the court decided that the factory should pay for the impairment of the plaintiffs' use of land, but even if conditions were so unhealthful that the plaintiffs could not remain on the land the court would not grant an injunction to shut down the factory.

Fraud and Misrepresentation

Fraud is a false representation of fact intended to deceive and that deceives another who relies on it to his legal detriment. Deceptively simple to state, fraud is a concept fraught with nuance and complexity.

Part of the complexity stems from the fact fraud is a communication tort. The same subtleties available to experienced novelists can be employed in negotiations over property, commercial business dealings, and all forms of economic transactions. Defining exactly what was represented can be difficult when negotiations go on for months, and when people use evaluative terms such as "the best on the market," "enormously capable," and "you can't miss with this stock." Moreover, the range of possible business dealings to which the tort may be applied is extensive. Negotiations may go on for months; conditions may change; people anxious to secure a transaction may puff their abilities or the capacity of the thing being sold.

The simplest cases of fraud involve the transfer of property. Frank tells a blind purchaser that his hogs weigh 350 pounds when they only weigh 300 pounds, and the trusting buyer overpays. Or, I assure you that the historic mansion you are about to buy from me has never had termites, knowing full well the statement is false, and you commit to the transaction unawares that the buggers have decimated the ancient woodwork and dramatically devalued the property. Although these are straightforward illustrations of fraud, most cases are not so simple.

Suppose, for example, that Frank misread the scale; or that the hog buyer isn't blind but simply failed to look at the scales; or that Frank weighed the hogs as a favor to the seller and didn't benefit from the sale; or the hogs' weight was estimated; or that the scales are defective; or that an ordinary buyer would have realized the hogs couldn't weigh so much; or that the weight was correct at the time of weighing but not at the time of sale; or that the hogs were being purchased for breeding rather than slaughter, so the weight differential was insignificant. We can add more variations, but the one thing clear about fraud cases is that every permutation imaginable has ended up in court at one time or another.

The legal requirements for proving fraud obscure the difficult cases. A plaintiff claiming fraud must establish five elements:

1   A false statement of a material fact,
2   Knowledge on the part of the defendant that the statement is untrue,
3   Intent on the part of the defendant to deceive the alleged victim,
4   Justifiable reliance by the alleged victim on the statement, and
5   Legally relevant injury to the alleged victim as a result.

Of these factors, we will discuss elements one and four.

False Statement of a Material Fact

This element is designed to reduce the types of representations that might be made about a thing or transaction to those that are misrepresentations of fact. This means that the used car salesman who promises "the ride of your life," or who guarantees sexual bliss with that Red Camero has no liability. The advertisement promising "relief," or the billboard showing a hunky cowboy enjoying a smoke, is considered *puffery*—not representations of fact.

By requiring that misrepresentations be about material facts, courts are attempting to thwart lawsuits in which factual misrepresentations likely had no bearing on the outcome of a negotiation. So if you're going to misrepresent the condition of that pricey mansion, better state that the porch was painted 8 years ago (instead of 10), or that the heating bill is only $550 per month (rather than $600). Little lies aren't fraudulent, at least not in law.

What if the seller of property knows about a condition that would be clearly material to a transaction, but merely fails to tell the buyer? In other words, the seller fails to disclose rather than actively misrepresents. The first cases that came up involved sellers who covered over obvious defects in order to hide serious hazards or defects (e.g., painting over termite damage in order to hide the defect). Even in a caveat emptor environment, courts found the distinction between affirmative misrepresentations and active concealment insignificant: both prevented the careful buyer from obtaining necessary information.

Nondisclosure presents a different type of problem, however. In many transactions (e.g., the stock market) someone may have information s/he has discovered through careful research that s/he thinks may affect the price of the good. Must she disclose the results of her research to potential buyers? If you find an antique lamp marked for $1.00 at a yard sale, must you disclose your superior judgment to the seller? In cases of nondisclosure, courts have tended to approach the problem by class of transaction. Housing real estate sales (which often involve inexperienced parties) may be treated differently than commercial real estate sales, where courts assume the parties are on a relatively equal standing.

In general, courts have been unwilling to require affirmative disclosures except in certain situations such as residential real estate transactions; or cases in which one party was in a trusting relationship with another; or cases in which the party has a legal duty to speak out (such as the buyer's agent); or to correct an earlier statement that is no longer correct; or when someone does speak about a something to provide a full accounting rather than a half-truth.

Justifiable Reliance by the Alleged Victim on the Statement

Plaintiffs must establish that they relied on the defendant's false statement, and that their reliance was justified. If the plaintiff believes or has reason to believe the statement is false, the reliance is not justified. If a person would have entered into the transaction anyway, she cannot establish that she relied on the statement when she entered the transaction.

Sometimes a speaker makes an affirmative misrepresentation to one person, and a different person hears about the statement and thereupon acts upon it. May the second person sue for fraud? Courts generally say that a representation can only be relied upon by those to whom it is directly made, or those to whom the statement may reasonably be expected to learn of it and rely on it (e.g., relatives or partners).

If the plaintiff claims reliance on an obviously false statement ("that car will get 100 miles per gallon!"), courts will generally say the reliance was unreasonable. However, in this instance courts will take into account a victim's special vulnerability—for example, if the victim is ignorant, illiterate, aged, or gullible, and the defendant knew about and took advantage of the victim's condition.

Other Business Tort Claims

Many other business torts and statutory causes of action are available to challenge unfair or unwarranted commercial advantages. Claims such as interference with others' contracts, misappropriation, breach of fiduciary duty, and civil conspiracy are sometimes available. Additional torts that may be available to businesses and others include claims against insurance companies for failure to pay legitimate claims; misuse of legal process; and unfair competition. Recent years have also seen a proliferation of statutory torts, including racketeering (or civil RICO), antitrust claims, securities fraud, and trademark and other intellectual property disputes. Many states have enacted statutes that cover these and other wrongs.

Defenses to Intentional Torts

Even if the plaintiff establishes a prima facie case of intentional tort, the defendant may still avoid liability if it can establish an affirmative defense, or show that it was engaging in privileged conduct that resulted in interference with plaintiff's interests. In a trial setting, the defendant ordinarily has the burden of establishing the elements of an affirmative defense. When a court recognizes a privilege, it essentially says to the plaintiff, "even though your interests have been interfered with by defendant, the defendant is permitted to do so."

The process of creation and destruction of privileges provide an important insight into the tort system. When judges (or legislatures) recognize a privilege, they are engaging in an important type of balancing of social interests, often evaluating whether it is better for society to recognize the privilege or not. In addition, once a privilege is created, judges must then decide its scope: should it be broadly construed or narrowly defined?

The legal system recognizes many defenses and privileges to interfere with another's interests. For example, courts will recognize defenses such as consent; self-defense and defense of others; defense of property and privilege to "recapture" chattels; official privilege (including arrest); privilege of necessity;

and privilege to compete. Some privileges are no longer recognized, such as the ability of husbands to "discipline" (beat) their wives. Some privileges, such as the privilege to "discipline" children are gradually being narrowed by the courts in view of much greater attention to child abuse.

These defenses often raise difficult questions themselves. Take consent for instance. If two people engage in a bar fight, have they consented to injuries inflicted by the other? Or, if a woman has consensual sex with her husband, not knowing that he is infected with an STD (but he does know and fails to tell her), has she consented to a subsequent infection?

With respect to the bar fight example, courts are split. Given the social objective of discouraging bar fights, it isn't clear to courts whether allowing the fighters to sue each other is more or less likely to deter fighting. But in the case of the unwittingly-exposed spouse, courts are more sympathetic. If the spouse has in fact contracted a serious disease through sex, and the other party was aware of the infection, courts are likely to treat the consent as effective for the sex but not for the exposure to the disease.

The Negligence Tort

The tort of negligence is generally considered to be the most important tort. It is important because it covers most instances of *unintentional* harm that occurs. It is also the tort that covers most instances of professional liability, such as that of accountants, physicians, engineers, architects, and lawyers. Thus, if a person inadvertently injures another, s/he is liable for the injury only if s/he acted negligently.

Lawyers use certain terms of art to describe the negligence rules. Every claimant must establish four elements: **duty, breach, causation,** and **damage.**

- **Duty.** Tort law tells you what degree of care you must exercise to avoid injuring others. The duty is usually stated at a high level of generality, and usually applies to everyone. For example, the negligence tort duty is "to act as a reasonably prudent person under the circumstances." In most tort situations, the judge is responsible for deciding what duty applies to a particular situation.
- **Breach.** Tort law also tells you how your behavior might depart from the level of care. For example, if you unintentionally bump into someone at a bar, and the person tumbles to the floor, tort law will not hold you responsible for the injury unless your behavior was unreasonable. So, if you exercise the specified level of care towards others, and the plaintiff is still injured, the plaintiff cannot recover. At trial, assuming the plaintiff has offered enough credible evidence, the jury decides whether a defendant has departed from the standard of care (i.e., "breached his duty"). Negligence law ordinarily requires that you take into account foreseeable risks and avoid unreasonable risks of injury to another.

- **Causation.** The claimant must show that your breach or negligence caused the harm, and the harm wasn't caused by something else. This causal link requirement imposes enormous hurdles in cases of medical error or toxic harms since it is often not clear whether the plaintiff would have suffered the harm in any event.
- **Legal Damage.** The plaintiff must establish legal injury. Usually, the injured person brings a lawsuit seeking damages or injunctive relief.

Establishing Duty and Breach

The Reasonable Person

To determine whether a person's conduct departs from the generalized standards of care defined by negligence, courts have created a mythical person, called the *reasonable person*. A person is said to act negligently if his conduct falls below that of the reasonably prudent person (RPP) facing similar circumstances. The RPP is assumed to have the knowledge, intelligence, experience, and perception of an ordinary person. However, the RPP does not reflect the average or even necessarily the majority way of doing things.

"I Can't Help It If I Am Not Possessed of the 'Highest Order of Intelligence'"

In a 19th-century case arising out of England, a farmer who stacked wet hay tightly was advised by his neighbors that the haystack would ferment and catch fire. He said he would "chance it." Instead, he tried to cool off his stack by creating a "chimney" in the center of the stack, which had the unintended effect of adding oxygen to the combustion. Unfortunately, the farmer's stack did catch fire and burned another neighbor's buildings. On appeal, the farmer argued that his conduct should be judged against the standard of which he was subjectively capable, that would take into account the fact that his level of intelligence and reasoning ability was not as strong as his neighbors'. The court rejected this approach, stating that the RPP standard was "objective"—the farmer's conduct would be judged against the reasonable person standard, not the standard of which he was capable.

Vaughan v. Menlove, 132 Eng. Rep. 490 (C.P. 1837)

For example, even if most people speed through a school zone, a jury must evaluate whether a RPP would speed.

The reasonable person is presumed to possess certain knowledge about his community, culture, and technology. An RPP knows that electrical cords should not be placed in water; that ice is slippery; that automobiles require a certain distance to stop; that raw chicken might contain harmful bacteria; and that a ball rolling into a street might be followed by a child. In the farmer case, the court said, in effect, that "everyone knows" that wet hay when stacked may ferment and catch fire, suggesting that the knowledge held by the RPP is culturally dependent.

Beginners, too, are held to the same standard as the reasonably competent person. A beginning sailor is held to the same standard as the person who's been operating sailboats for 30 years. To some, holding beginners to a standard they cannot meet may seem unfair. But, paraphrasing what Oliver Wendell Holmes said in *The Common Law* in defense of the objective standard, a beginner's slips are no less troublesome to his neighbors than if they sprang from a guilty neglect.

Suppose, however, that our hypothetical RPP engages in activities requiring special knowledge—such as operating a schooner or flying an airplane. Most people don't know how to do either. In that event, the operator is judged by the standard of a reasonably skilled, competent, and experienced member of the group authorized to engage in that activity. This standard is particularly important when evaluating the conduct of professionals—such as doctors, lawyers, and engineers—under a branch of negligence law known as *malpractice* (discussed below).

When defining the characteristics of the reasonable person, courts take the person's physical characteristics (e.g., blindness, infirmity) into account. However, in accordance with a general distrust of our ability to judge mental capacities, courts refuse to consider intelligence, memory, emotional stability, or psychological disability. For example, a blind person who trips into an unguarded excavation is not negligent for failing to see it; but a person suffering from a delusion that the excavation was a swimming pool would not be excused for diving into it.

In contrast to adults, children are held to a slightly different standard: the standard of a child of similar age, intelligence, and maturity. In this respect the child standard is both objective (holding all children of similar age to the same standard of care) but also more particularized (taking into account subjective factors such as intelligence and experience). Also, in contrast to the intentional torts, where children are held strictly liable provided they have the capacity to form the requisite intent, many states presume that children below a certain age (often seven years old) are incapable of negligence.

A key exception to this rule for children also applies. If a child is engaging in an adult-like activity—such as driving an automobile—the child is held to the adult standard. Many states have seen controversies over what constitutes an adult activity, as opposed to a child activity. In some parts of the country, hunting with a rifle would be seen as quintessentially adult, but in certain states courts have found such activities are appropriate for children.

"Don't Shoot!"

Along with most other states considering the use of firearms by children, the Arkansas Supreme Court held that an adult standard of care should not be applied to a sixteen-year-old hunter who injured a companion with a high-powered rifle. The court had "no doubt" that deer hunting is dangerous but could not say that deer hunting is an activity normally engaged in only by adults. According to the court, "[a] child may lawfully hunt without a hunting license at any age under sixteen. . . . We know, from common knowledge, that youngsters only six or eight years old frequently use .22 caliber rifles and other lethal firearms to hunt rabbits, birds and other small game."

The court also feared that, if it imposed an adult standard on child hunters, it would have to explain why the adult standard should not apply where the minor was hunting rabbits, or where a six-year-old was shooting at tin cans with an air rifle, "[n]ot to mention other dangerous activities, such as the swinging of a baseball bat, the explosion of firecrackers, or the operation of an electric train."

Purtle v Shelton, 251 Ark. 519, 474 S.W. 2d 123 (1971).

Departures from RPP Standard: Government Regulations and Statutes

If the standard of care is to act like a reasonable person under the circumstances, how does one establish that someone has departed from that standard? Courts have developed a number of techniques. One mechanism of proving negligence permits a plaintiff to show that the defendant's conduct violated a relevant federal statute, municipal ordinance, or administrative regulation, and that violation is causally linked to the plaintiff's injury. For example, if a statute specifically prohibits the activity (e.g., requiring a full stop at a stop sign) and the defendant failed to do, the defendant's actions are considered per se negligent.

Departures from Customary Safety Precautions

Suppose a hotel guest is injured when the glass door to her shower suddenly breaks and the spears from the glass cut her severely. If she can establish that other inns typically use safety glass in their shower doors, the hotel's departure from customary practices is evidence of negligence. Such evidence typically goes to a jury, which then must still decide whether the hotel was negligent, and whether the guest would have been injured even if safety glass had been employed.

Evidence of compliance with customary standards is also relevant to the negligence inquiry. If the hotel establishes that other companies in the industry do not employ safety glass in their shower stalls, that may also be considered by the jury. A caution should be noted, however. Following the practice of others does not insulate one from charges of negligence. As Judge Learned Hand stated decades ago in the famous case known as *The T.J. Hooper*, "[a] whole calling may have unduly lagged in the adoption of new and available devices." Thus, even if a company is following common practice, it is nonetheless possible that a jury may find the common practice unsafe.

Expert Testimony

In many cases, it will be necessary to call an expert witness to assist the jury in assessing the reasonableness of the defendant's behavior. Expert testimony is almost always required in cases alleging professional negligence, injuries resulting from complex products, or toxic harms. For example, most jurors would not be able to assess whether a physician overprescribed a particular medicine without hearing from medical experts about the proper standard of care. Or, suppose the claim is that an automobile was poorly designed by positioning the gas tank behind the rear axle. In such cases, experts in auto safety and design must be called upon to explain the alternatives and to articulate why the particular design is unsafe.

"First, Do No Harm"

A patient diagnosed with appendicitis was put under anesthesia for surgery. Several nurses and physicians had control of his body during the time he was unconscious. After surgery, the patient awakened with a debilitating pain in his right shoulder, and was unable to rotate or lift his arm. He had experienced no previous injury or pain in the shoulder area. The treating team could not explain how the injury occurred, but argued that it was due to infection not trauma. However, the trial court credited expert medical testimony that concluded that the patient's condition was caused by trauma.

On appeal, the California Supreme Court held that "all those defendants who had any control over his body or the instrumentalities which might have caused the injuries may properly be called upon to meet the inference of negligence by giving an explanation of their conduct." The decision is significant for placing the burden on the treatment team to explain how the traumatic injury occurred. If they were unable to give a satisfactory explanation, all would be held jointly liable to the patient for the injury.

(*Ybarra v. Spangard*, 25 Cal.2d 486 [1944])

Circumstantial Evidence

In some cases, courts permit a jury to infer negligence from circumstantial evidence. Sometimes the mere fact that an injury occurred is evidence of negligence. Suppose while driving behind a big rig on the highway, a spare tire from the rig suddenly bounces loose crashing into your windshield. Or, suppose a pedestrian in an urban business district is suddenly hit by a potted plant dropped from a third-floor window. In such cases, courts permit a jury to infer that whoever was in control of the injury causing device (the tire; the potted plant) was negligent.

Foreseeable Risk

In the absence of a statute, custom, and so forth, plaintiffs may employ one other broad mechanism of establishing that the defendant's conduct fell below that of the reasonable person. In general, a reasonable person is bound to foresee certain types of risks his conduct imposes on others. If you're driving on a country road and encounter a place where the road has

---

How Lack of Foreseeable Risk Explains Why a Plaintiff Might Lose a Case

The following is a copy of an actual answer filed by a railroad company in the 1930s to a complaint for damages against it:

> The defendant [the railroad] further specially excepts to said petition [the complaint filed by the plaintiff] where it is alleged that the plaintiff, upon discovering that the wooden stool was wet, raised the same and squatted with his feet poised on the porcelain bowl of the commode, from which roosting position he says his foot slipped causing him to fall to the great detriment of his left testicle, for the reason that it is obvious that the said commode with its full moon contours was rightfully and properly designed for the comfort of sitters only, being equipped with neither spurs, stirrups nor toeholds for boots or shoes: this defendant, therefore, was not legally required to foresee that the plaintiff, traveling on its modern, air-conditioned deluxe passenger train would so persist in his barnyard predilections as to trample upon its elegant toilet fixture in the barbaric style of horse and buggy days.
>
> For further answer, if needed, this defendant . . . specially pleads that the plaintiff should not be allowed to recover any sum against it for the reason that the plaintiff. . . . should have, therefore, in the exercise of due care deferred taking the Crazy Water Crystals until such time when he could be at home secure and sure-footed on his own dunghill or with his feet planted solidly on the flat board of his own old fashioned two-holer.

Excerpted from Rodney Jones, Charles Sevilla, and Gerald Uelman, *Disorderly Conduct: Verbatim Excerpts from Actual Cases* (Norton 1999) 37–38.

flooded, you are bound to anticipate that driving through the flood might kill the engine or reduce the efficacy of your brakes. If the stairs leading to your house are severely cracked, you are bound to anticipate that a guest might fall through and break a leg. This general standard of care permits courts to apply the rule with significant flexibility. It means, in general, that if a defendant could not foresee a particular risk of injury suffered by the plaintiff, the defendant cannot be found negligent.

Establishing Causation

General Principles

Even if the plaintiff can establish that the defendant acted negligently, the plaintiff must still establish that the defendant's negligence caused him harm. For example, a driver who runs a red light does not commit the negligence tort unless s/he hits someone. Driving negligently might constitute a criminal violation, but it does not create a tort unless the negligent act causes someone damage.

Moreover, the plaintiff must establish a causal link between her harm and the defendant's negligent act. For example, suppose someone suffers salmonella poisoning after eating at several restaurants. Even if it is certain that *one* of the establishments served him contaminated food, the plaintiff is required to establish *which* establishment served food that caused his illness.

Toxic torts create special problems of proof. Did exposure to asbestos cause plaintiff's cancer? Did the toxic dump created by defendant 30 years ago pollute the groundwater leading to the birth defects suffered by the neighbors? The film *Erin Brockovich* portrays a lawsuit against the Pacific Gas and Electric Company, which contaminated land by improperly dumping hexavalent chromium, a deadly toxic waste that allegedly poisoned the residents in the area. Based on real events, the film necessarily passes over several difficult causation issues. To prevail on causation in a toxic case, the plaintiff would typically have to establish *substance*, *source*, and *exposure*:

- **Substance**—that the substance in question can cause the particular disease;
- **Source**—that the defendant was source of substance; and
- **Exposure**—that the plaintiff was exposed to the substance in way that caused her disease.

The plaintiff would ordinarily employ different experts to establish each of these elements. Thus, to prevail in a toxic tort lawsuit is both very expensive and very difficult.

Complicating Causation

A number of difficult causation questions arise with great frequency. Here we will address three separate issues: **multiple causal factors; intervening causes; and limitations on responsibility (proximate causation).**

Multiple causal factors. Difficult issues arise when two different actors apparently cause plaintiff's injury. For example, in *Summers v. Tice* (1948), two bird hunters negligently fired shotguns in the direction of a third hunter; birdshot hit him in the eye and lip. It could not be determined which gun fired the pellets that caused the injuries, but it was certain that both hunters were negligent and at least one of them had fired the shell that injured plaintiff. The two hunters argued that plaintiff must demonstrate which shot caused his injuries. Since plaintiff could not do so, neither could be held liable. The California Supreme Court disagreed, and shifted the burden of proof on causation to the two hunters to exculpate themselves if they could; otherwise, both would be considered joint tortfeasors and held jointly and severally liable.

A joint tortfeasor is someone who the legal system has determined should share with another mutual responsibility for an injury. There are different types of joint tortfeasors. Sometimes two people act in concert with each other, such as where two drag car racers on the highway run a third person off the road.

More frequently, two people act independently of each other but their actions intersect in such a way as to create a common injury. For example, if two people unknown to each other negligently start separate fires that burn out of control, and the two fires combine before destroying plaintiff's house, both are jointly liable for the loss. The *Summers* case is also an illustration of this second type of joint causation since, even though they were on a common hunting trip, each hunter fired independently of the other.

Joint tortfeasors are jointly and severally liable for the injury they cause. This means that each tortfeasor can be held fully responsible for the injury, an important principle if one of the negligent parties is insolvent. If both defendants are solvent, each remains responsible to the other to pay a portion of the loss.

The principle of joint and several liability has been targeted by many business groups, who prefer an approach that would limit each defendant's responsibility to a proportionate share. In response to intense lobbying campaigns, many states have adopted statutes limiting joint and several liability. Although the statutes differ from state to state, most hold joint tortfeasors responsible for only a proportionate share of losses, usually assessed based on relative degrees of fault. Consumer groups contend that the result of these limits is to reallocate losses back to innocent victims. These groups argue that it is fairer to hold negligent defendants fully responsible, and further that the risk of a defendant's insolvency should be born by those who created the harm.

Intervening causes. Sometimes other events intercede between the defendant's wrong and the plaintiff's injury. For example, a negligently operated ship collided with another ship at sea. After several days floundering, the damaged ship sank. The first ship owner claimed that he was only responsible for the damage caused by the initial collision, but not the subsequent loss of the ship and cargo since so many other factors contributed to the eventual loss. However, the court disagreed: the defendant was responsible for the loss since the ship was disabled as a result of the collision and was unable to return to port.

Intervening But Not Supervening Cause

A negligently operated train caused a collision with plaintiff's horse cart, after which the driver was too stunned to protect his scattered goods. While the railroad's detectives secured the train, thieves made off with the driver's goods. On appeal, the train conceded liability for harm caused by the collision, but the question was whether the train was liable for the theft of the plaintiff's goods. The court held that the risk of theft after collision was foreseeable, and therefore fairly attributable to the defendant.

Brower v. New York Central Railway (1918)

"Supervening" Causes

A train negligently failed to let the plaintiff off at her stop. The railroad's agents delivered the plaintiff to a hotel. Because of the hotel's negligence, a fire started that injured the passenger. Was the railroad liable? The court answered no, finding that the passenger's injuries were too remote from the railroad's negligence and thus it was not responsible for the passenger's injuries caused by the fire.

Georgia RR v. Price (1898)

Limitations on Liability (Proximate cause). A notoriously confusing subject (even for lawyers) is a set of limitations on liability that fall under the rubric *proximate cause*. Suppose that a negligently operated automobile causes a train to derail, which then simultaneously smacks a pedestrian and produces loud reverberations that cause expensive china in a nearby shop to crash to the floor. The automobile driver is clearly liable to the train that derailed, and to the pedestrian. But is he also liable for the broken china? This question raises the issue of the issue of the ambit of responsibility for one's negligent acts. Mrs. O'Leary negligently placed her lantern near her cow, but is she responsible for the entire destruction of Chicago?

In resolving this question, most courts examine the question at the time the defendant acted negligently. At that point, could the defendant *foresee* the particular type of injury that manifested itself? A court is likely to find that a negligent driver can foresee injuries to other vehicles, pedestrians, and nearby structures such as light poles. And courts agree that where to draw the line of responsibility (to include or not to include responsibility for the broken china) is a policy judgment. This policy analysis by no means results in certain or predictable outcomes. And, where a defendant asks to be relieved of more extensive responsibility, the outcome often depends on the ability of counsel to "fit" or analogize the case at hand to prior cases.

Despite the general confusion about where the line is to be drawn, some rules are clear. For example, suppose that a bicyclist negligently runs into a pedestrian, who suffers a heart attack because of an unusual heart condition. Even if no other person would have suffered such an injury, the defendant is liable for the actual harm caused. This is known as the *thin skull* rule.

Suppose that our heart attack victim is being rushed to the hospital, and the ambulance collides with another car further injuring the heart attack victim. Most courts would hold the bicyclist liable for the additional injuries (jointly liable if the second collision occurred because of negligence).

"Danger Invites Rescue"

The plaintiff and his cousin Herbert boarded a train one evening. The conductor did not shut the doors before the train got underway, and Herbert fell out and over a bridge as the train rounded a corner. The train continued to the other side of the bridge, whereupon the plaintiff got out and walked back along the dark bridge to look for his cousin. While looking, he fell off the bridge in the darkness. He sued the railroad for negligence, claiming that the failure to close the door was the cause of his injury because he was trying to rescue his cousin.

In a famous opinion, New York Court of Appeals Justice Benjamin Cardozo argued that "Danger invites rescue." He reasoned that it was fair to hold the original wrongdoer liable for rescuer injuries as well as to the injured person. "The wrong that imperils life is a wrong to the imperiled victim; it is also a wrong to his rescuer."

Wagner v. International Ry. (1921)

Damages and Other Relief

Suppose a plaintiff wins her case, and the defendant does not have any defenses? What damages may a person ordinarily recover? In general, a successful tort litigant may be eligible for three different types of relief: injunction; compensatory damages; and punitive damages.

Injunctive Relief

An injunction (court order) is available only if necessary to achieve a specific result not available through the payment of money. For example, if the defendant has been stalking plaintiff, a court may order the defendant to stay a certain distance away. Or if the defendant's tortious behavior continues, a court may order the defendant to cease and desist. If the defendant's wrongdoing resulted in unwarranted profits, the transfer of property, or the completion of business transactions, a court may order their unwinding in order to put the plaintiff back in the position s/he would have been but for the wrong.

Compensatory Damages

Compensatory damages comprise the chief form of relief to which an injured person is entitled. The purpose of compensatory damages is to put the plaintiff back in the position s/he was in prior to the injury. They are not designed to increase the plaintiff's overall well-being.

Depending on the specific circumstances, compensatory damages may include compensation for direct harms, such as physical injuries, medical expenses, and lost pay and benefits. They may include the cost of home medical care (including specialized medical equipment such as beds or wheelchairs), or property damage such as might result from an automobile collision.

Compensatory damages may also include monies for intangible injuries such as loss of privacy, injury to reputation, pain and suffering, and emotional distress occurring because of the defendant's behavior.

Punitive Damages

Punitive damages are rarely awarded, and are available only in instances where the defendant's behavior is particularly egregious. Punitive damages are designed to punish and deter wrongdoers and others from engaging in similar conduct in the future. In recent years the Supreme Court has added constitutional limits to when punitive damages may be awarded, as well as limitations on their amount.

Defenses to Unintentional Torts

Most courts today recognize at least one of three defenses to unintentional torts: **contributory negligence; comparative fault;** and **assumption of risk.**

Contributory Negligence

When the plaintiff herself has acted carelessly toward her own safety, and her carelessness was a factor in her injury, the defendant may assert the defense of *contributory negligence*. Under the strict common law regime, which today is followed in only a handful of jurisdictions, a plaintiff whose own negligence contributed in any way to her injury was completely barred from any recovery.

Although both primary negligence and contributory negligence doctrines use the same language, one important distinction between them must be noted. When someone exposes *others* to an unreasonable risk of injury, we say that person has acted negligently. But the person who is merely "contributory negligent" has acted unreasonably with respect to her *own* safety. Many legal scholars therefore place contributory negligence in a different category of risky behavior since it does not expose *others* to injury. Note that a person could be both negligent towards others and contributory negligent: if I run a red light at a busy intersection, my behavior risks injury to others as well as to myself.

Comparative Fault

Because the all-or-nothing rule of the common law contributory negligence regime prevented even slightly negligent plaintiffs from recovering anything from negligent defendants, most states changed their contributory negligence rules during the last two decades of the 20th century.

Most states now follow a rule of *comparative fault*. Although states vary in their particular practices, most states now permit a negligent plaintiff to recover at least a portion of her losses by having the jury apportion the loss between the plaintiff and the defendant based upon their relative degrees of fault.

Assumption of Risk

A third defense, assumption of risk, permits a defendant to escape liability where it can be shown the plaintiff voluntarily agreed to encounter a known risk created by the defendant. Assumption of risk actually encompasses two separate defenses, *express* and *implied*. Most courts today treat these two defenses very differently from each other.

An *express* assumption of risk concerns an actual, advance acknowledgment by a person that she is aware of a particular risk and consents in advance to encounter it. Express assumption of risk arises frequently in sports and recreational activities such as hockey, football, mountain climbing, or horseback riding. In these situations, a player who is aware of the risk of injury typically agrees to assume the risk in order to play.

In the sports and recreational contexts, many courts will enforce an explicit assumption of risk provided that the express agreement truly offers the player a choice, does not impose undue risks to the public, and is not overreaching.

However, some express agreements to shift risk of injury can be highly problematic. For example, one California hospital attempted to require all patients to waive any claims for negligent treatment as a condition to providing care. If they were permitted to do so, other enterprises would shift the risk of product defects or poor treatment onto trusting consumers. Many of these "agreements" are reviewed carefully by courts for fairness.

In contrast, an *implied* assumption of the risk is one that a person does not explicitly agree in advance to accept, but after the fact a court infers that the person was aware of the risk, had a choice to avoid taking the risk, and the person's behavior indicated that they voluntarily encountered the risk. In the 19th century, courts routinely said that workers who "voluntarily" worked under negligently maintained and dangerous conditions "assumed the risk" if they were aware of the risk and were subsequently injured. The courts held that the employees were free to quit and to go work at another (dangerous?) factory.

Most courts today have greatly limited the "implied" assumption of risk branch, and have concluded that implied doctrine should be incorporated into the comparative fault inquiry.

"No Duty"

In all the negligence cases discussed thus far, someone has acted, and his/her act has caused another harm. But what if the harm is caused by some other event, and the defendant is a "bystander"? Are there circumstances in which a bystander could be responsible for the injury, or at least responsible for failing to protect the victim from further injury?

A classic example illustrates the problem. A baby is lying face down in a mud puddle. You happen to come by, notice the baby drowning, and do nothing to assist. The general rule is that, provided you have done nothing to create the situation, you have "no duty" to aid the baby, even though you could do so with minimal effort. This rule, known as the "no duty" rule (or no duty to rescue doctrine), is a very important rule in American law, and one that is often taken for granted even by people who consider it morally repulsive. Many European countries (and some states) reject this rule.

The basic notion is that people should not have to assist others in need. The rule reflects a strong version of autonomy (some would say selfishness). The legal system can impose great demands on you *if you act*, but if you simply refrain from acting, generally speaking the system does not impose an affirmative duty on you.

In the 19th century, the "no duty" rule was strictly observed. However, in more recent decades, state courts have found reason to create a number of exceptions to the no duty rule. There are three commonly recognized exceptions to this rule: first, where two persons are in what the law defines as a "special relationship," and the more vulnerable person is injured; second,

The American Rule of "No Duty"

Leroy Iverson liked to gamble, and often brought along his 7-year-old daughter, Sherrice. Sherrice would play while Iverson gambled into the early morning hours. One Memorial Day weekend in 1997, Iverson brought Sherrice to the Primadonna Casino in Las Vegas. Later, film from security cameras showed Sherrice playing hide-and-seek with a stranger, an 18 year old named Jeremy Stohmeyer.

At 3:48 a.m., the security films showed Sherrice running into the women's bathroom. Seconds later, Stohmeyer followed. Shortly after 5:00 a.m. Sherrice's half-naked body was discovered on a toilet seat. She had been sexually molested and strangled to death.

Stohmeyer confessed to the crime and was sentenced to life imprisonment as part of a plea agreement. However, while Stohmeyer was molesting and strangling Sherrice, a teenaged friend of Stohmeyer's, David Cash, stood on a toilet seat in the adjoining stall and watched while Stohmeyer molested Sherrice, but did nothing to stop the brutality. Later, during interviews, Cash said on air, "It's a very tragic event, OK, but the simple fact remains I do not know this little girl." "I do not know starving children in Panama. I do not know people that die of disease in Egypt. The only person I knew in this event was Jeremy Stohmeyer."

Under the American "no duty" rule, Cash was not required to assist Sherrice, or interfere, or to call the police. Recently, several legislatures have adopted statutes requiring reporting of certain crimes. California, for example, enacted a statute known as the "Sherrice Iverson Victim Protection Act" in response.

Facts based on: Marcia M. Ziegler, Nonfeasance And The Duty To Assist: The American Seinfeld Syndrome, 104 Dick. L. Rev. 525 (2000)

where someone promises to aid, but then doesn't do so; and third, where the defendant is himself involved in the event himself, even if he didn't cause the injury.

The special relationship category is somewhat flexible, but generally requires that the person needing aid have a pre-existing relationship with the person who is expected to assist. If a guest collapses on the patio of a motel, the innkeeper cannot simply ignore the guest: at a minimum, the innkeeper must call for assistance.

Other courts have found duties to aid based upon social or economic relationships such as innkeeper/guest; employer/employee; and school/pupil. For example, if a passenger on a train becomes severely ill through no fault of the operators, most courts will find that the agents must assist the ill passenger to obtain medical attention.

Some courts have expanded the notion of a "relationship" and imposed a duty to aid based on a common venture. For example, in one case two buddies went drinking and chasing girls. During the evening, they were chased by angry boyfriends who caught and severely beat one of the fellows. His friend placed the battered buddy in his car and drove around for several hours before driving him home and leaving him there in the car, unconscious in the back seat, where his family discovered him the next day. The friend died. The court held that their friendship and common quest to party and look for girls justified finding that the friend owed a duty to aid the beating victim.

Courts also find duties where one person makes a promise to aid, and the other person relies on the promise and is hurt when the assistance is not forthcoming. In a well-known case, a woman visiting a store was bitten by a housecat. She feared rabies, so asked the owner to keep the cat under careful observation for a month, to which requests the owners readily agreed. However, the owners subsequently allowed the cat to slip away for several days, so the bitten woman was compelled to undergo a series of painful rabies shots that later turned out to have been unnecessary when the cat turned up healthy. The court held that the promise to keep the cat under observation was reasonably relied on by the victim, and allowed her to sue the owners for failing to carry out their promise.

A very important illustration of the "special relationship exception arises from psychotherapeutic relationships. In the 1976 decision, *Tarasoff v. Regents of the University of California*, the California Supreme Court imposed important duties on treating physicians to warn potential victims of violence threatened *by their patients.*

In *Tarasoff*, a university student named Prosenjit Poddar was seeing a psychologist at the university's student health center. The psychologist recognized that Poddar was dangerous because he had a pathological attachment to a girl who had spurned him, Tatiana Tarasoff. Poddar also stated he intended to purchase a gun. The therapist notified the police both verbally and in writing, but did nothing to alert Tarasoff or Tarasoff's family. After questioning Poddar, the police accepted his promise to stay away from Tarasoff. Two months later Poddar killed Tarasoff.

The Supreme Court of California held that the therapist had a duty to warn Ms. Tarasoff or her family of the danger. The key determination is that the psychotherapist had made a judgment that Poddar posed a serious danger to Tarasoff, which warranted imposing a duty.

Many states have now codified some version of the *Tarasoff* duty, and in some instances have expanded the duty to protect. In particular, most states have imposed new duties on teachers, medical personnel, child care workers and others in authority to report any signs of child abuse in children under their care. In these cases, the statutes impose a duty of due care (i.e., a duty to act non-negligently) in responding to the statutory mandate.

A third major exception to the no-duty rule involves circumstances in which the defendant has been involved in some way with the event leading to the injured person requiring assistance. For example, a hobo was attempting to "jump" a railroad car when it was moving, but fell between the cars. The court held that the railroad was required to obtain aid for the hobo, and couldn't simply ignore the fact the hobo was trespassing.

This exception often involves people who are involved in auto accidents. If someone runs into me and is injured in the collision, courts generally say that I am under an obligation to call for assistance even though I didn't cause the collision.

To sum up, the "no duty" rule governs situations in which a person who is in a position easily to rescue another fails to do so, and as a general matter courts refuse to impose liability on the grounds that no person is required to act to protect another. However, in recent years courts have created important exceptions to this rule, and begun imposing a duty to aid on those who are in an important pre-existing relationship with the victim, or who have promised to assist (and fail to do so). The last category of exception, where the defendant was involved in the event, imposes liability not for the original injury, but for failing to assist once it's become clear that someone was injured.

Strict Liability

Thus far, this chapter has addressed intentional torts and the dominant negligence tort involving unintentional wrong. But there are some special situations in which courts impose very high standards of care under the doctrine of strict liability.

Strict liability should be contrasted with the negligence tort since both involve unintentionally created harms. As described earlier, the general negligence duty imposes a requirement to act reasonably under the circumstances. In contrast, where the strict liability doctrine applies, a defendant may be held liable where its actions have caused injury *even if the defendant acted carefully.*

The doctrine has been most frequently applied in four contexts: the keeping of known dangerous or wild animals; the storage, transportation or use of blasting materials; a more general category of "abnormally dangerous activities;" and certain contexts involving defective products.

Wild Animals and Blasting

If you keep a tiger in your back yard, and use extraordinary care to keep the tiger in but the tiger nevertheless escapes, you will be held liable for any injuries the tiger causes. A similar rule obtains with the various steps involved in blasting.

Abnormally Dangerous Activities

In the case of "abnormally dangerous" activities, one who maintains such a condition or activity on his premise, or engages in an activity that involves a high risk of harm to the person or property of others may be liable for losses, even though s/he exercised reasonable care to prevent such harm. What constitutes an "abnormally dangerous" activity is determined by reference to open-ended factors such as the utility of the activity to a particular place, the "commonness" of the activity; and whether the activity carries a high degree of risk of harm to others.

Because the factors used in determining whether a given activity is or is not to be adjudged under the strict liability doctrine are vague, the rule has greatest utility as a "backstop" doctrine employed when dangerous activities result in harm but it's impossible to pinpoint exactly where someone was negligent.

For example, in a Washington State case a tanker truck pulling a trailer loaded with gasoline spilled thousands of gallons of gasoline when the trailer inexplicably came loose and fell onto the road. The plaintiff was driving on the freeway when her car encountered the pools of gasoline and burst into flame, killing her. Finding that tanker trucks loaded with gasoline was "abnormally dangerous," the Washington Supreme Court held the operator liable even though any evidence of negligence had burned in the flames.

Similarly, an Idaho case imposed strict liability on the operators of a fireworks display at a public fairgrounds where one of the rockets went awry and injured a spectator, even where it was evident that the operators had used care in constructing the display.

Products Liability

The doctrines associated with products liability have become controversial at the end of the 20th century. During much of our history, manufacturers were insulated from liability for defective products that collapsed or proved injurious to life and limb. The first cracks in the limited liability bulwark came in the early 20th century, but not until the 1960s and 1970s did product liability begin to have a major impact on manufacturers.

Beginning in the 1960's courts began imposing a form of strict liability on manufacturers where their products contained defects that injured users or bystanders. Over the past 40 years, however, the doctrines have evolved so that most products cases contain a mixture of strict liability and negligence doctrines.

Today most courts recognize three different types of product defects for which manufacturers may be held liable:

* **Manufacturing Defects**—where an unintended serious flaw is introduced into a product, such as a dead mouse in a beer bottle, or defective steel in an automobile fan blade
* **Design Defects**—where a design flaw injures a user or bystander, such as a punch press without safety guards
* **Inadequate Warnings**—where a manufacturer fails to warn of a known hazard in its product, and a user was injured by the hazard

Manufacturing defects that injure consumers are typically judged under a strict liability standard. In contrast, most design defect and inadequate warning claims have a heavy *negligence* aspect, even though the complaint often asserts strict liability.

Contemporary Controversies Concerning Tort System

A Comment on Competing Theories of Responsibility

In recent years many of the consumer torts have become politically controversial. Business groups have established political action committees to critique the tort system, and to propose "reforms" that restrict many important doctrines. Consumer groups, civil rights organizations, and plaintiffs' lawyers are arrayed in opposition.

As a result of the political power struggle between these groups, competing theories of responsibility have been put into public play. Over the last hundred years, courts significantly expanded the types of behaviors and the range of actors who might be held liable for loss.[2] During that period, debates about the reach of the tort law were frequently confined to the law reviews and in arguments before appellate courts. Today, the arguments have spilled into public debate—and often at the national level. Let us consider just one example.

Former President Ronald Reagan was an avowed critic of the tort system. In a 1986 speech, Reagan described what he considered a ridiculous lawsuit as follows: "In California, a man was using a public telephone booth to place a call. An alleged drunk driver careened down the street, lost control of his car, and crashed into a phone booth. Now, it's no surprise that the injured man sued. But you might be startled to hear whom he sued: the telephone company and associated firms!"[3]

In fact, Bigbee, the fellow in the phone booth, had his leg severed after a car hit the phone booth in which he had been trapped. This type of enclosed booth, very common at the time, had an accordion door. When Bigbee saw the car coming, he tried to escape. The door jammed as he tried to flee, and he couldn't free himself. The accident left him unable to walk, severely depressed, and unable to work. Because the phone company had placed the booth near a known hazardous intersection, and because the door was defective, keeping him trapped inside, he sued the phone company for compensation.[4]

Reagan's anecdote seems to suggest that the only possible "responsible" party is the one who was the immediate cause of the collision—the allegedly drunken driver. Reagan's view also seems to suggest that there couldn't be multiple "causes" or several possible parties who might share responsibility for Bigbee's injuries. So, one view of "responsibility" for injury is to look to an immediate causal factor and limit the scope of liability to that causal agent. Indeed, this was a common view in the 19th century.

Most contemporary tort theorists have rejected President Reagan's view of causal responsibility. It is important to understand why.

First, tort law has been shaped in part by modern understandings of causation. It is possible for a contemporary lawyer to imagine several different parties each of whom might have contributed in a substantial way to the fact Bigbee was so severely injured:

1   The driver, for losing control
2   The telephone company for locating the phone booth within a few feet of a hazardous intersection
3   The repair company (which might also be the phone company) for failing to repair the door on the phone booth even after being notified of the hazard, so that Bigbee became trapped inside
4   Bigbee himself, who potentially should have been more alert under the circumstances (although there are no facts in the case itself to support this)

In short, a causally responsible party need not be the "last" or the "immediate" cause of an injury to be held liable.[5] A *causally responsible* party need only be shown to have failed to take *reasonable precautions* that would have avoided a *foreseeable injury* to a *foreseeable person*.

The fact that one party is *causally responsible* doesn't mean that that party would necessarily end up paying all the losses associated with the injury. Indeed, if all the "causally responsible" parties were amenable to suit, and all had resources available to pay damages, most courts would require that the losses be apportioned among the negligent parties based on their relative degrees of fault. Still, let's suppose the telephone company is the only party that is amenable to suit. (This could result from the drunk driver being judgment proof, for example.) Let's assume further that Bigbee is not contributory negligent. In that case, a causally responsible negligent party such as the phone company could be held liable for the entire loss under the rule of "joint and several liability."

As described above, "joint and several liability" means that when two (or more) parties are all negligent and causally responsible for a loss, each may be held liable for the entire loss. This rule, which is frequently challenged by tort critics, is said to be justified by a number of arguments. Key justifications include: as between the wrongdoer and an innocent party, the wrongdoer should pay; the rule maintains appropriate incentives upon those in control of unsafe conditions to repair those conditions; and the rule increases the chance that injured parties will receive full redress. If the plaintiff recovers the full amount from one of the negligent parties, then his judgment is satisfied, and that defendant is left to obtain "contribution" from the remaining defendants.

Second, contemporary tort law is infused with another core claim. That claim is that it is important for the well-being of all that actors take precautions for others' safety in order to reduce, *overall*, the social costs of accidents. President Reagan assumes that since a driver careened off the freeway out of control, if you take away that driver's negligence the problem is solved. However, the problem isn't solved: there's still a telephone booth located a few feet from a hazardous intersection and the door to the booth is still stuck. Tomorrow the same situation could occur and meanwhile society would now have two legless citizens incapacitated from being productive members of society.

To sum up, we can see that there are two approaches to the question of how to define legal responsibility for tort losses, moral and economic. Within each category, there are competing moral and economic arguments. Reagan's view of social responsibility is largely moralistic, and reflects one side of the moral divide. Reagan would significantly limit the scope of responsibility; the only "blameworthy" actor is the driver. However, a competing view of moral responsibility (and one that most courts today adopt) would hold that the telephone company is also "blameworthy" by failing to repair the booth and by locating the booth so close to the intersection that it foreseeably put Bigbee and all other users of the booth at risk of injury or death.

Tort scholars will also generate an economic incentive argument in favor of liability: liability should be placed in such a way as to encourage actors to reduce overall social losses when they can easily foresee how their failure to take appropriate precautions could injure another person.

Thus, a relatively inexpensive move in this case—to relocate the booth or to fix the stuck door—would reduce foreseeable hazards to all users of the booth. Under this (economic) rationale, damages are awarded not so much to "make whole" the victim as to induce those whose activities risk harm to others to "internalize" the cost of injuries. The theory is that the enterprise should rationally calculate the amount of loss it is creating, and will take steps to reduce that loss by adopting prudent precautions. The difficulty with the economic approach lies in determining "how much" incentive towards investment in safety the system should provide.

As seen by most courts today, the major goals of contemporary tort litigation are (1) to compensate parties injured by tortious acts of others, and (2) to incentivize tortfeasors to avoid creating the conditions that led to injury. As to achieving the second goal, it important to the overall goal of inducing reasonable safety precautions *that benefit all* that tort claims for injuries continue to be brought. Indeed, tort lawsuits are "essential if tort is to play its central role in discouraging dangerous behavior."[6]

One final point about Reagan's perspective—and one often ignored in many controversies about the tort system: If we roll back the clock to a 19th century understanding of causation or a narrow view of responsibility, who will pick up the tab for Bigbee's losses? Who should pay for Bigbee's future health care? If he cannot work, who will bear the loss? Who will pay for his prosthetic leg and medical treatment? Will government provide for his health care under a new social program not yet developed?

Injuries and their associated costs will not be going away anytime soon. In 1997, for example, estimates pointed to nearly $154 billion in spending for medical injuries (approximately 20% of the nation's health care spending) and lost work time associated with such injuries added another $100 billion to the figure.[7] The pretense of some high officials[8] that the *tort system* creates the unnecessary expense, and that the losses would suddenly disappear with tort reform ignores the fact that these costs are present because people have been *foreseeably* and *avoidably* injured by the activities or products of those being held liable. Many legitimate criticisms of the civil justice system may carry weight; but to pretend that the injuries will disappear if the tort system is "reformed" is belied by the facts.

Whatever defects might accompany our civil justice system, and there are many, few tort critics have proposed alternative mechanisms that would address the inadequacy of the social safety net—whether for accidents generally or preventable accidents in particular. If the tort system is significant altered, one question that needs to be asked is: WHO should pay for losses caused by preventable, foreseeable behavior that causes harm to other people?

Civil Lawsuits and Torts

Some literature put out by advocacy groups sometimes gives the impression that tort claims comprise the bulk of all civil litigation. In addition, some politicians (e.g., the second President Bush) have emphasized what they regard as a high number of certain types of tort claims, such as medical malpractice and products liability suits. In considering these implications, it may be helpful to review some patterns of civil litigation overall.

Note that not all torts are of the "personal injury" variety. Indeed, many torts lawsuits are filed by businesses against other businesses and involve claims of unfair dealing, fraud, interference with business relationships, unfair competition, misappropriation, and so forth. When PeopleSoft objected to Oracle's takeover bid in early 1994, it filed a $2 *billion* lawsuit against Oracle in California state court alleging unfair competition. State Judicial centers have observed that contract litigation and business litigation (businesses suing other businesses) has been on the rise.

Other tort suits are filed by businesses against individuals who, it is argued, are interfering with some important aspect of the business. For example, when Intel objected to a former employee sending email to current employees, it sued him for "trespass to chattels (personal property)"—its computer system. And when Food Lion objected to the ABC's *PrimeTime Live* investigative report over its meat handling practices, it sued ABC and its employees for deceit, fraud, trespass, and breach of fiduciary duty.

In a detailed study of civil litigation trends in 1992 in the most populous counties in the country, researchers discovered that only 10 percent of all civil suits were tort suits. Roughly an equivalent number were contract lawsuits—usually filed by businesses. Of the tort lawsuits, 60 percent were auto accident cases and 17 percent were premises liability cases. Only 8 percent of all tort filings in those states involved the hot button "tort reform" issues of medical malpractice (5% of tort filings), products liability (3%), and toxic substances (2%).

Furthermore, other studies reveal that only about 5 percent of tort suits go to trial (slightly higher percentage for malpractice and products, depending on jurisdiction and year, perhaps 10%). Of the tort cases that do go to trial, defendants win about half, though defendants win a majority of the medical malpractice cases (roughly 70%). Thus, whenever someone complains about trials and juries one must keep in mind that the person is speaking about a tiny fraction of the total volume of civil litigation.

For example, if we use the above figures to approximate civil litigation cases, for every million civil lawsuits:

- 10 percent of civil suits = 100,000 are tort cases
- 8 percent of tort suits = 8,000 are hot button malpractice, products, toxic tort
- 10 percent tried to jury = 800 of the hot button cases are tried to a jury
- of those tried to a jury = 400 hot button trials result in verdict for plaintiff; 400 for defendant

Thus, much ink is spilled over what is, in fact, relatively speaking a small fraction of the entire civil justice system.

Notes

1 Samuel Warren and Louis Brandeis, "The Right to Privacy," Harvard Law Review vol. 4 no. 193 (1890).
2 See, for example, Nockleby (with Shannon Curreri). 2005. 100 Years of Conflict: The Past and Future of "Tort Retrenchment." 38 *Loyola of Los Angeles Law Review* 1021.
3 As reported on the website of the Nevada Trial Lawyers Association http://www.ntla.org/ff-mcdonalds.htm.
4 This account is taken from the website of the Nevada Trial Lawyers Association at http://www.ntla.org/ff-mcdonalds.htm which in turn based its description on Nader and Smith, *No Contest: Corporate Lawyers and the Perversion of Justice in America* (New York: Random House, 1996). The actual case is reported at *Bigbee v. Pacific Tel. & Tel. Co.*, 665 P.2d 947 (Cal. 1983).
5 Many 19th-century courts, like Reagan, adopted a narrow view of causal responsibility. See, for example, *Ryan v. New York Central R.R.*, 35 N.Y. 210 (1866) (holding that railroad that negligently started a fire that burned down its own shed could not be held liable for the loss to neighbors when the fire spread). The *Ryan* view was been universally rejected by 20th-century courts. See, for example,

Kirincich v. Standard Dredging Co., 112 F.2d 163 (3d Cir. 1940) (defendant liable for not having proper rescue equipment even though did not contribute to decedent's fall into sea); *Kingston v. Chicago & N.W. Ry.*, 211 N.W. 913 (Wis. 1927).

6 See Richard Abel, 1987. The Real Tort Crisis—Too Few Claims, 48 *Ohio St. L.J.* 443, 460 (1987).

7 American Trial Lawyers Association, Fact Sheet: The TRUTH About the Civil Justice System, at http://www.atla.org/ConsumerMediaResources/Tier3/press_room/FACTS/frivolous/THETRUTHciviljusticesystem.aspx, citing M. Susan Marquis and Willard G. Manning, 1999. Lifetime Costs and Compensation for Injury, *Inquiry*, 1 Oct, p. 244.

8 See, e.g., Dan Quayle: the tort system creates a "self-inflicted competitive advantage." Vice President Dan Quayle, Remarks at the Meeting of the American Bar Association (ABA), Atlanta, Georgia (Aug. 13, 1991); Dick Armey and Newt Gingrich: "Americans spend an estimated $300 billion a year in needlessly higher prices for products and services as a result of excessive legal costs." Newt Gingrich, Dick Armey, et. al., *Contract with America* (New York: Times Books, 1994), 143. The $300 billion figure is not verifiable, but is claimed to represent the cost of all tort litigation.

6 Contract Law

Victor J. Gold
Fritz B. Burns Dean and Professor of Law,
Loyola Law School, Los Angeles
Senior Vice President, Loyola Marymount
University

Introduction: What Are Contracts and Why Do We Make Them?

You make contracts every day. Every time you order a meal in a restaurant, use a credit card, or even just make an appointment to meet a friend, you have entered into a contract. While the average person makes hundreds or even thousands of contracts every year, large businesses annually engage in billions of transactions that are governed by contract law. As we will see, modern society would be impossible without contracts and without the law that regulates their creation and enforcement.

Contract law is unlike most other law. Most laws are rules imposed by the government upon individuals and businesses. Government often does this to validate widely accepted norms of conduct. This is true for criminal law, tort law, and most other aspects of law described in this book. But contract obligations are different because those obligations are *voluntary* and generally are not compelled by moral or ethical norms. By entering into a contract, the parties usually assume obligations and secure rights that no government authority imposes upon them. Thus, contract law is sometimes referred to as *private law*, whereas criminal law and tort law are considered aspects of public law. Of course, the government is not totally out of the picture since the parties to a contract might file a lawsuit asking that a court enforce their contract. And we will see that both the legislature and the courts have something to say about what private agreements will be enforceable and how they may be enforced. But we will also see that the basis for enforcing contracts is rooted in economic rather than moral considerations. Thus, what sets contract law apart from all other law is the voluntary and morally neutral nature of the obligations it imposes.

We begin our discussion of contract law with two definitions. First, what is a contract? A *contract* is a promise that the law will enforce. What, then, is a promise? A *promise* is a commitment to do something or not to do something in the future.

These definitions help explain why people make contracts: Contracts allow us to plan by making some contingency about our future a bit more certain. For example, assume a company that makes computers enters into a contract with a supplier under which the supplier promises to sell and the computer company promises to buy a certain quantity of microchips each month for five years. Having secured a source of supply of microchips, an essential component for computers, the computer company now can do some additional planning. It can build an assembly plant, hire employees to work in that plant, and establish a system for the distribution and sale of the finished computers. The microchip supplier also can make plans, such as arranging to purchase the raw materials it needs to manufacture the microchips. Without a *promise that the law will enforce*, planning like this would be impossible and our complex economy would collapse.

Of course, even our best-laid plans often go awry. One of the parties to the agreement might become unable to perform or simply decide to breach its promise because the deal turns out to be disadvantageous. But this does not mean that planning was futile. If the agreement contains promises the law will enforce, the party aggrieved by the breach can sue and recover compensation for its losses and, in some cases, even obtain a court order that the breaching party must do exactly what it promised (as discussed in detail later in this chapter).

The definition of contract, "a promise the law will enforce," suggests that the law will not enforce all promises. So the next question is, what makes a promise enforceable?

Enforceable Promises: The Requirement of Consideration

A promise is enforceable if the party making that promise (the *promisor*) received from the person to whom the promise was made (the *promisee*) something in exchange for the promise, and the promisor's motive for making the promise was to receive this very item. For example, our computer manufacturer promises the chip maker money and receives a promise of microchips in exchange. The microchip promise is precisely what the computer manufacturer wanted in exchange for its promise of money. In such a situation, the law would say that the chip maker has given *consideration* for the computer manufacture's promise of money. Consideration is defined as a *bargained for exchange*. By *exchange*, we mean that each side gives something and each side gets something. By *bargain*, we mean what each side gives is what the other side wants. If a promisor does not receive consideration for its promise, the law usually concludes that the promise is unenforceable. This means that the person making the promise can breach it without fear that a suit for breach will result in a judgment against the promisor.

It is easier to understand the idea of consideration if you think about what sorts of promises are not supported by consideration. The classic example is a promise to make a gift. Thus, if your rich uncle promises you a new sports car for your birthday and asks nothing back in exchange, there is no consideration for his promise. This means that, if he then changes his mind and gives you a sweater instead, you have no grounds for a lawsuit. This type of promise, called a *gratuitous promise*, usually is unenforceable.

Consideration problems often arise in connection with an attempt by the parties to an existing contract to modify that contract after it was made. Assume, for example, you have a contract to work for your employer for one year at $50,000. After six months of work your employer realizes you are grossly underpaid and volunteers to double your salary for your promise just to do the *same* work you were obligated to do under the original contract. The boss's promise of the extra money is unenforceable because you failed to give consideration for that promise. Your promise to do the work was not given in exchange for the $100,000 promise because you already gave that promise in the original contract. Since you already were obligated to do that work under an existing contract, this is called the *pre-existing duty rule*. In other words, since the promisor already gave her promise to do the work, she is giving nothing for the promise of more money. How, then, can you and your boss arrange to get you a raise that would be legally enforceable? You must promise something new or different from what you previously were obligated to do. For example, if you were previously obligated to work for one year at $50,000, the boss's promise to double your salary is enforceable if you promise to work an extra year at the new salary or change your duties in some other way that your boss wants. Your pledge to do something new or different would then be consideration for the boss' promise of the extra money and would make that promise enforceable.

At this point it would be reasonable to ask the following question: why doesn't the law enforce all promises, even those that are not supported by consideration? After all, if you and your boss want to modify your contract, why does the law make that difficult? And since your uncle obviously is a jerk to give you a sweater after teasing you with dreams of a Ferrari, why let him off the hook? To understand the answers to these questions, you first have to consider why our courts enforce *any* private promises. As described above, contracts are obligations that private parties impose on themselves. So why should the government care whether any private promises are enforced? Why bother to build courthouses and hire judges to enforce contracts?

There are many possible answers to this question, but one of the more sensible answers has to do with the economic benefits contracts produce for society. Recall that we have said that promises are essential to planning for the future and that a modern economy would be impossible without the ability to plan. This suggests that society at large has a stake in seeing that even private promises are enforced.

But not all promises produce the widespread benefit of a thriving economy. How, then, can we tell what promises are worth enforcing? In a capitalist economy, we usually assume that individuals are in a better position than the government to know how to spend their money. This is because when people have their self-interests at stake, they tend to make more careful and better decisions than some government bureaucrat empowered to spend tax dollars. Capitalist economic theory suggests that when government allows individuals to make these decisions, the benefits flow not just to the individuals in question but also to society in general because the resources of society are being utilized in an efficient, value-maximizing way. Thus, when people *bargain* for something, they tend to make contracts that have a payback for all society. But when people simply promise to make a gift, the promise is motivated by squishy sentiment and does nothing for the rest of us. Of course, the morality of this "greed is good" philosophy might be debatable, but it does provide a utilitarian justification for the traditional law of consideration.

Rest assured that modern contract law recognizes there is more to life than the pursuit of self-interest. In the past hundred years or so, the law has developed several legal theories for enforcing a promise even if it is not supported by consideration. The most famous of these theories is the doctrine of *promissory estoppel*. Under this doctrine, a promise is enforceable even without consideration if it was foreseeable to the promisor that the promisee would rely on the promise, the promisee did in fact reasonably rely on that promise, and the promisee would suffer some injury as a result of that reliance if the promise was not enforced.

For example, assume that your rich uncle, who lives in Los Angeles, calls you in New York and promises to let you stay for a weekend in his guest house for free. In response, you buy a plane ticket and fly to Los Angeles. The act of flying across county is not consideration for your uncle's promise unless your uncle was bargaining for your visit, as might be the case if he was lonely or ill. Let's assume neither that he is not bargaining for your visit but simply offering you a free room if you choose to come. So, with visions of sunny days and movie stars in your head, you buy a ticket, fly to Los Angeles and arrive at your uncle's home. Can he refuse to live up to his promise on the ground you gave no consideration for it? No. Even without a bargained for exchange, it was foreseeable to your uncle that you will have to buy a plane ticket to take advantage of his promise of a free room thousands of miles away from your own home. In such a situation, it seems unfair to let the uncle avoid responsibility for your detrimental reliance on his promise. Accordingly, the law of promissory estoppel makes the uncle's promise enforceable.

Notice that not all reliance on promises is foreseeable and reasonable. Assume, for example, that after your uncle promises you a free place to stay for the weekend, you quit your job because your boss wants you to work that weekend. This act in reliance on your uncle's promise might not be foreseeable to your uncle and certainly might not be a reasonable reaction to your uncle's promise. If so, the uncle's promise is not enforceable under the theory of promissory estoppel.

The Mechanics of Assent: Offer and Acceptance

Now that we have a sense of *what* promises the law will enforce, we need to consider *how* people make contracts. Often a contract consists of a single document signed by all the parties to the contract. If the parties are not able to sign the document at the same time and place, sometimes the parties separately sign different copies of the same document. These are called *counterparts*, which is a legal term meaning each copy is considered an original and of equal evidentiary value. But contracts can be created in other ways as well. Some contracts are created orally without anything in writing. We will discuss the enforceability of such contracts later in this chapter. Many contracts are created through a series of communications between the parties, some of which might be oral and some in writing. For example, our computer manufacturer might fax a written purchase order to the microchip maker, which might respond with an e-mail or phone call agreeing to the terms of the purchase order or proposing some additional or different terms. When a contract is established through separate written or oral communications by the parties rather than in a single document, we say that the contract has been created through the process of *offer* and *acceptance*.

An *offer* is defined as an unequivocal statement of willingness to enter into a bargain using language such that the person who receives the offer would be justified in concluding that his acceptance will complete the transaction and establish a contract. The person who makes the offer is called the *offeror* and the person who receives it is called the *offeree*. To connect this concept to the law of consideration, which tells us when a promise is enforceable, think of the offer as a promise. Thus, an offer says something like, "I offer [or promise] to sell you 5,000 microchips for $100,000." By way of contrast, consider a tentative statement aimed merely at exploring the possibility of a deal, such as, "I might be willing to sell you 5,000 microchips for $100,000." This is not an offer but, instead, merely an effort to negotiate. Thus, an unequivocal "You got a deal!" in response to such an effort at preliminary negotiation is not an acceptance and does not create a contract. But such a response might itself constitute an offer if it meets the definition of offer given above.

Assuming an offer, an *acceptance* is an unequivocal statement of willingness to be bound to the terms of the offer. To connect this concept to our consideration discussion, you can think of the acceptance as a promise given in exchange for the promise in the offer. But remember, we have seen that consideration requires bargaining—the item given in exchange must be exactly what the offeror bargained for. This explains why a response to an offer that varies the terms of the offer is usually is not an acceptance.

For example, assume the seller responds to the offer to sell microchips for $100,000 with, "I accept, but I will not pay more than $90,000." This is a *counteroffer*, not an acceptance. Traditionally, contract law has required an acceptance to mirror the precise terms of the offer, with even trivial differences leading to the conclusion that the statement is a counteroffer. This is called the *mirror image rule*. In some cases, however, modern contract law will permit the recognition of a valid acceptance even where a statement is not the perfect mirror image of the offer, so long as the differences are relatively trivial. But the general idea behind the mirror image rule still prevails: The offeror determines the circumstances under which she is willing to be bound. This means not only that the offeror determines the terms of the contract, such as price, quantity, and quality, it also means that the offeror decides how a valid acceptance can be made. Thus, the offeror can dictate whether the acceptance must be in writing or may be verbal, whether the acceptance is a return promise or a performance, when the acceptance must be given, how the acceptance may be communicated, where it must be sent, and who can accept. All of this is simply an application of the law of consideration, but in another guise. In other words, if the response to the offer varies from the terms of the offer, then the offeree has failed to give consideration for the offeror's promise since the offeror is not receiving what she bargained for.

Since both offer and acceptance involve a statement of willingness to be bound to a contract, the next question is whether that willingness is judged based on an objective or subjective standard. In other words, what if something reads like an offer but the person sending that offer was just joking or for some other reason was not serious—is it still an offer? The answer is, the law does not care if the parties really meant what they said. The only thing that counts is objective appearances. For example, if what the microchip seller wrote or said would convince a reasonable person in the position of the computer maker that the seller made an offer, it does not matter if the seller was joking—she still is bound to her promise. This is called the *objective theory of contract formation*. Our embrace of the objective theory is consistent with the notion that contracts are essential to planning. Since we cannot read each other minds, a person can plan only based on what is outwardly apparent. Thus, contract law gives no effect to unspoken, secret intentions.

Termination of Power to Accept: Revocation, Rejection, Lapse

Once an offer is made, the offeree has the power to accept, thereby creating a contract. But several things can happen before acceptance to terminate this power. For example, the offeror might *revoke* her offer. Recall that an offer is an unequivocal statement of willingness on the part of the offeror to make a contract. A revocation is a statement or conduct inconsistent with this willingness. Thus, the offeror revokes if she says to the offeree anything like, "the deal is off," or "I revoke," or even just "I am not sure I want to go through with this." Since an offer must consist of an unequivocal commitment, an expression of doubt or equivocation is enough to constitute a revocation. Similarly, conduct that communicates such doubt or makes it impossible for the offeror to follow through on her promise also is regarded as a revocation. Thus, where Joe offers to sell his car to the Sue and then sells the car to Betty, the act of selling the car to Betty is a revocation of the offer to Sue.

A *rejection* by the offeree also terminates her power to accept. The offeree rejects an offer if she responds with "I reject," or "I am not interested," or any similar statement indicating a lack of willingness to make a commitment to the terms of the offer. Further, the offeree usually is assumed to have rejected an offer if she makes a counteroffer. For example, assume the owner of a car offers to sell it for $10,000. The buyer responds, "I'll pay $5,000." If the seller refuses the counteroffer, the buyer cannot change her mind and accept the $10,000 offer. This is because her counteroffer already rejected that offer.

The interplay of offer, acceptance, counteroffer, revocation, and rejection often is a matter of timing. In other words, the order in which these events occur often determines whether a contract was formed. Events that occur prior in time to other events are given priority over those subsequent events. If, for example, an offer was accepted before it was revoked, there is an enforceable contract. Conversely, if the offeree rejected the offer and then changed her mind and sent what looks like an acceptances, the attempt to accept fails and there is no contract.

Since there often is a time lag between when a communication is dispatched and when it is received, the law needs some rules to determine at what point in time these events are given legal effect. For example, an offer, revocation, and rejection are all given effect only when they are received. In contrast, an acceptance is effective on dispatch. This is called the *mailbox rule* since an acceptance is effective as soon as it is put in the mailbox or dispatched in some other fashion. Thus, a contract is formed if an acceptance is mailed before a revocation is received.

Timing also becomes important in another way. Even if the offeror does not revoke and the offeree does not reject, the power to accept an offer will terminate if too much time passes after the receipt of an offer and before the acceptance is dispatched. If too much time goes by, the offer is said to *lapse*, which is the legal equivalent of saying the offer dies of old age. An offer lapses after either the time stated in the offer, or after a reasonable time if no time is stated. Thus, if the offer says it is good for five days, an acceptance dispatched on day six will not create a contract since the offer previously lapsed. If the offer said nothing about how long it lasts, we have to consider the relevant circumstances to determine what might be a reasonable time to accept. If, for example, the offer is to sell something that fluctuates in value quickly, such as stock in a publically traded company, the offer probably needs to be accepted almost instantly since no reasonable person would think she has the luxury of watching and waiting to see which way the stock market is going before accepting such an offer.

Defenses to Enforceability: Statute of Frauds

Assuming a valid offer and an effective acceptance and further assuming that there is consideration for the promises made by the parties, the next question is whether there are grounds for a court to refuse the enforce the agreement. One such ground was alluded to in a previous section: Certain contracts must be in writing to be enforceable. This rule is called *the statute of frauds*.

The statute of frauds was originally enacted in England several hundred years ago to address the concern that litigants might bring fraudulent claims based on alleged oral contracts that were, in fact, never made. Since an oral contract is by definition not reduced to writing, there is no way to prove with certainty who is telling the truth—the plaintiff who alleges the contract was made or the defendant who denies it. Thus, the statute of frauds performs the useful function of preventing fraudulent claims based on fictional oral contracts.

But the statute also presents some problems. First, the statute of frauds could itself facilitate fraud if it permitted parties to escape from obligations they incurred under real, not bogus, oral contracts. Second, it is impractical to put some transactions in writing, either because they take place too quickly, too frequently, or are too small in value to be worth writing down. Thus, an overbroad statute of frauds might discourage people from making some useful contracts.

For these reasons, the statute of frauds applies only to certain types of contracts, leaving people free to make enforceable oral agreements of other sorts. Among the contracts subject to the statute of frauds are contracts conveying an interest in real estate that lasts in excess of one year, a contract involving a promise of marriage, a service contract that by its terms cannot be fully performed within one year, and contracts for the sale of goods of a substantial amount. But while oral contracts not within the statute of frauds are enforceable, there is still a problem proving the existence of these contracts. This is because, while one party may insist that such a contract was made, the other party may swear that it was not made. This is a problem that the law leaves to the jury to resolve by deciding which witness to believe.

Other Defenses: Problems of Status, Behavior, and Fairness

There are many other defenses to the enforceability of contracts. These defenses arise because of three types of problems. The first type of problem concerns the status of the parties to the contract. The second type of problem arises where one or more of the parties engaged in some type of bad behavior. The final type of problem has to do with contracts that have unfair terms and/or arise out of a bargaining process that is unfair.

Status

Status problems arise where one of the parties to the contract has some characteristic that calls into question her ability to make rational choices. Recall that contract obligations are voluntary and that we enforce contracts because we assume that people can make intelligent decisions about how to spend their money or allocate other resources. But that assumption is simply not valid for certain categories of people. This includes minors, people with serious mental illnesses, and intoxicated persons. All of these people are said to lack *capacity* to make a contract. In the case of minors (usually defined as anyone under the age of 18) the defense is absolute in that, even if the minor looks and sounds like an adult, the defense still applies. This is a rare instance where the law abandons what we referred to above as the *objective theory of contract formation*—the notion that the law of contracts gives credence only to what a reasonable person would conclude based on the facts that are objectively apparent. The reason for making an exception in the case of minors is that there is a strong public policy in favor of protecting minors and that policy is no weaker (and might even have greater justification) where the minor looks like an adult. But in the case of people with mental problems or intoxicated persons, we adhere to the objective theory of contracts. Agreements made by such persons are unenforceable only if the other party knew or should have known about the problem. So if a person was intoxicated and insane when she made a contract, but she appeared sober and lucid, the contract is enforceable.

Behavior

Defenses to the enforceability of a contract also will be recognized where one party engages in certain types of bad behavior in connection with the inducement or performance of that contract. These are the defenses of *duress, misrepresentation, mistake,* and *illegality*.

Recall that contracts are voluntary. *Duress* is a defense because it calls into question the volitional nature of the obligations incurred by the target of that behavior. For example, in the movie *The Godfather*, the Godfather, played by Marlon Brando, famously instructs his henchmen to approach a business rival and, "make him an offer he can't refuse." Of course, the Godfather is not referring to an offer in the sense described above. He is instructing his boys to put a gun to the head of his rival and make him sign the contract. Since a deal induced by such conduct is not the product of actual bargaining and free choice, the economic and utilitarian reasons described above for enforcing contracts are irrelevant. Thus, where a person is induced to enter into a contract by a threat of injury to himself or others, the contract is unenforceable because the defense of *personal duress* applies.

While the vast majority of contracts do not involve personal duress, it is common to encounter pressure of other sorts that might call into question the volitional nature of the resulting contract. In fact, most modern contracts are made under some sort of economic pressure. For example, because you needed a job and had bills to pay, you may have signed an employment contract agreeing to take less money than you thought you should receive. Or perhaps because of competition and other market forces, your former employer had to sell her business to a multinational corporation at a fraction of what she believed that business was worth. Are these contracts unenforceable because of duress? Common sense suggests that the answer must be no, since otherwise virtually no contracts in a modern economy would be enforceable.

For once the law conforms to common sense. *Economic duress* is a defense only where a person is induced to make a contract because of economic pressure and the party taking advantage of that pressure engaged in some wrongful conduct that created that pressure or made it worse. We will again turn to Hollywood for an example. There are dozens of old Western movies with the essentially following plot: a good-hearted rancher (with, of course, a beautiful daughter) is the victim of cattle rustlers and has to mortgage his ranch under harsh terms to pay his bills. The owner of the bank is the evildoer who hired the thugs to rustle the cattle so that he might force the rancher into the mortgage contract. Because the bank owner engaged in a crime or tort to create the economic pressure that induced the contract, it is unenforceable for economic duress.

What if a party enters into a contract not because of pressure but because of ignorance of facts material to the deal and those facts are known to the other side—is the knowing party's failure to disclose those facts a defense to enforceability? For example, assume you make a contract to buy a house that looks sound and sturdy. The seller knows that the house is infested with termites but says nothing. Is the contract enforceable? Typically, the answer is yes. The reason is an ancient doctrine called *caveat emptor*—let the buyer beware. The idea is that knowledge is a valuable commodity and the law should not compel anyone to give away something of value for free. If one party happens to have knowledge material to the contract, the other side should not expect that knowledge will be disclosed. Instead, each side should do its own investigation and homework into the details of the transaction. Statutes create various exceptions to the idea that the knowing party may remain silent. For example, where a corporation publically issues stock, it is obligated to disclose its finances and other facts pertinent to the issuance. Similarly, many states require the seller of a home to disclose defects to the buyer. In such a state, the contract described in the example at the start of this paragraph would not be enforceable if the seller failed to disclose the presence of termites. And where the buyer and seller are in a fiduciary relationship, the law imposes a higher than usual duty of candor, which means that *caveat emptor* does not apply.

The most important exception to *caveat emptor* arises where a party to a contract is not just silent, but actually says or does something to mislead the other party about facts concerning the subject of the contract. For example, the seller of the termite-infested house might paint over the evidence of the infestation or might simply say to the buyer, "This is a termite-free house!" In such a case the contract is unenforceable on the basis of *misrepresentation*. This is a defense to the enforceability of a contract because the party taking advantage has said or done something to discourage the other side from investigating and discovering the truth about the facts. Thus, the above-described rationale for *caveat emptor* evaporates. But here the law makes an important distinction between misrepresentation of the facts and the mere expression of an opinion about the subject of the contract. The latter provides no basis for a defense. In other words, there is no defense if the seller simply says, "This is a great house!" This expression of opinion, common in any negotiation, should not mislead any reasonable person into thinking there is no need to investigate the facts.

Assuming no misrepresentation but one or both of the parties are ignorant about some important facts, the law might recognize a defense to the enforceability of the contract for *mistake*. The applicable law is different, depending on whether the case involves *bilateral mistake* or *unilateral mistake*. In the case of bilateral mistake, both parties are mistaken as to a material fact concerning the subject of the contract. For example, assume two art dealers enter into a contract under which one agrees to sell and the other agrees to buy what both are convinced is an original Van Gogh. After the contract is made, a Van Gogh expert establishes that the painting is a fake through painstaking research (demonstrating that Van Gogh never painted an image of dogs playing poker). The contract is unenforceable. In the case of unilateral mistake, only one party to the contract makes a mistake as to a material fact concerning the subject of that contract. In that case, the law gives the mistaken party a defense only where the nonmistaken party knew or should have known that the other party was mistaken. For example, assume that a person takes an unusual looking stone to a jeweler for appraisal. The jeweler carefully looks at the stone with is eyepiece and declares it to be worthless. Another person overhears the conversation and asks to take a look at the stone. He has a better eye than the jeweler and immediately recognizes that it is a valuable gem. The bystander offers the owner $1 for the stone and the owner accepts. The contract is unenforceable for unilateral mistake since the owner was mistaken as to a material fact concerning the subject of the contract and the other side knew of the mistake, since he overheard the jeweler misinform the owner.

An important limitation on these mistake defenses is the notion that no such defense applies if the party seeking to use the defense *assumed the risk* of the mistake. A party assumes the risk if she enters into a contract aware that she might be wrong about her assumptions. For example, assume the buyer of the bogus Van Gogh was pretty sure it was genuine but knew that the only way to tell for sure is to have the painting evaluated by an expert. If the buyer is willing to make the contract under these circumstances, she is not mistaken but just assumes the risk. The law does not save gamblers from a bad bet. Note that there was no assumption of the risk in the example of the contract to sell the gem, since the owner investigated by taking the item to the jeweler. Once the jeweler, who is an expert, pronounced the stone worthless, the owner would have been certain of that fact and would not assume the risk of her mistake. Compare that example to the sort of story that often makes its way into the news on an otherwise uneventful day—someone buys for a few pennies what appears to be a worthless item at a swap meet or in a thrift shop. To the surprise of both buyer and seller, it turns out to be a valuable antique worth thousands of dollars. The contract for sale is enforceable and the buyer gets to keep the item because sellers at such venues typically do not consult experts to appraise or otherwise investigate the provenance of their inventory. This is because it normally would not pay to do so. Thus, those sellers assume the risk of mistake because they are aware of the fact that they do not know the full truth about their wares.

Illegality is the final defense related to the behavior of the contracting parties. A contract is unenforceable if performance of the acts called for in the contract are illegal, or the acts in question are legal but one of the parties has an illegal purpose for entering into the contract. An example of the former is a contract for murder. Needless to say, if an employee hires someone to murder his boss and the shooter only wounds the boss, you will not find a judge willing to hear a complaint for breach of contract. An example of the second type of illegal contract is a contract to rent a car which the renting party intends to use in the commission of a crime, such as running over his boss. So long as the car rental company was innocent and did not know of the renter's illegal purpose, it can sue under the contract and collect for failure to pay the rental fees. But the party with the illegal purpose, the disgruntled employee, cannot sue under the contract if the car has mechanical trouble and is not able to function in a homicidal fashion.

Fairness

Since contracts are voluntary, traditionally the courts have refused to examine the terms of a contract for fairness. The idea is that people should have the freedom to make any legal contract, even if the contract appears to be a very bad deal for one of the parties. The fact that one party has more bargaining power than the other and is able to extract extraordinary concessions from the weaker side usually is not a problem. Rather, the traditional view has been that this is merely an economic fact of life in a capitalist economy.

But in the second half of the twentieth century, contract law began to recognize judicial power to refuse to enforce the terms of a one-sided contract, especially where the process of bargaining that led to the formation of such a contract raised questions concerning whether the weaker party really knew or understood what she was getting into. This is the defense of *unconscionability*. For example, imagine you purchase a new car and, buried in the multipage sales agreement, there is a provision in fine print and in complex legalese that states the seller is not responsible to repair any defects in the car and will not compensate the buyer for personal injuries caused by brake failure, even immediately after purchase. There are two problems with the fairness of this contract. First, the process that led to the agreement seems unfair in that, given the complex manner in which the provision is worded and even how it is printed, it is unlikely you were aware of that provision or its meaning at the time you purchased the car. This is called *procedural unconscionability*. Second, the term of the contract limiting the seller's liability is unfair in that it is grossly one-sided and there does not appear to be a commercial or business justification for limiting the seller's obligations to this degree. Compare this contract to a more balanced warranty limitation that provides that the seller will repair the car and pay for damages caused by defects for the first 50,000 miles, but is not responsible for problems thereafter. Further, from a social standpoint it is probably a very bad idea to permit the maker of consumer goods like automobiles to insulate itself from liability for personal injuries caused by defective merchandise. These sorts of problems raise questions concerning the fairness of the terms of the contract. This is called *substantive unconscionability*. In most states, the defense of unconscionability applies where the defendant shows the contract was both procedurally and substantively unconscionable. While the defense of unconscionability is still recognized, it now enjoys somewhat less popularity than in did in the heyday of sensitivity toward consumer protection issues in the 1960s and 1970s. More recently, there has been a political and judicial trend against government regulation and in favor of the traditional notion that people should have the freedom to make any sort of contract they want, even one that to the outside observer appears manifestly unfair.

The ebb and flow of the judicial popularity of unconscionability makes an important point about contract law in particular, but also about law in general: Law is not handed down on stone tablets from the heavens. It is created by flesh-and-blood judges and legislators. Thus, law reflects the political and social biases of those people. The law described in the next section of this chapter provides some vivid examples of this.

What Are the Terms of the Contract?

If a contract is properly formed and there are no defenses to its enforceability, the results of a contract lawsuit usually will depend on the terms of the contract. For example, assume that a buyer withholds payment for goods delivered under a written contract because the buyer claims that the seller delivered the goods late or even delivered the wrong goods. The seller then sues, claiming the buyer's failure to pay was a breach of contract. Typically, the buyer then countersues, alleging the seller breached first by delivering the wrong goods and/or delivering late. Who wins? It depends on the terms of the contract pertaining to the nature of the goods in question and when they were supposed to be delivered.

Determining the terms of the contract depends on *three basic questions*. First, if the contract is in writing, do the terms of the contract consist solely of what is in writing or can they be augmented by what the parties agreed to during negotiations? Second, assuming we know the terms of the contract, how should those terms be interpreted? Finally, if the parties never agreed to a term that pertains to the subject of the dispute that has developed between them, how does the court resolve that dispute? We turn now to the first question, the resolution of which depends on the application of something called the *parol evidence rule*.

The Parol Evidence Rule

Imagine that the buyer and seller in the example described above began the process of reaching an agreement by negotiating over the phone. They started their negotiation with the buyer describing the goods she wanted and the seller quoting a price for those goods. Let's assume that the buyer said she wanted widgets and the seller offered a price of $10 per pound. The buyer responded by saying she was agreeable to that price. The parties then discussed the other terms of the agreement until the buyer mentioned that she needed delivery within one week. The seller said that, for one-week delivery, he would have to charge $12 per pound. After a bit more negotiating the seller prepared a written contract, signed it, and faxed it to the buyer. The written contract called for the seller to ship widgets and the buyer to pay $12 per pound, but it said nothing about delivery date. The contract also stated, "This is the final agreement between the parties." The buyer signed the written contract and faxed it back to seller. The widgets were delivered two weeks later. The buyer refused to accept or pay for the goods, asserting delivery was late. The seller then instituted a lawsuit for breach of contract, seeking damages based on a contract price of $12 per pound.

At trial, the buyer took the witness stand and offered to testify that, during negotiations, the parties agreed that seller would deliver the goods within one week. Should testimony like this be something the judge and jury may consider in determining the terms of the contract? On the one hand, it seems likely that the parties intended their agreement to include the one-week delivery deadline since they discussed the subject and the written contract adopts the $12 per pound price that is associated with one-week delivery. On the other hand, the written contract says nothing about delivery date. Can a contract include terms that were agreed to during preliminary negotiations but were never expressed in the final written contract?

The answer is yes. The parol evidence rule assumes that, even where the parties have signed a document entitled, "Contract," their agreement can in fact can consist of more than what is on the piece of paper. This is a somewhat difficult concept to grasp: When we put an agreement in writing, our contract is not the document itself. Rather, our agreement is something intangible that exists independent of the physical piece of paper that might memorialize only a part of that agreement. This is because, when people negotiate a contract, they frequently agree to terms that they fully intend to be part of the transaction but then omit those terms from the written version of the contract. Evidence of such additional terms agreed to during negotiations is called *parol evidence*. The rule regulating the use of such evidence is called, not surprisingly, the parol evidence rule.

The rule is complex. This is because the rule has to balance two important values that come into conflict in a situation like our widget case. On the one hand, we want parties to a written contract to be able to rely on what they wrote down. Remember, we have said that the importance of contracts is that they allow us to plan by making some contingency about our future a bit more certain. There is a danger that when a party testifies as to terms not in the written contract, that witness is lying. A convincing perjurer might be able to sway the jury and upset all the planning of the party on the other side, who thought she could rely on the written contract. On the other hand, we know that parties to a contract often do not write down everything that they agreed upon. If we want to give effect to the complete and true intentions of the parties, sometimes we need to be open to evidence of additional terms, especially where it seems that the risk of perjury is small.

The parol evidence rule tries to accommodate both the value of being able to rely on a written contract with the need to give effect to the intentions of the parties. Thus, the rule provides that where the parties make a written contract that is the *final* version of their agreement, but is not their complete agreement, evidence may be admitted to show that the parties agreed to *additional consistent terms*. Evidence of *inconsistent* terms is not admissible. Applying this part of the rule to our widget hypothetical, the trial judge would first take note of the fact that the written contract in question says it is the final version of the contract between the parties. Thus, the parol evidence rule applies. If the writing was only a draft, or anything short of a final agreement, the parol evidence rule would not apply. Next, the trial judge would permit the buyer to testify that the seller promised delivery within one week.

This is because the written contract says nothing about time of delivery. Thus, the parol evidence on that subject relates to an additional, consistent term. Finally, the trial judge would not permit the buyer's testimony regarding the $10 per pound price. This is because it is inconsistent with the express terms of the written contract, which calls for payment of $12 per pound.

The parol evidence rule also provides that, where a written contract is both the *final and complete* version of the agreement between the parties, parol evidence of both consistent and inconsistent terms is inadmissible. For example, imagine that the written contract for widgets not only stated, "This is the final agreement between the parties," but also contained a provision stating, "There are no promises, verbal understandings, or agreements pertaining to this contract other than those specified herein." In that case the trial judge would conclude that the written contract is both the final and complete agreement between the parties. Accordingly, the court would refuse to admit the buyer's testimony as to both the time of delivery (the consistent term) and the $10 price (the inconsistent term).

Interpreting Terms

Assuming we know what terms the parties agreed upon, the next problem is interpreting those terms. This is a common problem since, as every writer knows, language is an imprecise tool for expressing intention. So how do courts resolve ambiguities in contracts? The answer is by employing common sense and by considering evidence outside the written contract itself.

Common sense rules of interpretation are numerous and usually intuitive. For example, imagine that a written apartment lease states that the tenant is entitled to keep "cats and dogs" in her apartment. Can she bring a hamster home? Common sense, captured by an ancient Latin phrase, *expressio unius est exclusio alterius*, suggests that the hamster will be evicted. Translated, the phrase means that the expression of one thing is the exclusion of another. In other words, by expressly permitting dogs and cats, the lease meant to exclude all other animals. Or imagine that the lease stated that the tenant could keep "cats, dogs, goldfish, and like animals." Can the tenant now adopt a hamster? How about a tiger? The Latin expression, *ejusdem generis*, suggests the hamster can take up residence. Translated "of the same kind," this phrase suggests that the hamster is a "like animal" since it is similar to a cat, dog, and goldfish in the sense it is relatively harmless. Under this standard, the tiger probably does not qualify as a "like animal." But what if the tenant argues that the tiger is covered by the word *cat*? The phrase, *noscitur a sociis*, meaning, "it is known from its associates," suggests that "cat" must refer to just small, domesticated felines who would feel at home with associates like dogs and goldfish.

More difficult is the question whether a court can interpret language in a contract by resort to matters other than logic or common sense. For example, can a court consider evidence that reveals what the parties may have intended when they used certain language in the contract? Evidence of intention can take many forms. *Parol evidence* is one example—the parties may have had a discussion during their negotiations that bears upon the question of what they had in mind when they used a particular word or phrase in the written contract. Or the parties may have given some hint of their intentions by their performance of the contract. This is called evidence of *course of performance*. Or if the parties had prior dealings, that history might give some hint as to what they intended by their current contract. This is called *course of dealing*. Finally, the parties might be members of a particular trade or industry in which the word or phrase in question has an established meaning. This is called *trade usage*. Parol evidence, course of performance, course of dealing, and trade usage are all referred to as *extrinsic evidence* in that each of these types of evidence exist *outside* the written contract itself. Courts generally take one of two approaches to the question whether extrinsic evidence may be used to interpret language in a written contract. Which approach they take depends on how they answer the following philosophical question: what is the most important value to be served by contract law?

For some courts, the most important value is certainty—the ability to plan for the future. In a jurisdiction that follows this philosophy, it is vital that the literal language of a written contract be given effect, if at all possible. This is the contract law equivalent of something many people are familiar with in the area of constitutional law—some members of the U.S. Supreme Court have been called *strict constructionists* in that they purport to interpret the language of the U.S. Constitution literally without reference to historical materials bearing on the era in which it was written or to modern social and political realities.

For courts that apply this conservative approach to interpreting contracts, the language of a contract is to be given its plain meaning if possible. Thus, if the language does not on its face appear ambiguous, extrinsic evidence is inadmissible to interpret. Assume, for example, that a contract calls for the seller to deliver to buyer a quantity of "three-pound" widgets. Assume further that, in the widget industry, it is well established that any widget weighing between 2.9 and 3.1 pounds is called a "three-pound" widget, since it is not possible to more precisely control for weight in the manufacture of widgets. Courts following the traditional conservative approach would not permit evidence of this trade usage to be considered since the term "three-pound" has a plain meaning and is not on its face ambiguous. These courts reject the trade usage evidence, claiming that it would not be possible to rely on a contract and plan for the future if a word as simple as "three" is not given its clear meaning.

Other courts reject this traditional approach in favor of more flexibility. For these courts, the prime value of contract law is to give effect to the intention of the parties. These courts reject the plain meaning approach on the ground that language is plastic and inherently ambiguous. For these courts, plain meaning is a fiction. Thus, these courts are more open to the admissibility of extrinsic evidence so long as that evidence is offered to prove an interpretation to which the language in the contract is at least reasonably susceptible. Under this standard, trade usage suggesting that "three" can equal anything between 2.9 and 3.1 would be admissible. Anyone familiar with the idea that numbers are sometimes rounded up or down could conclude that "three" is reasonably susceptive to such an interpretation. But extrinsic evidence that three equals one or five might not pass this reasonableness test.

Gap Filling

Assuming we know what terms the parties agreed to and what those terms mean, there remains a third question concerning the content of a contract— what happens if a dispute arises between the parties and the contract says nothing on the subject? For example, imagine that our contract for the sale of widgets makes clear the price, quantity, and quality of the widgets as well as calling for a specific date of delivery. But the contract says nothing about where delivery is to be made. Does this mean that delivery is at the loading dock of the seller's warehouse? At the buyer's store? The answer to this question might be consequential since the costs of transporting the goods could be substantial. In such a situation, the contract is said to have a *gap*. Where a lawsuit turns on a question that the contract does not answer, the courts have the power to fill the gap.

The law calls for courts to fill certain types of gaps in specific ways. For example, where a contract for goods fails to specify their price, the court fills the gap by looking at evidence of market price. Where the contract fails to specify place of delivery, the law typically calls for filling the gap by calling for delivery to buyer at seller's place of business. Where the gap pertains to a more obscure issue and the law does not have an established rule for gap filling on that subject, the courts have the general power to fill the gap with whatever seems reasonable under the particular facts and circumstances of the case.

Third-Party Issues

In the immediately preceding sections we addressed a *what* question— what are the terms of the contract? Now we turn our attention to a *who* question—who has rights and duties under a contract? The most obvious answer to the *who* question is that the parties to a contract have rights and duties under that contract. That is a correct, albeit incomplete, answer. Other people can have rights and duties under the contract as well.

This takes us to the subject of *third-party beneficiaries, assignments*, and *delegations*.

Third-Party Beneficiaries

People who are not parties to a contract sometimes have the right to sue to enforce that contract if the contract was made for their benefit. For example, imagine Sue retains an interior decorator, Joe, to work on the remodel of her house. Joe makes a contract with Construction Corp. that states, "Construction Corp. will deliver remodeling materials directly to Sue and install them in Sue's house." The contract is between Joe and Construction Corp., but Sue is entitled to enforce the contract because she is considered a *third-party beneficiary*. Sue gets this status and right because the contract specifically identifies Sue as the beneficiary of Construction Corp.'s promise and calls for performance to be rendered directly to Sue. But not all third persons who might benefit from a contract have the right to enforce it. For example, it might be that the contract between Joe and Construction Corp. provides a benefit to Sam, who is Sue's neighbor, in that the remodel of Sue's house increases the value of her house and, in turn, also increases the value of the property next door. Sam might benefit from the contract, but does not get the rights of a third-party beneficiary because he is not named in the contract and is not receiving the performance of Construction Corp. The law deems Sam to be merely an *incidental beneficiary* and gives him no rights to enforce the contract.

Assignment and Delegation

We have seen that a third-party beneficiary exists where that person is identified in the contact and the contract call for performance to be rendered directly to the beneficiary. This means that third-party beneficiary rights are created at the time the contract is made. But third-party rights and even duties also may be created after the contract is formed. This is done by *assignment* and *delegation*.

An *assignment* is created when, after a contract is made, one of the original parties to the contract transfers the right to receive a performance under that contract. The party transferring the right is called the *assignor* and the party receiving that right is the *assignee*. The person who is to perform under the right assigned is called the *obligor*. For example, after making the contract with Joe, Construction Corp. might decide to transfer to its parent company, Mega Corp., the right to receive Joe's payment under that contract. The law typically places few restrictions on assignments. In fact, even if a contract expressly prohibits the assignment of rights, the law usually permits an assignment. But the law sometimes will refuse to enforce an assignment, especially if the assignment will change the character of the performance involved. For example, Sue cannot assign to her neighbor Sam the right to receive Construction Corp.'s performance if Sam's house is more difficult to fix or even just presents different remodeling issues. In contrast, the assignment by Construction Corp. to Mega Corp. of the right to receive payment from Joe raises no similar issues since Joe's performance remains the same—he writes a check for the same amount no matter who is the payee. Assuming an effective assignment, the person receiving the rights assigned can sue to enforce those rights.

Delegation occurs when, after a contract is made, one of the original parties to the contract transfers duties to perform under that contract to some third person. The party transferring the duties is called the *delegator* and the person receiving those duties is called the *delegate*. For example, assume that Construction Corp. finds it is overloaded with building projects and cannot do the work for Joe and Sue. It might decide to transfer its duties under that contract to BuildCo., another company in the construction business. A delegation of duties will be effective unless the original contract prohibited it or unless it would aversely affect the rights of the party entitled to receive the performance in question, called the *obligee*. Thus, if BuildCo. is new in the business and not as competent as Construction Corp., the attempt to delegate the duty to BuildCo. might fail. Even if this delegation is successful, however, this only means that Joe and Sue must accept the performance of BuildCo. and cannot demand that the work be done by Construction Corp. It does not mean that Construction Corp. has washed its hands of its obligations. If BuildCo. fails to properly perform, Joe and Sue still have a claim under the contract against Construction Corp.

Conditions

Contracts are constructed of two things: promises and conditions. Promises create obligations while conditions qualify those obligations. Contract lawsuits are always based on an alleged breach of promise. The result in the lawsuit frequently is dictated by the conditions in the contract because a condition protects the person who made a promise from having to perform on her promise and, thus, breaching that promise.

For example, a contract to sell a house might read something like this: "Bill promises to convey title to his house to Alice, and Alice promises to pay $1,000,000 on condition she gets a mortgage loan at not more than a 6 percent interest rate." Notice that there is a condition on Alice's promise. She is not obligated to buy the house unless a certain event occurs, namely, she gets a loan at not more than 6 percent interest. If she does not get that loan, she is not required to buy Bill's house and will not be liable for breach of contract. This leads to the following *definition of condition*—a condition is an event that must occur or be excused before the person whose promise is conditioned is obligated to perform on that promise. In other words, a condition works like an insurance policy. So long as that policy is in effect, the person making the promise that was conditioned is protected against breach.

But the protection of a condition can be lost, just like the protection of an insurance policy is lost if you forget to pay the premium. When this happens we say that the condition has been *excused*. There are several ways this can happen. For example, under the doctrine of *prevention* or *failure to cooperate*, a condition is excused if the party whose promise was conditioned had some control over whether the event that was the subject of that condition would occur, and that person either acts to prevent its occurrence or fails to try to bring about its occurrence. Imagine that Alice, the buyer in the house contract described in the preceding paragraph, never applies for a mortgage loan. If Alice then fails to perform her promise to buy the house and Bill brings a lawsuit for breach of contract, can Alice defend the suit on the ground that the condition concerning the 6 percent loan was never satisfied? The answer is no, even though it is true that she never received a 6 percent loan. This is because Alice had some control over whether the condition on her promise would be satisfied, namely, she could have applied for a loan. Since she did apply for a loan, the condition on her promise is excused for her failure to cooperate.

Recall that Alice promised to buy the house "on condition" she got a mortgage loan at not more than 6 percent. This is called an *express condition* because it is explicitly stated right in the contract. But imagine if the contract did not contain language of express condition. It might read something like this: "Alice promises to pay Bill $1,000,000, and Bill promises to convey title to his house to Alice." Even though there is no language of express condition here, is it true that there are no conditions in this contract? Are Alice and Bill promising to perform unconditionally? If so, that would mean that Bill is obligated to convey title to the property even if Alice does not pay the money. It would also mean that Alice is obligated to pay even if Bill refuses to convey title. Neither proposition seems to be consistent with what the parties had in mind—it is hard to imagine that either Alice or Bill thought they were obligated to perform on their respective promises even if the other party failed to perform its promise. If fact, there is a common-sense principle of law that leads to the conclusion that the promises of both Alice and Bill are conditioned in some way that is not directly stated in the contract. This takes us to the idea of *constructive conditions*, sometimes called *implied conditions*.

A constructive or implied condition is exactly what it sounds like. It is not directly stated by the parties but is something inserted into the contract by the law to make the contract conform to what the parties obviously intended. For example, where a contract calls for the parties to render performances that can be done simultaneously, the law implies that each party's promise is conditioned on the other party tendering its performance. So in a contract calling for the sale of a house, the payment of money by the buyer can be simultaneous with the conveyance of title by the seller. In such a case, the law says that the buyer need not turn over the cash unless the seller is tendering the deed, and the seller does not need to turn over the deed unless the buyer is tendering the cash. The promises made by Alice and Bill are each subject to a constructive condition.

The law implies conditions in other situations as well. For example, imagine that Alice is now the proud owner of a house and enters into the following contract: "Alice promises to pay $1,000 to Paul, and Paul promises to paint her house." Again, there is no express condition in this contract. But notice that this is a contract in which the performances cannot be rendered simultaneously. It takes much longer to paint a house than it does to write a check for $1,000. In this situation, the law implies a condition different from the one described in the preceding paragraph. Here is the applicable rule: where the performance of one of the parties will take longer that the performance of the other party, the rendering of the longer performance is a constructive condition on the promise of the party whose performance will take less time. In other words, Paul must paint the house before Alice has to pay. This is perfectly in accord with how the world usually deals with service contracts. Normally, unless something is said to the contrary, we assume that the worker will perform first and only then the employer pays for the service. So if Paul never paints, Alice is not obligated to pay and cannot be in breach of promise.

One last point about conditions: remember we defined condition as an event that must occur or be excused before the party whose promise is conditioned is obligated to perform. What does it mean to say the event "occurs"? Judges and lawyers ask that question using different terminology—what does it take to *satisfy* a condition? The answer depends on whether we are talking about an express or constructive condition.

Recall our example where Alice promised to pay for Bill's house "on condition she gets a mortgage loan at not more than a 6 percent interest rate." Assume she gets a loan at 6.125 percent. Is the condition satisfied? The answer is no. In the case of express conditions, the condition is satisfied only if the event that is the subject of the condition occurs exactly as described. *Close does not count* when it comes to satisfying express conditions.

But constructive conditions are subject to a different standard of satisfaction. Recall the contract where Alice promised to pay Paul $1,000 and Paul promised to paint Alice's house. We saw that the law implies into such a contract a condition on Alice's promise—the condition is that Paul paint the house. Until he paints, she does not have to pay. But assume Paul paints the entire house except for one closet that he overlooks. Is the constructive condition on Alice's promise satisfied? The answer is yes. This is because constructive conditions are satisfied when the event that is the subject of that condition occurs *substantially*. In other words, in the case of constructive conditions, *close does count*. This means that the condition on Alice's promise is satisfied and she is obligated to perform or else she will be in breach of her promise.

But this raises a further question—what is the effect of Paul's failure to paint that closet? Does he get a pass on that? Is Alice obligated to pay the entire $1,000 even though she did not get all that Paul promised? This takes us to the law of performance and breach.

Performance and Breach

If all the conditions on a promise have been satisfied or excused, the promisor usually must perform to avoid breach. The only exception is where the duty to perform is first discharged.

Discharge of Duties

The idea behind discharge is that something can happen after a contract is formed to make all the duties under that contract simply evaporate. This can happen in two ways. First, the parties to the contract can make a new agreement that wipes out the obligations under the old contract. This is called *discharge by agreement*. Second, an event might occur after formation of the contract that is so inconsistent with the expectations of the parties that the law concludes it would be best if we just let the parties walk away from their agreement. This second basis is called *discharge by operation of law*.

An example of discharge by agreement occurs where parties to an existing contract agree to modify it by making a new contract to substitute for the old one. *Modification* effectively discharges duties under the old contract so long as the new contract is itself enforceable. This means that all the issues previously discussed that have a bearing on enforceability, such as the requirement of consideration, could be raised in connection with an agreement to discharge duties under a previous contract.

Imagine that a major league baseball player is under contract to play for his team for two years at $1,000,000 per year. The player wants to make more money and the team wants to keep the player bound for a longer period of time. Thus, they agree to modify their contract to call for the player to be bound to the team for five years at $2,000,000 per year, while leaving unchanged all the rest of the terms of the original contract. The modification is enforceable under the law of consideration since each side has promised something new—the team has promised more money and the player promised to be bound for three additional years. The duties under the original contract are now discharged and the duties under the contract modification go into effect. But what if the player simply refused to bind himself to the additional years—could the parties make an enforceable contract calling for the player to get $2,000,000 per year for just the original two-year term? The answer is no, because the player would have given no new consideration for the team's promise to pay $2,000,000 per year. The player's promise to be bound to the team for two years would not be consideration for the $2,000,000 promise since the player was already bound to the team for that period. This is an application of the *pre-existing duty rule*, discussed above in the section on consideration. In such a case, the duties under the original contract would not be discharged.

The second basis for discharge, by operation of law, can occur in several situations. Duties are discharged for *impossibility* where, after formation of the contract, something happens that makes it impossible to perform the promises in that contract. This usually occurs where one of the parties needed to fulfill duties under the contract dies or becomes physically incapacitated. It also may occur where the subject matter of the contract is destroyed. For example, imagine that the baseball player in the preceding example suffers a career-ending injury right after signing the contract with his team. Assuming the contract does not provide otherwise (and most major sports contracts *will* provide otherwise), performance is impossible and the duties under the contract are discharged.

Duties are discharged for *impracticability* where something occurs that was unforeseeable at the time of formation that now makes it unreasonably difficult or expensive for one side to perform under the contract, even though performance is not impossible. For example, imagine that a real estate developer makes an agreement with a building contractor to construct a project on some vacant land for a set price to be paid to the contractor. When the contractor begins the work, he discovers that the land is very rocky. This is a geologic condition unheard of in the area and will make construction of the project two or three times more costly than anticipated. The duties under this contract are discharged for impracticability. Notice that there would be no discharge for impracticability if the project was to be built in New Hampshire, the so-called Granite State, because the presence of rocks there would be foreseeable at the time the contractor agreed to do the work.

Finally, duties are discharged for *frustration of purpose* where a party's purpose for the contract is destroyed by some unforeseeable event and the other party knew of this purpose at the time of formation. For example, imagine that a person leases for New Year's Day the penthouse suite at the top of a hotel overlooking the route of the Rose Parade. The hotel normally charges $400 per day for the suite, but charges $4,000 as a premium for New Year's Day because of the excellent view of the parade from the penthouse. After the lease agreement was made, an aphid invasion destroys all the roses in the area and the parade is cancelled. The tenant's duties are discharged, meaning he can cancel his reservation and owes the hotel nothing. Note that under these facts it is neither impossible nor impractical for the tenant to perform since the bug blight does not make his performance, payment of money, more difficult. But his purpose for making the contract, to have a place to watch the parade, has been destroyed by an unforeseeable event, and the owner of the hotel certainly was aware of the purpose at the time the contract was made.

Performance

If all conditions on a promise have been satisfied or excused and the duty of the promisor has not been discharged, that duty must be performed or there is a breach. As we will see in the next section, the victim of a breach may sue and recover a money judgment to compensate her for certain damages suffered as a result of the breach. But the full legal effect of a breach is a matter of its magnitude. Where the breach deprives the innocent party of most of the benefit it sought from the contract, it is called a *material breach*. The effect of a material breach is twofold. First, the innocent party's damages are calculated as if the breaching party *did nothing*. Second, as we saw in the section on conditions, the innocent party is not obligated to perform on her promise since the constructive condition on that promise is not substantially satisfied. But where the innocent party still receives most of the benefit it sought from the contract, notwithstanding the breach, the breach is called *immaterial*. In that case, the innocent party's damages are reduced by the value under the contract of the performance rendered by the breaching party. Further, the innocent party is obligated to perform on her promise since the constructive condition on that promise is substantially satisfied.

For example, recall the contract between Alice, a homeowner, and Paul, a painter, under which Paul promised to paint her house and Alice promised to pay $1,000. Since this is a service contract, we learned in the section on conditions that Paul's painting of the house is a constructive condition on Alice's promise to pay. Assume further that Paul painted the entire house except for one closet. This is an immaterial breach since the performance gives Alice most of the benefit she was to derive from the contract. Alice is entitled to damages based on the reduced value of the performance caused by the unpainted closet, but she otherwise is obligated to pay the rest of the $1,000. This is because the constructive condition on her promise to pay was substantially satisfied. Now assume that all Paul painted was one closet, but left the rest of the house unpainted. This is a material breach, meaning that Alice is entitled to damages without giving Paul credit under the contract for the painting of the closet. She is not obligated to perform her promise to pay because the constructive condition on that promise was not substantially satisfied. On the other hand, if the painting of the closet did bestow some economic benefit on the homeowner, we would discount the damages recoverable against Paul by the reasonable value of that benefit without regard to the contract price. This is called a recovery for *unjust enrichment* and leads us to our last topic, remedies for breach.

Remedies for Breach

A breach of promise occurs where (1) all the conditions on a promise have been satisfied or excused, (2) the duties under that promise have not been discharged, and (3) the promise was not fully and properly performed. This section describes the remedies available for breach.

Damages

The damages awarded for breach are intended to put the victim of the breach in the position it would have been in but for that breach. These are called *compensatory damages* in that they are intended to compensate the plaintiff for its losses. This is different from another type of damage award you may have heard of, *punitive damages*. Courts award punitive damages not to compensate the plaintiff for its loss but to punish the defendant for its conduct. Punitive damages are not awarded for breach of contract. This is because breach of contract is not considered a morally blameworthy act, like a crime or a tort. As described at the outset of this chapter, contract obligations are not compelled by moral norms but, instead, are made voluntarily. We have also seen that the reason society enforces those obligations is to promote economic interests rather than moral norms. Thus, so long as the plaintiff in a contract lawsuit is compensated for its economic losses, the law sees no sense in punishing the defendant for its breach.

There are several types of compensatory damages, the most important of which are *expectancy* and *consequential* damages. Expectancy damages are equal to the difference between the value of what was promised and the value of what was received, if anything, from the breaching party. For example, imagine a restaurant makes a contract with a produce company calling for the latter to supply the restaurant with Grade A tomatoes. The produce company delivers a shipment of Grade B tomatoes, which have a lower market value. Assuming the restaurant accepts the lower grade tomatoes, its expectancy damages are equal to the difference in market value between Grade A and Grade B tomatoes. If the restaurant does not want to accept the lower grade tomatoes, it is entitled to *cover* by purchasing substitute Grade A tomatoes from another supplier. If the restaurant covers and has to pay a higher price than the contract price, its damages are equal to the difference between the cover price and the original contract price. If restaurant rejects the Grade B tomatoes and does not cover by purchasing Grade A tomatoes elsewhere, its damages are difference between the market price at the time the restaurant learned of the breach and the contract price.

Notice that in all these examples we focus only on a narrow category of losses that the restaurant might have suffered—losses associated with the value of what was promised to the restaurant. But the restaurant also might have incurred other, even more substantial losses. For example, the restaurant might lose revenue because it needed the tomatoes for a dish it planned to put on the menu but now cannot. The restaurant might incur expenses because it purchased other ingredients for that dish that now cannot be used. It might even be the case that the tomatoes were needed for a special catering job that now, for the want of those tomatoes, the restaurant cannot perform. And this loss of business might be the final straw that pushes the restaurant into bankruptcy, resulting in economic losses that dwarf the value of the tomatoes. These are all called *consequential damages*. The victim of a breach is entitled to recover consequential damages only if, at the time the contract was made, it was reasonably foreseeable to the breaching party that a breach would inflict this damage upon the victim. For example, assume that at the time the restaurant made its contract with the tomato seller, the restaurant owner made it clear that she would have to dispose of other ingredients she had purchased if she if did not get Grade A tomatoes. The owner did not, however, suggest that breach of the tomato contract could have any other economic ramifications. Under these facts, the seller would be responsible for the losses associated with the wasted ingredients since those losses were foreseeable to the seller at the time the contract was made. But if the restaurant was thereby plunged into bankruptcy and went out of business, these economic losses incurred by the restaurant owner might not be recoverable since the restaurant owner failed to say anything that make this possibility foreseeable at the time of formation.

Some contracts contain a clause that specifies what the amount of damages will be in the event of a breach. This is called a *liquidated damages clause*. These clauses are enforceable only if, (1) at the time the contract was made the actual damages for breach were difficult to estimate, and (2) the liquidated damage amount is a reasonable forecast of the actual damages. If either of these elements is missing, the clause is not enforceable since it then would be considered punitive in nature and, as indicated above, punitive damages are not awarded for breach of contract. For example, assume that our tomato contract called for the restaurant to pay the seller $2 per pound for 100 pounds of Grade A tomatoes. Assume further that Grade A tomatoes were available in any supermarket for $3 per pound. The contract has a liquidated damages clause calling for the seller to pay $1,000 in the event it fails to deliver the required tomatoes. The clause is unenforceable. Damages for breach were not difficult to estimate at the time the contract was made since tomatoes had a known market value of $3 per pound. Thus, it was easy to estimate that, should the seller fail to deliver the 100 pounds of tomatoes at $2 per pound, the restaurant would have to pay at the supermarket an extra dollar for each of the 100 pounds needed. Further, the amount of liquidated damages would not be a reasonable forecast of the actual damages since $1,000 is 10 times the amount of the actual damages of $100. Where, as in this example, the liquidated damages clause is unenforceable, the courts simply award the plaintiff its compensatory damages under the standards described above.

Sometimes the victim of a breach is not limited to recovering its economic damages but may also get a court to order the breaching party to do exactly what it promised to do. Such an order for *specific performance* is rare since, as we have seen, the justifications for contract law are mainly economic. This means that if the breaching party can with money restore the victim to the position it would have been in but for the breach, there usually is no reason for the law to require anything more. This logically leads to the rule regarding specific performance—this remedy for breach of promise is only available where money damages would not be an adequate remedy. Typically, this is the case where the subject of the breached promise is unique. For example, imagine a contract calling for the sale of a one-of-a-kind antique or piece of art. If the seller breaches and refuses to turn the item over to the buyer, an award of money damages to the buyer would not be an adequate substitute for such an item, since the buyer could not go into the marketplace with that money and find a substitute. This is where the courts will order specific performance. But where the item in question is generic, like tomatoes, specific performance is not ordered since the buyer could take an award of money damages and easily purchase replacements.

One final point about remedies for breach—it is important to remember that the remedies of compensatory damages and specific performance are available only where the contract is enforceable. As we have seen throughout this chapter, there are many legal hoops to jump through before it is possible to conclude that the parties have made an enforceable contract. Often it is impossible to know if the contract is enforceable until a lawsuit is filed and a court gives a judgment in that case. But long before the lawsuit is filed, one or both of the parties may have already performed—delivered tomatoes, painted a house, conveyed title to real estate. What happens if in the ensuing lawsuit the court concludes the contact is unenforceable? Does this mean that the party who already received the benefits of that contract gets to keep them for free? Both common sense and the law tell us that the answer is no. Whenever one party bestows a benefit on another party, the party thereby enriched is liable under a theory called *unjust enrichment*, sometimes also called *quasi contract*. Under this theory, the law implies an obligation to give up any unjust enrichment by either returning the specific property value received or paying its reasonable value.

7 Intellectual Property

F. Jay Dougherty
Professor of Law (Copyright Law and Trademark Law), Loyola Law School, Los Angeles

Karl M. Manheim
Professor of Law (Patent Law), Loyola Law School, Los Angeles

The term *intellectual property* is a relatively modern phrase, usually referring to several rather different bodies of law, namely, copyright, trademark, and patent law. Various other related business torts, such as trade secret law or unfair competition, might also be considered within this rubric. However, this chapter will focus on the three areas of law at the core of what we call intellectual property—copyright, trademark, and patent law.

Copyright provides a set of exclusive rights in original works of expressive authorship. Patents also provide exclusive rights for new and useful products and processes. Trademark law applies primarily to distinctive words, symbols, and other devices that indicate the source of goods or services, and protects them from use by competitors of confusingly similar marks. This chapter will consider each of those bodies of law in somewhat more detail.

Normally, when one thinks of *property*, tangible objects come to mind, either *real property* (land) or *personal property* (other physical assets). By contrast, intellectual property deals with intangibles—creations of the mind. These are often considered forms of property because of the rules that protect ownership and use of the creations. As with ownership of real property, these rules provide a legal basis to exclude others from certain conduct or uses of the subject matter. Thus, it is not unusual for an injunction, that is, a court order to do something or to refrain from doing something, to be awarded where an infringement, or even merely a likely infringement, is found.

It is not uncommon for nonexperts, including journalists, to confuse these different bodies of law. For example, one sees a news story about a legal dispute over the title of a film or the name of a pop band.[1] The story might describe the dispute as a "copyright battle," although titles and short phrases are not generally protected by copyright, but rather are sometimes given legal protection under a type of trademark law. We will now consider in more detail each of the principle forms of intellectual property. You will understand the distinctions and the fundamental ideas within each by the end of this chapter.

Copyright Law

A Brief History

Before the existence of technology that permitted relatively cheap and easy reproduction of expressive works, there was little need for law to protect the exclusive right to copy or distribute copies of those works. For example, prior to the invention of the printing press, books were reproduced by hand, often painstakingly by monks. To do that took a long time and much skill that the average person lacked. Hence, although there are certainly examples of recognition of an exclusive right to copy or distribute works in earlier history and in other cultures, the origin of modern copyright is usually traced back to the printing press. After the printing press was introduced in England in the 15th century, books could be relatively cheaply reproduced and the publishing trade flourished. This would, of course, have incredible impact on society and culture.

The predecessor to formal copyright law was a system that developed in England as a result of a growing publishing trade within an authoritarian monarchical society. Publishers wanted to limit competition in the printing of popular books, such as the Bible and schoolbooks. The king wanted to control the dissemination of ideas, particularly heretical or seditious ones. Craftsmen and businessmen involved in the book trade became organized eventually in the Stationers' Company, chartered by the king. The company had developed an internal system of exclusive rights called the *stationers' copyright*. Meanwhile, the printing of any book had to be licensed by the monarch. A complex system of stationers copyrights and royal *patents* (as the license from the monarch was called) developed, both to organize and limit competition and to facilitate censorship. That system essentially lapsed at the end of the 17th century.

Shortly thereafter, publishers lobbied for a law to protect the exclusive right to copy and distribute a book. Although the earlier system focused on rights of publishers, virtually ignoring the author, publishers emphasized the natural rights of authors to persuade Parliament to create the first copyright statute in the Western world, the 1709 Statute of Anne. This statute, which provided exclusive rights to copy books for a very limited period of time, became the model for colonial and then U.S. States' copyright laws. After the American Revolution, all but one of the states passed similar laws. It became evident that a uniform federal law was desirable, so the Constitution granted Congress the power to legislate copyright law. Hence, among the powers granted Congress were the power "to promote the progress of science and the useful arts, by securing for limited times to authors . . . the exclusive right to their respective writings."[2] This clause also included a grant of the patent power, which will be discussed below.

Copyright Theory: An Introduction

Why should government protect copyrights? There are numerous theories addressing this fundamental question. These rationales sometimes suggest different contours for copyright. It is useful to have some acquaintance with at least some of these theories as they play an important role in legislation and are often asserted by parties and judges in copyright disputes. Often, the United States and England have been described as having a view of the purpose and nature of copyright very different from that in the rest of the world, particularly the rest of Europe. The U.S./English system, with its roots in the publishing industry's interests, seems to have focused on the economic importance of copyright. A utilitarian, instrumental rationale for copyright is certainly important in our system's history. The idea is this: authors create something of value to society. But once their creation is made available to the public, anyone may copy it without payment to the author. In order to give sufficient incentives to authors to create works of value to society, society must give the authors a legal right to limit exploitation of their works, at least for a sufficient time to return enough value to the author and to those who invest in reproducing and distributing their works. Notice that this theory would suggest a copyright minimal in duration and scope—just enough to incentivize creation. Note, too, that it focuses not on some natural right of an author to own or control the products of her mind, but rather on the ultimate benefit to society. One might say that the introductory language in the constitutional provision above, "to promote the progress of science," recognizes the instrumental function of copyright. The "limited times" restriction might also reflect that thinking.

By contrast, another set of rationales views copyright as a natural right of authors. Often, the systems in other European countries are described as reflecting that view. Indeed, even the name for the right reflects this distinction. In the United States and Britain, we call it *copyright*, but in much of the rest of the world it is called *authors' rights*. There are various types of philosophical theories that assert natural rights of authors to their works, not just the economic value but also other interests. Some of these theories view works of the mind as extensions of the personality of the author. Hence, not only should authors benefit economically, but also they should have the right to control changes to their works (especially changes that might reflect negatively on their honor or reputation) and to receive attribution or credit for them (and not be blamed for the works of others). These latter types of rights (along with a few others) are often referred to as *moral rights* or by the French equivalent, *droits morals*. As with any rationale, there are some questions about this one. For example, some works are more personal than others. Is computer program or a database a reflection of personality in the same was as a song or a poem? If not, should it have less protection? How long should these rights last?

Another type of natural right theory is based on the work of the philosopher John Locke. Locke posited a general justification for private property, and it can be extended into the intangible world of copyright. Under Locke's "labor theory," when a person applies his labor to something in the public "commons," he should be entitled above others to the fruits of his labor, provided there is "enough and as good" left for others to labor upon. One question about this rationale relates to the "enough and as good" part, the so-called proviso. If copyright is too extensive, is there really a robust "commons" of material to be used by other intellectual laborers? What about works that don't take much labor to create? Should they have less protection? If so, you can see some line-drawing problems.

The utilitarian incentive rationale discussed above is based in economic ideas and suggests minimal copyright. A more modern economic rationale is based on what is called *neo-classical economics*. This can be quite complex, but basically the theory is this. If a resource is in the public domain and anyone can use it, it will be overused and potentially wasted, which is bad for society. But if it is privately owned, the owner can sell it or license parts of it to those users who value it most highly. Assuming the cost of those transactions is low, this will create allocative efficiency, which maximizes social welfare, as economists define it. Unlike the earlier economic rationale, this one would support very extensive copyright protection, because the more private control, and the smaller the public domain, the better it is for social welfare. Only in limited circumstances where desirable transactions are costly or highly unlikely, that is, where there is a market failure, should there be limitations or regulation. Note that in a way this approach leads to an extensive copyright much like the natural rights theories' authors right. Because this rationale is popular in the United States, to the extent this theory is followed, we have come full circle around to something more like the authors rights systems in continental Europe.

There are several other types of ideas relating to the desirable function and extent of copyright. Some focus on the realpolitik of interest groups and their impact on copyright legislation. Another line of thought emphasizes the importance of availability of prior works for use by other authors, and, hence, the value of a robust public domain. A third notes a structural role of copyright in a democratic civil society, liberating authors from the government or rich patrons and facilitating an active marketplace of ideas.

Each of these ideas has implications for the nature and extent of copyright in our society. One can hardly do them justice in such a short space as this chapter, but the reader can get a flavor for some of the types of rhetoric underlying arguments about copyright.

Copyright Doctrine

Unlike some other bodies of law in the U.S. system, copyright is based primarily on a statute, that is, legislation passed by Congress. Copyright law in the United States is rooted in a federal statute, the Copyright Act of 1976 (1976 Act), which became effective on January 1, 1978. That act was the result of 20 years of revision studies and legislative activity. Interestingly, some of the delay resulted from Congress's difficulty in addressing new technologies of the time, namely, photocopying, cable television, and computer programs. The 1976 Act changed U.S. copyright from the prior law, the 1909 Copyright Act, in many important ways, some of which will be pointed out below. It has been amended in several very important respects after 1976, some of which will also be discussed below. The 1909 Act was short and somewhat general in its language, leaving much to the courts to interpret. The 1976 Act was much longer, and it has become even longer, more complex, and, in parts, more detailed as a result of the post-1976 amendments. Indeed, it has been argued that the whole nature of the copyright legislative process has changed, so that certain powerful interest groups or stakeholders negotiate a detailed resolution of a problem, and hand it over to Congress for enactment. Some parts of the 1976 Act certainly read that way. I tell my students that I fell in love with copyright law in law school in the late 1970s, and it's like my significant other gained 300 pounds. I still love it, but it's harder to get my arms around it.

There are many ways one might break down copyright law's doctrines. For the most part, journalists will cover disputes over copyright and existing or potential litigation.

One way to break down the issues would be to address each of the questions below. In any particular dispute, many of those questions will have a simple answer, and the core of the dispute will be one or more of the other questions.

As a preliminary matter, what statute applies? Most current disputes involve issues under the current version of the 1976 Act, but because the law has changed over time and some older works may give rise to issues relating to events in the past, sometimes an earlier version or statute may be important. For example, there was litigation over the film *Woodstock*. Because the famous festival took place (and the film was created) in 1969, while the 1909 Copyright Act was in effect, some of the issues as to who owned the copyright had to be resolved under that act.

Subject Matter

Is the work involved in the dispute within the general subject matter of copyright? The copyright statute protects only "original works of authorship fixed in a tangible medium of expression." Thus a work must be original. In copyright, this does not mean that the work is unique or novel, but only that it owes its origin to the author rather than having been copied from something else. This is quite different from patent law's requirement of novelty, discussed below. Some works are just too simple to merit protection or are basic building blocks of expression, such as simple geometric shapes, words or short phrases, or colors. Perhaps such material is not original enough, or perhaps there are simply policy reasons not to give someone rights of copyright in such a work. Secondly, some very slight degree of creativity is required, perhaps implied by the word *author*. The Supreme Court has said that this is a constitutional requirement (remember the word *author* is used in the constitutional grant of copyright power, too). Almost anything would satisfy this requirement, but the Supreme Court held that the way of selecting and arranging information in the white pages of a telephone book was too commonplace to be sufficiently creative. Finally, the work must be *fixed*, that is, capable of being perceived or communicated for more than a transitory duration. Exactly what is fixed and the medium of fixation is very broad and flexible. For example, there was an early dispute over whether the audiovisual appearance of the arcade game Pac-Man was sufficiently fixed. After all, the way the game looks is to some extent determined by the player and varies from game to game. But the court found that the elements of the game were embodied in a computer ROM chip and the game's attract mode (the screen shown when no one is playing) is the same each time, all of which made for sufficient fixation. Another decision with incredibly significant ramifications for computers and the Internet found that simply loading a program into a computer's temporary RAM memory (the part that's erased when you shut down, if you don't save to a more permanent memory device) was a fixation. One reason this is so significant is that there are many short-term, transient copies made when material is sent or viewed on the Internet. Because those constitute "copies" in the copyright sense, they potentially infringe copyright.

There are also some general exclusions from copyright-protected subject matter. Copyright does not protect any "idea, procedure, process, system, method of operation, concept, principle, or discovery" regardless of how it is explained or embodied in a work. Some of these exclusions dovetail with patent law, which, as you will see below, can protect procedures, processes, systems, methods of operation, and discoveries under certain circumstances. A recurring problem in intellectual property is keeping protection under the appropriate system, because the requirements for, and scope of, protection is quite different. The *usefulness* of something is to be protected, if at all, only if it qualifies under patent law and then only for the short term of a patent. Thus, for example, in a formative 19th-century case, the Supreme Court found that a book describing a system of bookkeeping may be copyrightable and its words—its specific form of expression—may be infringed. But that will not prevent someone else from using the system described or writing another book describing the same system in different words. An interesting more recent dispute arose over copyright protection for a particular series of yoga poses, described by its practitioner as the only series that would achieve good health. The dispute was settled at an early stage of the litigation, but I would submit that the series should be viewed as a useful system or method that should not be protected by copyright in the book describing it.

Denying copyright protection to the ideas embodied in a work is of fundamental importance in our system of free expression. Indeed, this principle is viewed as one of the ways that copyright can be consistent at all with the First Amendment's freedom of speech. One difficulty, of course, is deciding where an abstract idea becomes concrete and specific enough to be protectable expression. This is not only a problem as to scope of copyright, but also as to determining whether works that are not literally identical are similar enough that one infringes the other. There seems to be confusion about this concept in the press, because one sometimes reads of a copyright dispute implicating the theft of another's ideas. As a matter of copyright law, it is simply not an infringement or theft to take another's idea. However, many states' courts will provide some limited protection for ideas under some circumstances, primarily when there is an express or implied agreement to pay for the use of an idea. But this is not federal copyright law.

A further limiting concept related to the exclusion of protection for systems and ideas is the complex merger doctrine. Under that doctrine, if there is only one way, or possibly only a very few ways, of expressing an idea or system, then the expression might be found merged with the idea or system, in which event the expression itself may not be protected, or might be accorded a thin copyright, which is protection only against a verbatim or near-verbatim copy. Although this is an esoteric concept, it arises in many contexts, from disputes over very simple works like jewelry or contest entry instructions to complex modern works, such as computer operating systems.

Assuming the work is within the general subject matter of copyright, what kind of work is it, and are there limitations on what is protected by a copyright in that type of work? The 1976 Act lists several categories of works of authorship that might be protected, but it is not exclusive. Those are: literary works; musical works (including lyrics); dramatic works (including accompanying music); pantomimes and choreographic works; pictorial, graphic, and sculptural works; motion pictures and other audiovisual works; sound recordings; and architectural works. Some courts in Europe have recently found perfume to be potentially protectable by authors' rights, but the United States has not gone there . . . yet. In addition to those specific categories, copyright may protect more complex forms of work: "derivative works" (works based upon or adapted from other works) and "compilations" (an original selection, ordering or arrangement of material, which material may or may not be itself copyrightable). Space precludes a detailed discussion of the definitional contours of each of those categories, some of which are further defined in the 1976 Act, and others of which are not.

Instead, I will discuss a few interesting issues, to give the reader a sense of the potential complexities.

As to literary works, for example, one limiting concept arises from the general exclusions discussed above. A factual work is certainly copyrightable. Of course, nonfiction journalism is copyrightable. But copyright in a work does not extend to the facts contained in the work. It does not give exclusive rights even to unique historical or other theories that may or may not actually be true, or even provable, if they are purportedly factual. Copyright also does not protect the hard work and investment that goes into researching and discovering facts and disclosed in only one work. An interesting example of this concept was a lawsuit against Dan Brown, the author of *The DaVinci Code*. Another author had written a book that proposed several historical theories, some of which also were critical to the plot of Brown's extremely successful novel. It wasn't a coincidence. Brown's wife, who helped him research *The DaVinci Code*, admitted that she used the factual book. But the original author's claim was not successful.

With respect to "pictorial, graphic and sculptural works," an important limitation relates to artistic design elements of a useful article (i.e., something that has an "intrinsic utilitarian function"). This limitation reflects the policy mentioned above as to protecting useful things under patent rather than copyright (note that there is also another type of patent for a novel ornamental design itself, as discussed below). Many useful articles incorporate artistic elements. But too much copyright protection might permit long-term exclusive rights in something that might not even qualify for a utility patent. To resolve that, the 1976 Act permits such design elements to receive copyright protection only if they are "separable" from the useful parts of the article. There is uncertainty about what kind of separability is required. It might be "physical separability." For example, the hood ornament on a Jaguar automobile can physically be separated from the car and stand on its own as a sculpture. However, most courts require only "conceptual separability," presumably easier to achieve than physical separability. The problem is determining what is "conceptual separability"? Different courts and scholars have developed various proposed approaches to resolving that question, none of them very satisfying or easy to apply. Examples include the "necessity to the utilitarian function" test, the "designer judgment" test, and the "likelihood of marketability" test (there are others, too). The first looks at whether the aesthetically pleasing features are necessary to the function of the item. If not, they may receive copyright protection. The second focuses on the design process, and asks whether the designer was motivated more by concerns of utility or by aesthetic goals. The third asks whether the item would be likely to be purchased if it were not useful. Because of its importance in the modern commercial world disputes involving this problem are not infrequent, but are difficult to assess. An interesting development in this area relates to fashion design. Clothing is a type of useful article.

Hence, it has very limited copyright protection, even though fashion design can be very valuable. Before the Internet, the problem of cheap knock-offs of the latest haute couture was of limited impact. This is in part because the designer had market lead time to sell the expensive high fashion version of the item before cheaper imitations became known and available. With the Internet, knock-off manufacturers can have photographs of the latest Paris or Milan fashions instantaneously, say, in China, and the knock-offs can be in stores perhaps even before the designer versions can be made available. Some other nations, such as France, provide greater protection for fashion design. As this chapter is being written, legislation to add a limited form of copyright-like protection for fashion designs to the law has been proposed (it exists now, but only for "vessel hull designs").

Finally, what is a "sound recording" and how is it different from a "musical work"? This is a distinction that I often find people have difficulty understanding, but it is key to understanding the music and record businesses. A sound recording is a work consisting of sounds, but, by definition, not the sounds accompanying a motion picture. Essentially, it is what we used to call a *record*. Often it will embody a specific performance of a musical work, that is, a song. The song is what might be written on paper as sheet music by a songwriter. The songwriter is the author of the song. There might be many different sound recordings of the same song. In fact, since the first time a right to make records of a song was included in copyright law in the 1909 Act, songs have been subject to a *compulsory mechanical license*. It's called a *mechanical* license because the early technologies for such things (piano rolls and early phonographs and records) worked on completely mechanical principles. It's *compulsory* because, once the song copyright owner (usually a music publisher) has permitted one recording of the song to be distributed in the United States, anyone can require the owner to grant them a license to make and distribute their own recording of that song. For example, many artists have recorded their own versions of Beatles songs. Each one is a separate sound recording, with separate authors. Who is the author of a sound recording? Normally, the author of something is the person who originated the creative expression. For a record, that would be the performers—the singers and musicians—and the producers or perhaps even an engineer (assuming he's not just adjusting things under instruction from the others but is making his own creative decisions).

One reason it is important to distinguish the musical composition from the sound recording is that the bundle of rights is different with respect to each of those types of work. In most countries, what we call sound recordings are not protected under copyright or authors rights at all. Performers and producers are not considered authors, but rather a lesser form of creator, more like a translator. They do receive protection, under a system of *performers rights*, which is a type of right that neighbors, or is related, to copyright, but is not copyright. Since 1972, when sound recordings were effectively added to the subject matter of U.S. copyright, the United States treats sound recordings as a type of copyrightable work, with a full term of protection, but gives them a different group of rights. For example, with respect to other works, imitating the work, that is, creating something based on the work that is not a verbatim copy, is an infringement. For sound recordings, as a matter of copyright law, the rule is different. One is free to imitate a prior recording—so-called soundalike recordings are not copyright infringements (there could be problems under state right of publicity laws, at least if used in advertisements, but that's another story). On the other hand, for other types of works, taking a very small, virtually unrecognizable part of the work would be a de minimis taking, not an infringement. But for sound recordings, taking any part, no matter how short or how recognizable, has been found to be an infringement (there may be another defense available—fair use—to be discussed below). This issue is important in the world of hip-hop music, where digitally sampling a small piece of a prior recording is a common artistic practice. But perhaps the most important difference between the right in a song and the rights in a sound recording is that the owner of a song copyright has an exclusive right of public performance. That right will be discussed further below. For now, what that means is that when a song is played in a public place, like a bar, or broadcast to the public on radio or television, for example, the party playing or broadcasting has to get a license to publicly perform the song. By contrast, they do not currently require a license to publicly perform a record that embodies the song. In the 1990s, the record companies were successful in persuading Congress that the ability to transmit recordings over digital networks threatened their very existence. Congress amended the 1976 Act to provide a "digital audio transmission" right in sound recordings, for the first time giving a limited public performance right to sound recording copyright owners. The statutory provision is enormously complex, and the right is subject to numerous detailed limitations and exceptions. Certain types of digital transmissions are subject to a type of compulsory licensing. Performers and sound recording copyright owners (usually record companies) have long lobbied for a broader public performance right, and as this chapter is being written, legislation to give them that, at least as to broadcasts, has been proposed in Congress.

The following are just a few examples of the types of limitations as to particular types of works. They are some of the important ones, but there are many others.

Duration and Formalities

Assuming the work involved in a dispute is potentially copyrightable, one must ask if this particular work is still protected by copyright. This involves issues of duration of copyright and sometimes questions as to whether copyright may have been lost because of a failure to comply with certain formalities. The duration of copyright is quite different for works published before 1978 and those created or published after that. Earlier laws, including the 1909 Act (and going back to the Statute of Anne and the first U.S. copyright law), provided for two terms of copyright. Under the 1909 Act, a work had an initial term of 28 years from first publication or registration in the Copyright Office, plus, under certain circumstances, a second renewal term of an additional 28 years. The renewal term was extended by the 1976 Act for those pre-1978 works, and then again by the 1998 Sonny Bono Copyright Term Extension Act, so that the total term can be as much as 95 years. There are various complex issues relating to renewals, mainly who gets them, and whether they may be transferred ahead of time. As to newer works, essentially, those first published after 1977, there are two types of terms. For works created by an individual author, the term now (after the 1998 extension) is until 70 years after the death of the author. The United States recognizes another type of work called a *work made for hire*. These are works made by an employee within the scope of her employment, and, under some limited circumstances, a work commissioned from an independent contractor. The term for those works is generally 95 years from first publication. Notice the significance of publication in connection with these questions. What constitutes a publication for copyright purposes is itself a complex issue. For example, you might think a public performance in front of an enormous audience would "publish" a work, but it doesn't. There are other technical issues. An area of recent controversy that will arise more frequently in the future relates to the 1976 Act's provisions permitting grants of copyright to be terminated after a certain period of time. One recent example of such a dispute related to Winnie the Pooh, a very valuable merchandising property. It has been anticipated that there will be some very complex issues regarding artists attempting to reacquire their master sound recordings under these provisions in the coming decade.

If a work is still possibly within its term of protection, it is still possible that the copyright has been forfeited. Until 1978, an author had a state or common law copyright until her work was *published* (a term of art). The author most often secured federal copyright by publication of the work with a proper copyright notice. If an author published a work without the right notice, it lost its copyright and entered the public domain. The 1976 Act greatly expanded the reach of federal copyright, so that it covered all original works of authorship that are fixed, whether or not published. It also moderated the potential for forfeiture by creating some ways an author could save her copyright, even if notice was absent or erroneous. These types of formalities are prohibited by the most important international copyright treaty, the Berne Convention. The United States desired to sign on to the Berne Convention, which it did, effective on March 1, 1989. In order to do that, some changes were made to the 1976 Act. One change was eliminating the notice requirement entirely as to copies published after that date.

Some people believe that one secures copyright by registering it with the copyright office. This is not true. However, until 1992 one did have to register and file a renewal registration too, in order to preserve her copyright. In 1992, future renewals became automatic, so registration really wasn't required at all any more. An exception is that U.S. works must be registered before one can bring a copyright infringement suit. There are also some other benefits from an early registration of a work. A related copyright myth is that one gets some rights by mailing a copy of a work to oneself and keeping the envelope sealed. This may come from certain entertainment industry internal dispute resolution systems around the end of the 19th century. But it is of no benefit in terms of copyright law.

Ownership and Transfer

Assuming the material is copyrightable and still protected by copyright, who is the owner? This has been discussed to some extent above. Note that a copyright may be owned by someone other than the author of the work. Other than the work-made-for-hire situation discussed above, copyright vests initially in the author, that is, the individual(s) who originate the creative expression. Hence, the author is also usually the initial owner of the copyright. But copyrights are treated as property, in that they may be transferred to others, for example, by contract or by will, or by operation of law. Most copyright grants are required to be in writing and signed. Some interesting disputes arise when there are multiple contributors to a work, who might or might not be joint authors. The consequences of joint authorship can be surprising. The statutes contain some rules and courts have developed various others to determine when that form of ownership exists. Another interesting problem area is the question of whether copyrights are community property, in states that require that between spouses. There have not been many judicial decisions on that, and they did not agree at one point. But now, for the most part they do agree that copyrights can be community property. Finally, it is important to distinguish the ownership of copyright in a work from the ownership of a particular copy or copies of a work. This distinction was not always clear historically, but the 1976 Act is quite clear. Acquiring a copy of a work (even the only copy [e.g., an original painting]) does not mean one acquires the rights of copyright (e.g., the right to make reproductions of the painting). As mentioned above, there must be a signed, written transfer for the copyright to change ownership.

Rights Protected

What rights does the copyright owner have that might be infringed? It is an infringement of copyright to do or to authorize any of six rights: reproduction, distribution to the public, preparation of a derivative work (for example, a film adaptation or a translation), public performance, public display, and the digital audio transmission right in sound recordings (discussed above). In addition, Congress added a very limited set of moral rights with respect to works of *visual art* (a defined term, essentially covering single works of fine art or certain limited sets of reproductions). Each of those rights has limitations and exceptions of various kinds, which are too numerous to describe here. I will give one example of an important limitation on the distribution right. That limitation is often referred to as the *first sale doctrine*. The owner of a particular copy of a work that was lawfully made in the United States is entitled to sell or rent or otherwise dispose of it without the permission of the copyright owner. This doctrine was very important in the development of the home video business. Because of the doctrine, film copyright owners could not stop stores that bought copies of videocassettes from renting them out. On the other hand, record companies and computer software companies were successful in persuading Congress to prohibit rentals of records or computer software (subject to some exclusions, including videogames).

Infringement

When is a copyright infringed? As mentioned above, unauthorized exercise of any right of copyright is an infringement. Where a defendant engages in literal or verbatim copying (reproduction) and distribution of an entire work that is protected by copyright, the only question will be whether there is some defense. But many works are influenced by prior art, and have non-literal similarities to that prior material. How do courts deal with deciding when that similarity amounts to an infringement? This is a surprisingly difficult problem that courts have always struggled with and still do not have a simple, bright-line test for. Actually, they haven't always struggled with it, because until the second half of the 19th century, only a literal duplication of virtually an entire work could be an infringement. Congress changed that, and expanded the scope of rights protected by copyright, after a case involving an unauthorized translation of Harriet Beecher Stowe's *Uncle Tom's Cabin* was found not to be an infringing copy of the novel. Since that expansion in the rights protected, then, courts have struggled with this problem.

Different courts have different approaches to determining when a work is an infringing copy (or adaptation) of another work. I will briefly describe the approach of the Second Circuit (the federal appellate courts based in New York and some neighboring states). The Second Circuit courts handle many copyright disputes, and their approach makes more sense than the other biggest copyright circuit, the Ninth Circuit, in California and some neighboring states. Under that approach, a plaintiff must show: (1) ownership of valid copyright, (2) actual copying, as opposed to independent creation of a similar work, and (3) sufficient copying of copyright-protected elements from the plaintiff's work, sometimes called *substantial similarity* between the works or *unlawful appropriation*.

We've already covered the first element, ownership and copyrighted subject matter. How does the plaintiff prove actual copying? Recall that in copyright it is not an infringement that two works are similar, or even identical, unless one was copied from the other. Occasionally, there is direct evidence or a defendant admits that he used the plaintiff's work and asserts some other defense. Otherwise, the plaintiff introduces two types of indirect or circumstantial evidence. First, she shows that the defendant had access to her work, that is, he had a reasonable opportunity to see or hear it. Maybe it was widely published, or maybe there is some more specific chain of events by which the defendant could have seen the work. That access must be combined with a showing of similarities between the two works that tend to prove copying. This is called *probative similarity*. Occasionally, there is similarity that is so unusual that it is highly unlikely to exist absent copying, called *striking similarity*. For example, in the phonebook case mentioned above, there were some made-up names and phone numbers that appeared in both the plaintiff's and defendant's phonebooks. Copying wasn't denied in that case, but if it had been that kind of striking similarity might have satisfied both the access and probative similarity elements to show actual copying. Determining substantial similarity is the most difficult element. Judges have tried to articulate approaches to this, but in the end, it seems to be a case-by-case, subjective determination, made from the point of view of the so-called ordinary observer. Would such an observer "unless he set out to detect the disparities . . . be disposed to overlook them, and regard their aesthetic appeal as the same"?[3] That is one approach articulated by a highly respected judge in the Second Circuit, Learned Hand. In a much earlier case involving two popular plays, Hand articulated the problem in what is often referred to as the *abstractions test*. It is not really a test, but an observation that works may be similar at a high level of abstraction without infringing. If they are still similar as one looks at them in more concrete, less abstract detail, at some point infringement exists.

Indirect Infringement

A final aspect of infringement that has gained a great deal of importance in the digital era concerns the question of indirect infringement. The person who actually engages in copying or the exercise of another right of copyright is a direct infringer, but what about others who are involved in the infringing conduct in some way? The highly publicized Napster and Grokster cases have pulled this question into the public eye. There are two forms of indirect infringement, with very different requirements. Incidentally, although it was the high technology peer-to-peer file sharing systems that has popularized this concern, it was a case involving an old-fashioned flea market that articulated the current requirements and clearly distinguished the two forms of indirect liability. First, one may be a *vicarious infringer* if one has the right and ability to supervise and control the conduct of the infringer and can obtain a financial benefit from that infringement. This has developed from the more general concept that an employer is responsible for the conduct of her employees on the job. Second, one might be a *contributory infringer* if one has knowledge of the infringement and materially contributes to it or actively induces it. Notice that the vicarious infringer may be liable even without proof that she had knowledge of the infringement, and the contributory infringer may be liable even if she obtained no financial benefit. Because Napster operated a central server with an index of available recordings, had knowledge about at least some infringing acts, and stood to make substantial money eventually, it was liable under both theories. Grokster and related technologies were more difficult to analyze legally because they were far more decentralized. Ultimately, the Supreme Court focused on the "active inducement" type of contributory liability to find that the defendant could be liable. Many questions remain open concerning the relationship between copyright owners and makers and distributors of technologies that have infringing uses, but perhaps also non-infringing ones. Scholars and others had hoped that the Supreme Court would clarify its Sony Betamax decision in the Grokster case, but instead the majority resolved the issue on a somewhat different basis, failing to agree on how to properly interpret Sony.

Defenses

Assuming infringement is found, are there any defenses? There are various ways to defend an infringement claim. Some are standard defenses used in other areas of law. Others involve rebutting one or more elements of the claim. Perhaps the most interesting and important copyright defense is called *fair use*. This was developed by judges in the 19th century, and eventually codified for the first time in the 1976 Act. In addition to the idea/expression dichotomy discussed above, fair use may reflect important freedom of speech limitations on copyright. This is an enormous and complex area of copyright law, and there are many points of view about what the defense represents and how it should be approached, which cannot be done justice in this short chapter. Briefly, certain types of uses of copyrighted works, for example criticism, teaching, and news reporting, are viewed as having social value and are of limited harm to the copyright owner. In some cases, such as parody, the use is considered important to free expression, but unlikely to be licensed by the copyright owner (i.e., there is a market failure).

Doctrinally, the statute directs courts to consider four factors in assessing fair use. The Supreme Court said that those factors are not to be assessed individually and counted up, but rather to be carefully balanced as a whole

262   F. Jay Dougherty and Karl M. Manheim

based on the facts of each case. Numerous facts can come to bear on each factor, and I will mention only a few. First, the purpose and character of the use is to be considered. A commercial use is less favored that a nonprofit educational use, for example. After the Supreme Court's decision involving whether Sony was indirectly liable for copyright infringement by making and selling the Betamax VCR, a great deal of emphasis was placed on whether the use was commercial. If so, most courts found it to be presumptively not a fair use. In the Supreme Court's last decision concerning fair use, which involved a rap parody of Roy Orbison's rock-and-roll classic, "Oh, Pretty Woman," the court instead emphasized considering whether the character of the use is "transformative"; that is, does it add new expression, adding new meaning or a different purpose from the original, as opposed to verbatim copying. If so, it is less likely to act as a substitute for the original and more likely to be a fair use. Since that decision, most courts emphasize transformativeness in their fair use analyses. Second, courts look at the nature of the work copied. It is more likely to be a fair use if that work is a factual one than if it is a creative or artistic work, for example. At one point there were several judicial decisions that emphasized whether the work used had been published or not. They suggested that if it was not previously published, fair use would be virtually impossible. This was so disturbing to scholars and others that Congress was persuaded to add a provision to the statute rejecting such a conclusive presumption. Third, the court will consider the amount and substantiality of the portion used. For example, short quotations used in a review are much more likely to be fair use than long excerpts. This can be quantitative or qualitative, because a short excerpt might constitute the qualitative "heart" of the work. Finally, the court assesses the effect of the use on the potential markets for or value of the work. This is a very important factor. Is the defendant's use likely to act as a market substitute for the work used? If so, it would likely undermine the very incentives copyright is meant to provide. The same could be said as to markets for adaptations and works based upon the plaintiff's work, whether the plaintiff is actually in those markets or they should reasonably be expected to be in the control of the copyright owner. Some cases are rather expansive in their view of the copyright owner's markets. For example, in one case the defendant created a book of trivia questions about the *Seinfeld* television series episodes. Of course, they had to describe certain aspects of the episodes. This was found not to be a fair use, largely because the court was persuaded that the copyright owner of the show should have the right to control such an ancillary market.

Conclusion

There is much more to say about copyright law. We haven't covered entire topics, such as what remedies are available and when federal copyright law preempts state laws. The world of international trade and digital communication, issues presented by user-generated content, and many other current developments test the limits of copyright as it has historically existed. The controversial Digital Millennium Copyright Act of 1998 facilitated the use of technologies to limit access or use of copyrighted works, signaling increasing reliance on technology and self-help by at least some copyright owners as an alternative to traditional copyright. But we must move on to consider other forms of intellectual property!

Trademark Law

Introduction and Historical Roots

Trademark law is a branch of a much broader group of business torts known as *unfair competition*. A *trademark* is a word, name, symbol, device, or other designation, or combination of those, that is distinctive of a source of goods and distinguishes them from the goods of others. A *service mark* is similar, but is used to distinguish services, rather than products. This chapter will refer primarily to trademarks, but most of the concepts will also apply to service marks. Trademarks may be words or slogans, but may also be other types of material, such as designs (subject to some limitations), trade dress (the configuration, features, or packaging of the product itself, as long as it indicates source and is not functional), colors or combinations of colors (subject to some limitations), sounds (if not distinctive, they require secondary meaning, which will be discussed below), and even a distinctive fragrance (as long as not functional—the fragrance of a perfume, for example, is functional). The federal trademark law also provides for other categories of marks, namely certification marks and collective marks, discussion of which is beyond the scope of this chapter.

The roots of trademarks may go back to craftsmen's use of identifying marks on their goods in the ancient Middle and Far East. That type of mark affixation was certainly common, and regulated, in the middle ages. Such marks became an indicator of the source of origin and likely quality of goods. More recently, the 19th-century English and American antecedent of contemporary trademark law was common law protection against "palming off" or "passing off" goods as the goods of another. For example, if I were to manufacture a cheap suit and place an Armani label on it, or advertise it using photographs of an Armani suit, I would be attempting to confuse consumers into thinking that my suit originated from the source of Armani suits. I would be taking advantage of Armani's reputation in the marketplace (i.e., its "good will") deceiving consumers as to the quality of my suit, and engaging in palming off.

Thus, trademark law in part is to protect consumers from being deceived as to the source of origin of goods, and the accompanying assumptions about sponsorship, association, and quality. Trademarks also protect the good will and reputation of commercial enterprises from being unfairly appropriated by competitors and others. Among the various modern rationales for trademark protection are that it reduces consumers' information search costs, by symbolically telling them something about where their purchases originate. This lowers transaction costs and contributes to economic efficiency.

Unlike copyrights and patents, Congress is not expressly granted the power to provide trademark rights in the Constitution. In fact, the first federal trademark statutes, enacted in the middle of the 19th century, were found to be unconstitutional. Congress was later able to enact federal trademark legislation under its interstate commerce power. Of course, in order to do that, the trademark must be used in interstate commerce. Hence, trademark rights arise primarily under state common law. They may be enhanced by state registration systems, and are further enhanced in certain ways by federal trademark legislation once they are used in interstate commerce. The current federal trademark law was passed in 1946 and is known as the Lanham Act. Because one acquires trademark rights by use in commerce as a trademark, registration is not required. But registration does accord certain benefits, which will be discussed in somewhat more detail below.

Generally, the elements of a trademark infringement action are: (1) ownership, (2) ownership of a valid, protectable mark, and (3) a likelihood of confusion as to the source of origin, approval, sponsorship, or association of another with the product. Each of those elements involves terms of art and some complex concepts, which we can only introduce in this chapter.

Ownership

Unlike copyrights and patents, trademarks are not owned as property as such. In U.S. law, unlike the laws of many nations, trademark rights are acquired by use of a mark as a trademark—an indicator of source—in commerce. They are not acquired simply by adopting or registering them. Generally, the first person or entity who uses the mark as a trademark for specific goods or services obtains rights in that mark for that type of goods (and possibly types of goods he'd be likely to expand into), in the geographic area in which it's used and in potential areas of expansion (this geographic expansion can be limited under registration systems such as federal registration). The person who is in a position to control the nature and quality of the goods or services would usually be the proper claimant. For example, there was a dispute between a record producer/manager and the members of a popular R&B group called New Edition over ownership of that service mark. Although the producer was very involved in the commercial success of the group, the members had used the name before they worked with the producer and the court determined that it was ultimately the group members who controlled the quality of the services, so they owned the mark. Generally, trademarks must be affixed to the goods or used on labels or marketing materials used closely with the goods. Federal law is somewhat more restrictive than common law as to the affixation requirement.

Trademark lawyers say that trademarks cannot be owned or transferred in gross, that is, apart from the sale of business as to which they are appurtenant and its good will. Trademarks can be licensed for use by third parties, subject to many restrictions to assure that the trademark owner continues to be involved in how the mark is used and in the quality of products with which it is used.

Traditionally, one obtained rights with respect to the use of a mark on the specific type of goods as to which the mark was used as a trademark and in the geographic area in which it was so used. One who innocently adopted the same or a similar mark in another geographic area could also use the mark in their own area. This makes sense, since consumers would not be confused as to the source of goods if they weren't aware of the distant producer. One advantage of federal registration is that everyone in the United States is deemed to have constructive knowledge of the claim of trademark rights of the federal registrant. Effectively, this gives the federal registrant nationwide rights in the mark as to subsequent adopters of a similar mark, though there is provision to protect those who are already using a mark in a geographic area.

Federal registration is a somewhat specialized practice, although anyone may do it, without a particular license (unlike patent applications, for example). The registrant must give examples of the mark as used in interstate commerce and indicate which classes of goods or services it is used in. (In recent years, the Lanham Act was amended to also permit an "intent to use" (ITU) trademark application by someone who has a good faith intent to use the mark in commerce and satisfies some other requirements. Such a mark won't be registered until after the Trademark Office has been notified that it actually has been so used, within a certain period of time after the ITU application.) An examiner considers whether registration should be refused based on any of several potential exclusions, including what other marks have been registered that might be confusingly similar, and often initially rejects the application on that basis. The applicant has the opportunity to persuade the examiner that there is no real likelihood of confusion. We will discuss factors that show a likelihood of confusion below. If the applicant is successful, the mark is published in the Official Gazette of the Patent and Trademark Office, and others who have a reasonable basis for believing that they will be commercially damaged by the registration have a short period of time during which they may oppose the registration through proceedings before the Trademark Trial and Appeal Board (TTAB; a group appointed by the Commissioner of Patents and Trademarks). If it is not opposed, or if the opposition is unsuccessful, the mark is registered (and the registration published in the Official Gazetteer), and the registrant secures the benefits of federal registration (availability of some remedies is dependent on the registrant's use of a notice of registration, such as the r in a circle). Certain affidavits of continued use must be filed in the 6th and 10th year after registration in order to avoid cancellation of the registration, and federally registered trademark protection can continue in 10-year periods forever, so long as the mark continues to be used in commerce and an affidavit of that is filed in the 10th year of each 10-year period.

Trademark protection can be lost if the mark is abandoned (i.e., no longer used in commerce with no plans to resume commercial use). Under federal law, abandonment is presumed after non-use for three years, but that can be rebutted by explaining the suspension and proving plans to resume commercial use.

Validity

A *valid* mark is one that is used as an indicator of source and not simply to describe or decorate the product. It must be used in the ordinary course of business to produce an association between the mark and the source of the goods. Pre-sales marketing may suffice, as long as the use was to create that kind of association. For example, merely registering a domain name doesn't give one trademark rights. For purposes of federal registration, there are several types of marks that are barred from registration. Some types of marks are absolutely barred, including immoral or scandalous matter (this one can only be raised by a third party, not the examiner), disparaging or possibly disparaging (e.g., to persons or beliefs or national symbols), deceptive matter (including geographic deception) marks, or marks that falsely suggest a connection with persons, institutions, beliefs, or national symbols. Because of international agreements, marks that misdescribe the geographic origin of wine or spirits is also within this group of prohibited marks. An interesting example of the absolute bar was a dispute regarding the name for the Washington Redskins. The TTAB found that it was not "scandalous" because the term is acceptable to a substantial part of the population. But several years later a group of Native Americans successfully persuaded the TTAB to cancel the registration because the term was "disparaging" to a substantial group of Native Americans. Some other categories of material for which federal registration is barred are: marks consisting of the flag or insignia of nations, states, or municipalities; the name, portrait, or signature of any living person without permission, or of any president of the United States so long as the widow is alive; a mark that is so similar to another mark registered or used in the United States that it is likely to cause confusion, mistake, or to deceive (note that such a mark is also subject to cancellation for five years after registration); marks merely descriptive or deceptively misdescriptive; primarily geographically descriptive marks (unless they have developed "secondary meaning," which will be discussed below) or geographically misdescriptive; marks that are primarily merely a surname (unless they have achieved "secondary meaning"); and material that, as a whole, is functional.

Distinctiveness

To be protectable a mark must be distinctive. Several types of marks are considered inherently distinctive and may become protectable as marks as soon as they are used as such in commerce. The more distinctive a mark, the stronger it is considered to be. Perhaps the strongest type of mark is a *fanciful* or coined mark. This might be a word that is not part of the language, but that was invented for use as a trademark. Exxon would be an example. Another type of inherently distinctive mark is an *arbitrary* mark. This is a mark that is a real word, but one that has nothing to do with the product as to which it is used. Apple for computers might be a good example. The third type of inherently distinctive mark is a suggestive mark. This one is a little more vague. It is a real word that has only an indirect, suggestive connection with the product, one that requires some operation of the imagination to associate it with the qualities of the product. For example, Bronco suggests toughness, perhaps power, and a little wildness. Hence, it is suggestive as a trademark for trucks.

By contrast, words or marks that describe a product—*descriptive* marks—are not inherently descriptive. Of course, there is some risk in permitting a single entity to obtain somewhat exclusive rights in terms that describe its products. One risk is limiting the ability of competitors to describe their own similar products without a lawsuit, or otherwise limiting the use of a descriptive term. This might even reduce consumers' ability to obtain information about a product, rather than enhance it. However, even descriptive terms can become protectable as trademarks, if the user can prove that she has used the term in such a way that it has become recognized by the consuming public as having a meaning beyond its primary descriptive meaning, as an indicator of source. That type of meaning is called *secondary meaning*. There is no bright-line test for secondary meaning. Rather courts have developed various multifactor tests. Usually, they include the length and exclusivity of the use (the longer it has been used as a mark and the fewer other uses of a similar mark, the more likely secondary meaning); sales volume (greater sales, more likely secondary meaning); amount of advertising (more advertising and advertising expenditures tends to show secondary meaning); promotion of the connection between the mark and the claimant's products, either by the claimant or others (more promotion, more likely secondary meaning); consumer surveys (not required, and sometimes methodologically faulty, but can be helpful); consumer testimony that they think of the term as a source identifier rather than just as a descriptive term; intentional copying of the claimant's mark by the defendant (can imply secondary meaning). Note that the Lanham Act provides for a presumption of secondary meaning if a mark has been substantially exclusively and continuously used as a mark in commerce for a period of five years before it is claimed.

If a term is generic, it is not protectable as a trademark at all, at least as to that for which it is generic (e.g., *apple* is generic for fruit, but arbitrary for computers). A generic term is one that is understood by the public to represent a genus or class of products. A word that was as a protectable mark may become generic. Indeed, some well-known trademarks have suffered from "genericide." Aspirin, elevator, and zipper were all at one point trademarks. In modern times, companies perhaps are more sophisticated about this problem, so they are often careful to use a generic term together with their marks to try to avoid a claim that the mark itself has come to represent the genus of product. For example, one generally doesn't hear just "Kleenex" in an advertisement for that product, but rather, "Kleenex brand facial tissues." One wonders how some popular companies with such a strong position in their product markets that people have started to use them to refer to a class of products or activity are addressing this, say, perhaps *Google* or *Xerox*.

Likelihood of Confusion

Finally, someone who uses, in commerce in connection with goods or services, the same or a similar mark as another's in a manner that is likely to cause confusion as to source of origin is potentially a trademark infringer. This is true whether or not the trademark has been registered. Federally registered trademark owners have certain advantages; for example, access to federal courts and a presumption of validity and ownership. The Lanham Act itself even has an important provision that permits infringement and other actions by plaintiffs without registered marks, generally known as Lanham Act Section 43(a). Notice that actual consumer confusion is not required, but only a likelihood of confusion. Like secondary meaning, there is no bright-line test for likelihood of confusion, but rather a list of factors that are considered and weighed, and that vary a bit among circuits. Generally, those factors would include similarity of the marks in appearance, sound, and meaning (the more similar, the more likely is confusion), similarity of the goods or services (if they are the same or competing, or in the same class, or related in the minds of consumers, confusion is much more likely), the strength of the mark (highly distinctive marks are more likely to be confused with similar marks used by another), similarity of marketing channels (if they advertised or sold in the same or similar places, confusion is more likely), sophistication and care of the relevant consumer (the more sophisticated, the less likely to be confused; the cheaper the product the less care is likely to be exercised in distinguishing similar products), proof of actual confusion (not required or dispositive, but can be probative of likely confusion), likelihood of "bridging the gap" (if the products are not similar or competitive, is it likely the plaintiff would be expected to expand into the defendant's market), consumer testimony or surveys (but surveys won't have much weight if they are not objectively well designed), the defendant's bad faith (for example, evidence that she intended to cause confusion). Courts may consider other factors, too. If a likelihood of confusion is found, and there are no valid defenses, there are various remedies, including injunctive relief, and sometimes damages, profits, and attorneys' fees.

Defenses

There are numerous potential defenses to trademark infringement claims, some of which can be quite interesting and raise important policy issues, such as the tension between exclusive trademark rights and freedom of speech. I will discuss of few of them here. But first, it should be mentioned that as to federally registered marks, they become incontestable five years after registration. This means that only a very limited array of defenses is permitted to be asserted. Obviously, this is a strong incentive to seeking federal registration.

There are several defenses that are common in many other areas of law or equity, such as laches ("sitting on your rights"), "unclean hands" (plaintiff engaged in some bad conduct), or the existence of a valid license to use the mark. Perhaps most interesting are the fair use and nominative fair use defenses. Note that *fair use* in trademark law is very different from *fair use* in copyright law. Fair use in trademark means that a person in good faith is using a mark in its descriptive sense rather than in a trademark sense. Often this will involve the use of a descriptive term that has acquired secondary meaning and become a protectable mark. However, it might also apply in comparative advertising. For example, a knock-off perfume might invite consumers to compare it with another perfume, identified by its trademark.

Nominative use or nominative fair use refers to use of a mark to name the plaintiff's product in describing the defendant's product. Here are a few examples. A car repair shop could use the trademark of the cars repaired, as long as the use wasn't excessive so as to likely cause confusion. Teri Welles, who was Playmate of the Year 1981, did not infringe Playboy's marks when she used that phrase in metatags on her website. A newspaper that conducted a survey as to who were the audience's favorite New Kid on the Block (a take on once-popular young pop band New Kids on the Block) could use their band name in the survey and in advertising, even though they made money from the survey, so long as they didn't do anything else to cause confusion about origin or sponsorship of the survey.

Another important and rather unsettled area is the interplay between freedom of speech and trademark rights. Different courts approach this in

various ways. Because often the type of speech involved can be characterized as *commercial speech*, which may receive somewhat less constitutional
protection than noncommercial speech, some courts simply apply the likelihood of confusion analysis. The Second Circuit has developed a somewhat
different approach that has been followed by some other courts in some
circumstances. In a case involving an Italian film called *Ginger and Fred*,
about a couple in World War II–era Italy who went by the name of that
well-known dance duo, the Second Circuit court looked to see if there is
"artistic relevance" between the use of the mark (in this case, Ginger Rogers was the plaintiff and claimed trademark rights, among others, in her
name). If there is artistic relevance, which the court did find there, since the
dance couple used that name, then there is only a trademark infringement
if the use of the mark is explicitly misleading in some way. For example,
presumably if the film title was *Ginger Rogers Presents Ginger and Fred*,
that very likely would have been an infringement. If there is no artistic relevance, then a court would apply the usual likelihood of confusion analysis.
This approach, which recognizes the First Amendment value of a work's
title, attempts to strike a better balance between free speech interests and
trademark/unfair competition interests. It has been followed, for example,
in cases dealing with a pop song entitled "Barbie Girl" (artistic relevance
found, no trademark infringement as to Mattel's Barbie Doll) and a rap
song entitled "Rosa Parks" (artistic relevance not so clear, so case remanded
for a determination of that relevance).

Titles and Selected Other Interesting Applications

Two other interesting applications of trademark law in the entertainment
and media industries relate to titles of works and the use of trademarks
within the content of media content, such as films. A title of a single work,
such as a book or a film, is not copyrightable, but may become protectable
as a trademark. Titles of single works are generally not registrable as trademarks under federal law, but the title of a series of works may be. Distinctive titles, character names, and other distinctive features of television and
radio programs may be registered as service marks, assuming they otherwise
qualify. For an ordinary single work, however, the title only receives trademark protection (as an unregistered mark) if secondary meaning is proved.
In a sense, a title is viewed primarily as the name of a product, not an indicator of source, no matter how distinctive the word or words used. Once
secondary meaning has developed, however, it may be protected against
use of the same or a similar title on another work. For example, the owners
of *Bridge on the River Kwai*, a film that won the Academy Award for Best
Picture in 1958, succeeded in a trademark infringement claim many years
later against a company that produced a film entitled *Return From the River
Kwai*. Many motion picture companies are parties to a consensual system

for determining rights in titles that is administered by the Motion Picture Association. But a motion picture's production counsel still has to consider whether there are likely to be claims based in trademark law by companies that are not parties to that system, which can be quite difficult.

Recently, there have been several cases involving uses of trademarks in the content of motion pictures. Time precludes a thorough discussion of this area. Film companies (and even more so, television companies) have complex guidelines about how they will use trademarks and items showing trademarks in their programs without consent from the trademark owner. Usually, they avoid at least disparaging or negative uses. We have not had space to discuss the concept of parody in trademark law, but suffice to say that it is sometimes permitted and not considered an infringement, notwithstanding its critical nature. Similarly, even some arguably negative, but humorous, uses of trademarked items in films have been challenged but found not to infringe the trademark. For example, in a comedy entitled *Dickey Roberts: Former Child Star*, a distinctive toy known as a Slip'n'Slide was misused, arguably to comic effect. The toy company sued unsuccessfully. As trademark owners' rights expand, this area will need further scholarly analysis and decisional law.

Trademark Expansion and the Future

There is much more to say about trademark law, which has tended to expand in scope in modern times. Historically limited to claims between competitors selling similar or related products, it has expanded greatly at least as to highly distinctive, famous marks. If famous marks are used, even on completely unrelated products, their owners claim that their distinctiveness may be blurred. If used in a negative context, such marks may be tarnished. Blurring and tarnishment are two variations of a type of claim called *dilution* of the mark. Initially recognized only in the law of certain states, the Lanham Act relatively recently added an anti-dilution section. Historically, marks have only received trademark protection in their use as trademarks in connection with goods or services. In more recent decisions, this has expanded to include rights as to the mark as a merchandising value in itself, rather than as an indicator of source. Other concerns at the frontiers of trademark law (or maybe closer than that) include the interplay between trademark law and Internet domain names, "cybersquatting," parallel imports and "grey market goods," and the development of an international system to relate the numerous and somewhat different national trademark systems. The Lanham Act has been relatively recently amended to add a provision addressing cybersquatting, and there have been important international developments too. It is an exciting area, and if nothing else, it is certainly clear that trademark law issues will continue to require journalists' consideration.

A Brief Guide to Patents

Background

As we move into the knowledge economy of the 21st century, patents and other forms of intellectual property become ever more important, both economically and legally. It is estimated that the value of intellectual property to the U.S. economy is at least $8 trillion, much of that in patent portfolios.[4] No wonder that patent practice is a major growth area of the legal profession. Patent law is also an inherently international matter. Patent rights typically operate only within a nation's borders. Thus, a company wishing to protect their inventions in the global economy often needs to obtain patents from each country where protection is sought. Several patent treaties make this process somewhat less daunting than it might otherwise be. Nonetheless, patent practice and enforcement is often a multinational process.

The First Patent Law—Sybaris

"If any confectioner or cook invented any peculiar and excellent dish, no other artist was allowed to make this for a year; but he alone who invented it was entitled to all the profits to be derived from the manufacture of it for that time; in order that others might be induced to labor at excelling in such pursuits."

Athenaeus, & Yonge, C.D. (1853). *The Deiphnosophists: Or, Banquet of the learned of Athenaeus*. London: H.G. Bohn. 12:20, p. 835.

The rationale for protecting inventions can be traced to the Greek Philosopher Hippodamus (fifth century B.C.), who wrote, "those who discovered anything for the good of the state should be honored." The first patent law is ascribed to Sybaris, a Greek colony in southern Italy, in the second century B.C. The Sybarite patent law, as with Hippodamus's theory, reflects the utilitarian argument for intellectual property. By reserving exclusive rights to an inventor, along with the profits to be made from the invention, skilled artisans and others will be motivated to discover and create new items for the good of society. This is the basis for U.S. patent law—to incentivize innovation, so as to promote technological and economic progress. European patent law also reflects the incentive theory, but goes further. There is a strong natural law tradition in Europe. According to John Locke, people have a natural right to the fruits of their own ideas and own labor. Under this theory, society is morally obligated to recognize and protect property rights in ideas. Thus, in Europe, unlike America, authors and inventors have certain moral rights (*droit morale*). This may require recognition (including remuneration) for inventors, even when they've purportedly contracted their patent rights away.

The Constitutional and Statutory Basis for Patents in the United States

Article I, §8, ¶ 8: "The Congress shall have power to . . . promote the progress of science and useful arts, by securing for limited times to authors and inventors the exclusive right to their respective writings and discoveries."

Congress has exercised this power by enacting Titles 17 (Copyrights) and 35 (Patents) of the U.S. Code. Regulations of the U.S. Patent and Trademark Office (USPTO) are found in Title 37 of the Code of Federal Regulations (CFR).

Certain features of the Constitution's patent clause are worth noting. First, only "inventors" may be awarded patents, for their "discoveries." This has been interpreted to mean that a device or a process must be novel (new) to be patented. Only one patent may be granted on any given invention. Although several people may independently be working on the same invention, only one of them will get a patent. Compare copyrights, where a work needs only be original and creative, it does not need to be new or unique. Second, a patent must "promote the progress of science and useful arts." It does this by "teaching" the full nature of the invention and how it works. This knowledge eventually becomes part of the public domain, where it serves as a basis for further innovation. Failure to fully disclose the invention in a patent application will result in rejection or invalidation of the patent. Third, inventors obtain exclusive rights to their discoveries. That means a patent will exclude others from using the patented invention, unless they have a license. But a patent does not guarantee that the inventor can practice the invention herself. For instance, the Patent Office may grant a patent on a drug discovery. But the patent holder (called the *patentee*) must still obtain permission from the Food and Drug Administration (FDA) to actually use or sell the drug. Fourth, exclusive rights can be granted only for a limited time. For most of our nation's history, the term of a patent has been 17 years (from date of issue). Recently, however, to conform to international law, the term was changed to 20 years (from the date of application).

Patents issue in the name of the inventor or an assignee (often the company or university where the inventor is employed). Once issued, they have many of the attributes of property. They can be bought and sold, and patent rights can be licensed to others. Every patent ever issued in the United States can be found on the PTO website and in private databases such as Google Patents.

A patent is based on an application filed by the inventor or co-inventors. The application must describe the invention in detail, through a "specification" and "claims." The former defines the invention in technical terms; the latter in legal terms.

The specification "discloses" the invention; particularly how to make and use it. It must "enable" persons of ordinary skill in the "art" (the relevant field of technology) to practice the invention. The specification also shows how the invention advances the technology over what was previously known in the field (called the *prior art*).

The "claims" define or limit the scope of the invention. They constitute the legal protection afforded by the patent. Patent claims are analogous to the description of real property in a deed "which sets the bounds to the grant which it contains." (Compare the specification, which might be analogized to a property's street address and directions how to get there).

A patent typically has several claims (legal descriptions of novel attributes). Since, it is the claims that constitute the protectable parts of a patent, an unauthorized use (say, a competing product) infringes one or more claims of the patent.

Types of Patents

U.S. law recognizes three types of patents: **utility**, **design**, and **plant** patents. Most patents are utility patents—meaning they cover "useful" and functional inventions. Most discussions of patent law and policy (including this chapter) are geared to utility patents. Design patents are issued on ornamental (non-functional) designs, such as automobile grills and body parts. Plant patents are given for breeding a new and botanically distinct variety of plants, such as the Ingrid Bergman Rose.

Some forms of sui generis intellectual property protection function similar to patents. For instance, the United States protects mask works (printed circuit designs), and Europe protects computer programs and biotechnological inventions, through regimes that may overlap patent law.

Exclusive Rights of a Utility Patent

A utility patent reserves to the patentee the following exclusive rights in her invention (see 35 U.S.C. § 171):

• within the United States—to make, use, offer to sell, or sell
• to import into the United States

Let's take a closer look at these two issued patents. The former, the '089 patent (patents are often referred to by the last 3 digits in the sequential patent number), claims an optical computer mouse; actually just an

> ### Examples of Patent Claims
>
> Patent number 7,324,089. "What is claimed is:
>
> 1. An improved optical device for an optical mouse, being installed inside a case body of the optical mouse, comprising: a LED, for providing light for the optical device; a fixing base . . .; a lens mount, supporting a lens . . .; a sensor . . .; and a digital signal processor. . . ."
>
> Patent number 4,736,866. "We claim:
>
> 1. A transgenic non-human mammal all of whose germ cells and somatic cells contain a recombinant activated oncogene sequence introduced into said mammal, or an ancestor of said mammal, at an embryonic stage. . . .
>
> 11. The mammal of claim 1, said mammal being a rodent.
>
> 12. The mammal of claim 11, said rodent being a mouse.

improvement on such a device (most patents are improvement patents). The latter, the '866 patent, claims a living biological mouse; again, just a variation. We'll talk about patenting life forms later in this chapter.

For the moment, look at the structure of the '866 claims. They start at the broadest level of discovery that the inventor reasonably can claim (all "transgenic non-human mammals" transfected with a gene containing the genetic sequence for cancer). Broad claims may not be granted or, if granted, withstand scrutiny. So, it is customary to narrow the claims bit by bit until a fairly specific discovery is claimed. In this case, claim 12 is limited to a transfected mouse (now known as an "oncomouse"). If I were engaged in cancer research, and wanted to experiment on an animal that carries the human cancer gene (rather than experiment on humans with cancer), I would probably need this patented oncomouse. If I created ("made") or used such a product (the mouse) without permission, I would infringe claim 12 of the '866 patent. If I made a transgenic higher life form, say a primate, for cancer experiments (which I might want to do before starting human trials), I wouldn't infringe claim 12, but might infringe claim 1 (if it were found valid). Claims in a patent typically progress from broadest to narrowest, as seen in the '866 patent above. Narrow claims are more likely to survive than broad claims. But because they do not cover as much technology, they are less likely to be infringed.

How Is a Patent Obtained?

Unlike copyrights, which arise as soon as an expressive work is fixed on a tangible medium, or trademarks, which must be registered with the PTO but do not involve extensive examination, patents must be approved. The patent application process is long, expensive, and complicated. The process is so complex that patent attorneys must have a science or engineering background and take a separate bar exam (the only federal bar exam) to be admitted to practice before the PTO.[5] Although some inventors still handle their own applications, most hire patent agents or attorneys to do so.

Once an invention has been "reduced to practice" (i.e., its operation is known, even if not perfected), a provisional patent application can be filed with the PTO covering the invention. A provisional application confers no rights, but it sets the priority date—when the application is deemed filed—in case there are competing applications or earlier inventions. The applicant has one year to complete experiments, obtain supporting data, refine the claims, and convert the provisional into a regular application (which will be given the earlier priority date).

The patent application is then assigned to a patent examiner, who "shall make a thorough study thereof and shall make a thorough investigation of the available prior art [what is already known] relating to the subject matter of the claimed invention." 37 CFR §1.104(a). After the initial examination, "if the invention is not considered patentable, or not considered patentable as claimed, the claims, or those considered unpatentable will be rejected." §1.104(c). A rejection occurs with most applications at first. This "office action" commences a dialogue with the applicant where she will either revise her claims to overcome the examiner's objections, or provide additional support as to why the claims are patentable (e.g., why they are novel). At some point, the examiner either accepts the claims as revised and gives a notice of issuance, or gives a final rejection. An applicant can appeal a final rejection to the Patent Trial and Appeals Board (PTAB),[6] an administrative body within the PTO, and thereafter to the Court of Appeals for the Federal Circuit (CAFC). The CAFC is the only federal appeals court with specialized and nationwide jurisdiction. It hears appeals from the PTO and from district courts in patent cases.

Only one patent can issue on an invention, even if two or more inventors develop it independently of each other. Between 1790, when the first patent law was adopted, and 2013, the patent would be awarded to the first to invent a novel device or method, even if another person filed first. However, the Leahy-Smith America Invents Act (AIA), signed into law in September 2011, switched the United States to a "first-to-file" regime (effective March 2013). Under the new law, in the case of competing applications, the patent is awarded to the first to file for a patent, unless she "derived" the invention from another (who would then get the patent instead). This switch brought the United States into line with nearly every other country, most of which have had a "first-to-file" system for years. However, the changeover, as with many features of the AIA, was controversial. Opponents argue that "first-to-file" rewards large companies with large patent budgets, since the "race to the patent office" can be expensive.

What Inventions Can Be Patented?

Patentable Subject Matter

"Whoever invents or discovers any new and useful process, machine, manufacture, or composition of matter, or any new and useful improvement thereof, may obtain a patent therefor, subject to the conditions and requirements of this title."

35 U.S.C. §101

A patent may issue on any novel process or product ("machine, manufacture, or composition of matter"), or "improvement thereof." Does this cover life forms, such as the oncomouse, or synthetic life? What about innovative business methods ("method" and "process" are synonymous under patent law), such as e-commerce websites or tax strategies?

The Supreme Court has held that "Congress intended statutory subject matter to 'include anything under the sun that is made by man'" (*Diamond* v. *Chakrabarty*, 447 U.S. 303, 309 [1980]). In that case, the court upheld the patentability of genetically engineered bacteria (used to "digest" and dissipate oil spills). Subsequently, higher life forms have been patented, such as the oncomouse above.

Patents are issued at the national level (except for Europe-wide patents, which are issued by the European Patent Office [EPO]), so what may be patentable in one country isn't necessarily patentable in another. When the assignee of the oncomouse patent (Harvard University) filed for patent protection in Canada, it was denied. In Canada, higher life forms are not patentable. In contrast, the EPO upheld the grant of a patent on the oncomouse. The U.S. patent on the Harvard transgenic mouse was never challenged.

Non-Patentable Subject Matter

U.S. courts have crafted certain exceptions to §101. Among them are mathematical algorithms (formulae) and laws and products of nature. Some otherwise eligible subjects are specifically denied patents in the United States, such as inventions useful solely in nuclear material or atomic weapons. Congress has considered other exclusions, such as for "tax planning methods," genetic material, human cloning, and so on. But for the most part, the statement in *Chakrabarty* that statutory subject matter "includes anything under the sun that is made by man" still applies.

The biggest area of difference among national patent laws concerns software and so-called business method patents. The United States began treating pure software as patentable subject matter in the mid-1990s.[7] The number of such patents has exploded in the past decade, often with controversial and sensational results. For example, Microsoft was accused of infringing an audio compression patent by including a few lines of patented computer code in its MP3 decoder (Windows Media Player). Any complex device, such as the Windows operating system, will inevitably embody hundreds or thousands of software patents. Obtaining clearance (permission) for each of these patents is a formidable task, not the least because it isn't always clear what a patent covers. As Bill Gates stated in 1991, "If people had understood how patents would be granted when most of today's ideas were invented, and had taken out patents, the industry would be at a complete standstill today."[8] Some believe that overpatenting of software operates as a disincentive to innovation, especially by small companies and individual inventors that lack the ability to engage in expensive patent searches (more fully discussed below). In the Microsoft case, the jury awarded Lucent Technologies (the patentee) $1.53 billion in damages.[9]

As controversial as software patents are, business method patents are even more criticized. The patent office had a standing policy until 1996 of rejecting patents on "methods of doing business."[10] However, in the mid-1990s the PTO changed its policy and awarded a patent on "a data processing system for implementing an investment structure . . . for mutual funds" (essentially a software-based portfolio system). In previous years, the "invention" would not have been considered patentable subject matter since it simply automates "mental steps." See *In re Abrams*, 188 F.2d 165, 168 (C.C.P.A. 1951;"it is self-evident that thought is not patentable").

But, in *State Street Bank & Trust Co. v. Signature Financial Group*, 149 F.3d 1368 (Fed. Cir. 1998), the CAFC upheld the patent. This unleashed a wave of business methods patents in the United States, such as Amazon. com's "one-click" method for placing and receiving purchasing orders.[11] Under the PTO rules, a business method was patentable so long as it involved some technical element, such as implementation by computer (it must still meet all the other criteria for patentability). A 2005 decision of the PTO did away with the technical element requirement, such that now any business method can be patented. However, in *eBay Inc. v. MercExchang*, 547 U.S. 388 (2006), Justice Kennedy criticized the "burgeoning number of patents over business methods, which were not of much economic and legal significance in earlier times [but now affected by] potential vagueness and suspect validity."

The United States is one of the few countries to recognize business method patents.[12] They are specifically prohibited in most other countries, as well as by the European Patent Convention (EPC).[13] In *Bilski v. Kappos* (2010), the Supreme Court held that "federal law explicitly contemplates the existence of at least some business method patents." While not outlawing them entirely, the court significantly cut back on their patentability, stating that many of them were non-patentable subject matter (e.g., mathematical algorithms).

The America Invents Act also effectively reduces the incidence of business method patents by creating a special procedure for third-party challenges. Tax strategy patents, which had become somewhat popular and troublesome (to accountants), are effectively barred by AIA.

Criteria for Obtaining a Patent

To be patentable, an invention must be "new and useful" (§101). The first of these terms give rise to the *novelty* requirement, and the second to the *utility* requirement.

Novelty and Prior Art

A patent will not be granted if the claimed invention was "patented, described in a printed publication, or in public use, on sale, or otherwise available to the public before the effective filing date of the claimed invention" (§102[a][1]). These items constitute the "prior art" and tell us whether a claimed invention is novel.

Additionally, a patent will not be granted if "the claimed invention was described in [an earlier] patent . . . or application for patent [that] names another inventor" (§102[a][2]). It is this section that implements the new "first-inventor-to-file" system.

A patent application will be rejected if the invention is already in the public domain; that is, can be found in the "prior art." Prior art is that sum of knowledge that has been disclosed to the public, or at least that segment of the public working in the particular field of technology.

Up until 2013, priority (in the case of competing applicants) would go to the first person to invent, irrespective of when the patent application was filed. Now, the patent goes to the first person to file. There is an exception. If the first person to file actually derived the invention from another (i.e., wasn't the true inventor herself), then the true inventor is awarded the patent, even if she is not the first to file.

Any disclosure of an invention (publication, sale, etc.) before a patent application is filed operates as a "statutory bar" to granting the patent.[14] This is true even if it is the inventor herself who makes the disclosure (e.g., presents a paper at an academic conference). However, this section creates a one-year grace period for the inventor's own disclosures. Most other countries do not afford a grace period. That means any publication (by the

Statutory Bar

"Prior art excludes disclosures made by the inventor herself, or by another who obtained the information from the inventor, but only if the disclosure is made one year or less before the filing date of the application" (§102[b][1]).

inventor or others) before the application is filed will defeat the patent. The lack of a grace period in other countries can catch U.S. inventors by surprise, if they later seek to file internationally.

Obviousness

"A patent for a claimed invention may not be obtained [even if it is novel] if the differences between the claimed invention and the prior art are such that the claimed invention as a whole would have been obvious . . . to a person having ordinary skill in the art to which the claimed invention pertains" (§103).

Closely related to the novelty requirement is that of obviousness. An invention may be new and useful, but is such an insignificant advance over the prior art (what was already known by persons in the field) that it would have been obvious to a person of ordinary skill in the art. Most rejections of patent applications by Patent Office examiners, and most court challenges to issued patents, are based on obviousness.

An applicant for patent has a duty of candor to the Patent Office. She must disclose all the relevant prior art, and then explain how the invention differs from it. Intentional concealment or misrepresentation of prior art, or other factor that might affect patentability, is considered *inequitable conduct*—a form of fraud on the Patent Office. Inequitable conduct is often pleaded as a defense in a patent infringement suit, since (if proven) it results in declaring the patent invalid.

An examiner's rejection based on obviousness (or any other ground) can be appealed to the PTAB. In a patent infringement lawsuit, an accused infringer will often put on expert evidence tending to show the state of pre-existing knowledge (the prior art) and, based on that knowledge, that a hypothetical person of ordinary skill would have considered the invention as obvious (i.e., an insubstantial extension of previously known technology). Although an issued patent is presumed valid, it is a rebuttable presumption. Defendants often try to show that either: (a) the applicant failed

Patent Searches

Finding the prior art requires a search, not only of already issued patents but also of marketing activity and publications that may contain background information. Searches must be conducted worldwide. As a result, patent searches are costly, and are often out-sourced to specialty firms. As information becomes more readily available (e.g., via the Internet), searching may become a bit easier, but more material must be searched. An applicant will try to "claim around" prior art (characterize the invention in such a way as to avoid anticipation by earlier knowledge). Failure to uncover or distinguish prior art may result in a rejection, or invalidation in court.

to disclose all the prior art; (b) properly understood, the prior art "anticipated" the invention; and/or (c) the invention is obvious in light of the prior art. This is the most effective way to show that one or more claims of a patent are invalid.

Utility

An invention must be "useful" to be patented. The utility must be known and disclosed. This may be a stumbling block for certain inventions, such as genes and biochemical compounds. A researcher can sequence a gene (learn its exact chemical composition), purify it (remove non-coding nucleotides), and synthesize it in the laboratory—all of which lead to an invention. But, unless she knows or can predict the gene's function (either in the cell or in a laboratory), the utility requirement is not met. The utility requirement makes many genetic discoveries, such as express sequence tags (ESTs) and alleles (mutations), unpatentable.

The Patent Office requires that an invention have "specific," "credible," and "substantial" utility. Thus, some generalized description of utility (e.g., "this gene affects cell function") will be insufficient. The invention must credibly operate as stated (thus excluding perpetual motion machines). Finally, it must be more than trivial (e.g., operates as a paper weight); it must be truly useful in some respect.

Patent Licensing and Infringement Suits

The exclusive rights of patent can be exceedingly valuable or have no value at all, depending upon the utility and market demand for the patented invention. A patentee can either:

- practice (make, use, sell) the invention herself, and thereby earn monopoly (above market) profits because of the exclusivity;
- license the invention to others either on an exclusive or non-exclusive basis; or
- keep the invention locked up (no one makes or uses it) during the patent term.

Patent licensing is a specialized form of business negotiation. Where the patentee makes the product herself, she may choose not to license at all, since competition could suppress prices for the product. If she isn't a producer, she will want to maximize profits through license royalties. In many industries, this requires exclusive licensing, so that the licensee now stands in the same position as the patentee originally.

Some patents are acquired, not to bring new products to market, but for strategic purposes. Non-practicing entities (NPEs) are patent holders who neither practice their inventions, nor license others to do so. Rather, they hold on to their patents until it appears that some other firm is marketing an infringing product. At that time, it is usually too late for the infringer to "design around" the patent (i.e., use a substitute technology or method), which it might have done had it known ahead of time that its product infringed. At that point, the patentee can extract above-market royalties from the infringer, or sue for infringement. Patentees employing these tactics are sometimes referred to as *patent trolls*. Most NPEs are not themselves innovators. Rather, they often acquire large patent portfolios when businesses fail or sell off assets. The patents are treated as investments, which often pay off when someone else starts practicing the invention.

In an infringement suit, plaintiff must prove both the scope of her patent claims (precisely what technology is reserved by the patent), and that one or more claims have been infringed by defendant. The "accused" product must "read on" the patent claim, meaning that the claim describes defendant's product or process. If successful, plaintiff obtains damages equal to its lost profits, but in no event less than a reasonable royalty. In some cases,

---

Markman Hearing

In *Markman v. Westview Instruments* (1996), the Supreme Court ruled that the interpretation of patent claims (called *claim construction*) was a "matter of law" for judges to decide, and not a "question of fact" for the jury. As a result, so-called "Markman Hearings," where the metes and bounds of a patent are determined, are usually held in front of the judge at the beginning of a case. Since claim construction can be dispositive of whether the defendant has infringed the patent, many cases are won or lost at the Markman stage.

the court will issue an injunction against the defendant, prohibiting its continued infringement. This is fertile ground for a battle of experts, both in the field of technology covered by the patent and for economists giving their opinions on patent value. Damage awards can run into the tens of millions of dollars.

Challenges to a Patent After It Is Issued

Someone wanting to use a technology that may be covered by a patent has four options: (1) negotiate for a license; (2) take his chances in a patent infringement suit; (3) beat the patentee to court by filing an action for "declaratory relief" (seeing a judicial determination of patent invalidity); or (4) challenge the patent in an administrative procedure at the patent office.

There are two ways for a challenger to have the PTO re-examine a patent. The first, which was adopted as part of AIA, is called *post-grant review* (PGR). A challenger may request PGR up until nine months after a patent has issued. It is a full reconsideration of the patent and can result in amendment or cancellation of claims. The second procedure is called *inter partes review* (IPR). IPR can be requested at any time during the life of a patent, but this challenge is limited in the type of prior art that can be used and the scope of the administrative hearing. The Patent Trial and Appeal Board conduct both reviews. Both PGR and IPR are discretionary with the patent office and will be authorized only if there is a serious question about the validity of one or more patent claims.

Innovation or Anti-Commons

The justification for awarding limited monopolies via patents is that they ultimately increase social welfare by incentivizing people to innovate and contribute to the public knowledge base. Some argue, however, that patents inhibit innovation, especially where research technologies are concerned. Consider a patented microscope or other research tool. Unless a researcher is able to pay the licensing fee, she cannot use that tool for her own research. Of course were it not for patent law, that improved microscope might not have been invented in the first place. Perhaps there are other means to incentivize people to innovate, such as through government grants. But the United States has taken the position that the marketplace is the best way to encourage innovation. In fact, under the Bayh-Dole Act (1980), any invention that is the product of a federal research grant to a university must be patented, or the rights to the invention revert to the United States. Bayh-Dole is credited both with spurring innovation and a whole host of start-up companies, but also with changing the culture of academic research. At the very least, one cannot deny that patents are extraordinarily important to the American economy.

Notes

1 See, for example, http://www.contactmusic.com/news/fear-factory-in-legal-battle-to-keep-name_1106806 (battle over Fear Factory name described as a "copyright" fight).
2 U.S. Constitution, Art. I, Section 8, Clause 8.
3 *Peter Pan Fabrics v. Martin Weiner Corp.*, 274 F.2d 487, 489 (2d Cir., 1960).
4 Kevin A. Hassett and Robert J. Shapiro, *What Ideas Are Worth: The Value of Intellectual Capital and Intangible Assets in the American Economy* (Washington, D.C.: Sonecon, 2011), iv. See also Patent Reform White Paper, U.S. Dept. of Commerce, April 13, 2010, 2 ("factors linked to innovation are responsible for almost three-quarters of the Nation's post-WW II growth rate").
5 One does not need to be an attorney in order to file and prosecute a patent application in the PTO. Patent agents take the same examination and generally have the same rights at the Patent Office, but they cannot take patent cases to court.
6 Prior to the Leahy-Smith America Invents Act, appeals from examiner decisions went to the Board of Patent Appeals and Interferences.
7 We use the term *pure* software to distinguish computer code written in stand-alone readable form (such as on a CD-ROM) from physical devices (such as computer chips) that may contain computer code elements. The latter has always been patentable. In other words, the presence of computer code does not make an otherwise patentable device unpatentable (*Diamond v. Diehr*, 450 U.S. 175 [1981]). But the former—pure software patents—are a relatively new phenomenon.
8 Bill Gates, *Challenges and Strategy*, internal memo to Microsoft employees (May 16, 1991).
9 The award was reduced on appeal and eventually lowered. The patent war between Lucent (the successor to Bell Labs) and Microsoft then escalated with reciprocal infringement suits in various venues.
10 There is historical precedent for this exclusion. The British Statute of Monopolies (1623) prohibited the grant of monopoly rights in various lines of business. Until the late 1990s, U.S. courts had consistently rejected business method patents as well.
11 Upon reexamination, some of the claims in the Amazon.com patent were found to have been anticipated by the prior art, and therefore unpatentable.
12 Japan and Australia do as well.
13 Article 52 of the EPC states: "(1) European patents shall be granted for any inventions, in all fields of technology, provided that they are new, involve an inventive step and are susceptible of industrial application. (2) The following in particular shall not be regarded as inventions within the meaning of paragraph 1 . . . (c) schemes, rules and methods for performing mental acts, playing games or doing business, and programs for computers."
14 Only public disclosures trigger the one-year "statutory bar" of § 102(b). For this reason, and to protect trade secrets, inventors typically use "non-disclosure agreements" (NDAs) when discussing their inventions with others, such as investors and collaborators.

8 Civil Procedure

Allan Ides
Christopher N. May Professor of Law,
Loyola Law School, Los Angeles

What Is Civil Procedure?

A civil lawsuit is a noncriminal legal proceeding filed in a state or federal court through which a plaintiff seeks a remedy, such as money damages or an injunction, against a defendant who is alleged to have harmed the plaintiff in some fashion. The subject matters of civil lawsuits are as varied as the range of the substantive law: from personal injury claims to breach of contract claims, from human rights violations to antitrust disputes, from simple property-line controversies to complicated adjudications involving the takings clause. The law of civil procedure consists of constitutional provisions, statutes, rules, and judicially created principles that regulate the how courts adjudicate such lawsuits. Despite the variety of potential subject matters, the law of civil procedure tends to be "trans-substantive" in that it usually applies in the same fashion regardless of the nature of the underlying controversy.

The goal of the law of civil procedure is to provide the parties to a legal dispute a fair and efficient manner through which to resolve that dispute. But this seemingly prosaic goal belies the profound nature of procedure. In providing a method through which to resolve legal disputes, the system

---

The Distinction between Substantive Law and Procedural Law

It is probably not possible to devise a perfect, all-purpose method for distinguishing between substantive and procedural law. But as a rule of thumb substantive law can be thought of as the law that regulates everyday human activity, that is, human activity that takes places outside of the world of litigation: the law of negligence, the law of contracts, the law of property, and so forth. Procedural law, on the other hand, is law that arises only in the context of litigation and operates solely within that special world. It provides the means, manner, or method for resolving disputes arising under substantive law.

of procedure transforms abstract rights into enforceable principles of law. In this sense, procedure precedes the recognition of legal rights, for a right without a remedy is no right at all. Indeed, rights at common law were defined through the procedures by which those rights were enforced. Hence, while procedure may have a somewhat mechanical side to it, providing the rules of the game, it also reflects profound choices regarding the enforcement of rights and obligations within our system of justice. In other words, without rules, there is no game at all.

The following discussion is designed to give the reader a sense of the range of procedural issues that arise in the context of civil litigation, as well as to provide some familiarity with the applicable nomenclature.

Commencing a Lawsuit: Pleadings

Civil suits are largely written creatures. Much of the work of a civil lawyer is in writing, not necessarily in a courtroom. The written document through which a party to a civil action either asserts a claim or a defense or denies the legitimacy of a claim or defense asserted by an opposing party is called a **pleading**. There are three basic types of pleadings (with some variations): (1) complaints, (2) answers, and (3) replies.

The **complaint**, as it is called in most jurisdictions, is the case-initiating pleading filed by the plaintiff. It describes plaintiff's claims against the defendant and requests some sort of relief, such as money damages or an injunction. It might also include allegations pertaining to jurisdiction and venue (discussed below). At one time, complaints were highly technical

---

Common Law Pleading—Back to the Past

Common law pleading was the system of pleading that developed in England in the centuries following the Norman Conquest. This legal system was "common" as opposed to local in that it represented the law *common* to all England. The common law system of pleading evolved over six centuries of practice and served as the foundation for the colonial systems of law. At its best, common law pleading represented an improvement over previous systems of dispute resolution, such as trial by combat and trial by ordeal. By the 18th century, however, the common law system had become rigid and weighted-down with devilish technicalities. A case could turn on a lawyer's failure to use the proper "law French" declension! By the late 19th century, the system was replaced by precursors to the modern fact and notice pleading systems. Therefore, journalists not engaged in time travel should have no need to comprehend the niceties of the intriguingly serpentine system of common law pleading.

pleadings, easily subject to a variety of arcane and sometimes fatal objections. That formalistic approach has given way to more flexible pleading rules that downplay the role of pleadings in the ultimate resolution of a case. The basic idea this modern approach is to resolve the case on the merits to the extent practicable, instead of on some procedural technicality.

In terms of measuring the adequacy of a pleading, and particularly complaints, modern courts apply one of two relatively deferential standards: **fact pleading** or **notice pleading**. Fact pleading requires the plaintiff to allege facts that, if believed, would establish each element of any legal claim the plaintiff wishes to assert. For example, if the plaintiff sues the defendant for negligence, the plaintiff must plead facts supporting each element of that tort—duty, breach, and causation. Notice pleading, on the other hand, requires only that the plaintiff provide a "short and plain" statement of her claim (e.g., the defendant crashed into my car). The adequacy of a complaint under a notice pleading standard is premised on whether the information provides the defendant with adequate notice of the general nature of the claim being asserted. In actual practice, fact pleading and notice pleading standards tend to converge, with notice being the measure of the sufficiency of the facts plead. There are, however, some types of claims where more specificity is required. Congress, for example, imposed more strict pleading requirements for lawsuits arising out of the Y2K controversy.

The defendant's response to the complaint is called an **answer**. The answer admits or denies the narrative or specific facts described in the complaint and may include challenges to plaintiff's jurisdictional or venue allegations. The answer must also include any **affirmative defenses** the defendant may have against plaintiff's claims. An affirmative defense is one that defeats the claim by a type of end run. It says, in essence, even if plaintiff's description of the facts and law is correct, plaintiff's claim is without merit. For example, plaintiff's failure to file within the applicable statute of limitations would be an affirmative defense since despite the potential validity of plaintiff's claim, the claim would be time-barred from enforcement. In addition, the answer may include any claims the defendant may have against the plaintiff. These are sometimes called *cross-claims* or *counter-claims*. In general, the same generous (or strict) rules of pleading that apply to complaints will be applied to answers.

A **reply** is a response to an answer. Usually, a plaintiff is not required to file a reply, but may do so in order to respond to any affirmative allegations in the answer. But if the plaintiff does not file a reply, most courts, including federal courts, will treat the affirmative allegations as denied. The plaintiff must file a reply if the court orders her to do so, or if the defendant has asserted an affirmative claim (as opposed to an affirmative defense) against her.

Although the complaint initiates a civil action and although the collected pleadings may well frame the basic contours of the controversy, there are several preliminary procedural issues that may require judicial attention before the parties proceed to litigate the merits of the controversy. We turn to these now.

A Court's Power over Persons or Property: Personal Jurisdiction

Suppose Hannah, a citizen of California, files a negligence action against Barbara, a citizen of New Mexico. The claim arises out of an automobile accident that occurred while Barbara was driving along the Pacific Coast Highway in California. Hannah claims that Barbara's negligence caused the accident. The suit is filed in a state court located in California. Let's assume that Barbara was officially given notice (in legal terms, *properly served* with notice) of the lawsuit after she had returned home to New Mexico. Does the California court have the power to issue a binding judgment against Barbara even though she is not a resident of the State of California and even though she was not served while in the state? Stated more generally, does the power of a state court extend beyond the territory of the state in which that court sits?

In the late 19th and early 20th centuries, the answer to both of the above questions would have been no. While state courts at that time could assert jurisdiction over their own citizens, even when those citizens were absent from the state, the same was not true with respect to nonresidents of the state. With few exceptions, the power of a state court over nonresidents was limited to those nonresidents who voluntarily submitted to the court's jurisdiction or who were properly served with the complaint and a summons while within the territory of the state. State courts could also exercise jurisdiction over the property of a nonresident if that property were found within the state. In this context, the court's power was limited to the value of the property found.

The modern law of **personal jurisdiction**, which developed as a response to the increasingly integrated nature of the national economy, including the relative ease of interstate travel, is much less restrictive of state court power. Under this modern approach, which is a product of the Fourteenth Amendment due process clause, a state court may exercise judicial power over a nonresident defendant so long as doing so would not offend "traditional notions of fair play and substantial justice." Whether that somewhat abstract standard is satisfied depends on two basic aspects of the defendant's relationship with the forum, the state in which the court sits. The first aspect is the nature and scope of the defendant's contacts with the forum state; the second is the relationship between those contacts and the claim asserted against the defendant by the plaintiff. Essentially, the greater the contacts and the closer the relationship between those contacts and the claim, the more likely it is that the court will be allowed to exercise personal jurisdiction over the defendant. The method for measuring the sufficiency of the

---

Why Is Jurisdiction Important?

Personal jurisdiction laws in the modern legal system help determine who can be sued where and for what. Together with laws on venue (discussed below), these laws help determine who can be sued in front of what judge and jury. The extension of modern jurisdiction statutes has helped created the phenomena that have appeared in popular discussions of the legal system—"judicial hellholes," forum shopping, and the like. The freedom to sue nonresidents has opened up justice with the expansion of commerce, but it has also increased the likelihood that corporations whose business crosses state lines will have to cross state lines to go to court.

---

contacts and their relationship with the claim is known as the **minimum contacts test.**

In order to satisfy the standards of the minimum contacts test, a plaintiff must demonstrate that the nonresident defendant has engaged in or initiated "purposeful contacts" with the forum state, and that the claim asserted arises out of or is related to those contacts. For example, suppose a manufacturer located in State X knowingly ships a product into State Y for retail sale there. The product is purchased by a State Y consumer who is later injured by the product when using it in its intended fashion. If the consumer files a products liability claim against the manufacturer in a State Y court, the manufacturer will most likely be subject to personal jurisdiction in that court since the manufacturer's purposeful contacts (the shipment into the state) are closely related to the claim asserted against it (injury caused by the shipped product). The exercise of jurisdiction under such circumstances is sometimes referred to as **specific jurisdiction** since the jurisdiction exercised is specific to the claim asserted.

Note, however, that if the consumer in the above hypothetical had purchased the product in State X, it might well be that the State Y court would be without power to adjudicate the consumer's claim against the out-of-state manufacturer, for it now appears that the manufacturer did not initiate any contacts with the forum state. To exercise personal jurisdiction under such circumstances would violate the due process rights of the nonresident defendant.

The Minimum Contacts Test—Specific Jurisdiction

Purposeful contacts with the forum state.
and
A claim that is sufficiently related to those contacts.

Suppose that a nonresident defendant does have purposeful contacts with the forum state, but that the claim asserted against that defendant is unrelated to those contacts. May a court of the forum nonetheless exercise personal jurisdiction over the defendant? Perhaps. If the nonresident's purposeful contacts with the forum state are continuous, systematic, and truly substantial, a court of the forum state might be empowered to exercise **general jurisdiction** over that nonresident.

There are two critical differences between general and specific jurisdiction. First, general jurisdiction does not require the presence of any relationship between the claim and the contacts. In other words, the second element of the minimum contacts can be ignored and the nonresident may, therefore, be subject to jurisdiction with regard to claims having no connection with the nonresident's forum contacts. Second, while specific jurisdiction can sometimes be premised on a single contact that is closely related to the claim, the contacts required to establish general jurisdiction must be significantly more extensive and systematic, essentially tantamount to the contacts a resident would have with her own state. Hence, this type of jurisdiction is very rare. The most likely context in which it might be established is when a business that is incorporated out-of-state transacts all or nearly all of its business within the forum state.

Long-Arm Statutes

A state court's exercise of jurisdiction must also satisfy that state's **long-arm statute**. Long-arm statutes define the scope of a court's *statutory* power to exercise personal jurisdiction over persons not found within the state. Some long-arm statutes, such as that found in California, permit the courts of the state to exercise personal jurisdiction over a nonresident so long as doing so would not offend the standards imposed by the due process clause. Other states, New York for example, have slightly more restrictive long-arm statutes that specify the circumstances under which a court of the state may exercise personal jurisdiction over a nonresident defendant (e.g., the defendant transacts business within the state, the defendant committed a tortious act within the state). And so forth. These state-imposed restrictions are in addition to the restrictions imposed by the due process clause.

If the standards of either general or specific jurisdiction are established, the nonresident defendant will be given an opportunity to rebut the presumption of "fair play and substantial justice." Any defendant attempting to do so faces sizable hurdles, however, as satisfaction of either standard establishes a strong presumption that exercise of jurisdiction is reasonable.

Returning to our hypothetical negligence claim, the answer is clear. The claim asserted by Hannah arises out of Barbara's purposeful contacts with the State of California, namely, Barbara's voluntary visit to the state. Accordingly, despite the fact that Barbara is not a resident of California and despite the fact that she was not served while in California, a California state court may exercise personal jurisdiction over her without offending "notions of fair play and substantial justice." Put another way, under the given facts, the minimum contacts test has been satisfied, and there is a strong presumption that the exercise of personal jurisdiction would be reasonable. Given the very strong interest a state has in protecting its residents from the negligence of persons operating motor vehicles within the state, Barbara would not likely be able to rebut that presumption. Of course, the exercise of personal jurisdiction over Barbara must also satisfy the California long-arm statute, but since California has adopted a due process–style statute (see *Long-Arm Statutes* box), satisfaction of the constitutional due process standards automatically satisfies the identical statutory standards.

What About Federal Courts?

Aside from a few narrow exceptions, federal courts must adhere to the same due process standards that apply in state court proceedings. In other words, the minimum contacts test applies to proceedings applied in federal court. In addition, in the absence of congressional direction to the contrary, a federal court must also adhere to the long-arm statute of the state in which the federal court sits.

Perhaps the most interesting context in which issues of personal jurisdiction arise today is those involving the Internet. The basic question is simply stated—under what circumstances may a state court exercise personal jurisdiction over a nonresident who never physically enters the state, but who maintains a webpage that can be accessed by persons residing within the state? In other words, how does one apply the minimum contacts test to this contemporary problem of e-contacts created by the world-wide web? In ways it would seem ridiculous that by creating a webpage one consents to go to court anywhere in the country, perhaps the world. In other ways, web sites can harm people anywhere they are accessed, and thus could cause harms in unexpected locales. The essential question is when or under what circumstances webpage access within the forum state counts as a purposeful contact with that state by the nonresident moderator of the webpage.

The courts have not settled on a single formula for Internet cases, but the trend is toward dividing webpages into three types: (1) active; (2) passive; and (3) hybrid. An active webpage is one in which there is an interactive relationship between the webpage moderator and users of the webpage, such as might occur with credit cards for purchases over the Internet—for example, the type of transactions engaged in on Amazon.com. A passive webpage merely posts information and allows for no user interaction. A hybrid webpage is one that allows some interaction (e.g., users may post messages, but does not involve active commercial exchanges). Wikipedia might fall into this category. Stated somewhat simplistically, in-state access to an active webpage will usually constitute a purposeful contact with the forum state by the webpage moderator. Passive web pages, in the absence of some additional facts indicating that the content of the page is directed toward users in the forum state, are unlikely to constitute purposeful contact. With respect to hybrid webpages, the determination of purposefulness will depend on the type of interaction allowed, combined with any other facts suggesting (or negating) purposeful contacts with the forum state.

Question: Where Is that Internet Casino?

Tom is a lucky guy. He won almost $200K gambling at the World's Largest Internet Casino ("WLIC") while sitting in the comfort of his home in Texas. In order to play online, Tom was required to enter a contract with WLIC and to use his credit card to purchase game tokens. When the WLIC refused to pay Tom his winnings, he sued WLIC for breach of contract in a Texas state court. WLIC sought to have the suit dismissed, arguing that it had no contacts with Texas, since the WLIC server was located in California. The court disagreed. In essence, the interactive nature of the WLIC's webpage, coupled with WLIC having knowingly entered a commercial transaction with a Texas resident, established the necessary minimum contacts with the state.

Answer: Wherever Internet access is available.

The modern law of personal jurisdiction has not eliminated all the vestiges of the traditional model of personal jurisdiction. Hence, it remains the case that a state court may exercise personal jurisdiction over its own citizens without any need to satisfy the minimum contacts test. Similarly, a state court may exercise personal jurisdiction over a nonresident who is served while voluntarily within the territory of the state. Finally, personal jurisdiction may be exercised over any party who either consents to the exercise of personal jurisdiction or who waives any objections to that exercise.

Notice and the Right to Be Heard

Due Process

Personal jurisdiction is not the only requirement for a court to issue a binding judgment. Just as due process requires a forum state to properly exercise jurisdiction, due process also requires that a defendant be given notice and an opportunity to be heard. This means, simply, that the defendant must be formally notified of the proceeding and be given a fair and timely opportunity to contest the plaintiff's claim.

There is no set formula for determining what constitutes sufficient notice or an adequate hearing. The measure is reasonableness under the circumstances. The general principal, however, is clear: "An elementary and fundamental requirement of due process in any proceeding which is to be accorded finality is notice reasonably calculated, under all the circumstances, to apprise interested parties of the pendency of the action and afford them an opportunity to present their objections" (*Mullane v. Central Hanover Bank & Trust Co.*, 1950).

Because of the protections of the due process clause—that life, liberty, or property will not be deprived without due process—the usual presumption is that both the notice and the hearing will *precede* any such deprivation. Moreover, in the specific context of civil litigation, the further presumption is that the hearing will be adversarial in nature and presided over by a neutral magistrate. Both of these presumptions can be rebutted. Thus, for example, a child protective agency may be allowed to remove a child from a dangerous home prior to a hearing if exigent circumstances are presented. The custodial parent would, however, be entitled to a prompt post-deprivation hearing. In short, the nature and timing of the hearing required by due process may vary according to the circumstances. But again, the presumption is for a pre-deprivation notice and hearing.

Service of Process

In the usual course of events, that is, in civil litigation unfreighted by an emergency or special circumstances, the parties are not left to the potential vagaries of due process. With respect to notice, every judicial system within the United States provides fairly specific guidelines as to the contents of the required notice and as to the proper method for serving that notice, the so-called **service of process** mentioned earlier in this chapter. These guidelines are usually found in either statutes or formal court rules. These statutes or rules also set out the procedure to be followed once service is complete, or in legal terms, perfect.

A typical service of process provision requires that the plaintiff formally deliver to the defendant a **summons** and a copy of the **complaint**. The summons notifies the defendant that he or she has been sued in a particular court. It also explains what steps the defendant would have to take to avoid entry of default judgment as well as various other steps the defendant may or ought to take in response. The complaint is the document that describes the plaintiff's claims against the defendant. Hence, the complaint should provide the defendant with notice of what the lawsuit is about.

The pertinent regulations also provide specific guidance as to the acceptable methods of delivery. In-hand or personal service, in which a professional process server hands the defendant a copy of the summons and complaint, is universally allowed. Some jurisdictions also allow various alternatives such as service by certified mail or service on a person of "suitable age" residing in the defendant's principal place of abode.

You've Got Mail!

Can service of process be effected through e-mail? Apparently so. In one interesting case a federal court allowed a plaintiff to serve a defendant by e-mail after the plaintiff had exhausted all conventional methods of service. Better read that spam!

Note that compliance with statutory or rule-based guidelines on service of process will not necessarily satisfy due process. For example, in-hand service on a person who lacks mental capacity might well fail the reasonableness test of due process despite the usual statutory authorization for this type of service. The question in such a case would be whether the in-hand service was "reasonably calculated, under all the circumstances, to apprise interested parties of the pendency of the action" (*Mullane v. Central Hanover Bank & Trust Co.*, 1950).

The Types of Cases a Court May Hear: Subject Matter Jurisdiction

Many courts can only hear certain types of cases, whether bankruptcy, probate, or, as with federal courts, subjects defined by more complex rules. A probate court might be limited to hearing matters pertaining to the distribution of a decedent's estate through a will or by operation of law. A juvenile court might be limited to hearing cases involving minors. The authority of a bankruptcy court could be limited to matters related to bankruptcy, and so forth. The **subject matter jurisdiction** for a court specifies those particular cases that court may hear.

A court's subject matter jurisdiction is typically defined by reference to the topic of the potential claims filed before it, some characteristic of the

¡Adviso! **Personal Jurisdiction and Subject Matter Jurisdiction Are Completely Distinct Concepts**

Personal jurisdiction defines the breadth of a court's power to bind a party to its judgments. As such, it pertains to the court's power over a person or a person's property. Subject matter jurisdiction is a wholly different concept. It pertains to the types of lawsuits that a court is authorized to adjudicate. In short, these jurisdictions are completely distinct concepts and the satisfaction of one has no bearing on the satisfaction of the other.

parties to the suit, the amount in controversy, or some combination of these factors.

In general, subject matter jurisdiction is conferred by a constitution, a statute, or a combination of both. The subject matter jurisdiction of state courts is largely defined by state law, and the subject matter jurisdiction of federal courts is completely defined by federal law. In most state court systems, a case filed in a court lacking subject matter jurisdiction can be transferred to the proper court within the state system. In federal courts, the absence of subject matter jurisdiction requires dismissal of the lawsuit.

For purposes of subject matter jurisdiction, there are two types of courts: **courts of general jurisdiction** and **courts of limited jurisdiction**.[1] A court of general jurisdiction is a court that is vested with a presumed authority to adjudicate all subject matters save those specifically excepted from its jurisdiction. Thus a state court vested with jurisdiction to hear all civil actions except those pertaining to probate, would be a court of general jurisdiction. A court of limited jurisdiction is a court whose jurisdiction extends only to those subject matters specifically vested in it. A court with

Concurrent and Exclusive Jurisdiction

State courts of general jurisdiction are presumed to have concurrent subject matter jurisdiction, along with federal courts, over claims premised on federal law, including claims arising under the U.S. Constitution. In fact, by virtue of the supremacy clause, a state court cannot refuse to entertain a federal claim if that claim is of the same generic type that the court generally hears. Congress does, however, have the power to rebut the presumption of concurrency by conferring exclusive jurisdiction over certain specified claims on federal courts alone. For example, Congress has vested federal courts with exclusive jurisdiction over claims arising under federal patent laws.

authority over only probate matters would be an example of a court of limited jurisdiction.

The issue of subject matter jurisdiction is most important and most challenging in the context of federal court jurisdiction. All federal courts, which are sometimes called **Article III courts**, are courts of limited jurisdiction. That jurisdiction is limited by Article III of the U.S. Constitution and by any further restrictions imposed by Congress. Most importantly, a federal court cannot exercise jurisdiction beyond that specifically conferred on it. Moreover, a federal court's subject matter jurisdiction cannot be waived. Thus, a challenge to subject matter jurisdiction can be raised at anytime by any party or by the court itself, including while the case is on appeal. The remedy for an absence of subject matter jurisdiction is an automatic dismissal. This is so regardless of the stage of the proceeding or of how much time and effort has been put into the case. (By way of contrast, in most state courts, an absence of subject matter jurisdiction usually results in a transfer to a court with subject matter jurisdiction.)

Article III of the U.S. Constitution limits the judicial power of the United States to nine specified subject matters. Accordingly, an Article III court cannot, under any circumstances, adjudicate a case that does not fall within one of these categories. The most significant of the enumerated categories (i.e., the ones that account for the vast majority of cases filed in federal courts) are of two types: (1) cases arising under federal law—so-called **federal question** or **arising under** cases; and (2) and controversies between citizens of different states—so-called *diversity of citizenship* cases. A case "arises under" federal law for purposes of Article III if some aspect of the case requires the application of federal law; a cases falls within Article III's definition of diversity of citizenship if any one plaintiff is diverse from any one defendant.

Even if a case falls within one of the nine specified Article III subject matters, a federal court cannot exercise authority over that case unless Congress has affirmatively authorized the court to do so. (There is a small exception for the Supreme Court's original jurisdiction, which does not require a statute, as it is executed directly by the Constitution. See chapter 2 for further discussion of the court's original jurisdiction.) Importantly, Congress has never vested the federal judiciary with the power to hear the full range of subject matters provided in Article III. Thus, although federal courts are empowered to hear diversity cases in which the matter in controversy exceeds $75,000, they are not empowered to hear diversity cases with a lesser amount in controversy since Congress has only authorized jurisdiction over the former.

Federal Question Jurisdiction: Statutory "Arising Under"

The federal question jurisdiction of a federal trial court (i.e., a U.S. District Court) is conferred and defined by 28 U.S.C. §1331. That statute vests

The Judicial Hierarchy

The Supreme Court sits atop the hierarchy of the judicial system of the United States. On the federal side of the equation, the court exercises direct or indirect appellate authority over U.S. District Courts and the Courts of Appeals (as well as over certain other specialized federal tribunals). The court may exercise appellate jurisdiction over a lower federal court case only if that lower court had subject matter jurisdiction over the case. In this sense, the Supreme Court's jurisdiction is **derivative** of the jurisdiction of the lower federal court. The Supreme Court also exercises appellate authority over state judicial systems with respect to cases in which a state court has decided a question of federal law. The question of derivative jurisdiction does not arise in this context.

district courts with jurisdiction over cases arising under federal law. While the phrase "arising under" also appears in Article III, the statutory usage of this phrase has been interpreted more narrowly than the "any federal ingredient" standard of Article III. As used in §1331, a case arises under federal law if and only if plaintiff's claim is either created by federal law or includes an essential federal ingredient. In other words, a federal defense will not normally suffice to vest a federal trial court with jurisdiction over the case, even though the presence of a federal defense would surely satisfy Article III's more inclusive definition of arising under.

Most cases satisfying the statutory arising under standard do so by virtue of the **creation test**. This test is simple to apply. If a plaintiff's claim is created by federal law, the claim arises under federal law for purposes of §1331. Thus, a claim asserted under the federal antitrust laws arises under federal law, for the simple reason that federal law created the claim itself. By way of contrast, a claim asserted under the state law of contract is not created by federal law, but by state law. The former arises under federal law, the latter does not. In very, very rare circumstances a federally created claim might not arise under federal law for purposes of §1331, but as a rule of thumb if federal law creates the claim, a district court has jurisdiction to hear it.

A claim that does not satisfy the creation test, typically a claim created by state law, may be treated as one arising under federal law if, under the particular circumstance of the case, establishing the case requires the resolution of an **essential federal ingredient**. For example, a claim premised on the state law of trespass might arise under federal law if the property at issue had been conveyed to the original owner by the federal government. In such a case, the scope of ownership rights, and hence the availability of a trespass claim, might well present a question of federal law and thereby insert an essential federal ingredient into the plaintiff's claim.

Statutory Arising Under

The Creation Test
or
The Essential Federal Ingredient Test

By way of contrast, a federal defense to a state law claim will normally not suffice to establish statutory arising under jurisdiction. Thus a plaintiff asserting a state law claim cannot invoke federal jurisdiction by alleging that the defendant plans to raise a federal defense to plaintiff's claim. This is known as the **well-pleaded complaint rule**, the essence of which is that only the elements of plaintiff's actual claim, and not some anticipated defense, may be considered in determining whether a case arises under federal law for purposes of §1331.

There is one circumstance under which a federal defense may be used to satisfy §1331. If Congress has completely supplanted state law in some particular field of law, in essence, federalizing all potential claims in that field, the federal defense will redefine plaintiff's state law claim into a federal claim. This is known as **complete preemption**. It's successful invocation as a basis for federal jurisdiction is relatively rare.

Note that statutory arising under jurisdiction is significantly narrower than Article III arising under jurisdiction. This simply means that Congress has vested federal trial courts with a narrower range of federal question jurisdiction than would be permitted by Article III. Moreover, given that the Supreme Court's power to review a decision of a lower federal court is derivative (see **The Judicial Hierarchy** box), the fact that a federal ingredient arises somewhere in the case will not suffice to validate the Supreme Court's power to review the lower court's decision. In other words, the jurisdictional defect cannot be cured by subsequent events. If the arising under standards of §1331 were not initially satisfied, all the Supreme Court can do is dismiss the case and order the lower federal court to do the same.

Diversity of Citizenship: Statutory Diversity

Unlike a federal court's federal question jurisdiction, its diversity jurisdiction allows it to entertain claims that are premised solely on state law. This type of jurisdiction was designed to provide a method through which an out-of-state party could avoid potential or perceived prejudice in a state court tribunal, essentially taking away the "home-court" advantage of an in-state party. The extent of any actual home-court advantage in state courts is subject to much doubt. Yet despite a rather constant drumbeat for the elimination of diversity jurisdiction, Congress has consistently refused to do so. It is called *diversity* jurisdiction because it allows for the adjudication of state-created rights so long as the parties are from different states—so long as they are "diverse" from one another.

A district court's jurisdiction over diversity claims is conferred by 28 U.S.C. §1332. Just as §1331 does not confer the full range of federal question jurisdiction permitted by Article III, §1332 does not confer the rule range of constitutionally permissible diversity jurisdiction. While Article III would permit the exercise of diversity jurisdiction so long as at least one plaintiff and one defendant were from different states and regardless of the amount in controversy, statutory diversity is more circumscribed. It requires **complete diversity** between all plaintiffs and all defendants, which is to say that no plaintiff can be from the same state as any defendant. In addition, even if the complete diversity requirement is satisfied, the federal court may exercise jurisdiction only if the **amount in controversy** exceeds $75,000.

There are a number of technical complexities that arise in the determination of whether the requirements of diversity have been satisfied. The major ones pertain to citizenship. Under the Fourteenth Amendment state citizenship is defined as the place where a person resides, sometimes referred to as person's *domicile*. Implicit in this definition is the right of a person to change his or her state of citizenship by moving to another state with the intent of remaining in that state indefinitely. As a consequence, a federal court exercising diversity jurisdiction must sometimes engage in a detailed factual analysis of the parties' actual states of residence. For diversity purposes it is the date on which the case was filed that is determinative of each party's citizenship.

Similarly, difficulties sometimes arise with respect to the amount in controversy. In cases involving monetary damages, the plaintiff's good faith allegations usually control. A defendant, however, can rebut that presumption by showing that even if plaintiff prevails, plaintiff cannot, to a **legal certainty**,

---

Injunctive Relief: Amount in Controversy

Steamboat v. Bridge Company

Steamboat claims that a recently constructed bridge owned by Bridge Company has created an unlawful obstruction to navigation. Basically, the bridge is too low to accommodate Steamboat's smoke stacks. Steamboat seeks an injunction requiring Bridge Company to reconstruct the bridge to a height that would allow Steamboat to pass under the bridge. It would cost Steamboat $10,000 to install shorter steam stacks; it will cost Bridge Company $100,000 to reconstruct the bridge. What is the amount in controversy? (The question is not who should pay, but whether, assuming the validity of Steamboat's claim, the amount in controversy exceeds $75,000.)

recover the jurisdictional minimum. This might occur, for example, if the contract under which the plaintiff is suing limits damages to $50,000.

As the hypothetical in the preceding box indicates, there are also amount-in-controversy difficulties that arise when the plaintiff seeks only injunctive relief. Should the amount be determined by the amount the plaintiff will gain if the injunction issues or by the amount the defendant will lose? A variety of approaches have been taken to resolving this problem. Some courts have measured the amount in controversy from the perspective of the plaintiff, some from the perspective of the defendant, and others from the perspective of the party seeking federal jurisdiction. (As we will see in the immediately following section, sometimes a defendant can successfully "remove" case to federal court.) A growing number of courts have adopted the "either viewpoint, whichever is greater" approach. This approach would appear to reflect the most realistic assessment of the amount actually at stake.

Supplemental Jurisdiction

Federal question jurisdiction and diversity jurisdiction are forms of subject matter jurisdiction that are sometimes described as forming an "independent basis of jurisdiction." This simply means that jurisdiction over the claim is established without reference to any other claims being asserted. There is also a dependent form of subject matter jurisdiction. It is called **supplemental jurisdiction**. A claim falls within a federal court's supplemental jurisdiction if the claim is sufficiently related to a claim over which there exists an independent basis of jurisdiction. The relationship is usually established by the factual overlap between the claims.

For example, suppose a plaintiff claims that his Fourth and Fourteenth Amendment rights were violated when a police officer entered plaintiff's home and engaged in a nonconsensual search of the premises. Plaintiff sues the officer under a federal statute that creates a cause of action for such violations (42 U.S.C. §1983). Since this is a claim created by federal law, there is an independent basis of jurisdiction over this claim, namely, federal question jurisdiction. But suppose the plaintiff also sues the officer for trespass and invasion of privacy, both of which are claims created by state law. Assuming that the plaintiff and the officer reside in the same state, there would appear to be no independent basis of jurisdiction over these claims. They do not present federal questions and diversity is not satisfied. On the other hand, supplemental jurisdiction would be satisfied since there is a close factual connection between the federal claim, over which there is an independent basis of jurisdiction, and the state claims, over which there is not. Hence, the federal court would be empowered to hear the entire case.

There are a number of technical difficulties that arise in the context of supplemental jurisdiction, but they operate at a micro-detail level that journalists will likely not encounter in their forays into civil litigation.

Removal Jurisdiction

In the usual case, it is the plaintiff who invokes federal jurisdiction by filing the case in a federal court. However, a defendant may **remove** a case from state to federal court if the case could have been filed in the federal court in the first place. This means that removal is possible only if the case satisfies the federal court's subject matter jurisdiction, including supplemental jurisdiction. If there are multiple defendants, the general rule is that all defendants must join in the petition for removal.

If the basis of subject matter jurisdiction is diversity, removal is not available if any of the defendants reside in the forum state. This limitation does not apply if the case is premised on federal question jurisdiction.

There is a special provision for removal that pertains to cases filed in state courts in which a **separate and independent** federal law claim has been joined with otherwise nonremovable state law claims. Presumably those state claims do not fall within the court's supplemental jurisdiction, as supplemental jurisdiction is based on claims having similar facts involved. This provision is designed to prevent plaintiffs from insulating a federal claim from removal by filing it in state court along with unrelated state law claims, for example, filing a federal civil rights claim along with an unrelated breach of contract claim against the same parties. The usual outcome in this type of removal is that the federal claims will be heard in federal court and the state law claims remanded to the state court. All the defendants need not join the petition for removal under this provision.

When a case that has been improperly removed and must be set back to state court, the case is technically **remanded** to the state court.

The Geographic Location of the Lawsuit: Venue

While personal jurisdiction, addressed above, dictates what jurisdiction's courts may hear a case and measures the scope of a court's power over parties and property, it does not help in determining where in that jurisdiction the case will be heard. A suit's **venue** refers to the geographic location in which a civil action has been filed. Venue assumes that the court has the constitutional power to hear the case, and it focuses on convenience factors that may impose further limits on what constitutes an appropriate location for the lawsuit. In contrast to personal jurisdiction, "location" in venue usually refers to a subdivision of the state and not to the state as a whole.

A defendant has a right to have a case heard in a proper venue; this right may, however, be waived by a defendant's failure to assert a timely objection.

The unit of geographic location used to measure venue varies from state to state, but typically proper venue is defined by reference to political subdivisions of the state, such as counties or cities. More populous areas may be further subdivided into branches or districts of the local court. In federal court, venue is measured by reference to federal judicial districts. All states have at least one federal judicial district; more populous states have multiple federal districts. California, for example, has four such districts.

In most cases, the convenience of a particular venue is not determined on an ad hoc basis. Rather, proper venue (and presumed convenience) is usually defined by reference to statutory criteria. While the details may vary between individual states and the federal system, the basic approach is relatively uniform. Venue is typically geared to the place where events giving rise to the claim occurred, where any property that is the subject of the lawsuit is located, where the defendant resides or is doing business, where the plaintiff resides or is doing business (less frequent), and in cases involving the government, where the seat of government or the appropriate subdivision of the government is located.

Given the range of criteria used, in most cases the plaintiff will have a choice among proper venues. In the case of lawsuits pertaining to real property, however, there is often only one proper venue, namely, the political subdivision in which the property is located.

If venue is improper and the defendant objects, the usual remedy is transfer to a court where venue would be proper. This, of course, assumes that venue would be proper somewhere within that particular judicial system. Hence, a court of State X may transfer case to another court of State X. It may not transfer the case to a court of a sister state or to a federal court. If there is no proper venue within the state system, the only remedy is to dismiss the action.

Do not confuse removal and venue. Removal presents a jurisdictional issue, the resolution of which has nothing to do with venue. Moreover, the state court plays no role in the removal process.

A federal court may transfer a case to another federal court, including a federal court located in a different state. If venue is improper in the federal judicial district where the case was filed, the federal court also has the option of dismissing the case. A federal court has no authority to transfer a case to a state court. Of course, a federal court can remand an improperly removed case; but, again, that has nothing to do with venue.

Even if venue is proper in the original court, the court may transfer the action to another court in which venue would also be proper. Usually, however, the plaintiff's choice of the original venue will prevail in the absence of strong showing that that the potential transferee forum would be a significantly more convenient forum. In making a transfer determination, a court will consider such things as the availability of witnesses, access to evidence, and other factors pertaining to the fair and efficient delivery of justice. Again, keep in mind, that transfer is intra-jurisdictional. A state court may transfer to another court of that same state. A federal court may transfer to another federal court.

Even if a case is properly filed, a court might still be able to dismiss the case in order to allow the parties to refile that case in a more convenient forum that is located in a different jurisdiction. The doctrine that allows this is called **forum non conveniens**, a common law doctrine followed by both state and federal courts. Since there is no such thing as an inter-jurisdictional transfer, forum non conveniens is a dismissal doctrine. From a state court perspective, the more convenient forum would be a court of another state or a court of a foreign nation. From a federal court perspective, the more convenient forum is most likely to be the court of a foreign nation, though it is at least theoretically possible that the alternate forum could be the court of a state other than the one in which the federal court sits. In order to apply this doctrine, the court must assure itself that there is a suitable alternate forum that would have jurisdiction over the case and the parties. Moreover, the party seeking a forum non conveniens dismissal must waive any potential jurisdictional or statute of limitations defenses in the alternate forum.

The Law to Be Applied in Federal or State Court

This section addresses a somewhat complicated and technical body of principles known as the *Erie* doctrine. The discussion here will be abbreviated since it is unlikely that journalists will find themselves in the sometimes swampy quagmire of *Erie*. Should such an unfortunate event occur, however, what follows should provide the hapless scribe with the basic lay of the land. If you find yourself in this situation, feel free to hail one of the authors of this text for assistance. Hopefully, you'll contact the right one!

So here's a quick overview of the *Erie* and universe of problems that surround it.

When a federal claim is filed in a federal court, we sensibly expect the federal court to follow federal procedural law and federal substantive law. Similarly, we expect a state court adjudicating a state law claim to apply state procedural law and state substantive law. In either instance, any other approach would seem exceedingly peculiar. But what law should a federal court sitting in diversity apply? Similarly, what body of law should a state court apply when it entertains a federal claim? Can a court end up applying mismatching substantive and procedural laws?

As a general matter, the answer to the foregoing questions is both easy and sensible. A federal court sitting in diversity applies federal procedural law and state substantive law. In other words, the federal court operates as an alternative forum for the resolution of the state law claim. In so doing, it does not operate as a clone of a state court; nor does it operate as a tribunal through which new principles of state law can be forged. Rather, it applies state law through the lens of federal procedure. The same approach applies to state courts adjudicating federal law claims. The state court retains its character as a state court by applying state procedural law, but given the federal nature of the claim, the state court applies federal substantive law to the resolution of that claim.

Believe it or not, this intuitively sensible scheme is of somewhat recent vintage, at least with respect to the federal court aspect of it. Up until 1938, federal procedure was a combined product of federal and state law. Thus, in a case seeking money damages, a federal court would follow state procedural law, while in a case seeking an injunction, a federal court would follow federal procedural law. More oddly, in diversity cases, federal courts were empowered to ignore state common law, such as the state's law of negligence. Instead, the federal judge would look to "general principles of the law" to determine what the state law ought to be. The result was jurisprudential chaos. Federal and state courts sitting in the same state would apply different substantive principles for the resolution of identical state law claims. And, of course, federal procedure would vary from state to state depending on the law of the state in which the federal court sat.

All this changed in 1938 with the adoption of a uniform body of federal rules of civil procedure, namely, the Federal Rules of Civil Procedure promulgated by the Supreme Court, and with a Supreme Court decision—*Erie Railroad v. Tompkins*—that overruled the precedent on which the previously described chaotic approach to diversity was premised. In essence, the *Erie* court ruled that all law is the product of sovereign power and that federal courts had no constitutional power to create or alter the substantive law of the state in which the federal court sat. Of course, under proper circumstances a federal court can declare the law of a state unconstitutional. Post-*Erie*, however, a federal court had no independent power to create or modify state law in the absence of any constitutional objection to that law. In other words, federal courts would now apply state substantive law, including state common law, to all state claims.

All of the foregoing is simple and uncontroversial. Federal courts sitting diversity apply federal procedural law and state substantive law. More particularly, as to the latter, federal courts apply the substantive law that a court of the state in which the federal court sits would apply. The difficulty arises, however, when we move beyond the formal labels of procedure and substance. For example, suppose a negligence claim is filed in a federal court under that court's diversity jurisdiction and suppose as well that under a principle of federal judge-made law, the filing is timely; yet, had that same claim been filed in state court, the state's statute of limitations would have barred the suit. Hence, the state court would have been required to dismiss the suit. Must the federal court do the same?

From the perspective of formal definitions, if we label provisions imposing time limits on the filing of law suits as procedural, then the federal court should follow the federal rule and retain the case. If such provisions, however, are more properly characterized as substantive, then state law should apply and the case should be dismissed. Here we arrive at the tyranny of formal labels. One can construct an argument in favor of both labels in this particular context. Statutes of limitations are procedural because they merely provide a time frame during which a party can process her substantive claim. Statutes of limitations are substantive because they allow a potential defendant to resist liability once the period has run; in this way, statutes of limitations extinguish the substantive right. Obviously, we need to move beyond the labels in order to resolve this and similar conflicts between federal procedural law and state law.

Thankfully, the Supreme Court has devised a system for resolving such conflicts. The basic rule is that valid federal law will trump state law to the contrary. In other words, valid federal law always wins. This rule is based on the supremacy clause of the U.S. Constitution, which declares that *valid* federal law is the supreme law of the law, state law to the contrary notwithstanding. The critical question in every case, therefore, is whether the federal law, which in this particular context would be federal procedural law, is valid. That determination depends on whether the law comes in the form of a statute, a formal rule, or a principle of judge-made (common) law. The details of the related formulas are beyond anything a sane journalist would want to know (at least as a matter of general knowledge) and can be left for your "life line." Suffice it to say that in most cases federal procedural law is deemed valid, and this is particularly so of statutes and formal rules.

Of course, federal procedural is not always valid. In such cases, the purported federal law must give way to state law. This is rare, but it does happen from time to time. For example, the above hypothetical in which the federal judge-made rule regarding the timeliness of a lawsuit conflicted with the state statute of limitations provides an example of a case in which the federal rule would be deemed invalid as applied, since application of the federal principle would lead the federal court to enforce a state-created right that was no longer enforceable as a matter of state law. To conclude otherwise would violate the *Erie* principle that federal courts sitting in diversity must apply state substantive law and not some altered form of it.

Now you can nod your head knowingly when you hear a law student or lawyer (or judge) moan about the *Erie* doctrine.

Discovery

> "If you scrutinize a legal rule, you will see that it is a conditional statement referring to facts. Such a rule . . . say[s] in effect 'If such and such fact exists, then this or that legal consequences should follow.'"
> Jerome Frank, Courts on Trial 14 (1949)

Discovery is the process through which lawyers gather the facts relevant to the claims and defenses that have been or may be presented in a civil action.

The discovery process begins with the initial client interview and proceeds in steps from the relatively informal activity of gathering and culling information provided by the client or available in public records to a formal process involving the exchange of information between the parties to a pending lawsuit. The focus of this section is on the formal process of discovery and when we use the word *discovery* it will be in this formal sense.

Discovery is a relatively recent addition to the Anglo-American system of civil justice. In traditional English law, there was virtually no discovery. Essentially, in terms of fact gathering, the parties were left to fend for themselves. There was, however, a limited amount of discovery available through courts of equity, and just as equity pleading served as the model for modern pleading, equity discovery set the foundation for the modern law of discovery. In fact, the move toward modern pleading practices was accompanied by a move toward formalizing discovery. Thus, in the 19th century, states that had abandoned common law pleading began experimenting with various discovery devices to complement their systems of fact pleading. The adoption of the Federal Rules of Civil Procedure completed this process by giving discovery a central role in the federal procedural system. Today, virtually every state has now adopted some version of federal model.

To state matters at a very general level, the parties to a civil action are entitled to discover all unprivileged information held by an opposing party that is or may be relevant to a claim or defense asserted in the proceeding. The word *relevant* is interpreted broadly to include any information that may be admissible at trial *as well as* any information that, although not itself admissible, is reasonably calculated to lead to the discovery of admissible evidence. For further discussion of admissibility of evidence, see chapter 9, "Evidence."

The process of discovery commences with the filing of the lawsuit. In some jurisdictions, the parties are required to exchange certain information automatically (i.e., without have received a formal request from the other side). These automatic disclosures are fittingly called **mandatory disclosures**. For example, a party to a lawsuit in federal court must, among other things, identify any witnesses she might use to support her claims or defenses. These mandatory disclosures are designed to promote an efficient exchange of information to which each side of a controversy is obviously entitled.

The rules of discovery also provide the parties with additional tools to discover information not included within any mandatory disclosures. For example, the rules of mandatory disclosure do not require a party to disclose witnesses she may call to rebut an opposing party's claims or defenses. These additional tools include depositions, interrogatories, requests for production and inspection, physical and mental examinations, and requests for admission. The use of these devices is regulated by statutes and court rules; however, the parties are often able to alter these regulations by mutual agreement.

A **deposition** is a device through which an attorney directly questions an opposing party or witness in a relatively formal setting. The questions posed must be answered spontaneously and under oath. Typically, a deposition is taken at the office of the attorney who has requested the deposition. Present at the deposition are the person being deposed (the *deponent*), the deposing attorney, any opposing counsel, and a court reporter who must make a record of the proceedings (e.g., stenographically or by way of some other acceptable recording device). While opposing counsel is allowed to note objections to the questions posed, with the exception of objections based on privilege (see box below), the deponent must, with rare exceptions, answer the questions despite the interposition of an objection.

Privileges

A privilege is a judicially recognized right to refuse to disclose otherwise relevant information. A matter is deemed privileged for purposes of discovery if it would be privileged at trial. Among the most common privileges are the Fifth Amendment privilege against self incrimination, the attorney-client privilege, the priest-penitent privilege, spousal privileges, and the state secrets privilege. Some jurisdictions also recognize a reporter's privilege to protect confidential sources. A more thorough description of privileges is found in chapter 3.

Depositions are considered by many attorneys to be the most effective discovery device since they permit counsel to fully probe the other party and her witnesses with little interference from opposing counsel. (Yes, there are overzealous attorneys who attempt to interfere with the taking of a deposition; such abuses, however, should, can, and often do lead to the imposition of sanctions.) Both the number of depositions a party may take and the length of any given deposition are regulated by court rules, subject to the discretion of the court to alter those rules in the interests of justice. For example, the base-line rule in federal courts is 10 depositions per side, each deposition limited to one day of seven hours.

A party's deposition can be used at trial for any purpose, including as direct evidence of a particular fact and as impeachment of that party's testimony at trial. A nonparty's deposition can be used for impeachment purposes if that nonparty is called to testify and may be used for any purpose, aside from swatting in the head, if the nonparty is either dead or otherwise unavailable at the time of trial.

An **interrogatory** is a written request for information that may be served on an opposing party and which must be answered by that party in writing and under oath. At one time interrogatories were used to bury one's opponents in an avalanche of questions. Today, however, most courts significantly limit the number interrogatories that may be asked. In federal court, for example, a party may serve a maximum of 25 interrogatories on any one party. Again, this number can be altered by mutual agreement.

There are two key distinctions between interrogatories and depositions. First, the answers to an interrogatory need not be spontaneous. The answers can be, and usually are, drafted by the responding party's attorney. This is an obvious drawback, as some attorneys are skilled at providing answers that minimize the useful information disclosed. Second, and this is a plus for interrogatories, while the answer in a deposition need reflect only the deponent's personal knowledge, the answer to an interrogatory must reflect the knowledge of the answering party, her agents, and her attorney.

Interrogatory Number One

Identify the person referred to as "Deep Throat" on page 71 of the book, *All the President's Men*, authored by you and Carl Bernstein.

Response

Objection. Calls for privileged information.

Interrogatories are most useful in gathering specific information such as the date and time of a specific incident, the custodian of certain documents, the whereabouts of witnesses, and so forth. In other words, interrogatories can be used to lay a foundation for further discovery such as the taking of a deposition of a particular party or witness.

Requests for production and inspection allow a party the discovery of any form of tangible evidence that falls within the broad standards of discovery relevance. This device allows a party to examine virtually any type of relevant document, including electronically stored information, or tangible thing that may be in the possession or control of an opposing party. Included within this vast domain would be contracts, reports, e-mails, the interior of a manufacturing plant, and so forth. If the item sought is not in the control of an opposing party, the party seeking the production or inspection must serve a subpoena on the nonparty custodian.

A party to a lawsuit may be required to undergo a **physical or mental examination** if that party's physical or mental state has been placed "in controversy" as part of the civil action. For example, in a tort case in which the plaintiff claims to have suffered permanent injury due to the defendant's negligence, the plaintiff's physical condition is in controversy. In the usual case, the parties agree to an appropriate exam without the intervention of the court. Failing such an agreement, a court may order a party to submit to a physical or mental exam within the confines of the in controversy requirement.

A **request for admission** is a written device through which one party asks another party to admit or deny the truth of a specific matter relevant to the pending action. The effect of an admission is to conclusively establish the truth of the matter admitted for purposes of the trial. The effect of a denial is to require the matter to be proven at trial. A party, who has denied a fact that is later proven to be true, may be required to pay the reasonable expenses incurred in establishing the truth of that fact.

Request for Admission Number One

Admit or deny that you disclosed Valerie Plame's identity as a C.I.A. agent to Robert Novak?

Response

Deny!!!

Courts are empowered to enter **protective orders** to shield a party or other person subject to discovery from, in the words of the federal rules, "annoyance, embarrassment, oppression, or undue burden or expense." A court may also enter an order in response to a **motion to compel** requiring a party to cooperate in discovery. Finally, a court may impose **sanctions** on a party or an attorney who fails to comply with a discovery order or to adhere to the basic rules of disclosure and discovery.

The Composition of Civil Action: Parties and Claims

At common law, the basic litigation unit was a civil action in which a single plaintiff filed a single claim against a single defendant. The ancient forms of action were premised on this model. While such streamlined cases are occasionally filed today, most modern litigation is more complex, often drawing in multiple parties and even more often involving multiple claims. The process through which such litigation is constructed is referred to as the **joinder of claims** and the **joinder of parties**. Virtually all jurisdictions throughout the United States have adopted relatively liberal rules of joinder. The result is that many civil actions exhibit a complex web of parties and claims.

The Web of Parties and Claims

Potential parties: plaintiffs, defendants, and third-party defendants. In addition, an absent party with a tangible interest in the proceeding may be allowed to intervene as a plaintiff or a defendant; and an absent party may be forced into the case if his or her presence is deemed necessary to a fair adjudication of the controversy.

Potential claims: original claims (the plaintiff's initial claims), counterclaims (responsive claims often filed by a defendant by potentially filed by any party who has been subjected to a claim), cross claims (initiating claims filed between co-parties); and third-party claims (claim filed against a third party).

The Federal Rules of Civil Procedure provide an example of the modern approach to joinder. Unlike the limited litigation unit available at common law, the federal rules are designed to accommodate and promote a litigation unit that encompasses a wide range of parties and claims. In a sense, when it comes to joinder, the rules seem to say "the more the merrier." That might be a bit of an exaggeration, but it makes the essential point: the rules are designed to give the broadest possible scope to a civil action, allowing multiple parties an opportunity to resolve a wide range of dispute between and among themselves. Keep in mind, however, that despite the liberality of the joinder rules, the standards of **subject matter jurisdiction** must also be satisfied as to each claim and party. Supplemental jurisdiction plays an important role in this context.

If the number of potential plaintiffs or defendants becomes too large, a case can be filed as **class action**. A class action is a lawsuit brought on behalf of or against a group of persons without having to include all member of the group as named parties to the suit. Instead, designated, named parties serve as representatives of the group or class. Any resulting judgment, assuming all the requisites of a class action have been satisfied, will be binding on all members of the class.

In 2005, Congress enacted the **Class Action Fairness Act (CAFA)**, which created a means for expanding federal jurisdiction to include a wider range of "diversity-style" class actions. CAFA was part of a tort reform package and was ostensibly designed to address perceived state-court abuses of the class action model. Basically, CAFA "gives federal district courts subject matter jurisdiction over plaintiff class actions involving 100 or more class members if the total value of all claims exceeds $5 million and there is at least minimal diversity between the opposing parties." Despite the foregoing simplified description, CAFA is quite complex and replete with mathematical formulae to be applied at the operational level. Whether CAFA will accomplish its goal of tort reform remains to be seen.

Resolving the Substantive Dispute Pretrial

Very few civil cases actually go to trial. Most are either settled or dismissed on nonsubstantive grounds such as an absence of personal or subject matter jurisdiction or improper venue. Others are dismissed voluntarily. Also, in some cases one or the other party may default by failing to appear or participate, leading to the entry of a **default judgment** or an involuntary dismissal. Even cases that have not settled or defaulted and that have otherwise avoided the dismissal gauntlet will not necessarily go to trial. Instead, the controversy may be resolved by a motion designed to test the substantive validity or factual adequacy of the claims.

The Demurrer or Motion to Dismiss for Failure to State a Claim

A **demurrer** is a pleading that allows a party to challenge the substantive validity of a claim or defense. It says in essence, even if the facts are as the plaintiff (or defendant) states them, there are no legal grounds for relief. So if a plaintiff were to seek damages against a defendant based on defendant's impolite failure to thank the plaintiff for services rendered, a demurrer would be appropriate, plaintiff having stated no legal claim for relief. After a successful demurrer, a party is usually given one opportunity to file an amended pleading that cures the legal inadequacy. If a no amended pleading is filed or if a second demurrer is sustained, the second dismissal is usually considered to be "on the merits."

Demurrers are technically not allowed in federal court. Instead, a party seeking to establish the legal insufficiency of a claim must file a **motion to dismiss for failure to state a claim on which relief can be granted.** This is sometimes referred to as a **12(b)(6) motion** since the motion is filed pursuant to Federal Rule of Civil Procedure 12(b)(6). It operates in the same fashion as a demurrer but within the context of the liberal rules of pleading. Using the "absence of gratitude" hypothetical described in the preceding paragraph, a federal court might deny the motion if it appeared that plaintiff had stated a claim for compensation under a Good Samaritan Law or the like. On the other hand if no such claim is discernible between the lines of plaintiff's complaint, the complaint will be dismissed with at least one opportunity to file an amended complaint.

Summary Judgment

Summary judgment provides a method for resolving a case, or parts of a case, before trial and after the completion of discovery. (Of course, settlement always remains an option even after a trial commences.) In a way, a summary judgment motion is the flip side of a demurrer or a 12(b)(6) motion. It presumes the legal sufficiency of a claim or defense, but challenges the factual adequacy of that claim or defense. In essence, it says, "You can't prove that." (Complete with MC Hammer soundtrack.)

Suppose a plaintiff delivered certain perishable goods to the defendant and the defendant refused to accept delivery. The goods spoiled before the plaintiff was able to find another buyer. Plaintiff then sues the defendant for breach of contract. Assume that the law requires that any such contract be in writing. Defendant denies the existence of any such contract and during discovery asks plaintiff to produce the contract or some evidence of its existence. Plaintiff fails to do so. Defendant responds by filing a summary judgment motion challenging the factual adequacy of the plaintiff's claim. The plaintiff is now be required to produce sufficient evidence of the contract such that a reasonable juror could (not would) find that such a written contract existed. If no such evidence is produced, the court must grant the summary judgment motion. The basic idea is that there is no point having a trial if no reasonable juror could make the finding necessary to a judgment for the plaintiff.

At one time summary judgment motions were disfavored and thought to be inconsistent with a party's right to a trial by jury. That is no longer the case and in the last two decades the successful use of the motion has increased dramatically.

Trial and Appeal

As previously noted, very few civil cases go to trial. For example during the years 2003–2004, only 1.7 percent of the civil cases resolved in federal court went to trial, with about two-thirds of those cases being tried to a jury. The numbers are slightly higher for state courts, but not dramatically so. If a case is tried without a jury, the judge decides questions of law and questions of fact. If the case is tried to a jury, the judge decides the law (and instructs the jury on that law), while the jury decides the facts and applies those facts to the law.

Trial by Jury

The right to trial by jury in a civil proceeding is protected by the Seventh Amendment to the U.S. Constitution, which provides, "In Suits at common law where the value in controversy shall exceed twenty dollars, the right of a trial by jury shall be preserved." The Seventh Amendment applies only to proceedings in federal courts. However, the right to a jury trial is also protected in most state constitutions as a matter of state law. In federal court and in most state courts, the right to a jury trial must be affirmatively asserted by one of the parties. A failure to assert the right is deemed a *waiver*.

Whether the right to a jury trial applies to a particular lawsuit depends on the nature of the relief being sought. If the relief is traceable to common law remedies, as would be the case if the plaintiff sought a **legal remedy** such as monetary damages, then the right attaches. However, if the relief being sought is **equitable** in nature (e.g., an injunction or specific performance of a contract), then the right to a jury trial does not attach. If the remedies being sought are both legal and equitable, then factual issues pertinent to the legal claim must be resolved by a jury prior to any decision on the equitable claims.

Usually the determination of whether a claim is legal or equitable is relatively easy to make. The determination is somewhat more difficult with newly created rights or remedies with no historical analogue. Under such circumstances, the court must determine whether a judge or jury is better positioned to decided the issue.

Taking a Case Away from the Jury

The fact that the right to a jury trial has attached in any particular proceeding does not prevent a judge from taking a case away from the jury if the judge concludes, after a properly noticed motion, that the evidence introduced requires a particular resolution as a matter of law. For example, in a case in which the plaintiff claims the breach of a written contract, if the plaintiff fails to produce evidence of such a contract during the case in chief, the judge may, on the defendant's motion, enter a judgment as matter of law in favor of the defendant.

The nomenclature used in this context varies from jurisdiction to jurisdiction. Under the traditional approach, a motion for judgment filed immediately after the presentation of plaintiff's case in chief is called a **motion for a nonsuit**; a motion for judgment filed at the close of all the evidence is called a **motion for a directed verdict**; and a similar motion filed after the jury has entered a verdict is called a **motion for a judgment notwithstanding the verdict** (or JNOV). In most jurisdictions, a party may not seek a JNOV unless she has filed a motion for judgment prior to the entry of the jury verdict (i.e., a motion for a nonsuit or a motion for a directed verdict). The nomenclature used in federal courts is simpler. Regardless of when the motion is filed, it is called a **motion for judgment as a matter of law**.

Regardless of nomenclature, the standard applied by a judge in deciding whether to grant any of the foregoing motions is identical from jurisdiction to jurisdiction, and it is the same as the standard applied in measuring the sufficiency of a motion for summary judgment—the no reasonable juror standard. Thus, the moving party's motion for judgment must be granted if, given the evidence presented, no reasonable juror could rule against that party.

A party against whom a judgment has been entered may also file a **motion for a new trial**. Here the remedy being sought is not a judgment in favor of the moving party, but a new trial. The standards for granting such a motion differ, therefore, from the "no reasonable juror" standard applicable to a motion for judgment as a matter of law. Stated generally, a motion for a new trial will be granted only to redress errors that may have undermined the fundamental fairness of the trial.

Appeal

In most civil cases, an aggrieved party has a right to appeal a final judgment to an intermediate appellate court. Review of the appellate court's decision by the state's highest court is usually within the discretion of the high court. The federal system is similar. A party has a right to appeal a final decision of a federal district court to the U.S. Circuit Court of Appeals with jurisdiction over the geographic region in which that district court sits. Review in the U.S. Supreme Court is discretionary. Additionally, the Supreme Court has discretionary authority to review cases involving federal law decided by a state court.

Under some circumstances, which vary from jurisdiction to jurisdiction, a party may be file an appeal prior to the entry of a final judgment or decision. Such appeals are called **interlocutory** and their availability is defined by statute.

The Finality of Judgments

Once a case goes to final judgment and the appellate process has been exhausted, the parties to the case are bound by that judgment. This means that the claims and issues resolved within the case cannot be the subject of further litigation between these same parties. There are a few limited exceptions to this rule, but for the most part it is ironclad.

This principle of finality is embodied in the doctrine of **res judicata**, which, roughly translated means that "the matter has been adjudicated." Actually, res judicata embraces two related doctrines. The first is called **claim preclusion**. Claim preclusion measure the extent to which a claim resolved in one proceeding precludes litigation on that same claim in another proceeding. The second doctrine is called **issue preclusion**. It measures the extent to which a specific issue decided in one proceeding precludes further litigation of the issue in a subsequent proceeding.

These doctrines arise only when there are two separate legal proceedings: one that has gone to judgment and one that has not. The question is whether something that was resolved in the first case should bind the parties in the second case.

As a general matter, the law of preclusion to be applied in any particular case is the law that would be followed by the court first rendering a judgment.

Claim Preclusion

Claim preclusion is a relatively straightforward doctrine. It prevents the litigation of claims that have previously gone to judgment. It applies if three elements have been satisfied:

1   The claims at issue in each case must be the same claim;
2   The judgment in the first case must have been final, valid, and on the merits; and
3   Both cases must have involved the same parties or those in privity with them.

Whether two claims are in fact the "same claim" depends on how broadly or narrowly one defines the word *claim*. Some jurisdictions, such as California, have adopted a *primary rights* approach under which the scope a claim is defined by reference to the particular primary right being asserted. Under this approach there is a primary right to enforce contracts, a primary right to be free from personal injury, a primary right to be free from damages to property, and so forth. Thus, in a products liability suit, the owner of a vehicle that was damaged in a rollover might sue the manufacturer for breach of warranty, personal injury, and property damage, each a separate primary right and, hence, a separate claim. Given that each primary right represents a different claim, a lawsuit resolving the one would not preclude litigation on another, for the simple reason that the claims are not the same.

The more modern approach focuses on the underlying factual **transaction**. Under this transactional model, a claim is defined as "a group of operative facts giving rise to one or more rights of action." Obviously, transactional model is more inclusive, for it is not defined by the right asserted, but by the factual transaction giving rise to the suit. Applying it to the "rollover" example discussed in the previous paragraph, we can see the practical consequence of this model. Since the three rights of action (warranty, personal injury, and property damage) arise out of the same set of facts—the rollover—each right of action is part of the same claim. Hence, a lawsuit resolving one of these rights of action would preclude further litigation on the others.

The second element—final, valid, and on the merits—is relatively easy to apply. A judgment is **final** if represents the completion of all steps necessary to the adjudication of the claim. A judgment that is tentative, provisional, or contingent is not final. A judgment is **valid** if the requisites of notice and personal jurisdiction have been satisfied. Other challenges to validity, such as fraud or duress, are usually addressed to the court that originally rendered judgment. Every final judgment in favor of the plaintiff is **on the merits**; on the other hand, a judgment in favor of the defendant is only on the merits if it is rendered on substantive grounds. Thus, a dismissal for improper venue (i.e., a nonsubstantive dismissal) is not on the merits.

The requirement that both cases involve the **same parties** is usually easy to apply. The underlying principle is that a person who is not a party to case should not be bound by the judgment in that case. If the parties in each suit are literally the same persons, then the requirement is satisfied. The issues become slightly more complicated when someone sues in a representative capacity, for example, as a trustee. Such a person will not be bound except in that particular capacity. The "same parties" rule extends to persons in **privity** with a party. Suffice it to say that privity is established by the legal relationship between the party and the person said to be in privity. For example, the beneficiary of the trust would be in privity with the trustee and thus bound by a judgment against the trustee pertaining to the trust.

Issue Preclusion

The doctrine of issue preclusion prevents the re-litigation of issues resolved in a previous legal proceeding. There are four elements to this doctrine:

1   The same issue is involved in both cases;
2   The issue was actually litigated in the first case;
3   The issue was decided and necessary to the first case; and
4   Both cases involve the same parties or those in privity with them.

As to same issue, an issue is not a claim. It does not define a legal right. Rather, an issue is a factual or legal assertion that may support or defeat a claim. For example, the speed at which the defendant was driving is an issue; the design integrity of a vehicle is an issue; the proper legal standard to be applied to resolve a claim is an issue; and so forth. Whether an issue decided in one case is the same as an issue decided in another involves the exercise of judgment: is it reasonable under the circumstances and given any factual or legal overlap between the issues, to treat them as the same for purposes of issue preclusion? In other words, what constitutes the same issue sometimes involves a policy judgment.

The **actually litigated** requirement is more straightforward. It is satisfied only if the parties to the first suit contested the issue during the process of litigation. Hence, the issue must have been raised, formally contested, and submitted to the court for determination. Note that there is no "actually litigated" requirement under the doctrine of claim preclusion. A legal right that was not asserted in the initial lawsuit may be treated as part "the same claim" adjudicated in that lawsuit even if that right was not raised in that proceeding.

The **decided and necessary** requirement is to make certain that the issue was given full and serious consideration by the court. If the court did not decide the issue or if a decision on the issue was superfluous to the judgment, then issue cannot be precluded in subsequent litigation.

The **same parties** and **privity** principles applied in the context of claim preclusion apply also in the context of issue preclusion, but with some variations. As was true with claim preclusion, a nonparty or nonprivy cannot, under issue preclusion, be bound by a prior judgment. But unlike claim preclusion, under some circumstances a nonparty to the first proceeding may be allowed to assert issue preclusion in a second proceeding against a person who was either a party or in privity with a party in that proceeding.

Originally, the **doctrine of mutuality** prevented this development. Under that doctrine, only a person bound by the previous judgment was permitted to benefit from that judgment. Most courts have abandoned this doctrine, at least when the party asserting issue preclusion is using that doctrine as part of his or her defense, so-called *defensive issue preclusion*. Some courts, including federal courts, have also allowed plaintiff to assert **nonmutual issue preclusion**, so-called *offensive issue preclusion*, but only when doing so promotes judicial efficiency and is consistent with principles of fairness. Thus, if a plaintiff in the second suit could have joined in the prior proceeding but sat back in order to avoid the risk of being bound in that proceeding, a court is unlikely to allow the plaintiff to use issue preclusion offensively in the second proceeding.

Note

1 The use of the phrase *general jurisdiction* in this context is completely distinct from the use of that same phrase in the context of personal jurisdiction.

9 Evidence

Laurie L. Levenson
Professor of Law and David W. Burcham
Chair in Ethical Advocacy, Loyola Law
School, Los Angeles

Introduction

Purpose of Evidence Rules

Trials are not free-for-alls. They are supposed to be decided on the evidence. **Evidence is the testimony of witnesses, tangible objects, and stipulations** presented during a case. It also includes the inferences from that evidence. It does not, however, include the lawyers' statements. The purpose of the lawyers' opening statements and closing arguments is to help jurors organize the evidence presented to them and draw the inferences each side would like, but these statements are not evidence. A judge's statements during the trial are also not evidence.

Development of the Evidence Rules

Prior to 1946, judges decided what would be admitted as evidence based upon their sense of fairness and a developing body of court decisions. However, in the 1960s and 1970s, states and Congress adopted evidence rules to guide judges in their decisions. Evidence rules may be found in the rules of a jurisdiction, or in their evidence codes. To a large extent, they merely codify the practices that were used by courts prior to enactment of the rules.

Judges' Discretion

Although there are evidence rules, judges continue to enjoy broad discretion in deciding what jurors may consider in their decisions. Moreover, not every evidentiary decision is covered by the rules. For example, the Federal Rules of Evidence do not set forth the rules of evidentiary privileges because they were adopted at a time when there was a concern over the political consequences of recognizing privileges. Rather, the Federal Rules direct federal judges to consider the common law on privileges.

How Evidentiary Issues Are Decided

At trial, evidentiary issues may come to the attention of the court in two ways. First, prior to trial, either side may file **motions in limine**. These motions seek pretrial rulings by the court as to whether certain evidence will be admissible. If there is an objection to evidence, the party that wants to introduce it typically **proffers** what the evidence will be and why it is admissible.

Second, the court may decide evidentiary issues on the spur of the moment as they arise during trial. The majority of evidentiary decisions are decided in this way. Although the court may hear brief argument by the parties, its rulings must be made quickly to avoid disruption of the trial. If the court **sustains** an objection, it means that the question and evidence are not allowed. If the court **overrules** an objection, the question and testimony are permissible.

Harmless vs. Plain Error

In any given trial, judges are bound to make many incorrect rulings. Even so, these mistakes are generally of little consequence because appellate courts are particularly reluctant to reverse a case because of a bad evidentiary ruling. Rather, the appellate courts may find the error to be **harmless error** given all of the other evidence in the case. Only the most significant errors, those that affect fundamental rights and could have made a real difference in the case, are deemed reversible or **plain error**.

Burdens and Presumptions

The evidence laws may also govern who bears the burden of producing evidence or convincing the jury that their side is right. In **criminal cases**, the prosecution has the burden of proof. It must prove **beyond a reasonable doubt** that the defendant committed the crime. There is no numerical quantification of what proof beyond a reasonable doubt means. However, it is the highest level of proof that one could expect in a case. It is not proof beyond all doubt, but proof that would give a person confidence that he or she is making the correct decision in the most serious of decisions.

In a **civil case**, the burden of proof is generally proof by a **preponderance** of the evidence. Preponderance means that the prevailing party has shown that it is more than 50 percent likely that it should prevail. In some **serious civil matters**, the burden of proof is **clear and convincing evidence**, which is somewhere between preponderance of the evidence and proof beyond a reasonable doubt.

Presumptions are sometimes used to put a thumb on the scale for one side or another. For example, criminal cases carry a presumption of innocence. In other words, the defendant starts with a clean slate and must be acquitted unless the prosecution proves its case beyond a reasonable doubt. In civil cases, presumptions may exist that guide the jurors in their decisions. For example, there may be a presumption that if a baby is born during a marriage, it is the natural child of the husband and wife. Some presumptions are rebuttable (i.e., the opposing party may disprove the presumption). However, some presumptions are irrebuttable, and the decision maker must take as true what the presumption establishes.

Judge's vs. Jury's Role

As a general rule, the judge decides what evidence is admissible, and the jury decides the weight of that evidence. However, in a **court (bench) trial**, the court decides both admissibility and weight because there is no jury. A defendant and the prosecution are entitled to a jury trial, unless both sides waive that right. Only certain types of civil cases (generally, those for damages) are entitled to a jury trial.

Relevance

Relevant Evidence Is Generally Admissible

The evidence rules **favor the admissibility** of all relevant evidence. In other words, it is supposed to be the exception, not the rule, that evidence will be excluded. When evidence is excluded, it is because special rules have determined that the type of evidence is not reliable or that there are other policy reasons for excluding it.

Relevant evidence is generally defined as "evidence having any tendency to make the existence of any fact that is of consequence to the determination of the action more probable or less probable than it would be without the evidence." (FRE 401).[1] In other words, to be admissible, evidence need not be the proverbial "smoking gun." Cases are frequently won because small bits of evidence, when seen together, make a persuasive case.

Direct vs. Circumstantial Evidence

Cases may be won on **circumstantial evidence** or **direct evidence. Circumstantial evidence** refers to the bits and pieces of small information that when collected together prove the case. For example, in a case without a video of the crime, fingerprints, or a confession, the prosecution may still win if it can show that the defendant had the motive or opportunity to commit the crime, was seen in the vicinity, had the victim's possession in his home, had a gun of the same caliber used in the crime, and other such evidence. Most murder cases are won on circumstantial evidence. Television shows like *CSI* have given the misimpression that criminal cases are routinely won on fancy physical evidence, like DNA tests. However, that is not the case. DNA, confessions, and videotapes of crimes are considered **direct evidence**; they are a goldmine for prosecutors but are not required.

Excluding Relevant Evidence

Relevant evidence may be precluded if it is not very helpful in deciding the case or its usefulness is **substantially outweighed by other factors,** such as unfair prejudice, likelihood of confusing the jury, amount of time it will waste, or needless presentation of cumulative evidence (FRE 403). All evidence is prejudicial to the extent that it helps one side or the other. However, when the court talks about "unfair prejudice," it means that the evidence will appeal to the jury more on an emotional basis than on a rational one in deciding a case. For example, if a defendant is charged with bank robbery, the prosecution might want to introduce evidence that the defendant loved to watch television shows about Jesse James and Bonnie and Clyde. Although this evidence has some marginal value, its value is greatly outweighed by its likelihood to confuse or mislead the jury into believing that because a person enjoys certain shows, he becomes a bank robber.

Other relevant evidence may be excluded because there are **policy reasons** for excluding that type of evidence. For example, confidential conversations between a person and his lawyer are considered privileged and are generally inadmissible because society wants to promote open communication between a person and his lawyer. The same exclusionary rationale applies to evidence covered by other **privileges,** such as the priest-penitent privilege or the psychotherapist-patient privilege. Privileges are discussed in greater detail at the end of this chapter.

Evidence rules also tend to exclude what we call evidence of **subsequent remedial measures** (FRE 407). These are steps a defendant takes after an accident to fix the situation. Although these steps may show that the defendant believed he was responsible for the accident, we exclude this evidence because we want to encourage people to fix dangerous situations. Similarly, because we want to encourage people to settle cases and cover the expenses of those that they may have harmed, we **exempt evidence of offers to compromise, plea discussions, and even liability insurance** (FRE 408–411). Finally, as will be discussed in more detail later, we **exempt evidence of a rape victim's past sexual behavior** so that the victim will not feel like she is on trial (FRE 412). While these exemptions have exceptions, they all derive from societal policies that outweigh the usefulness of the evidence at the proceedings.

Judicial Notice

Most evidence is admitted through the testimony of witnesses. However, on rare occasion, a party may ask the court to take "judicial notice" of some fact. If the court takes judicial notice of the fact, the fact is established conclusively for the jury (FRE 201).

Judges are reluctant to interject themselves into cases, so they prefer not to take judicial notice. When they do, they tend to take judicial notice of facts that no one could dispute, such as the fact that it was raining on a certain day or that New Year's Day is a national holiday.

Hearsay

One of the more complicated areas of evidence is hearsay. Hearsay is a secondhand account by a witness of what was said outside the courtroom about an event. At trial, we would much prefer to have the person who observed an event testify directly as to what he saw or heard. That is the person we want to cross-examine to make sure his recollection and observations are accurate. The account by a third party is less reliable.

Right of Confrontation

In criminal cases, the Constitution gives the defendant a right to cross-examine witnesses against him. This is known as the *right of confrontation*. Thus, there are constitutional reasons to preclude hearsay. In the recent case of *Crawford v. Washington* (2004), the Supreme Court barred the use of certain types of hearsay that had been traditionally allowed because it would violate the defendant's right of confrontation. If evidence is deemed **testimonial evidence**, the defendant has the right to cross-examine. Thus, the police cannot interview the victim of a sexual assault and present the victim's testimony under a hearsay exception because it will spare the victim the pain of testifying. The defendant has the right to cross-examine the witness. The hearsay rules apply in both civil and criminal cases, but the constitutional right of confrontation only applies in criminal cases. Moreover, not every second-hand account is considered testimonial evidence. For example, if the police talk to a defendant's co-conspirator while a conspiracy is ongoing, the police officer can testify to what the co-conspirator told him about the workings of the conspiracy. Testimonial evidence refers to the type of formal statements police elicit from witnesses.

Basic Hearsay Rule

The basic hearsay rule is that statements made outside of the courtroom are inadmissible, unless they fall within a hearsay exception. The only catch is that there are lots and lots of hearsay exceptions. The easiest example of what would be considered inadmissible hearsay is a witness in a car crash case testifying that he wasn't present at the crash, but that his neighbor told him that the defendant caused the accident by making an illegal left turn.

What we want is the neighbor to come into court and testify as to what he saw and why he thinks the defendant caused the accident.

Hearsay Exceptions

Many hearsay exceptions will allow out-of-court statements to be admitted in court. The easiest way to think of them is by category.

Admissions and Co-Conspirator Statements

Statements made by the parties or their agents outside of the courtroom are admissible. Thus, a police officer may testify that the defendant confessed to him about the crime. Similarly, a witness to a car accident may testify that the defendant said, "Gee, I wish I hadn't hit that lady." There are historical reasons for this exception, as well as the belief that a party wouldn't say something against his interest unless it were true. Moreover, in a criminal case, a defendant has the right not to testify during trial. Therefore, the only way to present his statement is to have another person relate it to the jury.

It is important to remember that admissions are only admissible if they are **offered against the party who made the statement.** A person cannot offer his own out-of-court statement because he would then get his story before the jury without being subject to cross-examination.

The admissions exception applies to statements by a person's **agents,** as well as statements by **co-conspirators** while the conspiracy is ongoing. Thus, if Bonnie and Clyde try to recruit Jesse James and tell him all about how they commit their robberies, James, who turns out to be a government informant, can testify to those statements in court.

However, the exception only goes so far. Timing of the statement is also important. If a co-defendant is arrested and later tells the police that he and the defendant committed the crime, the part of his statement relating to the defendant is inadmissible because the defendant cannot cross-examine his co-defendant without his co-defendant testifying.

Prior Statements by Witnesses

If a person testifies, some statements that he or she made outside the courtroom may be admissible. These include prior statements **inconsistent** with what the witness is now saying in court. Such statements are always admissible to show that the witness is a liar. This is known as *impeachment.* However, sometimes the parties want the out-of-court statements to be **substantive evidence** (i.e., proof that what was said outside the courtroom was what really happened). Under the federal system, those out-of-court statements must be inconsistent and made under oath to be admissible as substantive evidence. However, some jurisdictions allow any inconsistent statements to be admitted as substantive evidences.

Statements made out of court may also be admissible if they are **consistent** with what the witness is now saying and the witness has been attacked for recently fabricating his story. The out-of-court statements show that the witness is not actually making up the story and has been consistent in his remarks.

Finally, **witness identifications** made outside of the courtroom are admissible if the witness who made the identification testifies at trial. Identifications are admissible even if the witness at trial cannot remember who committed the crime as long as he made an earlier positive identification.

Reactive Statements

We tend to trust statements that are made spontaneously during an event because we don't think that the person had time to fabricate his account. Therefore, **spontaneous statements** made while a person perceives an event, or **excited utterances** made while the declarant is still under the stress of an event, are admissible.

We also allow statements made by a person as to what he is **feeling** or has in his mind at the time, so long as that person's **state of mind** is relevant to the case. Thus, if a defendant is claiming self-defense, his wife could testify that he had constantly said he was afraid of the person he ended up killing.

Finally, we allow **statements made to doctors or nurses for medical diagnosis or treatment** because we think it is unlikely people will lie to the doctor when they need help.

Other Exceptions

Regularly made **business records** are allowed into evidence because we think people will try to be as accurate as possible when creating those records. Certain **public records** and reports are also admissible, such as rosters of what happens in a government office, observations made by public employees (except **police reports, which are inadmissible in criminal cases**), and official findings of government investigations, such as FAA findings of what caused a crash.

Also, many other types of records have historically been admissible as hearsay exceptions. These include **birth, marriage, and death records; old family records; property deeds; documents more than 20 years old; market reports; treatises;, criminal conviction records; and reputation evidence.** **Dying declarations** are also admissible if made when the person believed he was facing imminent death.

Two of the trickier categories of hearsay exceptions are: (1) former testimony and (2) statements against interest. Under the **former testimony exception,** if a witness testifies in a prior case and is subject to cross-examination, the testimony from that prior case can be used in a retrial if the witness is no longer available. The same is *not* true of grand jury testimony. Because there is no cross-examination in a grand jury, grand jury testimony is not admissible under a hearsay exception. Also, in civil cases, prior testimony (including deposition testimony) can be used not only against the party who had a chance to cross-examine, but also against any party who has the same interest as that party.

Statements against interest may also be admissible if the declarant is no longer available to testify and the statement was contrary to the declarant's financial or personal interest when made. In other words, if the declarant could be subject to criminal or civil liability when he makes the statement, the statement may be admissible. However, this exception has limits. Suppose a defendant on trial wants to have another person take the rap for him. He cannot have a friend who is already sitting in jail assume blame for the defendant's crime and then introduce his hearsay statement. Unless circumstances corroborate the statement and show it is trustworthy, the statement is not admissible.

Another hearsay exception is **forfeiture by wrongdoing.** If a witness makes a statement out of court, and then the defendant kills the witness before trial, the statement may be admissible.

Finally, the Federal Rules have a catch-all provision for hearsay statements that have special guarantees of trustworthiness and are critical to a case. The party offering the hearsay can give notice to the court that it wants to use the **residual exception,** and the court then decides whether allowing the statement is in the best interest of justice.

Character Evidence

A basic principle of evidence law is that we judge people on their current actions and not what they have done in the past. Therefore, propensity evidence is generally inadmissible, i.e., a party cannot argue that simply because someone did something before, he must have done it again. Moreover, a party cannot generally argue that his or her opponent is the "type of person" who would commit the act. There are strict limitations on the admissibility of character evidence.

Character of the Defendant

Evidence of a defendant's character is inadmissible unless it is offered by the defendant himself or offered by the prosecution to rebut character evidence by the defense. For example, assume the defendant is charged with fraud. The prosecution cannot introduce character evidence that the defendant has the reputation for being a thief, unless the defendant puts on testimony that he has the reputation of being honest or law-abiding.

Prosecutors love when the defense calls character witnesses because it allows the prosecutor to cross-examine the defense witness on all the bad things that the prosecutor has heard about the defendant. The prosecutor can ask these questions to test the witness's opinion of the defendant's character. For example, assume that the defendant called a character witness to say that, in his opinion, the defendant is a law-abiding person. At that point, the defense has opened the door for the prosecutor to ask, "Would you have the same opinion if you knew the defendant had cheated in school, stolen from his mother, and was involved in insider trading?" So long as the prosecutor has a good faith basis for the questions, he can ask them.

Character evidence of the defendant is admissible only in criminal cases.

Character of the Victim

Character evidence is frequently offered in self-defense cases. If the defense claims that the victim had a violent character, the prosecutor can either present evidence that the victim was peace-loving, or attack the defendant's character by presenting character evidence that the defendant was really the violent character.

Specific Prior Acts

In most jurisdictions, character evidence is only admissible if it is in the form of reputation or opinion evidence. A witness is not allowed to refer to specific instances of conduct by the defendant or the victim.

However, evidence of other crimes or wrongs is admissible if used for a specific purpose, other than to show the defendant's general character. **Prior bad acts can be used to show the defendant's intent, motive, opportunity, plan, knowledge, or absence of mistake.**

For example, assume the defendant is charged with transporting cocaine. He claims that he didn't know that he had cocaine in his suitcase. Prosecutors could offer prior incidents in which the defendant was caught with cocaine to prove that he really did know what he was transporting. This other act evidence can be introduced even if the defendant was never charged with the prior crime or even if he was acquitted of it.

Prior acts are also used to show a defendant's modus operandi. For example, assume a defendant is charged with rape. In this particular crime, the assailant wore a Batman mask. Defendant had been caught years before wearing a Batman mask during an assault. Thus, this evidence would be admissible.

Impeachment and Character Evidence of Witnesses

There are many ways to impeach or attack the credibility of a witness. First, a witness can be **caught in a lie**. As instructions to the jury explain, if a person lies as to one thing, he or she may be lying as to others. Second, the cross-examiner may show the witness has a **bias or motive to lie.** Third, the opposing party may show that the witness has the **reputation for being dishonest.** Once a witness's character for honesty is attacked, the party who called the witness can present testimony that the witness actually has a character for truthfulness. Fourth, a witness can be **asked about other times when the witness lied.** If those other times are unrelated to the current action, the questioner is stuck with whatever answers the witness gives. Finally, a witness (including the defendant) may be impeached with evidence that the witness has a **prior conviction** for a crime.

Generally, we think that people who have committed crimes are less likely to be trustworthy. However, not every conviction sheds light on a witness's credibility, and we are also concerned that if the defendant is the witness, jurors will lapse into thinking that because the defendant has committed a crime before, he has committed one again.

Accordingly, under most rules, **any felony** can be used to impeach a witness, but only **those misdemeanors that involved dishonesty or false statement** can be used to impeach. The court ordinarily has the power to decide whether the probative value of the evidence outweighs its prejudicial impact. If a conviction is more than 10 years old, courts are often reluctant to allow it. Also, if a conviction was pardoned or was a juvenile conviction, the court may disallow it. However, a conviction on appeal can still be used.

Presentation of Witnesses

The judge has broad discretion in deciding on the order of witnesses and allowing parties to take witnesses out of order. If physical evidence is offered at trial, the parties must establish its **authenticity** (i.e., that the evidence is what it is purported to be). A party may establish authenticity either through a witness testifying to the authenticity or, often with records, by a certificate of authenticity. Duplicates of writings are admissible if they are authentic. The so-called **best evidence rule** does not require that original documents be introduced; it only requires that if a document or recording is available, it should be provided to the jury rather than someone characterizing or summarizing it.

The judge may allow **demonstrations** and the use of charts in the courtroom. The judge may also decide whether the jurors can take notes during the trial. In some jurisdictions, the court has the authority to allow **jurors to ask questions** throughout the trial. Ordinarily, these questions are presented in writing to the judge, and the judge then decides which juror questions will be asked of the witness.

All witnesses must take an **oath** to tell the truth. However, the witness can swear or affirm to tell the truth. The witness need not put his hand on the Bible and swear to God. There are no limitations on who may serve as a witness, so long as that person understands his obligation to tell the truth and can communicate his answers. Children can testify, as well as the mentally ill.

To prevent witnesses from colluding on their answers, the court may issue a **sequestration order.** Under the order, a witness cannot sit in the courtroom and listen to other witnesses testify. The only exception to this rule is for the parties and their investigating agents. Violation of the order can result in contempt sanctions and the striking of the witness's testimony.

Expert Witnesses

Both civil and criminal trials can become battles of the experts. A wide range of experts may testify at trial. Expert testimony can cover everything from DNA to fashion designs to child abuse experts. Before an expert is allowed to testify, the court must be satisfied that the witness is an expert and that the testimony will satisfy the standards for expert testimony in that jurisdiction.

Two fundamental tests determine the admissibility of expert testimony. In federal court, the judges use the *Daubert* test. Before a witness testifies before the jury, the court holds a hearing to determine if the witness has the specialized knowledge and qualifications to be an expert witness. The judge is the gatekeeper for experts, so if the judge thinks the witness is offering junk science or testimony that otherwise does not qualify as expert testimony, it may be excluded.

In many state courts, including California, the courts use the older **Frye** test to determine the admissibility of expert testimony. Under this test, the proffering party must show that the type of expert testimony and results being offered are generally accepted by experts in the field.

DNA evidence in now generally accepted by the courts, although DNA tests are changing all the time. The goal for a party presenting expert testimony is to simplify it to a level where the jury can understand it. If the jurors do not understand evidence, they are not likely to accept it.

Privileges

In an effort to encourage open communications, the law makes inadmissible privileged communications. The Federal Rules of Evidence leave it to the courts to decide which communications are privileged, although there is a great deal of common law on this issue. Most states specify in their evidence codes which communications are protected by privilege.

Attorney-Client Privilege

The best known privilege covers attorney-client communications. A client has a privilege to refuse to disclose and to prevent any other person from disclosing **confidential communications** made between the client and his lawyer. These communications may be oral or in writing. In order to be classified as confidential, the contents of the communication must not be disclosed to third parties. Secretaries and paralegals who work for the lawyer are exempted. Courts are divided on whether inadvertent disclosures to third parties, such as mailing memoranda to a wrong address, waive the privilege.

In order to be privileged, the communication must have been made to **seek or provide legal advice**. The privilege covers communications both from the client to the lawyer and vice-versa. Ordinarily, the client's identity or the fees paid by a client are not considered to be covered by the privilege. Also, the privilege doesn't cover pre-existing documents. Therefore, a client cannot shield a document by turning it over to his lawyer and claiming that it is privileged.

If a client seeks an attorney's service to commit a fraud, the **crime-fraud exception** applies, and the communications are no longer privileged. The court determines whether there is a crime-fraud exception.

The privilege applies so long as the client reasonably believes that he is speaking to a lawyer (or his representative) who can give him legal advice. It doesn't matter if the lawyer has been paid or if, in fact, the lawyer turns out to be a licensed professional. It only matters that the defendant reasonably believed that he was seeking legal advice from a lawyer. Also, because the privilege belongs to the client, the client can waive the privilege, regardless of whether the lawyer wants it to be waived.

It is the duty of a lawyer to preserve his client's confidential communications. Under separate **ethical rules**, a lawyer may be barred from disclosing secrets the lawyer knows about a client. The only universal exception to this rule is if the client reveals to the lawyer that he intends to immediately hurt or kill another person. Only then can the lawyer report his client's communication. However, if a client confesses to a past crime, the lawyer must remain mute. The duty of confidentiality to a client survives the client's death.

Because of sensitivity to the attorney-client privilege, prosecutors often use **special masters** when they conduct searches of law firms. The special master's job is to secure any privileged communication so that it will not be seen by the investigators.

A related doctrine is the **attorney work product doctrine**. This is not an evidentiary privilege, but a discovery rule. Under Federal Rule of Civil Procedure 26(b)(3), attorney memoranda that reflect the attorney's strategy and thought processes should not be ordered disclosed unless there is a compelling need for disclosure.

In order to pool defenses, attorneys sometimes enter into **joint defense agreements**. In these agreements, the parties agree to share information among themselves, but not with outsiders. Courts are divided on whether they will enforce these agreements.

Finally, **corporate clients** have privileged communications, but only for those who control the management of the corporation and not mere eyewitnesses in the corporation. Under a broader standard used by some jurisdictions, the privilege applies to communications by any employee on a subject matter within the scope of his job for the corporation.

Physician-Patient Privilege

Most states, but not the federal courts, recognize a physician-patient privilege. In order to encourage patients to give full and accurate information to their doctors, statements between patients and doctors are privileged. This privilege also covers the doctors' records and hospital records. An exception is made for a patient who puts his medical condition at issue in a case. In that situation, the patient waives the privilege. Statutes may also require the reporting of certain types of illness or injuries to a defendant, such as a gun shot or venereal disease. This privilege is ordinarily inapplicable in criminal cases.

Psychotherapist-Patient Privilege

Similarly, confidential communications between a patient and a psychiatric professional are ordinarily privileged, including in federal court. As with the physician-patient privilege, the psychotherapist-patient privilege is inapplicable if the patient puts his mental or emotional condition at issue in the case. Moreover, in the landmark California case of *Tarasoff v. Regents of University of California* (1976), the court recognized that a psychotherapist could be sued if a patient revealed his intent to kill or harm another person but the psychotherapist took no steps to warn the victim or prevent the harm. Therefore, there is an implicit exception to the privilege in those situations where a patient threatens serious bodily harm to a third party.

Marital Privileges

There are two types of privileges that may apply to persons who are or have been married: (1) the **spousal testimony privilege** and (2) the **marital confidences privilege**.

Spousal Testimony Privilege

The federal system and most states recognize a spousal testimony privilege. Under this privilege, a defendant's spouse can refuse to testify against the defendant, and the defendant may block a spouse from testifying against him. Under the federal rule, it is up to the witness whether to testify. If the witness spouse wants to testify, the defendant cannot stop the spouse. Some states give the decision to the defendant to decide whether the spouse should testify.

The spousal testimony privilege only applies while the witness and the defendant are still married. If the marriage is a sham, the privilege does not apply. It also generally does not apply when one spouse is charged with a crime against the other spouse or their child.

Marital Confidences Privilege

The marital confidences privilege protects private communications between spouses while they are married. Even if the party and witness are no longer married, the privilege may still be invoked so long as the communication occurred during the marriage. This privilege, like the spousal testimony privilege, does not apply to cases involving a crime against the spouse or minor child. It also doesn't apply if the communication is being used to involve the spouse in an ongoing or future crime.

Clergy-Penitent Privilege

Traditionally, communications between a person and his spiritual leader are privileged. The court can decide whether the spiritual leader really qualifies as clergy. This privilege does not cover marriage counseling or business discussions among clergy. Recently, the courts have also held that it does not cover the counseling of priests suspected of molesting parishioners. In the O. J. Simpson case, Judge Lance Ito held the conversations between O. J. Simpson and Rosie Greer, his jailhouse spiritual leader, to be covered by the privilege.

Reporter's Privilege

Some states have a reporter's shield law that protects a member of the media from disclosing his confidential sources unless there is a compelling need. The federal courts have not yet recognized this privilege. Thus, in the Scooter Libby investigation, *New York Times* reporter Judith Miller was jailed when she refused to disclose who had leaked the identity of CIA agent Valerie Plame.

Government Privileges

The government has numerous privileges, such as those for state secrets. State and military secret privileges can be absolute. However, confidential presidential communications are covered by the **executive privilege** and are not absolute. If there is a "demonstrated, specific need" for the information, it must be disclosed.

Informer Identity Privilege

The government does not have to turn over the identity of its informants unless the court finds that disclosure is necessary to ensure the defendant of a fair trial. Typically, the court will hold a *Roviaro* **hearing** to decide whether the defendant's interests in disclosure outweigh the need to keep an informant's identity secret. If an informant is a percipient witness, disclosure is more likely.

Rape Shield Laws

Though not technically a privilege, rape shield laws protect against the introduction of evidence of a victim's sexual past. Unless the victim's sexual behavior is relevant to show consent or who committed the sexual offense, it is not admissible.

Privilege against Self-Incrimination

The best known privilege is the privilege against self-incrimination. This privilege is set forth in the Fifth Amendment of the Constitution: "No person shall be . . . compelled in any criminal case to be a witness against himself." The privilege only applies to individuals, not artificial entities such as corporations.

As stated, the privilege only prohibits the use of the defendant's statements against him in a criminal case. It does not protect against the use of these statements in a civil case. If a defendant in a civil case asserts the privilege, the plaintiff can argue that the defendant has something to hide. However, in a criminal case, no adverse inference may be raised by the defendant's refusal to testify. If a prosecutor in closing argument directly or indirectly points to the defendant's failure to testify, this is known as *Griffin error* and can lead to reversal of a conviction.

A witness may assert the Fifth Amendment before the grand jury. However, the Fifth Amendment can only be asserted if the information can implicate the witness in a crime. It cannot be used to cover up merely embarrassing information or to protect another person.

In order to get around the privilege, prosecutors may obtain **use immunity**, which prevents the speaker's statements from being used against him at trial or in the investigation. **Transactional immunity** may also be given. It is broader and blocks all prosecution of the speaker. If a person is given use immunity, he must testify, but his statements and any evidence derived from them cannot be used to prosecute that person. Moreover, the government has the burden of showing that it did not use the immunized statements in building its case against the speaker. Typically, a **Kastigar** hearing will be held to determine if any of the government's evidence is tainted by immunized statements. In the famous case against Ollie North, the government lost its evidence when it could not show that its witnesses had not been influenced by North's immunized testimony before Congress.

In order to prevent evidence from being tainted, the government may create "clean" (without access to immunized statements) and "dirty" (exposed to immunized testimony) to conduct their investigation. This technique is frequently used in police misconduct cases because police testimony given by officers compelled to give a statement under the threat of being fired are protected by use immunity.

When the government requests documents, the documents themselves are ordinarily not privileged because the author was not compelled to produce them. However, the act of identifying and producing the documents is covered by the privilege.

Note

1 FRE refers to the Federal Rules of Evidence.

10 Ethical Obligations of Lawyers and Judges

Laurie L. Levenson
Professor of Law and David W. Burcham
Chair in Ethical Advocacy, Loyola Law
School, Los Angeles

Despite legal jokes to the contrary,[1] lawyers must abide by strict ethical codes. Each jurisdiction has its own code of ethical conduct. The vast majority of these state codes are based on the American Bar Association's Model Rules of Professional Conduct. Each state's state bar association has primary responsibility for enforcing these ethical rules, although judges may also enforce them, though through alternate means. To help ensure that attorneys learn and follow these rules, most jurisdictions require law students to take a class in legal ethics, and also require prospective lawyers to pass a separate ethics exam in order to become a member of the Bar.

Many of the ethical rules are built around one concept—that a lawyer is acting on behalf of the client. Thus, anything that would get in the way of acting with the full interests of the client in mind runs against a lawyer's duty. Also, any revelation or use of information that the client would not make is not permitted. However, this duty is somewhat limited by the fact that attorneys are also officers of the court of the jurisdiction in which they are admitted to the Bar. As can be seen from the rules below, at times, a lawyer's duty to act as a proxy for a client is mitigated by a duty to be truthful to a court. Attorneys thus walk a fine balancing act between their own interests (collecting fees for services), their clients' interests (keeping information secret and fulfilling client objectives), and the interests of the court (maintaining truthfulness in the courtroom). This chapter in meant to give a sense of the rules that govern lawyers' behavior and how they affect the practice and business of law.

Ethical Duties of Lawyers

Duty of Competence

One of the primary duties of all lawyers is to act competently. Representing the interests of another person does not do much good when it is done shoddily. The standard for a lawyer's performance is that a lawyer must perform with the "legal knowledge, skill, thoroughness, and preparation reasonably necessary" to represent a client.[2] To make sure that a client receives this level of representation, a lawyer may sometimes associate with another lawyer to help with a case, or refer the case to a more competent lawyer.

Lawyers who suffer from mental problems, addiction, or other such problems are not considered competent and should not be representing clients. Likewise, if a lawyer is overworked and cannot adequately represent a client, that lawyer is also not competent for the case.

Duty of Confidentiality

Another important ethical duty of a lawyer is to maintain client confidences. One purpose of this rule is to encourage candid communication between the client and the lawyer. This duty of confidentiality does not just cover information the client gives to the lawyer; it also includes anything about the client that the lawyer learns through representing the client. In this way, lawyers have a responsibility to keep secrets beyond the "privilege" or attorney-client communications that the law of evidence provides.

In most jurisdictions, the duty of confidentiality lasts forever. Unless a client waives this confidentiality, lawyers can *never* reveal confidential information about a client's past activities. Therefore, if a client tells a lawyer that he killed a person and buried him in the desert, the lawyer is not permitted under the ethical code to disclose this information to law enforcement.

On the other hand, lawyers may have the discretion to reveal a client's intention to commit a *future* crime. In most jurisdictions, a lawyer can only reveal such information if the client indicates that he is going to commit a crime that will cause serious bodily injury or death. Thus, if the client told his lawyer that he buried someone alive and that person may still be alive, the lawyer would be permitted (but not required) to share that information with law enforcement. Some jurisdictions even allow a lawyer to reveal a client's intention to commit any kind of future crime, including a nonviolent fraud crime.

Because of the duty of confidentiality, a lawyer cannot state on or off the record confidential information about a client. Nor may a lawyer discuss a client's confidential information with the court. In this way, a lawyer cannot be called upon to testify against a client in most situations. In certain circumstances, however, a client waives the duty of confidentiality by raising certain challenges to his lawyer's representation. Thus, a defendant who claims that a lawyer committed malpractice, breached their contract, or provided ineffective counsel, waives the attorney-client privilege, and a lawyer is allowed to share confidential communications and information about the defendant.

Unlike the Fifth Amendment, which applies only to natural persons, corporate defendants—through their representatives—also enjoy a duty of confidentiality. This means that lawyers representing corporations also cannot reveal confidential information about their clients. However, corporate directors may waive this privilege when there is an internal investigation of the corporation.

Conflicts of Interest and a Lawyer's Duty of Loyalty

Lawyers also have an obligation to be loyal to their clients. This duty goes beyond maintaining a client's confidences. A lawyer must also avoid situations in which the lawyer, or the lawyer's other clients, have a conflict with the client.

One clear example of a conflict would be if a lawyer represented opposing parties in a case, or more than one client concurrently when those clients have competing interests. A lawyer cannot represent a client on a matter that is contrary to and substantially related to that of a prior client. The real test of the conflict is whether the lawyer, in order to zealously represent the new client, will be put in the untenable position of revealing confidential information about a prior client. When faced with a conflict of interest such as these, the lawyer must either advise her clients of any conflicts and get a knowing waiver of those conflicts, or withdraw from representing either side of a case.

Another clear conflict of interest also exists when a client's interests are contrary to those of the lawyer. This includes conflicts created by a legal, business, financial, professional, or personal relationship that the lawyer may have with another party or witness in the same matter. In order to avoid

---

Sex with Clients? Bad Lawyer!

Although the ABA Model Rules Professional Conduct cautions against conflicts of interest, the complexities of human sexuality often blur the lines of acceptable behavior in the lawyer–client relationship. There have recently been some notable examples: the much publicized relationship of the late Anna Nicole Smith with her attorney Howard K. Stern; discipline by the Washington Supreme Court meted out to a former president of the state bar association for extramarital affairs with six women while representing them in divorce and child custody cases; and the case of an army lawyer found to have rendered biased counsel to his client to conceal an adulterous, homosexual affair with the client. The rules do not go so far as to bar relationships between a lawyer and the client, but they do make clear that any relationship must be consensual and that the lawyer cannot pressure a client into a sexual relationship.

---

conflicts, lawyers generally cannot enter into business transactions with a client unless the client consents in writing after being given an opportunity to consult with independent counsel. Some jurisdictions also have special rules that prohibit lawyers from taking literary interests in a client's case until it is resolved so that there is no question that the lawyer did not alter his strategy in order to write a better book.

Additionally, lawyers generally cannot act as an advocate and witness in the same matter. Some exceptions include when a lawyer testifies regarding an uncontested matter or the parties' consent to waive any conflict.

In addition to clear conflicts, a lawyer's duty of loyalty also requires that lawyers keep their clients informed about any significant developments in a case, including all settlement offers. Ultimately, it is a *client's* decision as to whether to accept a settlement offer or a plea bargain. The client also gets the final say as to whether the client will testify. In other words, the client drives the course of representation, whereas the lawyer drives the tactics and strategies of the case. As noted in the next section, however, the methods clients and lawyers can choose during the course of representation are limited by other rules.

Lawyer's Goals for Representation

Even if it might be in a client's interests, lawyers are limited as to the actions they may take in zealously representing a client. For example, the ethical rules prohibit a lawyer from bringing a case or raising a defense merely to harass another person. Lawyers are expected to have a nonfrivolous basis in the law or facts for raising a claim. This does not mean that new arguments never arise—a lawyer's good faith basis may be based upon arguments for an extension, modification, or reversal of existing law.

Likewise, lawyers are not allowed to advise clients to violate the law. Thus, if a client asks a lawyer to help him flee the jurisdiction, the lawyer is not permitted to assist the client with this request.

Lawyers are also not allowed to threaten an opposing party with criminal or administrative charges (such as "I'll report you to the state bar") in order to obtain an advantage in a civil dispute. A lawyer can report another party to the bar; she just cannot threaten to do so. Lawyers are also barred from having direct contact with a party who is represented by counsel unless counsel has consented.

Conduct During Trial

Despite what is portrayed in many popular television shows, lawyers cannot use any trick to win a case. Lawyers are prohibited from misleading the judge or jury by misstating either the facts or the law. Lawyers are not permitted to suppress evidence, have ex parte contacts with the judge, or intentionally fail to cite a case that goes directly against the lawyer's position. Lawyers also cannot hide witnesses or pressure them to provide false testimony. Until a case is finally over, lawyers are not allowed to have contact with jurors. Ordinarily, jurors get to decide if and when they want to talk to the lawyers after a trial.

Pretrial Publicity

The ethical rules also control a lawyer's behavior outside of the courtroom. The U.S. Supreme Court has held that lawyers may be barred from making statements to the press if they know or should know that those statements will have a substantial likelihood of materially prejudicing a case. In an effort to prohibit further O.J. Simpson–like cases where there was a perceived media circus, judges may use gag orders or the threat of reporting violating counsel to the state bar if they engage in inappropriate pretrial publicity.

Certain communications, though, are safe zones of sorts. For example, with only a few exceptions, lawyers are allowed to reveal matters of public record, the status of ongoing investigations, the next procedural steps in cases, and any requests for assistance in obtaining evidence and other necessary information. In a criminal case, the lawyers may reveal the identity, residency, occupation, and family status of the accused, and if the accused has not been apprehended, information necessary to apprehend that person.

Even more importantly, most ethical codes have a "tit-for-tat" provision that allows a lawyer to issue a statement in reaction to a prejudicial statement by opposing counsel. This exception opens the door for continuous communications by counsel with the media prior to and during trial.

The Business of Being a Lawyer

Many of the ethical rules relate to the business of being a lawyer. These rules range from limitations on advertising and solicitation to rules regarding fees and the termination of an attorney–client relationship.

In order to protect prospective clients from being pressured into hiring a particular lawyer, the ethical rules bar the face-to-face solicitation of clients on a particular matter, unless the solicitation is by a nonprofit legal entity, such as the ACLU. Under the First Amendment, lawyers are permitted to advertise, but solicitations, unless done by nonprofit legal agencies, is prohibited. State bars typically have regulations regarding lawyer's advertisements, such as the time, place, and manner in which such advertisements may be made. They also do not allow lawyers to be in a partnership with a nonlawyer because the lawyer must be responsible for the client. However, lawyers may hire nonlawyers to assist them in their representation of a client. Duties of confidentiality extend to those who work for the lawyer.

A client can fire private counsel at any time. When this occurs, the lawyer is required to return any unearned portion of prepaid fees, as well as the client's files. Lawyers often have clients advance funds to be used in representing the client. Some types of fees, however, are not required to be returned, as they are charged to keep the lawyer available to the client. This is called a *true retainer*.

For fees other than retainers, lawyers may use several different types of fees to charge clients. **Hourly fees** are generally used by big law firms,

Ambulance Chasing

The ethics rules permit advertising a lawyer's services, but not solicitation of clients. Thus, lawyers may use all types of media to advertise their services, including television commercials, printed ads, and internet listings, but lawyers generally cannot make face-to-face solicitations to clients. In fact, many states have specific laws prohibiting lawyers from contacting prospective clients in jails or hospitals. At most, lawyers may let medical professionals and others know that they are available to represent clients. However, lawyers cannot pay these individuals to recruit clients on their behalf. Capping fees to nonlawyers are prohibited.

especially for transactional work. Plaintiff's lawyers often work for a **contingency fee** that entitles the lawyer to receive a portion of any funds obtained for the client. Lawyers may also use **flat fees**, which charge the client a single fee for working on a particular legal project. Contingency fees are not allowed in criminal cases.

Legal fees can be quite expensive. It is not unusual for a lawyer to charge $300 to $500 an hour to handle a matter. For the most expensive firms, hourly rates may run as high as $1,000 per hour. Lawyers who get a client's money "up front" are expected to put it in special trust funds. Lawyers are not allowed to commingle personal money with the clients' funds, nor to withdraw money from the trust fund until it is earned under the terms of their retainer agreements.

In addition to normal fees for work done, some jurisdictions also allow lawyers to earn a *finder's fee* when they refer cases to other attorneys.

Lawyers are not allowed to be in a partnership with or to split fees with a nonlawyer. This is because the lawyer must be responsible for the client. However, lawyers may hire nonlawyers to *assist* them in their representation

Taking the Risk—Contingency Fees

Contingency fee arrangements often receive intense press coverage and raise eyebrows for the exorbitant sums collected. Lawyers may collect 30 percent or more on major judgments, as frequently happens in personal injury and products liability cases, including those against major defendants like the tobacco companies. While the attorney fees in these cases are high, they are permitted because the attorney takes the risk of receiving no payment at all if the attorney is unsuccessful in the case. Moreover, attorneys often must cover the costs of a case up front and wait until the case's completion to recover these costs. Contingency fees are designed to provide avenues for representation for those who cannot afford to pay hourly rates.

of a client. When a lawyer hires nonlawyers, the lawyer's duties of confidentiality extend to those who work for the lawyer.

Even though a client can fire his lawyer at any time, a lawyer cannot quit at any time. A lawyer can only withdraw from representing a client if there are grounds under the ethical code to do so and the lawyer has the permission of the court. Lawyers are **required to withdraw** from representing a client if the lawyer knows or should know that the client has no good faith basis for the client's claim or the client is asking the lawyer to do something illegal. Lawyers are **permitted to withdraw** if the client makes it unreasonably difficult to represent the client or doesn't pay his fees. A lawyer may also withdraw when a client asks a lawyer to violate her ethical duties or when a client's mental or physical condition makes effective representation extremely difficult.

Lawyers need not withdraw just because they believe their client is guilty. Under the Sixth Amendment of the U.S. Constitution, all criminal defendants are entitled to effective representation.

Clients Who Lie

Lawyers are put in a tough position when a client reveals that he or she plans to lie on the witness stand. A criminal defendant has the constitutional right to testify. If a lawyer "knows" that a client will lie on the witness stand, the lawyer cannot assist the client in this illegal and dishonest behavior. The lawyer should seek to withdraw. Judges, however, frequently do not grant these requests because they do not want to delay the proceedings. Rather, they allow the client to testify, but without the lawyer being involved in the examination of the client. The lawyer asks only a general question leading to a narrative by the client. The lawyer cannot use any false testimony by the client in closing argument. If a lawyer only suspects, but does not know, that a client is engaging in falsehoods, the lawyer may examine the client on the witness stand and argue the evidence to the jury.

Special Ethical Duties of Prosecutors and Defense Lawyers

Prosecutors and defense lawyers have special ethical duties under the ABA Standards Relating to the Administration of Criminal Justice. For example, prosecutors have the duty "to seek justice, not merely to convict." Accordingly, prosecutors may not file charges unless they believe there is probable cause to support those charges. Even after filing, prosecutors still have a responsibility to seek justice. They must reveal any exculpatory evidence to the defense and should not comment in a trial on the defendant's exercise of the right not to testify.

Defense lawyers, on the other hand, have the duty to fully investigate a case, keep their clients informed, and avoid illegal means in representing clients. If defense counsel receives physical evidence of a crime, they should turn it over to law enforcement, although counsel is under no obligation to disclose how it got the evidence.

In a criminal case, the client has the right to make the following decisions: (1) what pleas to enter; (2) whether to accept a plea agreement, (3) whether to waive jury trial, (4) whether to testify in his or her own behalf, and (5) whether to appeal.

Corporate Clients

Just as with individual clients, corporate clients are also entitled to a lawyer's duty of confidentiality and duty of loyalty. However, a lawyer who represents a corporation is not bound to maintain the confidences of or loyalty to any *individuals* involved with the corporation, including the corporation's directors or officers. Rather, the lawyer represents the *entity* itself. Thus, if a lawyer learns that a person at a corporation is engaging in illegal behavior, the lawyer has an obligation to report the problem to those higher up in the corporation. Disclosing this information does not violate the lawyer's duties of confidentiality.

Corporate Clients and the Chain of Command

Whistleblower statutes exist on both the federal and state level to protect employees from retaliatory measures by employers. In the wake of the Enron and other corporate scandals of the early 2000s, ethics rules for lawyers have been altered to allow for greater vigilance over corporate wrongdoing. The ABA Rules address attorney disclosure responsibilities when confronted with illegal actions by corporate employers. A lawyer must bring the questionable actions to the attention of the highest authority within the organization. If this higher authority is unreceptive or unwilling to address these activities, then the attorney may disclose this information to outside authorities (including government agencies) to protect the integrity of the organization.

Pro Bono Services

Pro bono services are legal services that lawyers provide for no charge, often to indigent clients or nonprofit organizations. Most ethical codes stop short of requiring lawyers to engage in pro bono services. Lawyers are encouraged, but not required, to represent clients even if they believe their clients are guilty or unpopular. Criminal defendants, enemy combatants, and controversial corporate entities are all entitled to representation.

Disciplinary Proceedings against Lawyers

Lawyers who violate ethical rules are subject to disciplinary proceedings by the governing state bar authority, as well as sanctions by the court. Typically, state bars will have a trial-like procedure in which the lawyer can defend against any allegations of misconduct. When judges discipline lawyers, it is often by holding them in contempt of court. If judges are going to use contempt powers against a lawyer, they too must go through formal procedures, unless the contumacious behavior occurs in the presence of the judge. Under such circumstances, the judge may immediately punish the lawyer with financial sanctions or even imprisonment of up to six months in jail.

Judicial Ethics

Judges are also bound by ethical codes. Not only must judges respect and comply with the laws (both on and off the bench), but a judge cannot give the appearance of impropriety. Thus, a judge cannot preside over a matter if his judgment will be affected by family, social, political, or other relationships. A judge cannot hold membership in an organization that discriminates.

Judicial Conduct and Speech

Judges are supposed to treat all parties and litigants in a dignified manner. Judges are not allowed to have ex parte communications with just one party in a case. They are also barred from commenting on an ongoing case, even if it is on appeal from the judge's courtroom.

In *Republican Party v. White* (2002), the Supreme Court held that judges have a First Amendment right to speak out with positions on legal issues, even those that might arise in their courts. However, judges have a duty to disqualify themselves in any proceedings in which their **impartiality might reasonably be questioned**. Thus, the standard is not whether the judge actually feels a bias, but rather whether the judge's fairness could reasonably be questioned. This standard is the basis for disqualification rules that bar judges from sitting on cases where they own stock in a corporation that is a party, or where they have close relationships with a party.

Judges have limited ability to participate in extra-judicial activities. A judge can engage in extra-judicial activities, such as teaching and writing, when those efforts relate to the administration of justice. However, a judge may not engage in fundraising or accept free trips for educational programs without following the applicable disclosure laws. Under the federal Hyde Amendment, judges are not allowed to give money to a candidate in a partisan race nor are most judges allowed to engage in any political activities other than supporting their own candidacy for a judicial position.

The Supreme Court

Ironically, the one court that is not bound by the standard ethical codes is the U.S. Supreme Court. The Supreme Court decides on its own standards for disqualification and ethical behavior. Not so many years ago, Associate Justice Antonin Scalia was criticized for his duck-hunting trip with Vice President Dick Cheney, who had a case pending in the high court. Justice Scalia wrote an opinion defending his behavior, even though it might have caused the disqualification of a lower court judge because it called into question the justice's ability to impartial in the case.

Judicial Disciplinary Proceedings

Just as they follow different rules from lawyers, judges are disciplined in different ways. In most cases, the matter is handled internally by court personnel or a Commission on Judicial Performance that has the power to reprimand or suspend a judge. Federal judges, who enjoy life tenure, are subject to the disciplinary processes of their circuit courts.

Legal Commentators

Currently, there are no mandatory codes of ethics for legal commentators, although some bar associations have been adopting voluntary standards for such commentators. However, lawyers and judges who provide commentary to the media on other people's cases are still bound by their respective ethical codes and, as a matter of principle, should act competently and without conflict of interest.

Notes

1 One of my favorite jokes is: "Q: What's the problem with lawyer jokes? A: Lawyer's don't think they're funny, and no one else thinks they're jokes."
2 ABA Model Rule of Professional Conduct 1.1.

Appendix

Legal Research for Journalists

Daniel W. Martin
Professor of Law and Director of Law Library,
Loyola Law School, Los Angeles

Introduction

Legal research for journalists is a subset of the legal research program taught to law students or graduate library school students. In this brief guide, there is no attempt to cover the expanse of material that would be presented in a full semester course. Print materials are almost totally ignored. There is a strong emphasis on free online sources although some commercial sites are briefly mentioned.

The reasons for this online emphasis are the ease of presentation at a journalists' conference and the reluctant acknowledgement that much legitimate research already makes use of free online research sources.

One point is especially important in doing online research: critically evaluating sources is the key to success. In the print world, critical evaluation of the sources is also necessary, but the high hurdle of finding a publisher willing to spend money on editing and printing narrows the number of titles that end up on bookstore and library shelves. Legal publishers must be highly selective.

In the online publishing world, there is a similar hurdle for the top commercial sites like Westlaw and LexisNexis. But for the most part, anyone can publish anything on the web. Elements of the critical evaluation process of online resources include: Is the website authoritative? Is it up-to-date? Is it an official governmental website? Is the author an authority in the field? Is there good editorial quality? Is site a new one? Is it likely to be around tomorrow? Functionality is important, too, but not as important as the authority of the site: Does the site have a good search engine? Are all of the materials on the site logically linked to each other? Are the site's materials linked to related materials on other sites?

The emphasis on online materials here does not mean that print resources should not be used or considered in doing research. There are many great print resources available at public libraries, university libraries, and law libraries. Much of the traditional secondary source material (books about the law—see chart below) is available in print format only. There are print research guides available to direct users to print resources. Two of the classics of legal bibliography are Barkan, Mersky, and Dunn, *Fundamentals of Legal Research*, 9th edition, Foundation Press, 2009; and Berring and Edinger, *Finding the Law*, 12th edition, Thomson West, 2005.

In Figure 1, note that the primary sources (the law itself) are available on both the free and commercial databases. In some cases a commercial publisher will post the official version for free, linked to an official website. Thomson West, the official publisher for the California Code of Administrative Regulations does this for the state of California. (see: http://govern ment.westlaw.com/linkedslice/search/default.asp?tempinfo=word&RS= GVT1.0&VR=2.0&SP=CCR-1000). In the secondary source box, note that law review articles are available both in print and online, but books with commentary on the law will more likely be found in libraries.

Online Legal Information

Lawyers today can choose from three main groups of online legal information suppliers. These groups could be compared to the Great Danes, Chihuahuas, and virtual pets of the canine world.

Great Danes

LexisNexis and Westlaw are the standard sources for most lawyers, law firms, major corporations, courts, and law libraries around the United States. The subscriptions are expensive, but the databases are massive, the editorial quality is high, the material is up-to-date, there is good historical depth, and there are reliable citators. (Citators provide the complete history

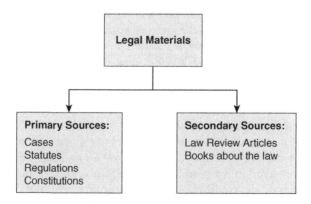

Figure 1

of the cited primary source and an overview of how later authorities have treated the cited source to let the user know if the law [case or statute or regulation] is still good law.)

http://www.lexisnexis.com
http://www.westlaw.com

Not quite a Great Dane, but certainly not a Chihuahua or virtual pet, Bloomberg Law has made good progress in the past couple of years. It's more like a Great Dane puppy. Of all the services challenging the seemingly captive legal research services market share of Westlaw and LexisNexis, Bloomberg Law has the best chance of making major inroads.

http://www.bloomberglaw.com

Chihuahuas

The Chihuahuas are the LexisNexis and Westlaw wannabees. They have some, but not all, of the features of the larger services. They are reasonably priced for what they provide. These companies would like to break into the big dogs' market, but they do not have the depth or quantity of resources that make the Great Danes what they are.

http://www.loislaw.com
http://www.accesslaw.com/
http://www.americanlegalnet.com
http://www.versuslaw.com/
http://www.fastcase.com
http://casemaker.us

Virtual Pets

Virtual Pet sources are mostly free. Some have individual features that could be found on Westlaw or LexisNexis, but all have some drawbacks that make them inappropriate for one-stop-shopping.

The Main Four

If a researcher only had access to a few free sites, Washlaw, Cornell's LII, Findlaw, and Hieros Gamos are the top ones for legal research. For the most part they direct users to other sites, but they do the hard work of organizing, listing, and linking all the free sites around the globe into a manageable whole. Washlaw and Cornell's LII are hosted at law schools and are mostly free of advertisements and links to commercial sites.

http://www.washlaw.edu (Washburn University School of Law's Legal Research on the Web)

http://www.washlaw.edu/reflaw/reflaw.html (Washburn University School of Law Virtual Reference Desk)

http://www.law.cornell.edu/ (Legal Information Institute at Cornell)

http://www.law.cornell.edu/states/listing.html (Legal Information Institute at Cornell, Listing By Jurisdiction)

http://www.law.cornell.edu/states/california.html (Legal Information Institute at Cornell, California Legal Materials)

http://www.findlaw.com (from Westlaw)

http://www.hg.org (Hieros Gamos)

Research Guides

In these sites there are some good research guides for general legal research (like the print classics in legal bibliography listed above) and for research in specific topics. The first two sites (LLRX and Zimmerman) are aimed at law librarians. The very useful Andrew Zimmerman guide is in a free part of the LexisNexis database.

Many of the 190 academic libraries in the United States have research guides posted on their web pages. The guides, or in some cases complete databases, are great places to do jurisdiction-specific research. For instance, Hastings College of the Law's library website has all of the California ballot propositions in digital format back to the first one in 1911 (see http://library.uchastings.edu/library/california-research/ca-ballot-pamphlets.html).

http://law.lexisnexis.com/infopro/zimmermans/
http://www.llrx.com/
http://www.llrx.com/columns/foia41.htm
http://www.ll.georgetown.edu/
http://www.ll.georgetown.edu/services/learn_research.cfm
http://www.ll.georgetown.edu/guides/labor_employment.cfm

U.S. Supreme Court

These sites will provide nearly all a researcher needs to know about the dockets, records and briefs, oral arguments, opinions, and audio recordings of the Supreme Court.

http://www.supremecourtus.gov/
http://www.law.cornell.edu/supct/index.html
http://www.oyez.org/
http://www.c-span.org/Topics/Supreme-Court/
http://www.c-span.org/Series/America-and-The-Courts/

Federal Courts

The Federal Courts websites are very helpful, but to get the briefs, users will still need to go to Westlaw or to the individual courts. Most court of appeals records and briefs are not available on free databases. Few audio recordings of oral arguments are available.

> http://www.uscourts.gov/
> http://www.uscourts.gov/News/InsideTheJudiciary.aspx
> http://www.uscourts.gov/courtsofappeals.html
> http://www.uscourts.gov/cgi-bin/cmsa2006.pl
> http://www.ca9.uscourts.gov/
> http://www.c-span.org/Topics/Supreme-Court/
> http://www.c-span.org/Series/America-and-The-Courts/

State Courts

This site directs users to the fifty state court systems. Cornell, Washlaw, and Findlaw will be useful for the same purpose.

> http://www.ncsc.org/Information-and-Resources/Browse-by-State/
> State-Court-Websites.aspx

California Examples

> http://www.courts.ca.gov/index.htm
> http://www.courts.ca.gov/selfhelp.htm
> http://www.courts.ca.gov/selfhelp-smallclaims.htm

Federal Legislation

Current federal legislation is easily researched and tracked using government websites. The Cornell site is helpful here, too, as in most other areas of legal research. Thomas (named for Thomas Jefferson) is the website for the Library of Congress serving the house members and senators. Thomas has one of the most up-to-date bill tracking systems.

> http://www.law.cornell.edu/
> http://www.law.cornell.edu/uscode/
> http://thomas.loc.gov/
> http://thomas.loc.gov/home/bills_res.html

State Legislation

In addition to the site of the National Conference of State Legislatures, Cornell, Washlaw, and Findlaw provide links to legislation in all fifty states.

http://www.ncsl.org/
http://www.ncsl.org/aboutus/ncslservice/state-legislative-websites-
   directory.aspx
http://www.law.cornell.edu/states/index.html

California Example

http://leginfo.legislature.ca.gov

Federal Agencies and Regulatory Law

U.S. government agencies are usually well covered by the individual agency web pages. FDsys, the website for the Government Printing Office, provides direct access to the Federal Register and the Code of Federal Regulations, the official publication vehicles for all U.S. regulations.

http://www.irs.gov/
http://sec.gov/
http://foia.fbi.gov/
http://www.gpo.gov/fdsys/
http://www.usa.gov/
http://www.usa.gov/Agencies/Federal/Executive.shtml

State Agencies and Regulatory Law

Cornell, Findlaw, and Washlaw provide links to the agency web pages and regulations in all fifty states. The Washlaw link for Alabama is listed below by way of example. It includes links to every agency in the state.

http://www.washlaw.edu/uslaw/states/alabama.html
http://www.washlaw.edu/uslaw/

California Example

http://www.oal.ca.gov/

The President

Users will want to avoid typing in www.whitehouse.com, which is a commercial site with no relation to the U.S. government.

http://www.whitehouse.gov/
http://www.whitehouse.gov/news/nominations/index-date.html

The Governors

California's governor's web page address is below. Researchers must use the "advanced search" feature to easily access proclamations, executive orders, and so forth.

http://gov.ca.gov/

Specialized Research

Covering Constitutional Law

These sites provide access to the U.S. Constitution and related documents.

http://www.law.cornell.edu/constitution/constitution.overview.html
http://www.archives.gov/historical-docs/

Local Law

Most cities have websites and many cities publish their municipal codes online. California local government codes and charters are listed at the UC Berkeley Institute of Governmental Studies site: http://igs.berkeley.edu/library/cagovdocs/

http://www.amlegal.com/nxt/gateway.dll?f=templates&fn=default.
htm&vid=amlegal:lamc_ca (Los Angeles Municipal Code)
http://qcode.us/codes/malibu/
(Malibu Municipal Code)

Blogs about Law . . . Blawgs

More and more law blogs are appearing—mostly on academic websites.

http://www.abajournal.com/blawgs/
http://electionlawblog.org/
http://legaldockets.com/NewPubBlog.html

Great Starting Place: Law Librarians!

Local public law libraries: http://www.publiclawlibrary.org/find.html (This list is just for California.)

LA Law Library provides free public access to LexisNexis and Westlaw: http://lalaw.lib.ca.us/

Academic law libraries (about 200 total): http://www.aallnet.org/sis/allsis/links/libraries.asp

Loyola's law library: http://library.lls.edu/

Four Additional Great Subscription Databases

Users may not want to pay for a subscription to these databases, but they should be able to access them in the local public, university, or law libraries.

Full text of American law journals (PDF): http://heinonline.org

U.S. Congressional Serial Set, 1817–1994: http://www.readex.com/readex/

22,000 historic treatises on Anglo American law: http://www.gale.cengage.com/pdf/facts/momlTreaties.pdf (this set will have some overlap with the free resource, Google Books: http://books.google.com)

Directories/Biographical Information

Lawyers

The California Bar website gives general information about all lawyers and detailed information about disciplined lawyers. Martindale-Hubbell, FindLaw (Find a Lawyer tab), lawyers' firm pages, LinkedIn pages, and Facebook pages provide directory information and are all available for free online.

http://www.calbar.ca.gov/state/calbar/calbar_home.jsp (attorney search box)

http://members.calbar.ca.gov/fal/Member/Detail/35901 (member resigned with charges pending)

http://www.marhub.com/ (free version of the LexisNexis-owned directory)

http://lawyers.findlaw.com (free version of the Westlaw Legal Directory)

Judges

The Los Angeles County Bar evaluates all judicial candidates: http://www.lacba.org/showpage.cfm?pageid=1829

Los Angeles Daily Journal Judicial Profiles (subscription only) provide detailed biographies of judges sitting in state and federal courts in California: http://www.dailyjournal.com/

Covering Foreign and International Law

These websites provide links to governmental web pages. WorldLII is affiliated with Cornell's Legal Information Institute. This 2008 article provides an LII overview:

> http://www.nyulawglobal.org/Globalex/Legal_Information_Institutes.
>   htm
> http://www.worldlii.org/
> http://www.nigeria-law.org/index.html
> http://www.washlaw.edu/
> http://www.loc.gov/law/guide/ (Library of Congress international law
>   links)
> http://avalon.law.yale.edu/default.asp

Miscellaneous/Legal Humor

The California Coastline project was seldom viewed until Barbara Streisand sued the site owners for posting a photo of her coastal property. Her losing lawsuit prompted a new term, *the Streisand effect*, and put the obscure website on the map. The University of Texas Law Library has a large collection of Law and Popular Culture resources, and its website surveys the collection's print and video offerings. The remaining web addresses in this section are for legal humor sites.

> http://www.californiacoastline.org/streisand/lawsuit.html
> http://tarlton.law.utexas.edu/exhibits/lpop/
> http://legalhumor.com/
> http://lawhaha.com/

Index

Made in the USA
Monee, IL
28 January 2022

90150170R00213